Gutenberg's Europe

to Henri-Jean Martin

Gutenberg's Europe

The Book and the Invention of Western Modernity

Frédéric Barbier

Translated by Jean Birrell

polity

First published in French as *L'Europe de Gutenberg. Le livre et l'invention de la modernité occidentale (XIIIe-XVIe siècle)*, (c) Éditions Belin, 2006

This English edition (c) Polity Press, 2017

Cet ouvrage, publié dans le cadre d'un programme d'aide à la publication, bénéficie du soutien de la Mission Culturelle et Universitaire Française aux États Unis, service de l'ambassade de France aux EU. This work, published as part of a program of aid for publication, received support from the Mission Culturelle et Universitaire Française aux États Unis, a department of the French Embassy in the United States.

Polity Press
65 Bridge Street
Cambridge CB2 1UR, UK

Polity Press
350 Main Street
Malden, MA 02148, USA

ISBN-13: 978-0-7456-7257-1
ISBN-13: 978-0-7456-7258-8 (pb)

A catalogue record for this book is available from the British Library.

Library of Congress Cataloging-in-Publication Data

Names: Barbier, Frederic, author.
Title: Gutenberg's Europe : the book and the invention of Western modernity / Frederic Barbier.
Other titles: Europe de Gutenberg. English
Description: Cambridge, UK ; Malden, MA : Polity, [2016] | Includes bibliographical references and index.
Identifiers: LCCN 2016013294 (print) | LCCN 2016041373 (ebook) | ISBN 9780745672571 (hardback) | ISBN 9780745672588 (paperback) | ISBN 9781509509928 (Mobi) | ISBN 9781509509935 (Epub)
Subjects: LCSH: Printing–History–Origin and antecedents. | Books–History. | Gutenberg, Johann, 1397?-1468. | Europe–Civilization. | BISAC: HISTORY / Social History.
Classification: LCC Z126 .B36513 2016 (print) | LCC Z126 (ebook) | DDC 686.1092–dc23
LC record available at https://lccn.loc.gov/2016013294

Typeset in 10.5 on 12 pt Sabon
by Toppan Best-set Premedia Limited
Printed and bound in Great Britain by CPI Group (UK) Ltd, Croydon

The publisher has used its best endeavours to ensure that the URLs for external websites referred to in this book are correct and active at the time of going to press. However, the publisher has no responsibility for the websites and can make no guarantee that a site will remain live or that the content is or will remain appropriate.

Every effort has been made to trace all copyright holders, but if any have been inadvertently overlooked the publisher will be pleased to include any necessary credits in any subsequent reprint or edition.

For further information on Polity, visit our website: politybooks.com

Contents

∂ↄ

Figures, Maps and Tables

∽

Figures

Maps

Tables

Foreword

✧

I hope in this book, by a discussion of the very first media revolution, that of Gutenberg in the mid fifteenth century, to offer some insights into the media revolution of the early twenty-first century. It is an essay, not an in-depth study or a scholarly work on the invention of printing – a subject on which a formidable bibliography already exists. It will ask how Western civilizations passed from one communication system (oral and manuscript) to another (printing); how this technological innovation developed and what were its consequences; and how the change in the dominant media influenced not only social structure as a whole, but a number of abstract categories and ways of thought. As a revolution of equal if not greater significance takes place before our eyes, it is important to be able to identify how the changes that accompanied phenomena of the same order came about in the past.

I have chosen not to encumber my book with a bibliography other than that provided by the notes, which refer only to material I have directly and regularly drawn on for this work. A supplementary and much more extensive bibliography on the history of the book may be found on the website of the Centre de recherche en histoire du livre,[1] which includes a complementary iconography specially prepared for this volume. Some of my notes refer to other relevant websites, in particular those of an iconographical nature.

I would like to thank all the colleagues and friends with whom I have discussed the themes developed in this book; and in particular to record my gratitude to the librarians and archivists whose books and records I have consulted over the years, sometimes importunately, in France and in other European countries: Mmes et MM. Jesus Alturo (Barcelona), Pierre Aquilon (Tours), Michella Bussotti (Peking), Max Engammare (Geneva), Sabine Juratic (Paris), Jean-Dominique Mellot (Paris), Matthias Middell (Leipzig), István Monok (Budapest), Philippe Nieto (Paris), Dominique Varry (Lyon) and Jean Vezin (Paris). I am grateful also to the Centre national de la recherche scientifique and the Institut d'histoire moderne et contemporaine for making it possible for me to carry out my research and bring my project to fruition.[2] Lastly, I warmly thank the members of my seminar on the 'History and civilization of the book' at the École pratique des hautes études,[3] where a number of the arguments developed below were first presented for discussion.

Abbreviations

⁀

Ad:	Archives départementales (followed by the name of the département)
Am:	Archives municipales (followed by the name of the town)
BEC:	Bibliothèque de l'École des chartes
BHR:	Bibliothèque d'humanisme et Renaissance
Blockbücher:	*Blockbücher des Mittelalters. Bilderfolgen als Lektüre* (Mainz, 1991)
Bm:	Bibliothèque municipale (followed by the name of the town)
BnF:	Bibliothèque nationale of France
BrB:	Bibliothèque royale of Belgium
BSB:	Bayerische Staatsbibliothek (Munich)
5e centenaire:	*Le Cinquième centenaire de l'imprimerie dans les anciens Pays Bas* (Brussels, 1973)
Charles V:	*La Librairie de Charles V* (Paris, 1968)
CMEL:	*Catalogue des manuscrits en écriture latine portant des indications de date, de lieu ou de copiste*, ed. C. Samaran and R. Marichal (Paris, 1954–84), 7 volumes have appeared
CNAM:	*Les 3 [Trois] révolutions du livre* [catalogue of exhibition at Conservatoire national des Arts et Métiers] (Paris, 2002)
Crousaz:	Karine Crousaz, *Érasme et le pouvoir de l'imprimerie* (Lausanne, 2005)
DEL:	*Dictionnaire encyclopédique du livre* (Paris, 2002) (vol. I, A–D, 2002; vol. II, E–M, 2005)

Delaveau/
Hillard: Martine Delaveau and Denise Hillard, *Bibles l'imprimées du XVe au XVIIIe conservées à Paris* (Paris, 2002)
Febvre et Martin: Lucien Febvre and Henri-Jean Martin, *L'Apparition du livre*, 3rd edn, with postface by Frédéric Barbier (Paris, 1999)
Gut. Jb.: *Gutenberg Jahrbuch*
HAB: Herzog August Bibliothek, Wolfenbüttel
Haebler: Konrad Haebler, *Die Deutschen Buchdrucker des XV. Jahrhunderts im Auslande* (Munich, 1924)
HBF: *Histoire des bibliothèques françaises*, vol. 1 (Les bibliothèques médiévales, VIe siècle–1530) (Paris, 1989)
HCL: *Histoire et civilisation du livre. Revue internationale*
HEF: *Histoire de l'édition française*, ed. Roger Chartier and Henri-Jean Martin, vol. I (Paris, 1982)
ISTC: *Incunabula short title catalogue*
JS: *Journal des savants*
Lehmann-
Haupt: Helmut Lehmann-Haupt, *Peter Schoeffer* (Rochester, 1950)
Le Livre: *Le Livre* [catalogue of the exhibition in the Bibliothèque nationale] (Paris, 1972)
Livres et
bibliothèques: *Livres et bibliothèques* (Toulouse, 1996) ('Cahiers de Fanjeaux', 31)
Mainz 1900: *Festschrift zum fünfhundertjährigen Geburtstage von Johann Gutenberg* (Mainz 1900)
Mainz 2000: *Gutenberg: Aventur und Kunst. Vom Geheimunternehmen zur ersten Medienrevolution* (Mainz, 2000)
Marchand: Prosper Marchand, *Histoire de l'origine et des premiers progrès de l'imprimerie* (The Hague, Vve Le Vier and Pierre Paupie, 1740)
Mélanges
Aquilon: *Au Berceau du livre: autour des incunables* (Mélanges Pierre Aquilon) (Geneva, 2003)
Mise en page: *Mise en page, mise en texte du livre manuscrit*, ed. Henri-Jean Martin and Jean Vezin (Paris, 1990)

Offenberg: Adri K. Offenberg, *Hebrew Incunabula in Public Collections: A First International Census* (Nieuwkoop, 1990) ('Bibliotheca humanistica & reformatorica')

Poitiers: *Le Livre à Poitiers* (Poitiers, 1979)

Prosopographie: 'Dictionnaire des imprimeurs et libraires lyonnais du XVe siècle', in *Au Berceau du livre: autour des incunables* (Mélanges Pierre Aquilon) (Geneva, 2003), pp. 209–75, illustration

RFHL: *Revue française d'histoire du livre*

Ritter: François Ritter, *Histoire de l'imprimerie alsacienne aux XVe et XVIIe siècles* (Strasbourg, 1955)

Roma 1997: *Gutenberg e Roma. Le origini della stampa nell città dei papi (1467–1477)* (Naples, 1997)

Rouzet: Anne, *Dictionnaire des imprimeurs, libraires et éditeurs des XVe et XVIe siècles dans les limites géographiques de la Belgique actuelle* (Nieuwkoop, 1975)

Schriftstücke: *Schriftstücke. Informationstäger aus fünf Jahrhunderten* (Munich, 2000)

Thesaurus librorum: *Thesaurus librorum. 425 Jahre Bayerische Saatsbibliothek* (Wiesbaden, 1983)

THR: 'Travaux d'humanisme et Renaissance'

Tours 1988: *Le livre dans l'Europe de la Renaissance.* [Actes du colloque de Tours] (Paris, 1988)

Trois révolutions: *Les Trois révolutions du livre…* [actes du colloque de Lyon, ed. Frédéric Barbier] (Geneva, 2001)

Veyrin: Jeanne Veyrin-Forrer, *La Lettre et le texte. Trente années de recherche sur l'histoire du livre* (Paris, 1987)

Wolfenbüttel 1972: *Incunabula incunabulorum. Früheste Werke der Buchdruckerkunst. Mainz, Bamberg, Strasburg, 1454–1459* (Wolfenbüttel, 1972)

Wolfenbüttel 1990: *Gutenberg. 550 Jahre Buchdruck in Europa* (Wolfenbüttel, 1990)

Introduction

The Media and Change

〽

I show neither sense nor reason, I am foolish indeed to take pride in a multitude of books. I am always wishing for and dreaming of new books, the substance of which I cannot grasp and of which I comprehend nothing...my house is decked out with books, I am content to see them often open without understanding anything inside them...

Sebastian Brant (1498)

Other Media Revolutions

As telecommunications and computing have spread into every aspect of life, the twenty-first century has experienced a spectacular 'media revolution'. For the historian, however, it is not the first. Other periods have also been marked by far-reaching changes in their systems of social communication. The two crucial periods with regard to written communication were the fifteenth century, with the invention of printing (typography with movable characters), and the nineteenth century, with the impact of the Industrial Revolution on the book and the periodical press, and the invention of the mass book trade.[1] In both cases, the system of communication was totally transformed and contemporaries felt they were living in a time of radical change, giving access to a higher level in the scale of civilizations. The humanists of the sixteenth century looked with such disdain on the medieval tradition of thought that the concept of the Middle Ages, with all its negative connotations, seems today to have been their 'invention'. At the end of the eighteenth century, Condorcet in his turn would present the progress and diffusion of the Enlightenment through the printed word as taking the human race to a new stage in its history, that of triumphant rationality, hence universal happiness. Such utopian discourse is not unique to the revolutions of the past – it has been revived in our own day, from the *Rapport Nora-Minc* commissioned by President Giscard d'Estaing in 1978 (translated into English as *The Computerization of Society: A Report to the President of France*, MIT Press, 1980) to the theoreticians of the media revolution: the technical progress of today, we are told, creates the potential for a much-expanded and universally shared knowledge, together with new ways of operating, characterized by the instantaneous circulation and processing of information.

I will begin by looking at other media revolutions in Western civilization. What we call the 'Gutenbergian revolution', in the mid fifteenth century, transformed the operating conditions of the societies it first affected, some of which rapidly experienced a phenomenon of mass mediatization. I will then examine the nature of the change. The invention of Gutenberg was essentially technological, and the very word 'revolution' that is generally used of it today implicitly emphasizes its novelty and its suddenness. Printing brought one period, the Gothic/medieval period, to an end and initiated another, which would be called the Renaissance, characterized both by its close relationship to classical antiquity and by its modernity; indeed it was in the fifteenth century that the word 'modernity' emerged in French. Gutenberg's invention had huge consequences for the evolution of Western societies, but it could only happen as a result of a number of earlier phenomena and changes. For the innovation to have practical applications, and for it to spread effectively, it had to be viable not only at the technological level but also at the economic level; it had to respond to a demand, and the conditions of production and distribution had to be such as to make its use possible.

It is this transition from one state to another that I shall discuss, in its three main phases: a slow rise, accelerating to a peak; the apogee of the invention; and the successive developments of its effects and of its appropriation by large numbers of people. These developments can only be perceived and understood in the medium term, with the passage of two or even three generations after Gutenberg, but their consequences were certainly more profound – and more modern – than might have been expected. In other words, there was a period of change preceding Gutenberg, of 'Gutenberg before Gutenberg'; but there was also a period of post-Gutenberg repercussions, when all the possibilities of the invention were not yet exploited or its consequences appreciated. The invention itself was the turning point, but

I will discuss it in the context of a much longer timescale, which first made this transformation possible then allowed its full potential to be exploited – opening the way to other changes.

My main argument concerns the structuring role of the media. Modernity gave texts a new status and radically changed their content, in ways that were particularly visible in the scientific sphere; however, these phenomena can only be understood through the change in the dominant media. The operating conditions of printing, including the practices linked to it, framed and oriented at every level the production of discourse and the models which underlay this very production.

The Carolingian Reformation

As regards writing and books, the change in Western Europe originated at the end of the first millennium, when the demographic and economic trends began first to fluctuate and then to go into reverse. Until the Carolingian period, the relationship with Latin antiquity had remained fairly direct: some of the monuments had survived, the artists followed Graeco-Latin models, the copyists reproduced such manuscripts as reached them, and the handwriting adopted in the great Carolingian scriptoria was directly inspired by Latin handwriting.[2] Whether concerted or not, the political project of Charlemagne and his entourage at Aix-la-Chapelle – to restore the Western Empire in the form of a Christian Empire governed by the emperor and the bishop of Rome – has to be understood from this perspective. Its failure marked the start of another period, less closely linked to the ancient models, but oriented towards the construction of a wholly original civilization – that of the Middle Ages proper. It was the dissolution of the Carolingian Empire that paved the way for change and, paradoxically, invention.

The project for Carolingian Reform supposed conditions that did not exist. It needed an effective concept of the state (*res publica*) and also the material means to ensure the independence of the sovereign and the integration of the territories he controlled. But the kingdom was still seen as a private possession, which the sovereign bequeathed to his successors, between whom it would be divided after his death. The Carolingian Empire disintegrated in the ninth century, to be replaced by the great entities of Western Francia, Lotharingia and Eastern Francia. In the West, in the absence of adequate mechanisms enabling integration, real power was divided between a multitude of local and regional officials who sought autonomy, with the result that the political, economic and cultural spheres fragmented. The break-up was aggravated by the Saracen, Hungarian and above all Norman raids, first signalled in 799; pirates devastated Frisia and then the Channel coasts, sailed up the rivers (sack of Chartres in 857, of Cologne in 881, siege of Paris in 885, etc.) and settled in Normandy (911), from which they conquered England (1066). It was not the distant and too often impotent sovereign but the local powers, the count and the bishop, who were able to organize and coordinate an effective defence against the plunderers. This led, eventually, to the rise of feudalism and the pre-eminence accorded to ties between persons, between the suzerain and his vassal and his sub-vassals. The sacred dimension of his status notwithstanding, the sovereign was in practice no more than the person who sat at the apex of the feudal pyramid.

From the fifth century to the end of the tenth century, the book remained, in the West, effectively confined to the ecclesiastical world, so much so that the word clerk, *clericus*, initially meaning a man of the Church, took on the meaning of literate and educated. It was the Church which, in the fifth century, when the cadres of state and administrative officials crumbled, took over from the Roman Empire and assured the preservation and transmission of ancient culture. In Gaul, the aristocracy of the Late Empire and the very Early Middle Ages was an aristocracy of Christians of ancient high culture; we need think only of Sidonius Apollinaris, or of Fortunatus, one of Martin's successors in the bishopric of Tours. Scriptoria and libraries were established in the monasteries and in some cathedral schools. The texts were in Latin and their content was primarily religious: the Bible translated into Latin by St Jerome at the end of the fourth century (the Vulgate), the writings of the Fathers of the Church, the lives of saints and martyrs and other liturgical works; to which should be added the texts transmitted from classical antiquity and those of pre-Carolingian and Carolingian authors.

A development of crucial importance followed from the linguistic diversity acquired in the ninth century: classical Latin was no longer either understood or used beyond a very narrow group of educated men, though it remained, in more or less degraded forms, the language of the Church, the administration and written culture. Most people now used the vernacular, Romance languages in the formerly Romanized territories, or Germanic languages where the invaders were in the majority. The vernacular remained essentially oral to the end of the first millennium; in the West, the written material known to us from the ninth century is reduced to very rare and fortuitous texts. Innovation came from the frontier zones: the *Oaths of*

Strasbourg were drawn up in 842 in that key city of the ancient *limes*. The *Canticle of St Eulalia* and the *Song of Ludwig (Ludwigslied)*, copied around 870 at the end of a Latin manuscript, came from another frontier, that of Flanders and Hainault.[3] In England, the king of Wessex, Alfred the Great (died 899), had the Latin classics translated into the vernacular. In Greater Moravia, Cyril and Methodius created an alphabet adapted to the language of the Slav peoples they evangelized (ninth century); they translated the Bible into Slav and used this language for the liturgy. We shall on several occasions return to the paradoxical role played in the process of innovation by frontier zones or by outlying geographical regions which one might expect, a priori, to be less favoured.

From its beginnings in the second half of the eighth century, the work of the Carolingian scriptoria, after that of St Martin of Tours, marked an important stage in the revival of classical Latin: in the perfecting of the new script, the 'Carolingian miniscule';[4] in the creation of models of book and page layout; and in copying, strictly speaking. The aim was the reform of the Church, with a view to producing a clergy of high quality and strengthening the structure of imperial power. The central role devolved on the small group that surrounded the emperor in Aix-la-Chapelle: Leidrade, born around 743–5 in Bavaria, was a clerk in Freising (a bishopric created in 739), where he followed the rise of the library and scriptorium under the influence of Bishop Arbeo (764–84); he was summoned to Aix in 782, to join the palace school which included Alcuin, Theodulf and St Benoît of Aniane. The latter, sent as archbishop to Lyon in 796 to impose reform on the diocese, created the school of singers and the school of readers, developed an active scriptorium, reorganized the chapters of the various churches and restored the Abbey of l'Île Barbe. Alcuin (died 804), abbot of St Martin of Tours in 796, also reorganized the school and the scriptorium, making this the most important intellectual centre[5] in the empire. Once again we find the frontiers as crucial zones. Leidrade was a Bavarian, Alcuin came from England (York) and Theodulf from Visigothic Spain. The latter, abbot of Fleury-sur-Loire and bishop of Orléans, reorganized the monastic school, while the scriptorium enriched the library. Great intellectual figures followed one another at Fleury in the tenth and early eleventh centuries, including Odo, Gerbert, the schoolmaster Abbo and Abbot Gauzlin, future archbishop of Bourges. Other centres existed alongside the monasteries, in particular in certain cathedral schools. The powerful oppidum of Laon was also the site of a school inspired by the presence of scholars from the British Isles, in the wake of John Scotus Eriugena (until 870). Its library was particularly remarkable for its Greek manuscripts. Much later, at the turn of the eleventh and twelfth centuries, Laon was once again made famous, by the teaching of Anselm of Laon, the master of William of Champeaux and enemy of the young Abelard.

Industrial Revolution and Economy of the Sign

Though population estimates for the Middle Ages remain speculative, it is possible to highlight the main elements in a dynamism that was increasingly visible after the year 1000. The demographic situation was fundamental, though linked to economic development, and it is in this context that the trajectory specific to writing and the book has to be discussed. With the turn of the tenth and eleventh centuries, everything changed, and Western Europe began once again to expand: the continent had some 40,000,000 inhabitants around 1100, but nearer 75,000,000 in 1300. France had perhaps 6,000,000 inhabitants in the eleventh century; according to the *État des paroisses et des feux* (State of parishes and hearths), instituted on royal orders in 1328, the number had risen to between 16 and 17,000,000, making it the most populous kingdom in Europe. In England, the population grew from 1.3,000,000 in 1087 to 3,500,000 at the end of the fifteenth century. And when Raoul Glaber spoke of the 'white mantle of churches' covering Western Europe in the eleventh century, he bore witness to the increasing number and size of the human communities.

The wonderful twelfth century and the apogee of the thirteenth century were followed, however, by more troubled times. A demographic plateau, from the 1340s (sometimes earlier, by 1270 in Castile), was followed by a dramatic decline that reduced the population to fewer than 50,000,000 inhabitants by 1400. Natural catastrophes (the Black Death was responsible for the deaths of at least 30 per cent of the European population between 1347 and 1350, perhaps even 50 per cent in the most exposed towns, such as certain Mediterranean ports[6]) added their toll to that of interminable wars, in particular the Hundred Years War (globally, from Crécy, in 1346, to Castillon, in 1453). Revolts, famines, massacres and underlying insecurity only intensified the crisis. It was not until the fifteenth century that some recovery was visible, and it was only at the end of that century that the population again reached the levels of the 1300s (over 80,000,000 inhabitants). Although this was still an age of underpopulation, and although recurrent crises persisted, aggravated by periodic revisitations of plague, the dynamic was once again more favourable.

Demographic growth, though fragile (as the crisis of the fourteenth century revealed), was made possible by advances in agriculture, transport and trade. Globally, the primary sector was dominant, but the rural world was experiencing profound change. In the eleventh and twelfth centuries, this took the form of assarting and the adoption of new techniques in agriculture and in certain processing operations: in particular watermills, then windmills, used for grain, textiles and forges, and eventually also for the manufacture of paper. In England, Domesday Book (1085–7) records more than 5,600 mills.

> Invented to grind grain, which remained its main use, [the mill] was very quickly used for other tasks: crushing bark for tanners, nuts and olives, ore and newly woven cloth that had to be fulled to give it strength...[7]

The reception of these innovations drove a growth that fed on itself: this was 'the first European industrial revolution' (Fernand Braudel), a horse and milling revolution, which happened between the eleventh and thirteenth centuries and which made it possible for more people to be fed.[8] The increase in production and the increase in population went hand in hand.

As well as these transformations in the rural world, another sector, and one crucial for my subject, was experiencing radical change: the increasing density of population resulted in a process of geographical interconnection and integration, while also encouraging trade and circulation. Although the barter of goods and services remained the norm at the local and even regional level, things were very different higher up. Decisive innovations in shipbuilding followed one after the other in the thirteenth and fourteenth centuries: improved sails, the invention of the sternpost rudder and the perfecting of the compass. New maritime routes were opened up and the tonnage of ships was greatly increased – hulks and galleys had a carrying capacity of 300 tonnes, the carrack up to 1,000. This meant that ports had to be adapted, and heavier investment was needed to allow trading operations on a larger scale, which led in turn to the development of improved financial techniques. Political development and the gradual invention of the modern state also depended on greatly increased financial resources.

Writing was central to the most important of these developments. Administrative practice saw the invention in Italy of accounting procedures (double-entry book-keeping at the end of the thirteenth century) and sophisticated instruments of exchange (bill of exchange, credit systems). Modern accounting was based on the definition of very precise calculation procedures and the keeping of series of accounts, and then of specialized books of account. This was also a period of growth in the monetary economy and of the rise of banks, which made it possible to mobilize larger capital sums and put them to use. As the rediscovery of Aristotelian thinking underpinned the growth of a new theory of representation and the sign, economic and financial operations, even political activity, seemed increasingly to belong to an economy of the written sign and of its techniques of manipulation. The invention of Gutenberg happened in a world in the process of rapid modernization, but it provided this very process with the means for a radically new development.

PART I

Gutenberg before Gutenberg

1

The Preconditions for a New Economy of the Media

Though [King Charles V] understood Latin well and there was never any need for it to be expounded to him, he was so farseeing, out of love for his successors, that he wanted to provide for them in times to come instruction and knowledge leading to all the virtues. For this purpose he had all the most notable books translated from Latin into French by the accepted masters and experts in all the sciences and arts...

Christine de Pisan

The Key Space of Modernity: The Town

Growth and tipping point

The modernity of the Middle Ages was based on the town. Though the growth of urbanization and of the innovation it encouraged assumed a major transformation in the countryside, it was also the main factor for change in the sphere of writing. The change was first socio-political: in the town, social structures, occupations and modes of representation were all renewed. The society of the early Middle Ages and the Carolingian period had been a rural society, but, beginning in the eleventh century, there was a step change; urban centres developed, which in their turn promoted innovation in every sphere, including that of the symbolic systems – and of writing. In the words of Fernand Braudel:

prompted by demographic expansion – never before had towns sprung up so thickly within such easy reach of one another. A clear distinction

Table 1.1 Large towns in the Middle Ages

	Beginning thirteenth century	
Population	>50,000	>20,000
Near East and Muslim world	3	7
Italy	0	2
The West, except Italy	0	0

For each period, the two columns indicate the number of towns with more than 50,000 or with between 20,000 and 50,000 inhabitants.

Table 1.2 Urban population and rate of urbanization in Europe, 1300–1500

Dates	Urban population	Rate of urbanization (%)
1300	7750 million	10.3
1400	7560 million	13.6
1500	8390 million	11.2

Source: Paul Bairoch, Jean Batou and Pierre Chèvre, *La Population des villes européennes, 800–1850: banque des données et analyse sommaire des résultats 800–1850: The Population of European Cities: Data Bank and Short Summary of Results 800–1850* (Geneva, 1988, p. 225).

of functions, a 'division of labour' between town and countryside, sometimes brutally felt, became the norm. The towns took over industrial activity, became the motors of accumulation and growth, and re-invented money.[1]

The geographical distribution of towns shifted westwards, whereas only the great Mediterranean civilizations, Byzantium and the Arabo-Muslim world, had previously been represented. Of the earliest European metropolises (more than 50,000 inhabitants), all, at the beginning of the thirteenth century, had still belonged to the Byzantine or Islamic worlds (Baghdad, Cairo, Constantinople), but the balance gradually shifted, first in favour of the Italian peninsula, then of other regions. By the middle of the fourteenth century, the list includes four Italian towns (Venice, Genoa, Milan and Florence), later to be joined by Naples. Around 1350, and in spite of the Black Death, it was the turn of North-western Europe, with Paris (80,000 inhabitants) and Ghent (60,000 inhabitants). The end of the fifteenth century was marked by the disappearance of independent Burgundy (and the decline of Ghent), but also by the increasing importance of the Iberian Peninsula: Valencia and Lisbon joined the list.

Table 1.1 (continued)

c.1350		End fifteenth century	
>50,000	>20,000	>50,000	>20,000
3	8	3	9
4	6	5	14
2	5	3	8

The shift was even more marked at the level of large towns (between 20,000 and 50,000 inhabitants). The pre-eminence of Italy, though still real, was lessened to the benefit of other areas, in particular, around 1500, the Iberian Peninsula – with Granada (the last Muslim capital in Europe, which passed into Christian hands in 1492), Seville, Toledo and Barcelona – and the Low Countries and North-western Europe (with Antwerp, Bruges, Brussels, Ghent, Lille, Cologne and London). Other towns had already almost reached this size, including Medina Del Campo, Valladolid and Zaragoza. In short, between the end of the twelfth century and the end of the fifteenth, the dynamic of urbanization shifted, initially to the advantage of Italy alone, then of Western Europe, by contrast with Byzantium and Islam.[2] For innovation, this was a decisive factor.

Models of urban success

Let us set aside the political dimension, and the distinction between communes, *bonnes villes*, 'residence towns' (*Residenzstadt*), etc. The distinguishing feature of urban society was the specialization of the crafts, by contrast with a rural economy characterized by the self-sufficiency of the community. The town, an agglomeration of persons dependent on external sources for their food supply (Werner Sombart), was the natural site for the invention of other models of consumption, hence of life.

Max Weber proposed, speaking very generally, three successful urban models, often found in combination. The first was the town of crafts, for example Chartres, economic capital of Beauce and town of markets. Large numbers of artisans congregated in the suburbs which grew up outside its walls in the eleventh century. Innovation was concentrated on the watercourses, where leather and wool were processed, before activities later diversified. The wealth of the town was given spectacular expression in the construction of the cathedral of Notre Dame, as also in the size of its chapter (seventy-two members!), whose prebends were among the richest in France. As might be expected, these very favourable conditions had consequences for the sphere of writing, whether in the case of the bishop, the chapter or the many religious houses or of the small schools and the prestigious cathedral school itself.[3]

The second model, which accounted for the most spectacular success stories, was that of the trading town, in particular the town of long-distance trade. This was the case in Italy, at a time when Westerners, Italians in the vanguard, established permanent settlements in Byzantium and the great centres of the eastern Mediterranean, whose trade they dominated. In the north, the Hanseatic networks were controlled by Bruges and Lübeck, though London should not be forgotten. In the fourteenth century, Bruges was the transit centre for wool and the entrepôt for the Hanseatic towns. This period of prosperity continued under the dukes of Burgundy (from 1384), when the presence or proximity of the court encouraged the growth of intellectual and artistic activities. As well as the men of the book (copyists and calligraphers, miniaturists, booksellers and then printers), there were artists, in particular painters, most notably Van Eyck (died 1441) and Memling (died 1494).[4] In the interior, it was the fair towns which were the chief hubs for the exchange, regulation and redistribution of merchandise and values, from the fairs of Champagne to the great Italian, French (Lyon), Spanish (Medina Del Campo) and German (Frankfurt on main) fairs. The lift-off of towns such as Leipzig in the fifteenth century was similarly related to their role as trading hubs, in this case connecting the Germanic and Slav worlds.

The third model was that of the princely town, home both to a more or less rich and spectacular court and to administrative services controlling a territory. In central France, in and around the Loire Valley, towns such as Nantes, Angers and even Bourges fall into this category. Let us look more carefully at this model: for the historian, understanding comes from the dialectic between different levels of analysis, from large units to the local level, the latter serving both as illustration and as opportunity for detailed scrutiny. The history of Bourges confirms the general trend, while also illustrating the transition from one model of success to another. In the Roman period, the powerful Gaulish city became capital of the province of Aquitania prima. As the Roman Empire disintegrated, a wall protected it from external attacks. Many buildings testify to the role of Bourges as a religious capital, assisted by the residence of the primate of Aquitaine. The urban renaissance of the tenth century saw the creation of parishes (St Bonnet) and 'bourgs' along the roads leading to the gates, which were home to a growing population which practised new crafts. The Benedictine abbey of Chezal-Benoît, founded in 1093, was a cultural centre and its rich library was completely reorganized in 1488 by Abbot Peter du Mas; it later passed in part to the Maurists.[5]

From the crafts to trade: a bourgeoisie of business and commerce gradually developed in Bourges, active first in wool (sheep farming in the Champagne berrichone), weaving, dyeing and trade (at the fairs). The supremacy of the town was based on its dominance over the surrounding countryside and on the creation of specialized trading networks. Its growth was further promoted by political factors: in 1100, Bourges became part of the royal domain; its walls were extended at the end of the twelfth century; above all, the rebuilding of the cathedral of St Stephen began in 1195. The chapter owned a very rich library, housed in a specially furnished room above the sacristy (1417).[6] The number of churches grew and new religious houses were founded. The apogee was reached with the 'residence city', when Jean de France, the king's brother, received the duchy of Berry as an apanage and made Bourges his capital (1360). He built a palace there, with a Sainte-Chapelle consecrated in 1405. The ducal administration expanded and the duke himself was a Maecenas and a collector, who assembled a sumptuous library.

In the fifteenth century, the wealth of the great bourgeoisie, its links with the court and royal administration and its role as patron of the arts are illustrated by the career of Jacques Coeur (Bourges, 1395/1400–Chios, 1456), but also by the dynasty of Lallemant. The Lallemant seem to have been immigrants arriving from across the Rhine in the thirteenth century. Originally dealers in fabrics and woollen cloth, they obtained important financial offices (general receivers in Normandy and Languedoc) and were later mayors of Bourges. They were involved in transporting works of art from Italy to Amboise (1495) and in various other schemes promoted by the kings in the region; they amassed a collection of illuminated manuscripts and were in contact with Clément Marot (who composed their epitaph) and the printer-bookseller Geoffroy Tory. Their hôtel, decorated with Italianate themes, was one of the most sumptuous in the town in the early sixteenth century. The explicit of a manuscript of the *Jewish Antiquities* of Flavius Josephus, completed in 1489, throws light on the relationships between the families of patrons and the copyists (in this case Nicolas Gomel) or illuminators:

> Cy fine le XXe et derrenier livre des anciennetez des juifs...lequel livre a fait escrire noble homme Jehan Lalemant, receveur général de Normandie...par son humble et obéissant serviteur Nicolas Gomel.[7]

(Here ends the XXe and last book of the antiquities of the Jews... which book the noble Jehan Lalemant, receiver general of Normandy had written... by his humble and obedient servant Nicolas Gomel.)

The university, founded by Louis XI in 1463, crowned the edifice and remained one of the most important in France in the Renaissance period. Nevertheless, the town succumbed to a certain lethargy as a result, amongst other things, of a fire in 1487, the decline of the fairs (in favour of Lyon), the difficulties caused by the periodic disturbances, the departure of the court and the end of the ducal dynasty of Berry. Other examples could equally well have been chosen: in Bourges, as in Poitiers and other towns, the initial period of expansion was dominated by factors of a general nature, mainly demographic and economic, while the second was more 'political'.

The power of the written word[8]

The principal development visible from the eleventh century in the world of writing was a general opening up. Writing had until then largely been an affair of the Church, and above all of the monasteries established in the countryside; now it began to permeate the whole of society: first the urban world, then, though to a lesser degree, the worlds of the castles and of even the big villages. This was made possible by the emergence of educational institutions, political rationalization and the growth of trade and an urban bourgeoisie. The town may have been the favoured site of innovation but it, in its turn, depended on the rise of a civilization of writing for the establishment and development of its power: written documents, titles of ownership, accounts, lists and finally books all first appeared in towns. The urban archives were the site of a 'bourgeois memory', largely in the vernacular, which was constructed in opposition to the 'noble memory' constituted by the cartularies preserved in castles and religious houses. It was also in towns, therefore, that technicians of writing and of written rationality first appeared, that is, notaries and other lawyers, administrators, great merchants, teachers and their students. The fixing of written law accompanied this process. The technicians of writing were gradually incorporated into the urban craft structure, as in Nimes in 1272, in the case of the lawyers and the physicians.

A town like Valenciennes, one of the most important and wealthiest towns in the Scheldt, had an organized archive by 1240. It was in regular correspondence both with neighbouring towns (Sainte-Amand, Le Quesnoy, Tournai and Cambrai) and with towns further away (Ghent and Bruges, Ypres, Ath, Nivelles, Brussels and Arras among others).[9] It was by its use of the charters of 1114 and 1302

– written documents – that it systematically extended its control over a surrounding countryside that included some 300 small towns and villages; it imposed its own interpretation of village charters, pushed for the customs to be put into writing and, in effect, created a structure prefiguring an Italian contado such as that of Florence.[10] In this latter town, the company of the Scarsella, founded by seventeen merchants in 1357, was in weekly correspondence with Genoa and Avignon; the letters took a fortnight to reach their destination. Further north, the Hanseatic counters maintained a network of correspondents covering the whole of their commercial zone, from London to Novgorod. Together with the specialization of functions, the principal tool of urban supremacy was the practice and the recording of writing. The chief and decisive advantage of the towns lay in their mastery of the spheres of rationality and of the techniques of communication and administration, and in the accumulation (including that of wealth) that this made possible.

Iconography confirms this means of conquest by the 'writing town' of the surrounding countryside. Brueghel pictures the *Census at Bethlehem* in a village in Flanders, in winter. There is not a trace of writing to be seen except in connection with the officials sent out from the 'residence' and installed in the village inn, where, armed with their registers, they conduct a census of the inhabitants and, we may assume, collect taxes.[11] Pieter Brueghel the Younger's *The Village Lawyer* illustrates a similar theme, but much later (1620): here, the lawyer has apparently come to the inn, where, almost buried under a mass of all sorts of papers, he sees his clients, while the peasants appear before him, some carrying a fowl by way of payment. There is an *almanach* (calendar) pinned to the wall, perhaps as a symbol of the system of measuring time linked to writing and to the labour of writing; we see the transition from the 'natural' time of the seasons and religious festivals to the time of the administrator (taxes!) and the financier (calculation of rents and rates of interest), an interpretation confirmed by the hourglass on the table – lawyers were paid according to the time spent on a case. Every detail is significant; they reveal the gulf between rural society and a modernity that combined mastery of the written word, the transition to a different perception of time and the invention of a different type of work. It was the categories linked to writing that more and more obviously assured the domination of the town and its administrators and merchants over the rural world.[12] It was in the town that the new type of work, intellectual work, was invented; whether it was proper for this work to be paid would be debated for centuries to come, even in the nineteenth century.

Though writing spread, it remained an affair of technicians and a minority. In towns, and even more in the rural world, 'publicity' was still ensured by proclamation, and the crier was a common feature of daily life. His job was both to 'publish' the decisions of the authorities and to represent them by spreading their word, hence a degree of ceremony and the use of a uniform or at least distinctive signs such as coats of arms. In the *Retable of St Bertin*, a man reads a charter written on parchment, whose red seal attests to the status of the issuing authority, before a crowd assembled outside the town (1459).[13] As late as 1515, the archduke of Austria wrote from Bruges to the magistrate of Valenciennes to inform him of the peace concluded with France and to instruct him to publicize it *en lieu où l'on est accoustumé faire criz et publicacions*.[14] Nevertheless, this was already the age of the 'empires of paper' (Marshall McLuhan), power systems in which the fluidity of the software (the paper and, above all, the sign) compounded a power and a wealth that it enhanced. The growth of urbanization was accompanied and reinforced by the growth of an artificial environment, one of signs and the spread of the written, and then printed, word; to which it should be added that we have today entered a new phase of abstraction through the sign, that of the generalization of the virtual.

Acculturation through the town

In a largely rural and feudal society, the towns were themselves frontiers where different worlds met. They were points of contact and exchange, not only of merchandise but also of texts, people, experiences, ideas and representations, ways of life, techniques and even aesthetic forms. Innovation was first a product of new social and political systems. The word 'bourgeois/burgess' described, in the etymological sense, the inhabitant of a 'bourg' (a small market town), then, by extension, someone who engaged in activities that lay outside the traditional tripartite society. The burgess – or townsman – did not live directly from the land, nor was he an ecclesiastic or a knight. He was part of a different system than that of orders and feudalism. Towns were a place of horizontal solidarities between individuals engaged in the same activity, in contrast to the vertical solidarities characterizing feudalism and its pyramidal system. Though initially subject to one or more lay or ecclesiastical lords, towns, as their power and prosperity increased in the eleventh and twelfth centuries, were gradually recognized as original and more or less autonomous entities – the communes.

Crucial to urban identity was the place accorded to work and to the wealth it could bring. And here, too, work meant also writing and the mastery of signs: trade, especially long-distance trade, and the crafts required command of the written word, which made it possible to conduct commercial correspondence, keep accounts and record and follow instructions, in short, run a business, even on a small scale. Around 1500, the portrait of the money changer, with his correspondence and his account books, but also often a more or less magnificent manuscript, was a classic motif of painting. The wife of the *Moneylender* of Quentin Metsys, *c.*1514, turns the pages of an illuminated manuscript Book of Hours, open at the 'Hours of the Virgin'.[15] The *Trachtenbuch* of Matthäus Schwarz presents the immensely wealthy Jacob Fugger, plainly dressed, at work with his secretary, who, seated at a table on which lie two registers, updates an account in the ledger. Letters already dealt with are scattered on the floor. In the background is a notary's chest, with drawers in which the letters received are filed according to the towns to which they referred – Rome, Venice, Ofen (Buda), Cracow, Milan, Innsbruck, Nuremberg, Antorff (Antwerp) and Lisbon. Nowhere is there any merchandise, but everywhere there are 'writings'; the ability rapidly to receive, control and process information was now a necessary precondition for wealth – we should remember that by the beginning of the fifteenth century the greatest Italian merchants wrote as many as 10,000 letters per year.[16] By this period, the portrait of the merchant or the financier shows him facing frontwards, in a sumptuous fur-trimmed robe, a purse and a few business letters in his hands. Writing was everywhere, seen from the dual perspective of utility (work) and distinction (wealth and *otium*).

And what was true of a minority was now also true of a majority:

> To live in these surroundings, then exceptional, gave specific features to daily life and social relations. Living crammed together, going to work when the clock struck, using coins on a daily basis, eating food that had been bought, being informed about events, even distant, because towns were the site of exchanges of every type: all this helped to create an urban ethos of liveliness, individualism and rationality which historians believe emerged in the twelfth century.[17]

The town acted as an agent of acculturation based on the rationality of the sign and of mediatization, in which all its inhabitants were involved to a greater or lesser degree. Mastery of time and space was made imperative by the need to use fixed references for correspondence and contracts, but also for the measurement of work itself. This explains the spread of mechanical clocks in towns and the more advanced regions:[18] first in Italy (Orvieto and Milan), then in the 'old Low Countries' (Valenciennes) at the very beginning of the fourteenth century. The famous clock of the Palais de Justice in Paris was built in 1370 by a technician from Germany. The technology was more widely disseminated by the mid-fifteenth century: perhaps most famous is the Great Clock of the king of Aragon's castle in Perpignan, but we may remember also the clocks in Windsor, Prague and Cracow, not forgetting several towns in southern and central Germany (Augsburg, Nuremberg, Frankfurt, Mainz). This geography of innovation prefigured in many respects, including with regard to lifestyles, that of the first typographical printing works.

Another major characteristic of urban civilization relating to my theme was the rise, alongside collective solidarities, of a sense of individual responsibility. Everyone was responsible for the conduct of his or her own affairs and susceptible to a form of uncertainty, which might lead to questioning of a religious nature. This encouraged not only the growth of pious practices, but also attention to books and the development of new reading practices and new 'lifestyles' in which an individual sensibility was an increasingly strong presence. Individual stories and autobiographies proliferated. A man like Ulman Stromer (died 1407), one of the principal men of affairs of Nuremberg and one of the first to introduce papermaking into Germany, left a manuscript in the vernacular recounting the history – that is, success story – of his family.[19] We can already see how these processes of innovation, theorized by Max Weber, could in the ascendant West link together the new importance of towns and the growth of a specific religious sensibility, combining literacy, the innovation of capitalism and the sense of individual responsibility.[20]

Nevertheless, distinctions need to be drawn and it is necessary to relativize. Though the towns grew in importance, and though there was a degree of geographical integration, this affected only a minority of people in Christian Europe, especially on the margins. Rural society, which was almost exclusively oral, was everywhere predominant. Even in the towns, those who could neither read nor write were in a majority, though a majority that was shrinking. Lastly, it was one thing to know how to read and write, if sometimes in a perfunctory and imperfect fashion, and even to engage in a little correspondence, but it was quite another to own one or more small books of piety; and yet another still, and very much rarer, to live in an environment where books of all types were relatively numerous and acculturation through the written word an accomplished fact. The world of the book, the world of workshops of copyists, libraries and the first specialized bookshops, could never affect more than a small number of people.

The Market in Education

Elementary and secondary education

The town was inseparable from the school. Nevertheless, we need to remember at the outset that education affected only a small part, even a tiny minority, of society. For the vast majority, education as such did not exist; one learned within the family and the community – village or parish – or through apprenticeship in the case of the crafts. This was a world in which the book and writing were notable by their absence, even if the beginnings of an opening up were visible. Guibert de Nogent could write, at the beginning of the twelfth century:

> In the time just before my childhood and even during it, the lack of schoolmasters was such that it was virtually impossible to find one in the small towns. They were scarcely to be found in the cities. Perhaps you might chance on one? Their knowledge was so meagre that it could not be compared even to that of the itinerant clerks of today.[21]

Little is known about the global results of this gigantic effort, but it is estimated that, around 1450, between 10 and 15 per cent of the population of Western Europe could read and write, though with huge variations from one region to another. In a town such as Reims, around 1300, literacy seems already to have been well established, and this was a factor that strengthened the ascendancy of the town over the countryside, where most people were illiterate.

Though writing and the book were no longer the exclusive preserve of the ecclesiastical world, the regulars still played a major role in the economy of instruction, and their schools, dynamized by the reform of the Church, were increasingly active. Benedictine reform began with Cluny in the mid-tenth century, before other religious orders appeared. Cîteaux was founded in 1098 by monks from Molesme who were seeking to return to the original Benedictine rule; the Premonstratensians were an order of regular canons established near Laon in 1121, and they spread rapidly all over Europe. Everywhere, education and the book played a central role. The first community of Carthusians was founded by St Bruno (died 1101) at the Grande Chartreuse (1084), and the order was organized in the first decades of the twelfth century (1140). The Carthusians accepted only young men of twenty and over, an age when the brethren had usually completed all or part of their studies. They devoted a large part of their time to copying manuscripts destined to enrich their libraries, and to reading and study. These religious houses all had a library and a school, and often also a copying workshop, some adding binding and later xylography, even typography (in the second half of the fifteenth century). The school of the Benedictine house of Saint-Denis, near Paris, was famous for the teaching of Greek, and the abbey's rich library attracted scholars and students: Suger was educated there and Abelard went there to consult its books. The collection is believed to have contained some 1,500 volumes at the end of the fifteenth century.[22] In Cologne, birthplace of St Bruno, the Charterhouse of St Barbara was also renowned for its very rich library.[23]

From the end of the eleventh century and throughout the twelfth, the network of cathedral schools was also revitalized. Under the direction of their schoolmasters, Chartres, Paris, Laon, Reims, Bamberg, Freising and Canterbury among others were required to train competent clergy, capable of supporting the reform of the chapters, and the schools were inevitably provided with libraries, some of considerable size. Similar developments followed all over Europe up to the turn of the sixteenth century. In France, vestiges of these ancient libraries still survive, at Noyon, Bayeux and Le Puy. At Chartres, the canons housed their library in a timber-framed house behind the chevet of the cathedral, and embellished the reading room with windows illustrating the disciplines taught in the university (1411).[24] In Spain, a library was created in the cathedral of Gerona, situated above the cloister and near to the school (1395). There were libraries in the cathedrals of Tortosa and Tarragona, and a new library was founded at Cuenca in 1401. At the beginning of the fifteenth century, there were books everywhere in the cathedral of Barcelona – in the sacristy and the library, but also in two cupboards installed in the choir, not forgetting the volumes placed on the lecterns and desks for the religious services and those available in the church. The chapter library in Seville was in existence by 1440, and by 1464 it had a librarian responsible for the care of the books. Gifts from the prelates were important in building up its stock, but we should also mention that of Hernando Colón (Colombo), son of Christopher (Columbus), who bequeathed his immense library (15,344 books) to the cathedral on his death (1539). The library at Léon was founded in the fifteenth century and the cathedral library of Salamanca around 1480. Though there were no institutional libraries, there were many manuscripts in the churches of Oviedo, Murcia and Jaca. These libraries were primarily intended for religious worship, of course, but they also sometimes included specialized works in other fields, especially canon law. The situation was similar at the other end of Europe, in Poland, where the cathedral libraries were also very rich. The oldest was that of Gniezno/Gnesen (eleventh century), while the inventory at Cracow listed fifty-two codices in 1110.

In the churches, too, there were books everywhere, as, for example, in the collegiate church of St Amé in Douai, for which inventories survive from the fifteenth century, including one dated 18 August 1463:

> ung viez missel qui soloit servir au grand autel...un autre missel neuf que donna sire Jaques Sturquin, auquel convient meltre cloaux; un missel neuf en deux volumes servant à présent au grant autel auquel les cloaus d'argent commencent de roiller...

> (an old missal which used to serve on the high altar...another new missal which was given by sire Jaques Sturquin, which is in need of new nails; a new missal in two volumes currently serving on the high altar, the nails of which are beginning to darken...)

This library had numerous other books, too, some chained, others awaiting binding (*à reloÿer*), many given by the faithful, some kept in cupboards, and not forgetting the '*mariologe que les enffans baisent*'.[25] This visible presence in churches, especially in the choir, was an important factor in familiarizing the whole community of the faithful with books. Educational opportunities were particularly plentiful in the largest towns. In Paris, in addition to the school of Notre Dame, made famous by Peter Lombard (died 1160), the abbeys of St Germain-des-Prés and St Geneviève attracted students by their teaching. Schools were also provided by the orders of regular canons, in particular St Victor. This abbey, founded by William de Champeaux near the Montagne-Sainte-Geneviève in 1113, owned one of the most remarkable libraries in Paris at the end of the Middle Ages. A new home was built for its books in 1508, with fifty-two desks holding 1,049 chained manuscripts.[26] This library was put to good use by the great humanist printer Josse Bade (1461–1535), who drew on it for texts to print.

And it was not only the Church; from the twelfth century, some urban magistrates were concerned to promote educational institutions. Nor should we forget the numerous private schoolmasters, remarkable evidence of whose existence occasionally survives, like the signboard painted by Holbein the Younger for a master of writing operating in Basel, though at a later date (1516).[27] Henri Pirenne has described the organization of schools in Ghent in the second half of the twelfth century.[28] Some of these schools achieved a remarkably high standard, like the Latin school of Sélestat, directed by a certain Gotfried at the end of the fourteenth century. Here, reading and writing, maths and singing were taught at an elementary level, then, at a higher level, came an initiation into the trivium (grammar, rhetoric and dialectic). Under the direction of Louis Dringenberg (died 1477), a former student of the Brothers of the Common Life, and later a student at Heidelberg, Sélestat became the first 'humanist school' in southern Germany. We cannot know the scale of this phenomenon, but an impression is created of a growing demand for education – hence books. And as the distribution networks for manuscripts were inadequate, it was the library, which allowed volumes to be shared, which provided the most appropriate response.

Universities and colleges

The culmination of the process was the foundation of the universities. Teachers and masters, if they were to survive, needed to attract pupils and to be paid for their work. But intellectual labour produced no objective good and did not fit into the ordinary categories of the market – a word to which we will return. So the masters of Bologna (1088), Paris (*c*.1150) and Oxford (1167) organized themselves into corporate bodies, called a *universitas*, to respond to an increasingly pressing demand. These first foundations were followed by Salerno (1173), Vicenza (1204), Palencia (1208), Arezzo (1215), Toulouse and Cambridge (1229). In Central Europe, political modernization was accompanied by the formation of universities, in Prague, Cracow (1364), Vienna and Pécs, and also Louvain (1425); and the creation of new universities accelerated during the Great Schism, especially in Germany (Erfurt, Cologne, Heidelberg, Leipzig, etc.). By the second half of the fifteenth century, Europe had some sixty-five universities, many of them specializing at least in part. Bologna took over from the schools of Roman law already active in the town, Salerno from those of medicine. Paris shone in theology and philosophy, and the fame of its professors attracted hordes of students, of whom some were famous: Bruno, born *c*.1032 in Cologne, and first a student at Reims, was made a doctor of theology and philosophy in Paris before becoming schoolmaster of the cathedral school at Reims – where the future Urban II was one of his students.

Little is known about the way these university libraries operated. That in Cologne was created soon after the foundation of the university in 1388. The library of the faculty of liberal arts, first documented in 1418, was located in a special room, furnished with sixteen desks for the books (1427). The catalogue of 1474, which has happily survived, lists 342 volumes, all manuscript. The increasing size of the collection made it necessary to devote two further rooms to the library in 1478. There were other libraries in colleges in the town (called *Gymnasien* by the 1490s). In Spain the constitutions of Alcalá, in the fourteenth century, laid down rules for the care of the volumes. In 1457, the library of Salamanca, the richest in the peninsula, received the books bequeathed by Juan of Segovia, archbishop of Maurienne, and, in 1480, it was installed in a special building.

The existence of a university presupposed that the students had access to the books necessary for their work. The demand could be huge – there were some 10,000 students in Paris around 1300.[29] In the largest centres, the spread of writing was on such a scale that shops specializing in writing materials began to appear; they sold parchment, then paper, sometimes already prepared, and everything needed for this activity.[30] Bologna was particularly well off in this respect, and the university world permeated the whole of urban society; the city has one of the oldest representations of a parchment-maker's workshop and shop, where all the paraphernalia of paper-making and writing was also sold.[31] Another fourteenth-century manuscript depicts a lecture in law: the professor is seated, in his red gown, his bundle of notes before him, his audience sitting on benches or the floor, some pen in hand, others following the lecture in books; and, at the right-hand side of the picture, we glimpse the street, where a lawyer gives a consultation and draws up an act, surrounded by plaintiffs, while a tonsured monk and another person are discussing a book. Everywhere, we see writing and references to writing.[32] In the university towns, copying workshops gradually appeared, over which the university exercised a degree of control. With the appearance and expansion of the *pecia* system, to which we will return, their control became more direct; soon, the bookshops began to trade in books whose owners had no further use for them. The transition to the bookshop proper was not far off.

The college system, linked to the universities, was introduced in the thirteenth century. These were foundations enabling poor students to follow courses, which, by the fifteenth century, were increasingly accepting paying students. The colleges were financed by rich patrons and often organized according to the origin of the students, as in Bologna, in the case of the Collegio di Spagna, founded in 1364 by the cardinal archbishop of Toledo and pontifical legate, Gil Carille de Albornoz. It accommodated twenty-four Spanish students, employed two chaplains and housed the legate's personal library. In France, the colleges of the university towns of the Midi, Avignon, Montpellier, Toulouse and Cahors, are well known.[33] At Montpellier, a university founded by Nicolas IV in 1289, the colleges of Pézenas, Saint-Ruf, Saint-Benoît and Mende were established in the fourteenth century, with others following. In Paris, the great abbeys also maintained their colleges, to which they sent monks with scholarships to be trained and to follow courses. The college of Saint-Bernard was opened in 1244 for the monks of Clairvaux, while the powerful abbey of Saint-Denis had a college in the city in the thirteenth century, used by a dozen students, as well as its school. The Sorbonne, the college founded in *c.*1257 by Robert of Sorbon (1201–74), was a special case. The college of Navarre was a royal foundation (1316) and the seat of the 'nation' of France, one of the four 'nations' of the university. Pierre d'Ailly, royal almoner, archbishop of Cambrai and cardinal, would be its reformer. Navarre and the Sorbonne both had famous libraries.[34] Paris eventually had some sixty establishments, including the colleges of la Marche and of Beauvais, the latter founded by Bishop Jean de Dormans (1370). There was a similar system in England, with Balliol College (1262), Merton College (1263) and University College (1280) in Oxford.

The books of the mendicant orders

The Church faced a serious crisis in the thirteenth century, most dramatically manifested in the heresies, and this, too, prompted further efforts to reorganize and reform. New religious orders were founded with the aim of promoting the evangelical ideal of absolute poverty and ministry. The most important were the 'mendicant orders' of the Dominicans (Preaching Friars) and the Franciscans (Friars Minor), but also of the Carmelites and the hermits of Augustine, whose austerity and commitment contributed to their success. They played a major role in education, assisted by the fact that, contrary to earlier practice, they were established in the towns. The Dominicans, founded in Toulouse in 1215 by Dominic de Guzman (died 1221), expanded with remarkable speed: by the fourteenth century they had more than 600 convents and some 12,000 brothers. When the Treaty of Paris (1229) ended the Albigensian crisis, the Dominicans were given the task of organizing the Inquisition (1232), and their convent of the Jacobins, in Toulouse, was home to the new university which Count Raymond VII was forced to establish. Wherever it went, the order engaged in teaching at a high level, as laid down by its founder in 1217–20, and as organized by successive chapters from 1259. It was based on convents, each with a 'doctor' assisted by a 'master of students' for the teaching of theology. Each province had one or two schools (*studia solemnnia*), whose best students progressed to one of the order's *studia generalia*. At the head of this organization was the faculty of theology in Paris, where the

Dominicans had two chairs, and where they trained masters equipped with the *jus ubique docendi* (universal right to teach). Their convent in the rue Saint-Jacques (hence the name Jacobins) was founded in 1221; it was the first *studium generale* and it had numerous famous masters, following in the footsteps of Albert the Great and Thomas Aquinas:

> This educational organization gave the Preachers an incomparable scientific influence; it ensured an effective decentralization of theological teaching, previously concentrated in Paris, and it made possible, in the mid fourteenth century, the creation of numerous faculties of theology in the universities.[35]

In Provence, the priory of Montpellier formed a *studium generale* with its own library.[36] As well as in Toulouse, the order settled in Avignon, in 1224, where it opened its third *studium* in the province. The library at Avignon was greatly expanded, especially after the arrival of the popes, thanks to substantial gifts and the work of copying carried out by the brothers:

> The library...had an almost contemporary collection...dynamic, growing rapidly and destined to be much utilized, in short, a working library for the use of the Preachers. The near absence of liturgical books, the most precious, suggests that it was a reference library.[37]

The network continued to expand and there were libraries in the less important convents: Saint-Maximin had a working library by the first decade of the fourteenth century, and twenty-five students were registered there at the end of the fifteenth century.[38] Aix was a special case, as the town was the seat both of an archbishopric and of a university. The order controlled the university when Avignon Nicolai, provincial prior in 1401, was appointed archbishop of Aix (1422), then elected chancellor of the university (1436). From then on, the two offices were linked. In Germany, the school of Cologne became a *studium generale* in 1248, well before the town had a university (1388). The Dominicans were in Strasbourg in 1224, where a general chapter met in 1260, a second following in 1294. Albert the Great was lector there, and the scholastic doctors of the thirteenth century preceded the mystic preachers of the fourteenth. In 1303, the order was in Erfurt, another centre of early modern mysticism. Everywhere, attention was lavished on the libraries, for which detailed legislation was drawn up, with the result that it is impossible to overestimate the role of the Dominicans in the world of the book. The provincial chapter of Avignon[39] proclaimed, in 1288, that their weapons are the books, and that, without books, no brother can be prepared to preach or to hear confession. As a result, we enjoin the priors and other brethren to strive to increase the number of books deposited in the common cupboard.

The Franciscans followed a similar path, though less systematically, with great figures such as Alexander of Hales and St Bonaventure (died 1274). Above all, however, the Franciscan missionaries played a major role along the Eastern routes, and even in China. Painting echoed this close relationship with the written word: in 1501, Holbein the Elder painted for the high altar of the Dominicans in Frankfurt the order's *Genealogical Table*, in which he portrayed the founder and the principal Dominican doctors and scholars, each with a book.[40]

The Emergence of the Political

The last major factor favouring acculturation through the written word was the increasing power of lawyers and administrators, to which we have already referred, together with the increasing rationalization of politics. In the Middle Ages, as today, to govern was also to be informed and in a position to make decisions in full knowledge of the facts.

Administration and rationalization

Once an administration had developed, not only round the most powerful princes and sovereigns but also round the urban magistrates, new needs emerged in the spheres of justice, finance and the army, not forgetting communications and what might be called, at the risk of anachronism, information and data management. These needs were catered for by technicians, administrators, councillors, lawyers, even professors of law, men who had increasingly often received a specialized training, themselves wrote expert treatises and were beginning to assemble their own libraries. In the background, we see the rise of the 'offices', while secretaries, messengers and ambassadors also made their contribution, as did historiographers: Carpaccio would portray them in his *Mission of Hippolyta*, where the young scribe, shown in profile, leans on his writing desk in the foreground of the painting.[41]

The aim was to rationalize the management of resources, so as to assure the wealth and power of the government, but also to theorize the political system and strengthen it in relation to the outside world.

The politico-administrative rationality was more precocious in certain states, the model being the Norman principalities, from Normandy to Sicily. The same trend may be observed, though at a later date, in the Capetian kingdom. True, the provosts (*prévôts*) appeared under Robert the Pious (996–1031), but they were still little more than private agents administering the king's demesne. The institutions were organized on a more stable basis from the twelfth century, with, around the sovereign, the rise of the palace and the gradual appearance of a centralized and specialized administration. Under Philip II Augustus (1180–1223), the provosts, of whom there were some 250, mostly in the Orléanais and the Gâtinais, began to become royal officials, and the power of the bailiffs (*baillis*) was spelt out in the king's 'Testament' (1190). The principal institutions were gradually put in place: the *Cour des comptes* (Court of accounts, 1203), the Parlement (1239), and the offices of the Chancellery with the group of educated technicians constituted by the notaries and secretaries of the king.[42] It was the same in Nuremberg, for which exceptional evidence survives of the administration's familiarity with writing, in the form of the notebook, with folding flaps, which the official responsible for the town fortifications carried with him on inspections in c.1425.[43]

As a result, the administrative and financial archives increased in volume, while the theoreticians of power set out to codify the material tools of public administration,[44] and also to provide them with conceptual frameworks. This systematization was based on the written reference and linked to the gradual introduction of juridical categories from Roman law. The 'legists' of Philip IV the Fair (died 1314) illustrate this well. The dauphin had received an excellent education, which had introduced him to the Stoics. Once on the throne, Philip was a 'fanatic of kingship' (Edouard Perroy), who surrounded himself with a group of faithful councillors with whom he worked. The *curia*, initially formed of the *seigneurs* of the royal domain, now included a number of men from the southern lesser nobility, in the wake of the Chancellor Pierre Flote and his pupil William of Nogaret, both connected to the university of Montpellier. It was these southern intellectuals, paradoxically, who most energetically theorized the superiority of royal power. The policy of Philip the Fair was designed to impose the king's will on the whole of the kingdom, and I will observe here only that, as regards writing, it was he who promulgated throughout the Midi the statute regularizing the profession of royal notary.[45]

Gradually, education came to offer a favoured route to social promotion and so numerous were the examples of men who rose in the Church or in the lay administrations through the 'talents' acquired in school and university that a new norm was established. A Constitution of Clement VII decreed, in 1378, that the members of the metropolitan chapters should at least have an arts degree; the chapter at Laon, studied by Hélène Millet, counted seventy-two graduates among the eighty-two canons in 1409.[46] This pattern spread beyond the ecclesiastical world. Admittedly, merchants, even at the highest level, did not for a long time to come need an advanced education; it is well known, for example, that Jacques Coeur was described as *sine litteris*, that is, 'without letters', by which we should understand not that he was illiterate, but that he had never followed a university course. Nevertheless, the remark suggests some surprise on the part of its author. From the second half of the fourteenth century, the old identification of clerks and university graduates was no longer so absolute, and lay graduates began to appear. This reveals both the increase in demand, especially in the legal sphere, and the fact that the university sometimes paved the way for a strengthening of social position for certain groups of families. In fifteenth-century France, the urban oligarchs of towns like Amiens, Reims, Senlis, Tours, Poitiers and Lyon sent some of their children to study for a university degree, especially in law. They soon occupied most of the decision-making posts in the magistracy and set their sights on public office.[47] As we shall see, there was a close relationship between the universities and the world of printing in its early days, in the case both of the financiers – such as Barthélemy Buyer in Lyon – and the typographers, beginning with Gutenberg himself.

The situation was similar in Florence, a commune where the contado was largely organized during the course of the fourteenth century, and where the councils made an effort gradually to rationalize an administration they wanted to achieve maximum efficiency.[48] Statutes were issued in 1408–9, a series of reforms were instituted in the 1420s, and attention was paid both to the choice of administrators and to the way they performed their duties. Administrative competence extended to economic matters, in particular fiscal affairs, but also to record-keeping, with a survey of the activities of the contado (1426) and then the compilation of a new cadastre (1427), on which the finances would be based, hence the reform of the state. Everywhere, based on the political rationality being established and developed, record-keeping was the prime management tool. In Florence itself, the lawyers, in the wake of Bartolus de Saxoferrato, intervened not only to guide and supervise action but also to give it a solid and effective theoretical basis. At the local level, administrative staff proliferated; there were about 100 *podestats* (captains and governors) in the different towns of the contado in the fifteenth century, each with an office and a staff of technicians, larger or smaller according to the size of the locality. In Pisa, the first official under the Florentine captain was a judge, required to be a graduate in law. This drive for politico-administrative rationalization seems, overall, to have had some success, especially in the economic sphere.

Distinction through the book

At the centre of the political systems gradually being established was usually a court (*curia*), which was an administrative tool, but also a site for the affirmation of a 'lifestyle' marked by a 'distinction' which justified the privileged status of a prince whose power was becoming more absolute.[49]

In fact, the cultural and artistic dimension became a key element in the contemporary political system, as the prince, those close to him, and, in their image, persons of high rank demonstrated the exceptional nature of their status by a form of representation that was often spectacular. It explains the sumptuousness of the environment (the castles, the gardens, the forest for hunting), the commissioning of works of art (including manuscripts), the patronage, the custom of dedication copies, the various events (festivals), and so on. Many illuminations in the *Très riches heures* of the duc de Berry depict scenes which are as mirrors of this sumptuous court life.[50] Through emulation, the model spread in part to the highest ranks of urban society, and certain types of princely book were found, imitated among a wider public – in particular Books of Hours. This lifestyle, a herald of modernity, is illustrated by the painting of the *Garden of Paradise* by a Rhenish master of *c.*1410–20: in a walled garden full of flowers and many-coloured birds, a group of people engage in refined activities, making music, conversing, picking fruit (cherries) – and reading. In the background, the painter has placed a light meal.[51] This is a society of leisure (*otium*), and we may note that the main persons shown in the painting are female.

This model of political organization favoured the 'residence cities' (*Residenzstadt*), the future capitals: first of all Paris, but also towns such as Lille, site of the principal institutions administering the Burgundian territories, or Heidelberg, residence of the Elector Palatine, and not forgetting the great Italian cities, capitals of kingdoms (Naples) or centres of territories of varying size. Florence was no principality, but the constant references to antiquity and to the 'virtue' (*virtú*) of the *res publica* gave written culture and the book a particular status in its political ideology. Leonardo Bruni was chancellor from 1427 to his death in 1444. Regarded as the theoretician of republican *libertas* as opposed to the tyranny of a city such as Milan and, like Cicero, defending the Republic against the rise of princes, he wrote a *History of the Florentine People*. After his death, the city decided to build him a sumptuous tomb in Santa Croce: the recumbent statue, swathed in the Roman toga, holds a book in his hands. It is not, however, as in the typical statuary of the age, a Book of Hours, or a devotional work, but the masterpiece composed by the deceased to the glory of his fatherland and the values it defended. It is not the author or the politician as such who is honoured, but the author as personification of the grandeur and freedom of the city and its state.

Libraries and communities

Viewed from this perspective, the collection of books, the library, served a dual function, at once practical and symbolic. The king of France, the dukes of Burgundy, Berry, and Orléans, the count of Artois, the great English lords such as the duke of Bedford,[52] German lords and Italian lords (the Visconti and the Sforza),[53] not forgetting Matthias Corvinus, king of Hungary,[54] vied with each other in the magnificence of the commissions and collections that helped promote a sovereign's prestige. The sons and grandsons of John the Good (1350–64), most notably Charles V (died 1380), were among the first bibliophiles of the age.[55] In Paris, there were signs of a stabilization that would lead to institutionalization. The king's library, transferred into a tower in the Louvre in 1367–8, had a 'keeper' in the person of Gilles Malet, vicomte de Corbeil (died 4011). The site was specially fitted out, the walls panelled with wood from Ireland, the ceiling lined with cypress, the furniture (benches and 'bookwheels') renovated, the doors remade and the windows protected by latticework against birds. An inventory of 1373 lists 917 volumes, and Charles V was the first sovereign to bequeath his books to his successor.

The king's library was innovatory in content, too, both in the type of text it contained and in the works created there. In 1371, resuming and extending a policy initiated by his father, the king instructed his councillor and chaplain, Nicole Oresme, dean of the chapter of Rouen, to translate the *Ethics, Politics and Economics* of Aristotle.[56] Oresme had already translated an astronomical treatise of Ptolemy, the *Quadripartitum*,[57] and Charles also commissioned translations of the works of Petrarch. These are all indicators of a degree of modernity, which is also visible in the inclusion in the collection of a number of scientific manuscripts, such as the *Catalan Atlas* (from Majorca) commissioned by the king, a record of the state of cartographical knowledge in 1375.

Also modern was the use made of this library, which served as a working and governmental tool, one might almost say resource centre, for the king and his close advisors, Nicole Oresme, Raoul de Presles, Philippe de Mézières and the chancellor Pierre d'Orgemont. The aim was political: to theorize the royal office, to lay down and apply the rules of good government and to conduct an effective diplomacy, in particular as regards England (the vassal status of the king of England for his French possessions must be proved). So Charles V, in 1372, had the *Livre de l'enseignement des princes* copied; then, in 1373, he commissioned the Carmelite Jean Golein (died 1430) to translate the *Information des rois et des princes*, a text composed for the son of Philip the Bold describing the qualities indispensable for good government.[58] Pierre d'Orgemont wrote a *Life* of John the Good and a *Life* of Charles V, but the most famous work in this regard was the *Songe du vergier*, a treatise on the relationship between the spiritual and temporal powers. Originally written in Latin in 1376, on royal orders, it was translated into French two years later. Lastly, the political function of the library was indissociable from its role as conveyor of a prestige that complemented the theme of 'glory': to increase the king's renown was also to confirm, even increase, his power. The *Livre du sacre*, written on royal orders soon after 1365, fixed the memory of a ceremony which was to become canonical; it was used to order the consecration of Charles VI in 1380.[59] The same applied in the case of the manuscript of the *Grandes chroniques de France*, written under the supervision of the king himself.[60] On the death of Charles V, the library contained some 1,200 manuscripts.

A similar approach was adopted by the Italian dynasties, some of which were linked to Spain. But there was already a shift of perspective, in favour of humanism. The king of Aragon, Alfonso the Magnificent (*c.*1394–1458), organized a humanist court in Naples, attracting scholars, chroniclers and artists. The king was himself a fluent Latin reader and he assembled a library of 1,140 volumes. The western Mediterranean was at this point a Spanish lake, and the solidarities between, on the one hand Catalonia and Valencia, and on the other Roussillon, the Balearic Islands, Sardinia, southern Italy and Sicily, would play a major role in the early days of printing. Lastly, it is impossible to discuss the princely libraries of the turn of the fourteenth and fifteenth centuries without mentioning the library of Burgundy, whose duke, in the words of David Aubert, was 'the prince in Christendom, without any reservation, who [was] best equipped with an authentic and rich library'.[61]

Two other factors also played a role in the evolution of libraries, especially in Italy: the concept of the common good (the library at the service of the community) and the reference to antiquity (hence a certain form of evergetism). With regard to the former, Petrarch bequeathed his library not to a religious community, but to the Venetian Senate, to be put at the disposal of the public. Though this legacy was never implemented, a precedent had been set. In Florence, the return from exile of Cosimo de Medici (1434) marked a further shift of the political regime towards a principality. It was the small group assembled around Cosimo that was responsible for 'the architectural, pictorial and literary discourse of the city' (Fernand Braudel). In the 'city of lilies', humanism ruled, and it is in this context that we should see the legacy of his library by Niccolò Niccoli to Cosimo, for it to be made available to scholars, who were actually the *familiares* of the prince (1437). It was to these 'friends' that, adopting a Petrarchian motif, Lorenzo the Magnificent dedicated his books, as proclaimed by the bindings bearing the formula *Liber Laurentii de Medici et amicorum*. Also in Venice, Cardinal Bessarion adopted a similar approach.[62] The library, the copying and printing workshops and the bookshop now structured an original social space, in which intellectual, economic and political functions all intervened.

Lastly, with the growth of the bibliophile, the combined commercial and symbolic value of books led to their movement from one great library to another, through legacies, gifts and purchases, but also by force, even by seizure in war – the latter one of the models of the 'travelling book'.[63] The French Bibliothèque royale provides a spectacular example of the 'recoveries' of the most precious books or collections. On the death of Charles VI (1422), as the political crisis became acute, the king's books were bought by the duke of Bedford and taken to England. Some of them passed to Louis of Bruges, lord of Gruuthuse, whose library was in its turn purchased by Louis XII.[64] Some books had a more chaotic history: the *Bible historiale* of Jean de Vaudetar, a councillor of Charles V, was offered by him to the king. It had been copied by Raoulet of Orléans, who had completed the task in 1372. After the king's death, the volume passed to the duke of Anjou, then to the duc de Berry, before returning to the Louvre in 1416. It disappeared from the royal collections in 1424, only to reappear in the seventeenth century among the books of the lawyer Bluet, then in the possession of the Jesuits of La Flèche, who offered it to the intendant Foucault. The manuscript was part of the Gaignat sale in 1764, when it was bought by Meerman. Finally, it was given by the latter's son to Baron van Westreenen, founder of the Museum Meermanno (formerly Museum Meermano-Westreenianum) in The Hague, where it has since remained. This *Bible* is all the more remarkable in that it contains 269 illuminations, of which one of the most famous is that on folio 2, signed by Jean Bondol, known as Jean de Bruges (1371): it shows the king receiving the volume as a gift from his councillor. It is one of the first examples of a painting whose subject was not inspired by a religious theme – and of a 'natural' portrait of the sovereign.[65]

2

The Economy of the Book

෧෮

When I was a child, open to instruction, I was given several books, whose contents I remember very clearly. I have held onto all I could, sometimes more, sometimes less, as I liked some subjects more than others, and of which some have been necessary to me, others useful, others glorious and laudable, others bitter and in bad taste, though beneficial nonetheless when they had been thoroughly dissected.

Georges Chastellain

The medieval world prioritized gesture, orality and hearing. Feudal ties were between persons, and materialized in a ritual in which writing generally played no part: the vassal spoke certain codified phrases, then placed his hands between those of his lord. Private acts (contracts, donations), even decisions that might be described as of a public nature, were the subject of written documents, but, to be recognized, these had to have the signature of a group of witnesses or be publicized by proclamation. Tradition was oral, custom and customary law prevailed in a society that remained largely illiterate, and this was still largely the case at the beginning of the early modern period.[1] The construction of rationality and the rise of modernity through writing happened only slowly and affected only a minority of the population; writing was the business of the clergy, obligatory intermediaries between the earthly world and God. It gradually became a prerogative of scholars who were no longer necessarily men of the Church, then of men of power, those who sought to assure and increase their wealth and their dominance – the sovereign princes and their entourages, the most powerful groups among the urban bourgeoisie.

Manuscript Production

An overall view

The consequences of the very general phenomena I have described are difficult to assess as regards the economy of the written word, given the impossibility of estimating the number of manuscripts produced either by period or by region. The available sources (the surviving manuscripts) are very imperfect: the catalogues are incomplete, and the manuscripts have not survived in the place or even region of their production. We are reduced to guesswork as to the proportion of manuscripts lost and the further back in time one goes, the greater the uncertainty. I will confine myself to tracing the broad outlines of a situation we cannot know in any detail; it is not so much the figures observed or calculated that matter as their distribution and the trends they reveal.[2]

We are best informed about the Holy Roman Empire, where, from the eighth century, the statistics reveal four distinct periods. First, the Carolingian lift-off of the ninth century was very marked, allowing a level of production not found again until the first decade of the thirteenth century. Second, this rapid increase levelled out in the tenth and eleventh centuries, though this was a period of consolidation rather than decline as the level remained nearly twice as high as in the eighth century, and the figures increased from one century to the next. There followed, from the mid-eleventh century and continuing in the twelfth, a marked recovery with a doubling of the number of manuscripts produced, an upward trend which continued in the thirteenth century, if less rapidly, and accelerated slightly in the fourteenth century; German production then grew notably faster than in Italy and even more France, where it failed to increase during the long crisis of the years 1330–1430. Lastly, in the fifteenth century, the number of manuscripts more than tripled compared with the previous period.

These figures bring out two points in particular: the 'crisis of the year 1000' did not exist, the lowest point seemingly reached in the first half of the tenth century; and never had so many manuscripts been copied in Germany as in the age of Gutenberg. The lift-off was probably earlier in Italy than in France, where it was slower to get under way. Recent research has provided us with a more accurate picture of the quantity of manuscripts available in certain regions: 2,600 manuscripts produced in Catalonia before printing have survived, to which should be added around 3,000 manuscripts of which

Table 2.1 Production of manuscripts in Germany, eighth–fifteenth centuries

Century	eighth	ninth	tenth	eleventh
Empire	33,564	134,905	57,862	63,711
Index	100	402	172	190

we have only fragments (because used for binding, etc.). This gives a total of 5,600 items, making no allowance for documents lost altogether; and, of course, the manuscripts produced locally were not the only ones to have circulated in the province, and we need also to allow for those that were imported, principally from Italy and France.[3]

The semiological turn

The history of innovation once again highlights the privileged position of the frontier zones (the *frontera* of the Spanish reconquest), where exchanges of every type were most numerous and most diverse. The transition from antiquity and the *translatio studiorum* first came about through civilizations external to the Christian West. At the 'House of Wisdom' in Baghdad (832), Aristotle, Ptolemy, Archimedes, Euclid, Galen and Hippocrates were copied for the purpose of study and discussion. The catalogue of Ibn al-Nadīm, bookseller in Baghdad, lists all the titles available in Arabic in 987.[4] Paradoxically, the dismantling of the caliphate spread such practice from the capital to the periphery. In the ninth century, Andalusian society was rapidly orientalized; Al Hakam II (961–76) founded the largest library in the West (Arab authors speak of 400,000 titles) and attracted Eastern scholars and men of letters to Cordoba. The intellectual milieu of twelfth-century Andalusia was outstanding. Averroes (died 1198) was the principal philosopher of the Arabo-Muslim world; his commentaries on Aristotle were known in the West in the 1220s, and were the basis for the developments in thinking of Albert the Great (died 1280) and Thomas Aquinas (died 1274).[5] The presence of Jewish communities throughout the Mediterranean basin further encouraged exchanges with the Near East (Cairo, Byzantium) and Andalusia, including of texts and books. Cordoba was also home to Maimonides (died 1204), one of the most important philosophers of medieval Judaism. When the Muslims retreated to the central Mediterranean, from the second half of the eleventh century, Sicily, too, became an intermediate space between several civilizations – Arabo-Muslim, Byzantine and Western. Under the rule of the Normans, Palermo, ancient capital of the Kalbite emirate, was one

Table 2.1 (continued)

twelfth	thirteenth	fourteenth	fifteenth
127,066	163,854	278,016	910,000
379	488	828	2711

of the greatest and most cosmopolitan cities in Europe. The figures of Frederick II (died 1250) and Manfred of Hohenstaufen may still be controversial, but the court of Palermo was indubitably one of the most brilliant and most cultivated of the thirteenth century.[6]

Events as diverse as the development of the thinking of Averroes and its diffusion, the seizure of Constantinople (1204), and the progress of the *reconquista* in Spain (victory of Las Navas de Tolosa, 1212), together with the policies of Frederick II, combined to open up Western thinking and bring it closer to its Platonic and Aristotelian heritage. Plato had posed the question of how to develop general knowledge on the basis of particular experiences born of experience: ideas were timeless, but they were part of the tangible world. Aristotle theorized the system of the word as linguistic sign: the word had to be a sign *of* something, hence linked to something external. Experience functioned as a superimposition of interconnected signs: tangible experience (*res*, the object) was apprehended as sign of the timeless idea, the spoken word as sign of the object, writing as sign of the oral. The power of this 'semiotic triangle',[7] a triangle that combined the sign (the word, *vox*), the signified (for Plato, experience), and the object itself (for Plato, the idea) was, from the twelfth century, the basis of the reorganization of human knowledge: we enter the world of mediation and representation, in which the reflection and the manipulation of virtual objects (the words and the discourses) were the foundation of knowledge and its practical applications. The proliferation of writings and of books, its scale revealed by recent quantitative studies, accompanied this process.

The tool of virtuality was extremely powerful. Increasingly, people began to reason in the abstract, and the world became a 'paper world', to the point, sometimes, of losing its objective immediacy. The thinking on cartography, astronomy and the natural sciences showed how the properties of the real were now perceived as apparent, while its true categories were both rational and hidden. Models were also constructed in a material form, and we should remember that the first terrestrial globe was made in Nuremberg, by Martin Behaim (himself a student of Regiomontanus), in 1492, the year Columbus crossed the Atlantic.[8] When Galileo (1564–1642) wrote that 'nature is written in the language of mathematics', he was pushing the argument to its limit: thinking was organized on the basis of representations which made it possible to make the tangible universe operate in the manner of a system of signs, in this case a mathematical model. The concept of the 'paper world' thus described all the categories, models and artefacts linked to writing, and with whose aid the external world was thought. The applications of abstract representation (modelling) could be of great practical importance: it was the reading of Ptolemy in an *Imago mundi* of Pierre d'Ailly published by Johannes de Westfalia, and reflection on the Ptolemaic model of the universe, that led the navigators to contemplate reaching the East Indies by turning their back on them and sailing West.[9]

This approach soon posed the problem of the status of religion and Revelation, since the global system of thought (Foucault's episteme) must always remain, in a sense by hypothesis, crowned by theology. The major conceptual shifts which, especially in the sphere of the text, bore on theology were gradually applied to other spheres. The theory of the sign was based first on the spoken word, which referred to a representation drawn from experience, then to the timeless idea on which it was based. The argument was extended to the sphere of writing: the written word was the sign of the spoken word, so the text became a collection of signs about which one could reason as such. Scholasticism (*scola*, school) developed a method of analysing discourse and its components based on a theory of the sign and making it possible to advance in argument. For scholasticism, the world was an organized whole, whose phenomena functioned as the signs of the perfect world of ideas – the world of God. Discourse, as a collection of signs, was instrumentalized as tool of a rationality, the strength of the demand for which had already been emphasized by Abelard (died 1142):

> My students demanded human reasons, they needed intelligible explanations rather than affirmations. They said that it is useless to speak if you do not communicate understanding of your words, and that no one can believe if they have not first understood.

For Thomas Aquinas (died 1274) and the Dominicans, dialectics made it possible to construct 'an intelligible theory of the real', which the Church crowned by the study of the Scriptures and tradition. Reason, first of the human faculties, could not prove dogma, but it demonstrated its likelihood. For William of Occam (died *c.*1349), signs did not describe real objects but the idea of them (concepts). Nevertheless, the status of the concept remained problematic: it could refer to the actual structure of the object (*in re*), to a prior reason of divine order (*ante rem*), or to a construction of the human mind (*post rem*). This meant that the concepts could in their turn be understood as signs that did not exist in themselves, but only in and through the human mind: metaphysics and rational theology became 'vain sciences', whereas 'he who we know on earth is another than God' and only revealed theology contributed. This nominalism prevailed in Paris in the second half of the fourteenth century and was the basis of the fundamental distinction between the scientific life and the religious life; Pierre d'Ailly, chancellor of the University, took up these ideas, as did his pupil and successor, Gerson.[10]

To give primacy to the (written) letter and the literal signification was protection against going astray in ill-founded developments. It assumed thinking about what the words meant, but also, in good scholastic fashion, being as precise as possible about the operating conditions of the discourse, especially as the problems of equivocations (homonyms), plurivocal signs, stylistic devices (tropes) and ambiguities of all sorts made the signifying/signified articulation more or less direct and restrictive. Intellectual material was divided, therefore, into sections and subsections of a normalized analytical framework: *partes*, *membra*, *quaestiones* and lastly *articuli*, at the level at which one tried further to refine the analysis. The history of reading also played a part in this development. Until the twelfth century, the semiotic triangle was not recognized because reading remained oralized, whether one was read to or read to oneself, aloud or murmuring. Hearing was the dominant sense, and there was no need to decode a particular text as a written object because it was not at first perceived visually. It was not, therefore, necessary for the layout of the page to analyse the written text in detail, by the separation of the words or the development of standardized systems of punctuation. There was a direct relationship between the meaning of the text, its reading and its understanding by meditating on it, the written and oralized text functioning as the visible tip of a larger complex. As the Apostle Paul had explained: 'the letter killeth, but the spirit giveth life';[11] it was therefore the Spirit that must be found when words as such were of little importance. Claudius of Turin confirmed this at the beginning of the ninth century: 'Blessed are the eyes which see the divine spirit through the letter's veil.'[12] And the historian Stanley Morison believes that 'understanding came not through such indirect means as words and images, but directly through the effects [of those words and images]'.[13]

It was this ancient construction that was challenged from the twelfth and thirteenth centuries by the conception of written discourse as a collection of signs and by the increasingly widespread practice of silent reading. The perspective remained teleological (Creation and history had a meaning), but the literal meaning (given by the words) gradually took precedence over the spiritual meaning: one must ponder the words and other components of the text, the result of this reflection being 'a product of research, and [not] a gift of the Spirit'. This explains the effort put into the study of the Scriptures, their content, and their *mise en texte*, that is, the structuring of the text, in Oxford and above all Paris. In his *Summa theologica*, Thomas Aquinas returned to and refined the doctrine of the quadruple meaning of a text: literal, allegorical (the text announced the coming of Christ), moral (it showed how to lead one's life) and eschatological.

Central to the change, therefore, was work on the text, and on the most important text of all, the Bible, which it might be possible to clarify and better understand by engaging in exegesis. The interpretation of the Scriptures became a science, which led to the definition of a method applicable to other fields of thought.

Change: The Contents

Though the twelfth and thirteenth centuries saw a huge increase in written production, they were also characterized by a contradictory process. Massively over-simplifying, we may describe this output as influenced by three different trends: first, a tendency to specialization;[14] second, and *a contrario*, a degree of standardization, through the enlargement of the reading public; and lastly the book could also become an object of social assignation or, to use the vocabulary of Pierre Bourdieu, of distinction, as well as a demonstration of power.

Specialized texts

Alongside the classics of every library, the sacred and patristic texts, liturgical works, etc., there were now specialized treatises, which proliferated in fields as various as medicine, the law, politics and other branches of knowledge, from the natural sciences to history. Scholasticism encouraged the extension of the inventory of curiosities to the whole of Creation. Albert the Great, professor of theology in Paris and teacher of Thomas Aquinas, was the author of a *De natura rerum* (1270) which is remarkable not only for the innovative nature of its aim (to catalogue the whole of the physical world), but for the method adopted to achieve it: he accepted the immutability of the species, then passed under review all living beings beginning with mankind, according to a logical classification and an alphabetic sub-classification. The latter, based on an abstract code, introduced the principle of a formal logic completely alien to the structure of the population described, but *a contrario* made it easy, even for a non-specialist, to consult the volume. The perfected genre of scholasticism was the summa, an encyclopedic form introduced by Alexander of Hales (*c.*1231), which culminated in the *Summa theologica* of Thomas Aquinas: the summa was the world in a book, and once again it was a 'paper world'.

These specialized manuscripts took one of two very different forms, depending on whether they were working notes or a more finished document. The clerks were perfectly at ease with writing, so a type of manuscript appeared which was characterized by a rapid cursive script, heavy abbreviation and, increasingly, the use of paper as support. The page layout was basic and the signposting throughout a very dense text confined to cursory and brief marginal notes. The models for these working manuscripts were provided by university books, student notes, and so on. Other, much more polished, special-ized manuscripts were veritable scientific treatises, dealing with sub-jects such as theology, astronomy, arithmetic and computation, and the care put into their manufacture meant that they could take their place if so desired in the most prestigious princely libraries; in which case they were often in the vernacular. The *Livre de chasse* of the count of Foix, Gaston Phoebus, is a spectacular example of the latter from the late fourteenth century; it deals with a specialized field, admittedly, but one of direct relevance for courtly life.[15]

The reversal of the problematic of the sign was accompanied in the twelfth and even more the thirteenth century by the increased importance of the written text seen as aid to order and rationality. In the case of the operating rules of the Church, this process was visible in the systematic organization of a body of specialized law, canon law, which was effectively applied to the whole of society.[16] The spirit of Gregorian reform encouraged a return to the sources as the basis for the labour of reflection and reorganization – a charac-teristic objective of the specialists in writing; it was first visible in Italy, particularly Bologna, and then France. This shift was given impetus by the demand from the new universities, where texts were needed to support teaching. So, the monumental juridical collections were gradually assembled: Ivo of Chartres, around 1140, set out to gather a mass of scattered elements into coherent collections, and the result of his work was the *Decretum* of Gratian, 'more than 4000 fragments, primarily from conciliar and patristic texts and to a lesser extent texts of Roman law' (A. Lefèvre-Teillard). The *Decretum*, foundation of canon law, was added to by collections of the decretals issued by successive popes: the *Decretals* of Gregory IX (1234), the *Sexte* of Boniface VIII (1298), the *Clémentines* (1317) and the *Extravagantes*. The same process was undertaken in the sphere of civil law, where the *Code* of the Imperial Constitutions was completed by the *Digest* (or *Pandects*), the *Institutes* and the *Novellae* (up to the thirteenth century), which together formed the corpus of civil law (*Corpus juris civilis*).

Not only did the search for written sources and their compilation and organization make it possible to put the law on a firm footing, but the written reference became the basis for rational thinking, because the text was itself a tool for the rationalization and manipulation of the world. Other texts were drawn up, therefore, which reflected the labour of thinking: specialized summae on the reading of particular texts (such as the *Decretum*) or on particular problems, and above all commentaries, some of which became classics and were taught in their turn. Accursius commented on the *Corpus juris civilis*, Bernard of Parma and Jean André on the essence of canon law, and other manuals were prepared for every sort of reading and discussion. Everywhere and always, it was work on the text and reference to the text which made it possible to develop thinking and organize discussion.

Towards a wider public

However, writing and the book now impacted on a wider public, albeit still a small and privileged group, and must respond to their needs. I will return to the question of the books of piety, and discuss here only the rise of the vernacular as a written language. As urban civilization increased in importance, the vernacular began to predominate in both documentary archives (administrative records) and business records. At the same time, a growing number of texts were written or translated and copied in the vernacular, in response to the demand from a wider public for recreation, prestige and documentation. The 'histories' met the first two of these needs, being both chronicles that were read out of interest (to study models) or curiosity and also texts with a political dimension – to glorify the exploits of a dynasty or an individual. The genre was particularly developed round the Capetian monarchy, after Geoffroy de Villehardouin (*c*.1150–1213), author of a *History of the Fourth Crusade*;[17] Joinville (1225–1317) wrote his *History of St Louis* at the request of Queen Jeanne de Navarre, wife of Philip the Fair; Froissart (1337–*c*.1410) lived in the entourage of various princes (the count of Foix, the English court, Guy of Dampierre) and wrote his *Chronicles* from 1373; Christine de Pisan wrote a biography of Charles V for Philip the Brave. And so on. This genre spread to the Burgundian court, where Philip the Good created the office of *indiciaire* (chronicler) to the duke, of which the first incumbent was Georges Chastelain. I should refer also to Philippe de Comines (1447–1511), career diplomat, who transferred from Charles the Rash to Louis XI (1472) and wrote his *Memoirs* from 1489.

The 'romances' were recreational texts in the vernacular. They frequently conformed to the ethic and values of chivalry – honour, loyalty, piety – and their themes mixed heroes of antiquity (Alexander) and more recent (Charlemagne) or mythical persons. There were references to Christianity everywhere, as shown by the example of King Arthur and his twelve knights, but also by the themes of pilgrimage and, above all, crusade. They were poems, and in France the most important of them appeared in the twelfth century and were intended to be read aloud: the classic example, from the beginning of that century, is the *Chanson de Roland*. Among the most famous are the courtly romances of Chrétien de Troyes (died *c.*1190): *Tristan et Iseut* (lost) and the Arthurian romances (*Lancelot*, *Perceval*, the *Knight of the Lion*, etc.). Jean de Berry owned a sumptuous *Livre de messire Lancelot du Lac*, bought in 1405 for 300 gold écus from the Parisian bookseller Regnault du Montet, and '*couvert de drap de soye vert à deux fermoers dorez et sur chacun ais a V boullons de cuivre dorez*' ('covered with cloth of green silk with 2 clasps of gold and on each side V screws of gilded brass').[18] The love, even erotic, interest gradually increased: the *Roman de la rose* of Guillaume de Lorris and Jean de Meung is the most famous example.[19] This text was found in numerous princely or private libraries, including once again that of the duc de Berry, who received the manuscript as a gift, in 1403, from Martin Gouge, general treasurer and future bishop of Chartres (1408–15).[20] Its success led to a characteristic controversy among the French pre-humanists: Jean de Montreuil (died 1418), chancellor of Charles VI, friend of Coluccio Salutati, and himself a fine Latinist, was one of the most ferocious defenders of the text. Its enemies included Gerson, who wrote a 'treatise against the Roman de la rose' in 1402 in which he explained that if he was to own a copy, and it was the only one in existence, and worth £1,000, he would still rather burn it than sell it for fear of contributing to its success.[21]

The same was true of the growing number of translations into the vernacular, to which I will return. In short, and contrary to ancient practice, a cultural multilingualism prevailed in the world of writing once it ceased to be the sole preserve of groups of specialized clerks. We should also add to this mix the manuscripts containing the classics of antiquity and the post-classical authors, together with the 'manuals', collections of letters (their very existence testimony to a more widespread use of writing) and books of medicine, falconry and hunting, even rural economy (the *Liber ruralium commodorum* (*Book of rural benefits*) of Pietro de Crescenzi). Many of these works were eventually also printed. Over time, the new written culture spread by reproduction among the nobility, and, gradually, also the urban bourgeoisie. The status of the author, too, began to change: attached to the person of the prince, he was often in minor orders (which allowed him to receive ecclesiastical revenues), but had no prospect of living by his pen. The first author to achieve celebrity status was Petrarch (1304–74), in Italy and Avignon, while, more generally, awareness of the author – and hence of the text – increased. In his *Philobiblion*, Richard of Bury made the books themselves complain (*c*.1343):

> Every day, ignorant compilers, translators and transformers diminish our nobility by giving us new names of authors. This ancient nobility changed, we degenerate more and more every time we are reborn in numerous copies; we are made to write in spite of ourselves words used by bad authors, and sons are robbed of the names of their true fathers...

Change: The Objects and Practices

Methods of manufacture

The book may have become increasingly secularized, but the tools and working practices nevertheless remained very close to what they had been before the year 1000. There are innumerable portrayals of the scribe, the most detailed dating from the early Middle Ages. He is absorbed in his work: preparing the parchment, sharpening his pen (the goose quill replaced the reed in the sixth century), then copying strictly speaking. From the codicological study of a volume or the manuscript production of a particular workshop it is sometimes possible to deduce the principles underlying their work and establish if the manuscript was made according to the system of imposition – in which the copy was made on the flat, before the quire was folded. The support was parchment, usually sheepskin, later paper. The scribe wrote on his knees, especially in the case of students, but sometimes on a trestle table or a specific and more or less elaborate piece of furniture. This was usually a sloping desk, with bookshelves underneath, though the books might also be kept in a small closed cupboard. At the side was a shelf for the usual tools, including inkhorns; copyists and illuminators prepared their own inks and colours, the recipes varying in detail. Above the desk, a folding shelf held the manuscript to be copied. The furniture might be more elaborate, as in the painting by Giovanni De Paolo made in Siena *c*.1465. The artist has chosen the scene in which St Jerome appears to St Augustine, who is hard at work on a manuscript, virtually submerged by books, seated at a desk with several levels and also some small cupboards; it stands next to another piece of library furniture consisting of two book cupboards and a folding shelf. There are books everywhere, but also the paraphernalia of the writer: an inkwell, a pair of spectacles, pens, etc. The painting is also evidence of the modern way of reading, that is, the extensive reading of many books consulted for the purposes of the work in hand, rather than the intensive reading of a single text constantly reread and pondered; a reading now more often individual and silent, rather than oralized or for the benefit of a circle of listeners.[22]

Either way, copying was slow work and its cost considerably increased by the price of parchment, not forgetting, once the job was completed, the possible later passage of the volume through the workshops of decoration and rubrication, painting and binding.

The text

The more widespread use of books also meant changes in the economics of the book. In the monastic scriptorium the cost of manufacture had been of little consequence, but things changed once a wider society was involved. The desire to reduce costs is apparent in the shift from an expensive support (parchment) to one that was more accessible (paper), while the density of the page was increased, even tripled in some cases. Another way of broadening access to books was the creation of libraries, in particular within universities and colleges.

At a quite different level, developments in the scholastic method influenced not only the conception and content of texts but also the disposition of the pages and the material form of the volumes, leading to new ways of using them. The form of the book, the reading practices associated with it, and the intellectual categories underpinning the appropriation of its content were directly connected.[23] Scholasticism assumed the progressive divisibility of everything, a divisibility which made possible its analysis and comprehension, and this conception, foundation of university teaching, was expressed in architecture as well as in writing.[24] In Gothic architecture, the play of the columns and vaults materialized the hierarchy of the forces at work in the construction of the building. As regards writing, the Carolingian miniscule disintegrated in the tenth and eleventh centuries, giving way to the new forms of gothic: the ductus was retained,[25] but it broke down into several successive strokes accentuating the contrast between the downstrokes and upstrokes. Gothic script might be said to have functioned as an analysis of the writing, its breaks echoing the play of architecture and referencing the developments of an intellectual analysis attentive to the connections between the whole and its parts. Its use all over Europe by the twelfth and thirteenth centuries means that it is possible to propose a complex typology according to regions and uses: gothic *de somme* (rotunda), perfectly written, was meant for scientific treatises (the summae), whereas textura (also called *Lettre de forme*) was primarily used for liturgical books and was adopted as model by Gutenberg for the characters of his *42-line Bible* (1455). Bastarda, lastly, slightly slanted, was used primarily for copying manuscripts in the vernacular. The most cursive forms were the most common, for legal documents and some university manuscripts.

In Carolingian manuscripts, the words had usually not been separated, which made an oralized reading necessary. Gradually, an increasing autonomy of the text developed together with the growth of silent reading, especially among scholars. This required a careful management of the written text so that it contained within itself the indicators that would make a productive reading possible. This led, especially from the eleventh century, to major changes in the *mise en livre*, with the separation of words, the division of the text into autonomous sections and subsections, the growth of indexes, etc.[26] Similarly, a standardized system of punctuation spread, especially in the twelfth century, with the period or full point (marking the principal scansion), the semicolon, the period or full point with a circumflex over (for secondary scansions) and the hyphen (for words split at the end of line).[27] Weak punctuation was indicated by an oblique line (/), a sign which evolved into the comma. The initial accentuated by colour marked the beginning of the sentence, and the pilcrow (¶) was used for our division into paragraphs. Quotations (such as passages from the Bible) were gradually given special treatment, designed to identify them as parts of reported discourse. The next main innovations emerged in Italian humanist circles, where the exclamation mark and brackets were gradually adopted (*c.*1400). This assemblage of signs organized into a code was taken further in printed books, with the aim of regularizing textual practices and establishing a method making it possible to identify with certainty the literal meaning of the text.

It would be hard to exaggerate the importance of these developments: once the reader found in the text only the literal meaning put there by the author, groups of readers with the same sensibility, sometimes called 'textual communities', could form around a certain corpus. This was probably one of the distant origins of the movements for Church reform, which aimed always at a return to the Word and to the early Church. The first book to be studied was the Bible, and the task was made all the more urgent by the need of universities and schools for a series of homogeneous manuscripts of the sacred texts. The Dominicans of the rue St Jacques were the pioneers, especially under the direction of Hugh of St-Cher, prior from 1233 to 1236: the Bible was corrected and revised according to the Vulgate of St Jerome; Stephen Langton introduced the division into chapters;[28] and the sacred text was widely distributed in the form of small manuscripts, on very fine parchment, in tiny script, with a hierarchized page layout. Thousands of copies of this 'University Bible' were produced, so many that it may well be that their dissemination was not unrelated to the speculation of Parisian bookshops. Work on the text also led the Dominicans to prepare Bible concordances: they combed through the text *in extenso*, classified all the words in alphabetical order and indicated all the various occurrences of each one, making it possible to identify and clarify the meaning. More than eighty manuscripts of the third and most developed version of these concordances survive, copied in Paris between 1280 and 1330.[29] Similar procedures were subsequently adopted outside the field of the Scriptures. When, for example, Nicole Oresme translated Aristotle, he completed his work with a 'table of noteworthy subjects', in alphabetical order; it amounted to an index of the principal themes addressed, with references to the books and chapters of the main text. He added a second working tool in the form of a table of 'key words of Politics', effectively a sort of specialized glossary. Always and everywhere, words were being processed and their possible meanings pondered.[30]

Ruling lines before copying structured a page layout which might often, from the eleventh century, be extremely complex, according to the levels of text. The structure of medieval teaching and the practice of the commentary meant that the text became inseparable from an apparatus of commentaries that was sometimes as long as the text itself – or even longer. The main text was copied in larger letters and the gloss (the commentary) might be placed next to the corresponding passage, in the margin and in smaller letters (marginal gloss), or it might be interpolated into the text itself (interlinear gloss). The two systems might be combined on the same page, depending on the level of the commentaries in question: the shorter commentaries (explaining a word) appearing in an interlinear gloss, the longer surrounding the main text. The construction of the page was even more complicated if it was necessary to insert commentaries on commentaries, as was often the case. The practice then was to include navigational systems making it possible to link each gloss to the passage to which it referred. The numbering of the leaves (foliation) or pages (pagination) spread only slowly from the twelfth century, though running titles were generally earlier.[31]

The organization of the discourse was made gradually more visible, first by the separation of the words, then by the differentiation of sections of text; the latter was done less by the use of paragraphs (with line breaks and first line indents) than by incipits distinguished, for example, by their larger letters or the use of coloured inks. The content of the passage was sometimes reiterated in the margin in a short review or simply highlighted by the insertion of a manchette.[32] The various reference systems were most highly developed in the biblical manuscripts, where concordances, tables and indexes emerged and developed, most notably in the work of the Dominicans.[33] Tables of chapters also began to appear, sometimes numbered, though usually without pagination. This rapid growth of reference systems implies that reading was no longer done *in extenso*, but that it was now possible to refer to a particular issue or passage at will. By contrast, in the fifteenth century, the humanist manuscript was centred on the text, presented alone on the page and in a new calligraphy (humanistic script), sometimes with a sumptuous painted decoration – for example in the manuscripts of the king of Hungary, Mathias Corvin. The page layout revealed from one period to the next the changed status of the principal text – and of its author.

The decoration of manuscripts, and even to a lesser degree their illustration, constituted a tool that was used not only to represent, but to clarify the textual organization. The illustration was sometimes an element in the modernity of the thought: the manuscripts of the *De natura rerum* of Albert the Great often illustrate each of their successive articles, revealing the desire to provide an image capable of objectifying the object described. The aesthetic aim is clear, but the image was also required to enrich the text from the perspective of pre-scientific information. But at the same time, the more or less spectacular and sumptuous nature of the decorative elements was organized into a scale which revealed the structure of the text through the hierarchy of its constituent sections and subsections. As we have seen, the incipit was given special treatment (a coloured ink, a script with larger letters or in a different character), but this treatment sometimes spilled over from the field of the writing itself: the beginning of the text might be emphasized by a border or frieze, a decorated or historiated letter, sometimes a painting or miniature. The Bible of Sawalo, copied at Saint-Amand in the third quarter of the twelfth century, consists of five folio volumes written by the same scribe and remarkably decorated. Aids for locating and searching appear throughout its leaves: table of the Gospels; concordances in an architectural frame of Roman inspiration; large letters decorated with interlaced patterns including animal figures; titles in capital letters; and each volume introduced by a *page-tapis* ('carpet page') initial signed by the painter.[34] In the Gothic period the decorated initial was sometimes integrated into the marginal decoration. One very common theme was that of the vine (*vigne* in French, hence the term 'vignette'), with its tracery of foliage, and which, especially in Parisian manuscripts, served as support for figures of persons or animals (the 'drolleries' or grotesques). Also widely found was the historiated initial (integrating a particular scene), for example the 'I' opening the text of Genesis (*In principio creavit Deus*...= In the beginning God created...). There were other common themes: the Old Testament identified the fool as he who did not believe (Psalm 53: The fool hath said in his heart, there is no God), and this explains the presence of the figure of the fool in the illumination of many capital Ds. This system of marking by elements external to the text continued in printed works.

The book was a material object, whose characteristics were for the reader inseparable from its contents. The form chosen for the book, its *mise en livre*, began with a bibliographical format, which was dictated by both the contents and custom. Large, even monumental, formats dominated in the case of the Holy Scriptures until the twelfth century, a model that persisted for a long time to come and was still adopted for some manuscript Bibles in the sixteenth century. The books used for divine service and the basic treatises of the reference libraries also usually had a monumental format – the Fathers of the Church, commentaries on the Scriptures, major legal treatises, etc. By contrast, classical texts were copied in smaller manuscripts, often quarto, in line with a tradition dating back to the Carolingian Renaissance. This form also predominated for university manuscripts from the twelfth century, a period when many manuscripts in smaller format appeared, especially Bibles. Lastly, manuscripts in the vernacular languages, which proliferated from the thirteenth century, took a variety of forms, depending on their contents and the status of their owner. The book became an indicator of social assignation: large monumental copies made for the powerful, smaller formats for readers of lesser status. Books of Hours, which are not strictly speaking liturgical books, needed above all to be easy to handle: they were tiny, beautifully made manuscripts, such as those whose praises were sung by Eustache Deschamps at the end of the fourteenth century:

> Heures me fault de Nostre Dame/Si comme il appartient à fame/Venue de noble paraige,/Qui soient de soutil ouvraige/D'or et d'azure; riches et cointes/Bien ordonnées et bien pointes,/De fin drap d'or très bien couvertes;/Et, quand elles seront ouvertes/Deux fermaulx d'or qui fermeronts,/Qu'adoncques seuls qui les verront/Puissent partout dire et compter/Qu'on ne puet plus belles porter...

> (I need Hours of Our Lady/as proper for a woman of noble standing,/ which are of delicate workmanship/ of gilt and blue, rich and elegant/ well designed and painted,/well covered in fine gold leaf;/ and, when they are opened,/two gold clasps which will close,/So that then those who see them/ tell and relate/that one cannot carry a finer one...)

The image

It is not my purpose here to engage in an art historical debate, but rather to emphasize a few points of particular significance. Erwin Panofsky constructed a chronology specific to the history of art which overlaps with that described here, distinguishing between the three levels of meaning of an image: (1) the *motif* is independent of any experience allowing a scene to be identified as, for example, that of Christ's Last Supper: at this pre-iconographical level, the motif would, in this particular case, simply be regarded as that of a meal taken in common; (2) iconographical analysis makes it possible to identify the *themes* represented through the scene, the problem being that of the interpretation by the artist and its subjectivity, and the articulation of the motif and the theme produces the image; and (3) lastly, there is the *content*, or intrinsic meaning of the image: this is the level of iconological analysis, which is applied to the symbols represented in the work and makes it possible to discover its precise meaning. Panofsky showed that the relationship between the two first levels changed between the tenth and eleventh centuries: in the Carolingian period the classic motifs were articulated with classical themes because the artists, including the book illustrators, still had classical models in their mind's eyes. Increasingly, however, the Middle Ages developed an original civilization, which combined classical motifs and non-classical themes, or non-classical motifs and classical themes:

> Wherever a classical image, that is, a fusion of a classical *theme* with a classical *motif*, has been copied during the Carolingian period... this classical image was abandoned as soon as medieval civilization had reached its climax, and was not reinstated until the Italian Quattrocento. It was the privilege of the Renaissance proper to reintegrate classical *themes* with classical *motifs* after what might be called a zero hour.[35]

The history of perspective confirms this chronology, returning by another route to the relationship between the world and its representation. If the painters of Graeco-Roman antiquity mastered perspective, it was through specific modes of construction, in a curved space and according to an aggregative representation. For the ancients, 'the totality of the world always remained something radically discontinuous',[36] so space was not susceptible to a homogeneous representation. The dislocation of the perspective in the paintings of the early Middle Ages relates to the reversal operated by Christianity: the world was the materialization of the Word of God, thus it formed a *continuum* which the artist reproduced by the representation of simple surface planes and by the play of lines and colours. If the Carolingian Renaissance reintroduced the motifs of the ancient perspective, the impossibility of integrating the data with a thinking based on the play of surfaces rendered the attempt short-lived: drawing was line drawing, the perspective remained inadequate, and the symbolic elements were many.

> The Middle Ages believed that everything was in God. There was no distance between things, because they were only the manifestation of a single essence. The representation of space by values, attributes of moral meaning, followed from this.[37]

The rediscovery of the Aristotelian doctrine of a finite space made it possible to approach the problem afresh. The invention was Italian, when Cimabue (died *c.*1302), Duccio (died *c.*1318) and Giotto (died *c.*1337) set out to reconstruct pictorial perspective through the use of geometry (vanishing lines and the idea of a constantly measurable distance) and according to a model which soon spilled over into the sphere of the book. Based on the elaboration of a mathematical theory of space and its representation, the construction of a unified space by the unicity of the vanishing point was, nevertheless, slow, which was related to a tendency for the possible objectification of the external world and implicitly posed in new terms the articulation between it and Revelation. The unity of space also made it possible to involve the spectator in the scene, becoming a realistic image of the tangible world: the space from which one observed the work was the same as that of the work itself. This mode of representation appeared first in Tuscany, but also in Naples, where Giotto once lived, Avignon, and Lombardy. Thus the 'Renaissance' style marks less a rupture than the systematization of the mathematical construction of space and the constancy of the reference to antiquity.

Once the model of strictly documentary illustration was left behind, the image also brought into play systems of codes, whether in the case of its content or its representation. The code of colours was particularly important: colours immediately signified in themselves and were organized into a hierarchy descending from red (prestige) to black (edification), to green (love, beauty), to brown, etc. The symbolism might be multiple, as with blue, colour of loyalty, but also of the royal house of France, and all these usages were eventually codified – for example in the *Blason des couleurs* of *c*.1458. But the book was also a symbolic object, part of more or less restrictive social codes. With the secularization of books and the developments of scholasticism, and then the emergence of the great princely dynasties, which gradually assembled extraordinary libraries, increasing attention was paid to illustration as evidence of wealth and prestige. In the princely manuscripts of the fourteenth and fifteenth centuries, the script is a calligraphy of large character, and the quality of the support (a beautifully prepared vellum) contributes to the aesthetic of the page. The manuscripts of the dukes of Burgundy and Berry were illustrated by the greatest Burgundo-Flemish and French artists of the age. The richness of the binding also contributed to making these books high luxury items, sometimes intended more for display than for reading or consultation – as their state of preservation reveals. They cost a fortune: the French illuminated manuscript of the *De proprietatibus rerum* ('Of the properties of things') of Bartholomew the Englishman was sold *'tout neuf et ystorié'* ('all new and histori-ated') to the duke of Burgundy, Philip the Bold, in 1400, for the enormous sum of 400 gold écus.[38]

Reading practices

Changes in reading practices were fundamental to these develop-ments. At the level of ideas, the theory of the semiotic triangle shows that the transition from intensive and oralized reading to a form of extensive and silent reading accompanied the construction of the theory of the sign. The expansion of the potential readership, though relative, led to major shifts at the sociological level: increasingly, from the eleventh century, the book emerged from the world of religious houses to permeate the whole of society, especially in the urban centres, and the conditions of production and dissemination of texts changed as a result. Lastly, at the level of practices, the ways of reading a particular text were conditioned by the material form given to the book: the transition from the book in the form of a roll (volumen) to the book in quires (codex) made new ways of reading possible; the invention of the miniscule was a necessary precondition for rapid reading (fourth century); the internal organization of the copy made or did not make silent reading possible, and the navigational systems made or did not make possible a type of consultative reading, as opposed to sustained reading, etc. Where modern readers, accustomed to handling numerous volumes, take it for granted that they can always and easily return to the text, the university scholar of the Middle Ages systematically prioritized memorizing, and made this task easier by observing the physical characteristics of the page, with elements such as the script, rubrication, and so on. Chant reading was another way of assisting memorization, to the point where, if regularly repeated, the book itself might be rendered redundant. Finally, reading was not the only way in which a book could be used, and the rise of the princely bibliophile explains those sumptuous manuscripts destined to glorify their owners as much if not more than to serve a regular practice of reading.

However, this schema needs to be nuanced. The history of reading is often presented as a continuous development, which moves through a series of stages on the way to an increasingly abstract and intellectualized practice: from oralized reading to silent reading, from intensive reading to extensive reading, and from a minority practice to a majority practice, eventually generalized in Western societies. Though it is true that reading practices were increasingly modernized, it is important to emphasize that the change came about only slowly (the history of reading is a history of the 'third level', to use the phrase of Pierre Chaunu), and its principal distinguishing feature was the unevenness of the distribution of each phenomenon at any moment. In other words, the consequences of certain innovations (for example the generalization of the codex) for the practice of reading were not felt immediately, but over the long term, and both modern and more archaic practices coexisted at all times. It was with some surprise that St Augustine, visiting St Ambrose in his cell in Milan, observed that the saint was already familiar with a form of silent reading:

As he read, his eyes travelled over the page and his heart sought out the meaning, but his voice remained silent and his tongue did not move. Anyone who wanted could approach him freely, visitors were not generally announced, so that often when we came to pay him a visit, we found him engaged in reading like this in silence, because he never read aloud.[39]

St Augustine also distinguishes in passing the elements that would characterize the construction of the semiotic triangle, with the page (the signs), scanned by the eyes, and the articulation with the heart (the signified). Nevertheless, the spread of silent reading did not lead to the disappearance of oralized reading, which, as we have seen, was based on a specific organization of the text and a very limited use of abbreviations. For Geneviève Hasenohr, this absence of abbreviations, especially in manuscripts in the vernacular, is:

> a sign ... that the reading ... of texts in the langue d'oc and langue d'oïl remained *la lectio romane*, an oral deciphering progressing word by word throughout the discourse in a slow diachrony, whereas university reading had become a synchronic reading, which no longer heard the text but looked at the page, the eye, guided by many analytical markers, seeking to encompass it as a whole.

As the new reading practices spread, it was inevitable that they would acquire an increasingly important sociological dimension, between the two extremes of those who might be described as 'elite readers', that is, the clergy, the educated and university graduates, and the vast majority who simply did not know how to read. As a result, with a history of reading which prioritizes the spread of practices, we are already, implicitly, touching on the paradigm of the economy of the book and the invention of the market, which will be the subject of the next chapter.

3

The Birth of the Market

∽

We [books] are sold like slaves or servants, and we are like hostages in
the cupboards without any possibility of ransom...We are handed over
to Saracens, to heretics...

Richard of Bury

The Market and its Regulation

What is the market?

The demand for education and reading grew in European towns;
through the universities, the schools and the colleges, writing and
books spread to a wider society. This resulted, over time, in a transformation in the nature of the object: the manuscript had been essentially, in the Carolingian period, an object to be consulted, borrowed
or exchanged; it now became an item of merchandise endowed with
a value, which meant that an economy of the book, strictly speaking,
could develop. What triggered these changes, until Gutenberg, was
the joint action of the market and capitalism.

The classical analysis of the categories on which the construction
of capitalism was based distinguishes three principal levels of
exchange: at the first level, 'material civilization' directly combined
production and consumption and took place without monetary
exchanges. It was overwhelmingly predominant in the rural world of
the Middle Ages. Nevertheless, reproduction of the ancient techniques and practices, and self-sufficiency, do not preclude some

circulation of products and services, even their shared use, but within
a single community. In the case of the book, this was a world of the
monastic scriptorium, which combined production and 'consumption': each religious house assembled the collection of books it
believed it needed and that it had the material means to acquire. The
duty of obedience meant that the initiative of the abbot or his representative was decisive in the enrichment and management of the
collection. So the schoolmaster of Saint-Pierre de Luxeuil could
explain, in 1104, at the end of a copy of the *Geometry* of Boethius:

> I, Constantius, sinner and unworthy priest...I have copied for [the]
> service [of the monastery] these books of Boethius on geometry in only
> eleven days...on the orders of the pious Abbot Milo.

It is in this context, consequently, that studies of the history of
libraries based on their contents are most fruitful, adopting the perspective of the 'pragmatic scripturality' explored by German medie-
valists,[1] because the manuscripts present in a monastery were by
definition those that had been copied or acquired for the express
purpose of making them accessible. There was no market in books:
volumes circulated, in very small numbers, as loans or as gifts, and
texts were copied by those who needed them. Scholars readily
arranged to have books brought to them, even travelled long dis-
tances to acquire them.

The second level was soon superposed on the first. This was still
a system dominated by proximity, but it allowed exchanges to take
place and develop. The producer sold items himself or through a very
small number of intermediaries. A demand existed, and it was met
by the increasing volume of trade, but the nature of the goods in
circulation changed greatly from one place to another: in the rural
world, trade consisted almost entirely of basic commodities, agricul-
tural production or its conversion (flour, etc.), tools, textiles and a
few items of clothing. The range of goods was wider in urban centres
depending on the hierarchy of functions they performed. In the
smaller towns, embryonic administrative services, or a tiny court, or
the presence or proximity of a religious house required very little in
the way of stationery (parchment, ink, pens, perhaps a few books).
It was very different in the larger and more dynamic centres, where
there was a concentration of functions, administrative, religious (seat
of a bishopric or archbishopric), economic or cultural (a network of
schools, even a university). The increasing diversity of functions went
together with increasing social diversity. It was at this level that a first

market in books could develop, often associating production (copying) and circulation (sale and resale of manuscripts).

Lastly, the third level was where merchants intervened between the producers and the market: they bought to resell, operated on a larger geographical scale (that of the major international trade routes and fairs), and sought to maximize their profits. Their techniques grew more refined, with, for example, advance purchases, maintaining stocks of merchandise or financial and banking techniques. At this point we emerge from the system of the transparent market to enter that of capitalism, which favours concentration and monopoly. If we ignore a few 'princely booksellers', the sphere of the manuscript remained external to these enterprises, except at the crucial level of the relationship between capitalism and technical innovation and its applications. In fact, it was the investors, familiar with the practice of venture capital through the financing of distant voyages in search of the luxury products so highly prized in the Middle Ages, who financed the 'R & D' which would result in a gradual transformation of the whole economy of the book up to the 'Gutenbergian revolution'.

A regulatory system: the *pecia*

First, a few words on vocabulary: the *librarius*, a word dating back to antiquity, means a person who works with books, a scribe, a bookseller strictly speaking, even a librarian. The *stationarius*, by contrast, appeared in Bologna and Paris within the orbit of the university world. The root *statio* refers to a locale, but also, in the Roman period, to a subordinate administration, so the word refers to a certain type of official position: the *stationarius* was a person in possession of a privilege from the university, to which he also had obligations. The key practice of the *stationarius* was that of the *pecia* (quire). Though the oppositions may be less clear-cut in reality (Jean-François Genest believes there was a very active 'free sector'), the purpose of the *pecia* was threefold: it was first necessary to verify and authenticate the text of reference, which would serve as a basis for teaching; then to ensure multiplication by copying with maximum accuracy, eliminating as far as possible errors in reading; lastly, the university supervised the tariffs, which limited any possible speculation, while at the same time providing it with a resource in the form of the corresponding taxes. The *pecia* was thus in effect a regulatory system. In parallel, universities and colleges began to respond to the demand for books by creating and enriching libraries for study, whose operating principle was as much economic (regulating the market) as intellectual:

> It was in this way that, little by little, urban communities of teachers and students – the colleges – were created, which not only assumed responsibility in whole or in part for accommodation costs, but...offered collective access to books 'in timeshare' which dispensed with the need for each person to own his own copy of all the works indispensable to the transmission of knowledge.[2]

So, the *stationarius* was in possession of a copy of the text to be reproduced, whose contents had been verified by the university authorities (the exemplar). The manuscript was divided into quires (the *peciae*), each of which was handed to a different scribe so they could all be copied simultaneously. This required a precise timetable, which was rarely adhered to (the text to be copied was not available, the scribe moved on to the next, the space set aside was no longer appropriate). The work was done either on commission (the *stationarius* entrusted a particular piece of work to a copyist) or on hire (the client or his representative hired the successive sections and copied them or had them copied); in theory, it took four days to transcribe one *pecia*. The *stationarius* drew up a list of the exemplars he could offer his clients, the *taxatio*, specifying the price for renting each one. The hierarchization of the vocabulary testifies to the standardization of the work: one *charta* was a bifolio (two leaves); one *pecia* was a block of four leaves, that is, one leaf folded twice; the *quaternus* was two *peciae*. Certain manuscript references reveal that the document in question had been copied by the *pecia* system – in particular the numeration of the *peciae* by final formulas such as '*fi*[nit] *x pe*[cia]' (= 'end of tenth quire').

Chronologically speaking, the institutional *stationarius-pecia* system was already fully operative in Bologna in the first decade of the thirteenth century, before it spread to the other great university towns – including Paris by around 1270.[3] In Bologna, the sector was controlled by the commission of the *peciarii*. In Paris, the earliest university regulation dealing with the book trade (1275) makes no distinction between *librarius* and *stationarius*, the single clause addressing the need for booksellers to do everything in their power to avoid faulty copies of exemplars and to sell books only at a reasonable price.[4] Regulation of the book trade was still in its infancy, but it developed in the last quarter of the thirteenth century (as shown by the university regulation of 1302). In 1316, the *librarius* was distinguished from the *stationarius*, and the university exercised jurisdiction over all the book trades – *librarii* ('*librere*') and *stationarii*, copyists ('*escripvain*'), illuminators, parchmeners, binders, etc. Their members swore an oath and were exempted from the taille. Most of them, at one time or another, engaged in several of these activities. One final example: in the north of Spain, at Lerida, an official act regulated the operation of the *stationarii* active in the town.

Thanks to the lists established by the *stationarii* and to codicological research, we are able to identify the limits of the corpus of texts disseminated by the *pecia*. A list of Parisian *exemplaria* dating from the years 1272–6 first offers the texts of the Fathers of the Church and the twelfth-century theologians, then

> treatises relating more or less directly to the faculty of arts: Bartholomew the Englishman [etc.], and finally Latin translations of Greek commentaries on Aristotle. Followed by three theological manuals in constant use in teaching: the *Summa de penitentia* of Raymond de Pennafort, the *Sentences* of Peter Lombard and the *Historia scolastica* of Petrus Comestor. Next came a rubric: *Ista sunt exemplaria in*...[the theological manuscripts follow...].[5]

The list ends with works classified by author, St Thomas Aquinas, St Bonaventure and Peter of Tarentaise, the glossed Bible, sermon collections, sixteen works of canon law and ten of civil law, in all a total of 138 items. Another Parisian list, of 1304, fixes the price of the *exemplaria* available in the shop of the *stationarius* Andrew of Sens: 156 items, but containing far fewer sermon collections, biblical commentaries, patristic texts and twelfth-century theological texts. Louis Jacques Bataillon has emphasized, however, that a survey of the surviving manuscripts produces a different corpus than that of these lists: for example, only three Bibles made by the *pecia* system survive, but, conversely, so do a whole range of manuscripts in *pecia* that do not appear in the lists. This reveals both the inadequacy of the documentation and that the *pecia* was not applied in a totally systematic and rigorous fashion.

The Religious Paradigm, or the Emergence of the Masses

The religious crisis and the growth of a mystical sensibility played a decisive role in the expansion of the demand for books and graphic material (pious images) among a much wider public. It was also a modernizing factor, encouraging individual reading and an increased use of the vernacular as a written language.

Mysticism and the experience of immediacy

I mean here by mysticism the individual experience of God, to which the faithful acceded through contemplation in their inner self. The mystical movement fused the reflection of the very deepest thinkers and the practice of the masses. It sometimes assumed a dimension of protest in the face of a grave religious crisis, and it had significant consequences for the economy of the book. As we have seen, nominalist theories, developed in the tradition of William of Occam, distinguished the spheres of human reason and of Revelation: if his reason only allowed man to know 'an other than God', it was nevertheless still possible for the faithful to have an immediate experience of God through revelation and ecstasy. The sanctuary of revelation was wholly internal: 'It is in the depths of the soul, under a light described as marvellous, that the divine truth, which is a hidden truth, is revealed' (J.-A. Bizet). The spread of mysticism was linked to that of the mendicant orders, the Franciscans (such as William of Occam), and above all the Dominicans. It involved, from an apostolic perspective, making available to the majority an experience previously reserved to a minority, in line with the order's motto (*contemplata aliis traderer* = to pass on to others the things contemplated). God could be found in each one of us:

> In the most private depths of our soul where he is more present than it is to itself...this search is pursued by meditation, which delivers us from the senses and images, from every form imported from the outside, and makes us inhabit ourselves; by interior renunciation, which attaches little importance to the operations of our reason and our own will, and delivers us from ourselves; by the abandonment, lastly, which allows the soul to return to its source and God to empty it of what is not his work in order to fill from himself the void he has made...[6]

Though God might be found in each one by each one himself, the search for him was still mediated through the word (the preachers and the apostolate), written documents and pious images. This was implicitly revolutionary: if each Christian could find God in himself, where did that leave the status and role of the first order, the Church, especially in a period when it was in the throes of a series of major crises? One last notable characteristic of these different movements was their relationship to the universities: the initiators were clergy, but their activities took place outside any institution and were aimed at the laity and the mass of the people in the towns. This was a factor of huge importance, for the expansion of the potential reading public or 'consumers' of texts and images, for the status of the intellectual and for the re-evaluation of the role of literacy in the society of the age.

Erfurt, Oxford, Prague

Erfurt, capital of Thuringia, was a town that had experienced huge social and economic change since the 1150s. A century later, the Dominican provincial, Johann Eckhart (died 1328), former professor in Paris, Strasbourg, and Cologne, preached in the city, in the vernacular, on the necessity of solitude and individual prayer.[7] The man, who soon became known as 'Meister Eckhart', spoke to each individual of the possibility of knowing God through mystical experience and revelation. A bull of Jean XXII condemned twenty-eight of his theses in 1327, but Eckhart died the following year. His influence remained strong in the regions of middle Germany and the Rhine Valley; among his disciples and successors were Tauler, in Strasbourg (died 1361), Heinrich Seuse called Suso (died Ulm 1366) and the Brabanter Ruysbroeck (died Groenendaal, 1381). The region between Thuringia, the Rhine Valley and the Low Countries was one of the great poles of Western modernity.[8]

Two generations later came the second great figure of the reform movement, John Wycliffe (died 1384).[9] A former student of Balliol College, Oxford, Wycliffe, too, was a true university product, made doctor of theology in 1372. His work, based on scholasticism, convinced him of the need for religious reform. In his *De Dominio divino* (1375), he developed his theory of Grace, which he extended by a critique of the institutional Church through the theory of the two Churches: to the Church of the Antichrist responded the invisible Church of the elect in a state of grace (the treatises *De Ecclesia* and *Doctrinale*). The official Church was not the Church of the elect; many of its institutions and practices were open to criticism, including the cult of images, the papacy (*De Dissensione paparum*), the material wealth of the regular orders and the practice of indulgences. For Wycliffe, the Bible was the sole source of the Christian faith and morality (*De Veritate Scripturae*, 1378), which posed as fundamental the problem of its reading and its possible interpretation. Advocating a primarily literal reading of the Bible, Wycliffe returned to the questions of the nature of the sign and the role of metaphor, etc., to which he devoted the *Postilla*, the *Trialogus* (the first of his texts to be printed, in 1525), the *De Veritate Sacre Scripture*, and the *Opus evangelicum*, as well as numerous sermons.[10] Lastly, he undertook the translation of the Bible into English.[11] In 1381, however, he was forced to leave Oxford for Lutterworth, where he died three years later.

Three theses of Wycliffe were condemned as heretical by the synod of Canterbury in 1382, including that on the Eucharist – once again a question relating to the nature of the sign: the bread and wine preserved their material substance in the sacrament, in which Christ was not physically present (treatises *De Eucharistia Confessio* of 1381 and part of the *Trialogus*). Wycliffe wrote in Latin, normal university practice, but his texts were translated into the vernacular, amended, and widely circulated, either orally (by preachers) or in writing. A particularly important manuscript was the *Floretum*, a summary in extracts of Wycliffian theses, in alphabetical order and with an index. The prologue stated that the work was intended for the *pauperes sacerdotes* (poor priests), and its influence is apparent in many sermons. These positions had major political consequences in England, with the movement of the Lollards ('babblers'); in Oxford circles this name was also applied to the rebellious peasants who seized London in 1381, and to groups of townspeople, members of the lower clergy, sometimes to nobles, even to people close to the court. The *Twelve Conclusions* posted in 1392 on the doors of Westminster Hall, during a session of Parliament, focused primarily on a critique of the Church and its reform. As in Prague at the beginning of the fifteenth century, and then in Wittenberg in 1517, we observe a modern system of publicity through the written word, and, to give their message greater impact, the Lollards wrote in English. In the first decades of the fifteenth century, the movement was increasingly directly associated with rebellion. The doctrines of Wycliffe were condemned by the Council of Constance in 1415; the body of the *doctor evangelicus* was to be exhumed and burned and his ashes scattered, a sentence repeated in 1427 and carried out in 1428.

Wycliffe's influence was also considerable in a quite different geographical area, that of Prague and Bohemia, where it was assisted both by the circulation of students and by the presence in London of Anne of Bohemia, queen of Richard II.[12] Once again, this was a very modern geography: it was the wealth provided by the silver mines that enabled the king of Bohemia to make himself the most important lay Elector of the Empire. The Emperor Charles IV of Luxembourg (died 1378) wanted to turn Bohemia into a modern principality, around its capital Prague. All sources of power were concentrated in the town and it was the seat of the court, the administration and the new archbishopric (1344). A university was founded there in 1348, which soon became the most important in the German-speaking zone, and to which, in 1366, the emperor added the new *Collegium Carolinum*. Charles IV wanted to be a prince of letters, and he attracted artists and intellectuals to his court and set in motion a vast programme of editing and copying, partly in Czech. The interest of a wider public explains the remarkable role of the vernacular as a written language: the Bible was translated by the end of the fourteenth century, and dozens of copies dating from the fifteenth century survive.[13] Nevertheless, problems were already accumulating; the battles between the different 'nations' of the university led to its decline, to the benefit of Leipzig, while the rivalries between Germans and Czechs spread to a clergy already marked by the gulf between the hierarchy and the lower clergy. As economic difficulties worsened and a period of political crisis loomed, appeals for the reform of Church and society multiplied.

One of Wycliffe's disciples, Jerome (Hieronymus) of Prague, played a major role in the early days, but from 1409 the movement was led by John Hus (1369–1415), a native of Husinec (southern Bohemia), a former student in Prague, a priest (1400) and rector of the university (1402–3). Hus preached in the vernacular in the new Bethlehem Chapel in Prague, wrote hymns, translated the *Trialogus* of Wycliffe into Czech, and reformed the language and orthography; he also entered into increasingly fierce conflict with the Church, which he in his turn criticized for its wealth, its temporal power and its secular practices. The radicalization of the movement accelerated the break. The archbishop of Prague, who had supported Hus, began to distance himself from his theses. Hus, who refused to burn his Wycliffian writings, was excommunicated in 1410. The disturbances spread to Prague, and worsened when he condemned the trade in indulgences (1411) and wrote his *De Ecclesia* (1412). Recognition of the immanence of the divine made the instrumentalization of the latter unthinkable and brought discredit on a religion of contract; a bull on indulgences was publicly burnt in Prague in 1412. Even more clearly than in Erfurt and Oxford, the written word was central to the struggle in Bohemia: Scripture was the sole reference, to which everyone should have direct access, which meant that the reform of the Church posed the question of literacy and the use of the vernacular. Hus withdrew to southern Bohemia, but was excommunicated by Jean XXII in 1412. He declared his readiness to explain himself before the council and received a royal safe conduct for his visit to Constance, but was arrested soon after his arrival, called on to retract, condemned, and burned at the stake (6 July 1415). The Czech reaction led to the first Bohemian Wars: the first Defenestration of Prague (1419) and the proclamation of the Articles of Prague, which established the Reformation (freedom to preach, poverty of the clergy, formation of a popular national army).

Hussitism acted as a major impetus to writing and to translation into the vernacular, Czech or High German, and Bible study was practised in Bohemia at all social levels. If the Hussites, like the Lollards, ultimately failed, unlike the Lutherans a century later, it was no doubt because they lacked access to printing to spread their message, but it was primarily because their activities posed a radical challenge to the social and political order – whereas Luther made a very different choice at the time of the Peasants War. From 1433, the camp of the moderates and the nobles in Bohemia turned increasingly against the radicals, who were ultimately crushed at the Battle of Lipany (1434). A deep sensibility to books has remained, however, a constant in Bohemia to the present day.[14]

The Lower Rhine: the *devotio moderna*

The new silent readers, immersed in the text and as if closed in themselves, were alone with the subject of their reading and their thoughts. It is hardly surprising that this new solitude was accompanied by the emergence of a new religious sensibility, more attentive to the text and the image, more oriented towards inner experience and often towards practices of individual devotion. This trend was at its strongest in the regions most deeply caught up in the modernizing process at the demographic (urbanization), economic and social levels. In the face of the changes happening all around, and also of the tragic uncertainties of the fourteenth century, there was unease, and the need to seek refuge in another relationship to the divine and to experiment with other forms and other practices of solidarity and responsibility within the community. This need for the mystic was strengthened by the general tendency towards more individual thinking, but strengthened also by the crises then shaking the institutional Church: the establishment of the papacy in Avignon (1305), the Great Schism (1378–1417), the scandalous rivalry between two popes who each excommunicated the other. The council which met, at long last, in Constance (1414–18), under the authority of the emperor, set out to restore the unity and the doctrine of the Church; reform was postponed, the popes of Avignon and of Rome were deposed, and Martin V elected. In France, the poet Eustache Deschamps echoed the uncertainty and misery which seemed then to be all around (1346–1406/7):

Tems de doleur et de temptacion,/Aages de plour, d'envie et de tourment,/

Tems de langour et de dampnacion,/Aage mener près du définement [decadence],/
Tems plein d'orreur, qui tout fait faussement,/Aage menteur, plain d'orgueil et d'envie,/
Tems sanz honeur et sans vray jugement,/Aage en tristour, qui abrège la vie...

(Time of grief and temptation,/Age of weeping, envy and torment,/ Time of weakness and damnation,/Age leading to decadence,/Time of error, which does everything falsely,/Age of lies; full of pride and envy,/ Time without honour and without true judgement,/Age of sadness, which shortens life.)

The *devotio moderna* was a spiritual movement that appeared in the Low Countries around 1375, close to the Carthusians, and also closely linked to the world of writing.

John of Ruysbroeck, called the Admirable, had probably heard talk of Meister Eckhart in Cologne. This former vicar of Saint Gudula in Brussels retreated to the Forest of Soignes to devote himself to contemplation and to write his two great works, in Flemish, the *Treatise of the Seven Cloisters* and the *Adornment of the Spiritual Marriage*. His teaching distinguished the active life, which aimed to destroy sin, the inward life, which aimed at the renunciation of the world and the imitation of Christ, and, lastly, at the highest level, the contemplative life, in which the intelligence was in union with God. Geert (Gerhard) Groote (died 1374) was born to a rich bourgeois family in Deventer – a town to which we will return. After studying there and also in Aachen, Cologne, Paris and Prague, he became a convert to mysticism (1374) and met Ruysbroeck in the house of the Augustine canons of Groenendaal, near Brussels (1377). Groote translated the *Spiritual Marriage* into Latin, withdrew to the Charterhouse of Munnikhuisen and preached throughout the diocese of Deventer. Here, he gathered around him a few poor students from the chapter school, then some laymen and some clerks, who formed the first group of Brethren of the Common Life: they did not take vows, but lived together, held their worldly goods in common and adopted a rule based on prayer and work, in particular the copying of manuscripts. As a boy, Josse Bade had his first lessons with the Brethren of Ghent, his native town; the school of Deventer was at the height of its fame in the two decades from 1470, when it was directed by Alexander Hegius (1433–90) and when its students included Thomas à Kempis and Erasmus. Louis Dringenberg (1410–77), rector of the school of Sélestat, was another former student of the Brethren in Deventer. Communities of the same type, including men and women, soon appeared in Zwolle,

Amersfoort and Delft; the movement then spread to the Rhineland and northern Germany, Brabant and Flanders. A convent of regular canons was founded in 1387 at Windesheim, near Zwolle; it followed the rule of St Augustine and was to become extremely influential.[15] Let us recall, lastly, that Gerson, dean of Our Lady of Bruges from 1397 to 1401, knew the Brethren of the Common Life and read the Latin translation of the *Spiritual Marriage*, while his own works circulated within communities that followed the *devotio moderna*.

The *devotio moderna* had a huge impact on the world of writing. The Carthusians were often integrated into the university world, as in the case of Bartholomew of Maastricht (died 1446), doctor of theology, professor, then dean and rector of the University of Heidelberg, before he withdrew to the Charterhouse of Roermonde, then to Cologne. Johann Heynlin, a student in Paris and a key figure in the introduction of printing to France, withdrew at the end of his life to the Charterhouse of Basel. However, the Brethren of the Common Life also encouraged the teaching of the 'little schools' and the spread of literacy throughout the whole of the old Low Countries and north-west and northern Germany. Their practice of reading and appropriating sacred texts went together with the huge increase in the number of copies and the spread of annotated manuscript collections, and they launched into the activities of printing and bookselling at a very early date (in Brussels, Marienthal and Rostock). An individual relationship was established between the reader and a text that had become primarily an aid to piety, and some of the texts written by the mystics enjoyed a steady success for centuries to come.

The great devout figures played a major role in this movement. Dynamic speech can never be ineffective and, in the third quarter of the fifteenth century, two figures played a crucial role in the *devotio moderna*. Denis the Carthusian (died 1471), born near Liège, produced an immense oeuvre, both theological treatises strictly speaking and mystical texts – he read and repeated everything, he copied and illuminated his manuscripts himself, he was the *doctor ecstaticus*:

> To see you [God], this would be for the spirit to see that You are altogether invisible, and the more it sees this, the more it contemplates You clearly...

The Carthusians of Cologne were the first to work on the thought of Denis and on editions of his texts, successively publishing his commentaries on the Scriptures. The second great figure was Thomas of Kempen (Thomas à Kempis) (died 1471), brother of one of the founders of Windesheim and a former student of Groote at Deventer.

Thomas had joined the congregation of Windesheim in 1406, and was very probably the compiler and part author of the *Imitatio Christi*. The *Imitation* is a collection of four treatises on the spiritual life, completed in 1441, which circulated very widely – 700 manuscripts, nearly 4,000 printed editions up to the modern period.[16]

Production: books and piety

The success of the Dominican Bible testifies to the aspirations of a clerical readership which wanted access to the sacred text in a compact and manageable form, and a well laid-out page. But the growth of mysticism also explains the increasing demand for a type of manuscript and printed matter that would support pious practices. Two different models responded to the demand to integrate piety into everyday life: on the one hand, pilgrimage, which acted as the *praefiguratio* of the ascent to heaven; on the other, and much more often, the books of piety, primarily the Bible and Books of Hours, but also texts like the *Imitation*, the *Art of Dying* and the *Mirror of the Sinful Soul*; nor should we forget devotional images. Prayer books for the use of the laity had existed since the ninth century, but it was only in the thirteenth century, and particularly in the Île-de-France, that it became common practice to bring together in a specific collection certain prayers and texts drawn from the Bible and the divine office. The vernacular was used from an early date in the free prayers, though the corpus of liturgical texts constituting the fixed and obligatory core of these new Books of Hours was rarely translated before the sixteenth century.[17] The innumerable portrayals of the Annunciation illustrate the devotion that now pervaded the whole of daily life: an intimate scene, an interior, with the Virgin deep in a book, probably her Book of Hours, at the moment when the angel visited her. But we should also remember the sewing Virgin, in the choir of the cathedral of Chartres: a young woman bent over her work, needle in hand, with, open on her knees, the little book of piety whose reading punctuated her day. Albert Labarre has observed that 'there were books of hours at every price for a varied public';[18] nevertheless, the archetypal example was a book of small format and high value intended for a person of note. Some richly illuminated examples are numbered among the masterpieces of world painting, such as the *Heures de Jeanne d'Evreux*, illustrated by Jean Pucelle and one of the jewels of the magnificent 'library' of Charles V; but also the *Heures d'Etienne Chevalier*, illustrated by Fouquet, and, most of all, the *Très riches heures* of the duc de Berry, the work of the Limbourg brothers.[19]

Alongside the texts were images, which the disciples of the *devotio moderna* saw as an immensely powerful aid to the labour of meditation.[20] The image, escaping more easily from the rational categories of discourse, made people see with greater directness the immensity of the divinity, in which they could lose themselves with delight. Words had already been rejected in favour of silence by Meister Eckhart, who wrote of 'the indeterminate abyss of the silent and unsociable divinity'. Tauler similarly spoke of 'tranquil silence', of the 'sinking [in which] all similarity and all dissimilarity are lost'. The image opened the way towards the naked and empty state of God and of eternity, and it combined sweetness of contemplation and vertiginous abysses of oblivion. Unsurprisingly, this form of sensibility was the source of considerable economic activity; the sale of objects of devotion such as pious images or pilgrimage mirrors is revealed by Gutenberg's researches in Strasbourg. Lastly, the economic dimension of the various phenomena associated with piety was made all the greater by the fact that they constituted a sort of template for the mass production of manuscripts and above all printed matter.

Writing: Work and the Professions

The age of the skilled craftsmen

An increasingly broad sector within Western society gradually acquired a degree of familiarity with writing. Once it had emerged from the exclusive world of the Church, and in particular the monasteries, to penetrate, in the first place, urban society, the activities associated with writing and with the book could develop. The number of libraries increased, and then, at a later stage (especially after 1300), workshops of lay copyists appeared and illustration and binding emerged as distinct artisanal or artistic activities. This was still largely a world of commissioning (a book was made only if a commission for it had been received), but the growth of the market led to the growth of a first society of craftsmen skilled in copying and selling. These developments were accompanied by a relative reduction in the cost of manuscripts: Ezio Ornato has estimated that, in France, the average price of a manuscript fell by half in the fifteenth century compared with the century before.

Nevertheless, specialization was still limited and in the vast majority of cases copyists and booksellers had another principal occupation, their work with books remaining secondary. Many copyists were students; some were ecclesiastics or lawyers or administrators (notaries, clerks of the court, secretaries) in need of a supplementary income. Their reward might on occasion, in addition to payment strictly speaking, be a less immediate benefit – earning blessings for the copyist and helping to assure his eternal salvation in the hereafter. Jean de Papeleu, a clerk in Paris, practised in the rue des Ecrivains, as revealed by the explicit of the *Bible historiale* of Guiart des Moulins dated 1317.[21] On 6 March 1382, a certain Jeannin Fromage wrote, not without some satisfaction, this explicit in a manuscript of *La Somme le roi* by the Dominican Laurent du Bois, which describes what might be called the 'manuscript circuit':

Cest livre est tout escript/ Priés pour celui qui l'a escript/
Et pour celui qui l'a fait faire/ Et pour celui qui l'exemplaire/
Nous a presté jusqu'en la fin./ Cil qui l'escript ot non Jehannin/
Et son seurnon estoit Froumage./ Diex nous deffende tous de damage,/
Amen.[22]

(This book is all written/Pray for he who has written it/And for him who had it done/And for him who has lent the copy/To us right to the end./He who wrote it is called Jehannin/And his nickname is Fromage./ God protect us all from harm,/Amen)

There are many similar examples, such as that of Mathias Rivalli, 'Poitevin clerk', who, in Paris, in 1364–5, copied a manuscript of the *Histoire ancienne* in French, which the duc de Berry then had protected by a binding displaying his arms.[23] In less important towns, the non-specialist copyist was even more prominent. In Dôle, where the university had been founded by Philip the Good in 1423, it is the religious, but also students, who have left traces of their work: Pierre Le Vannier, *bachelier en décret* and student of law, born in Artois, records having finished his copy on 24 December 1451 'at eight o'clock in the morning'. The appearance of printed books was very far from destroying the market in manuscript books. In 1472, a copy of the *Propriétaire des choses*, translated into French by Jean Corbechon, was commissioned by a Parisian bourgeois from a student who had no compunction in 'enriching' the text:

lequel livre je, Jehan de Bihays, maistre es-ars et escolier estudiant à Paris, ay copié et transcript le moins mal que j'ay peu en y adjoustant peu de chose que j'avoie veu tant par expérience que par la doctri[n] e d'aucuns docteurs, à l'instance et requeste de Nicolas de Blanchecourt, barbier juré et bourgeois de Paris...[24]

(Which book I, Jehan de Bihays, master of arts and scholar studying in Paris, have copied and transcribed the least badly I could, adjusting a very few things I wished to as much from experience as the doctrine of any doctors, on the authority and at the request of Nicolas De Blanchecourt, sworn barber and bourgeois of Paris...)

Nor did sales always take place within a specialized circuit. Private persons often sold one of their own manuscripts, or a moneylender or creditor might sell a book that had been handed over as security or in payment. This may have been the case with the 'juif Israêl' of Montpellier, from whom the metropolitan chapter of Bourges bought a Latin Bible for thirty gold francs in 1373.[25] And we should remember the famous poem in which an anonymous jongleur lists the towns in which he had been obliged to sell off one or other of the books from his library:

> Mon Lucain et mon Juvénal/ Oubliai-je à Bonival/
> Stace le Grand et Virgile/ Perdis aux dés à Abbeville/
> Mon Alexander est à Goivre/ Et mon Grécime est à Auxoire/
> Et mon Thobie est à Compiège/ Ne crois que jamais je le tiegne/
> Et mon Doctrinal est à Sens...[26]

(My Lucan and my Juvenal/I forgot at Bonneval/Stace the Great and Virgil/I lost at dice at Abbeville/My Alexander is at Goivre/And my Grecime is at Auxerre/And my Thobie is at Compiègne/I don't think I shall ever get my hands on it/And my Doctrinal is at Sens...)

Copyists and booksellers

The growth of the book trade in the principal towns led to the appearance of specialized socio-professional groups organized into guilds. At least 254 persons are known to have been active in the manufacture or trade in books in London between 1300 and 1520, of whom 117 were stationers, to which should be added the painters. There were separate guilds of copyists and illuminators in the city in the fourteenth century, which combined in 1403 to form a single guild of book craftsmen.[27] The book trade was concentrated near to St Paul's Cathedral.

Table 3.1 Book artisans in London in the fifteenth century

	1400	1410	1420	1430	1440	1450	1460	1470	1480	1490
Numbers	42	40	34	42	40	47	48	50	39	41

We are also well informed about the situation in Paris.[28] The number of specialists in the book trade remained small, even in a capital of such importance: in 1297, the register of the taille listed one bookseller on the Right Bank, eight in the Île de la Cité (rue Neuve-Notre-Dame) and the same number on the Left Bank, near the university. This traditional geography of the book has lasted until today: the Left Bank and the university quarter (rue Saint-Jacques), then the cathedral of Notre-Dame, to which the Palais was later added. In *c*.1250, a certain Herneis Le Romanceur was established in front of Notre-Dame, where he offered manuscripts in the vernacular:

Et qui voudra avoir autel livre, si viegne à lui, il en aidera bien à con-seillier, et de toz autres. Et si meint [demeure] à Paris devant Nostre Dame...[29]

(And whoever wants such a book, let him come to him, he will help to advise him about it; and about all others. And he lives in Paris, in front of Notre Dame.)

Also known at this period is the Sens family. Guillaume de Sens, copyist and *stationarius librorum*, is documented in 1275; he died before 1292, leaving Marguerite, his widow, '*marchande de livres*' in the rue Saint-Jacques. André de Sens (André l'Anglois) was also a bookseller and *stationarius* (1314), whereas Thomas de Sens was a bookseller and innkeeper (1313), then *stationarius* (1314). This family seems to have been close to the university and to the Dominicans, whose works they helped to distribute. Geoffroy de Saint Léger had a house in the rue Neuve-Notre-Dame, where he was known as *librarius juratus* ('sworn bookseller') in 1316 and the possible successor to Jean de Saint Léger. He worked with artists and illuminators for persons of the highest rank (Louis I of Bourbon, Queen Clementia of Hungary and Queen Joan of Burgundy),[30] who were interested in manuscripts in the vernacular: chivalric romances, the *Bible historiale* of Guiart des Moulins, the *Grandes chroniques de France*. Also operating in the rue Neuve-Notre-Dame at this period was Thomas de Maubeuge: the Countess Mahaut of Artois commissioned manuscripts from him for her library in Hesdin. He copied the following incipit at the beginning of the *Grandes chroniques* dated 1328:

Ci commencent les chroniques des roys de France...lesquelles Pierre Honoré du Nuef Chastel en Normandie fist escrire et ordener en la manière que elles sont, selon l'ordenance des croniques de Saint Denis, à mestre Thomas de Maubeuge, demorant en rue nueve Nostre Dame de Paris, l'an de grace Nostre Seingneur MCCCXXVIII.[31]

(Here begin the chronicles of the kings of France...which Pierre Honoré of Neufchatel in Normandy caused to be written down and arranged in the way they are, according to the arrangement of the chronicles of St Denis, by master Thomas de Maubeuge, living in the Rue Neuve Notre Dame de Paris, in the year of grace MCCCXXVIII.)

Also in the rue Neuve-Notre-Dame, Richard de Montbaston took the oath as sworn bookseller on 5 October 1338; he had a copying workshop, sold manuscripts, and is known to have produced the manuscript of the *Golden Legend* translated into French by Jean de Vignay (1348).[32] Others included Guillaume Lecomte (after 1368) and Jean Boquet, who was at one point bookseller to Charles of Orléans.[33] In 1398, Thévenin Langevin had Nicolas Oresme's translation of the *Ethics* of Aristotle copied for Louis d'Orléans, in two volumes, for 240 gold francs. This manuscript later came into the possession of Jean de Berry.[34] In all, a total of eleven *écrivains* or stationers and fourteen sworn booksellers are known for Paris in 1368, a number which changed little until the first decades of the fifteenth century. In 1488, the '*suppôts*' of the university of Paris included twenty-four sworn booksellers, four parchmeners, four merchants and seven papermakers and merchants, two illuminators, two binders and two *écrivains*. Some of these copyists became rich, like the Parisian Nicolas Flamel, also a *suppot* of the university, who, in 1407, built in the rue de Montmorency a beautiful house of three storeys with two shops for rent on the ground floor.

There were similar developments in the other main centres of production, in France and elsewhere. In Bruges, David Aubert worked regularly for the duke. A copy in twelve volumes of the *Roman de Perceforêt* (1459–60) has the explicit:

(Volume 1) Par le commandement et ordonna[n]ce de...mon très redoubté seigneur Phelippe...duc de Bourgoigne, je David Aubert comme l'escripvain me suis emploié de mettre au net et en cler françois certaines anciennes histoires...

(Volume 5) Cy fine le Ve volume...lequel a esté réduit en langaige moderne en la fourme qui s'ens [ui]t, pour le grosser et historier en vellin...[35]

((Volume 1) By the command and ordinance of...my mighty lord Philip...Duke of Burgundy, I, David Aubert, as *escripvain* have set

myself to write clearly and in lucid French certain ancient histories... (Volume 5) Here ends the fifth volume... which has been reduced
into modern parlance in the form which follows, to ?bind and decorate
it in vellum...)

In a region more profoundly affected by the *devotio moderna*,
however, like Utrecht, the role of the convents remained very important, with the Brethren of the Common Life, but also the Augustinians
and the Carthusians, and even the various houses of the third order.[36]
In a quite different environment, Diebold Lauber ran a copying
workshop between 1427 and 1467 in Haguenau, the town where
his father had probably been the messenger of the imperial bailiwick
and where he himself also worked as a teacher. A large body of his
work has survived, more than eighty manuscripts, most of them
illustrated. He probably received commissions, but he seems also
to have copied texts directly, or had them copied, so as to be able
to offer the books to potential customers. A catalogue of his stock
dating from the 1450s lists some forty-five titles for sale, intended
for a clientele of rich lay men and women: saints' legends, epistles
and gospels, psalms, romances (including the *Parzival* of Wolfram
von Eschenbach), as well as 'good' medical treatises; most of these
works were in the vernacular.[37] A number of copyists and illustrators
who were employed in this workshop are known, such as Diebold
von Dachstein, Johannes Port de Argentina (= Strasbourg) and Hans
Ott, a draughtsman documented in Strasbourg in 1427–49. Many
specialist craftsmen of German origin were established in the book
trade of towns like Barcelona and Valence, also Seville, etc., and it
even seems that some copyists were unfamiliar with the language in
which they had to work.

Like students and their teachers, these skilled craftsmen moved
from one town to another as necessary, according to the movements
of their customers and of those who supplied them with commissions:
Guilbert of Metz, a copyist documented in Paris between 1407 and
1434, is also found in Grammont, town of his birth, '*à l'escu de
France*', where he worked for Philip the Good.[38] At the international
level, the great business dynasties were not above investing in the
production of high-end luxury objects, and thus finding favour with
some of the most powerful princes of the age. The Rapondi were
merchants of Lucca, with a factory in Bruges, whose activities brought
them into contact with the Burgundian dynasty. In Paris, Dino
Rapondi was a financier and councillor of the duke, to whom he
offered manuscripts, including, at New Year 1400, a *Decades* of Tite-
Live, for which he received 500 gold francs as a reward. His brother

Jacobo was also active in Paris, where he specialized in the manufacture of precious manuscripts for Philip the Bold: a historiated *Bible* (600 écus, or 1,050 francs),[39] a *Golden Legend* (500 écus), a Boccaccio (*De Claris mulieribus*) in French (300 écus), etc. His particular speciality was secular texts, in a town where Jean L'Avenant and Yvon Le Gorgent, the latter an *écrivain*, produced liturgical manuscripts. It was Rapondi who, in 1402, lent some of the money necessary for the duke to be able to employ the Limbourg brothers.[40]

In every sector of the book trade, Italy was in the vanguard. Bologna, thanks to its university and its schools of Roman law, was a major centre for the production and distribution of books from the twelfth century; the town was home to all the trades associated with the manufacture of parchment and paper, but also writing (the two brothers Cardinale and Rugerino da Forli had a workshop there *c.*1267) and binding, and the *pecia* system was practised at an early date. Manuscripts from Bologna were exported to Paris, Montpellier, and the German university centres, while the sale of books between private persons within the town was, from 1265 and above a certain sum, to be the subject of a notarized contract.[41] But the most famous bookseller of the fifteenth century was probably Vespasiano da Bisticci (1421–98) in Florence, a man known as the *princeps librariorum* (prince of booksellers), who had a workshop offering every service relating to the book – copying, illuminating, binding and distribution.[42]

Painters and specialized workshops

Linked to the rise of a wealthy clientele, the figure of the painter emerges with increasing clarity from about 1400, as distinct from that of the illuminator, or even of the artist entrusted simply with the decoration of a manuscript. The problematic is that of the sociology of art: established in 'residence towns' (Residenzstadt), the painters were attached to certain princely bibliophiles, who gave them commissions. Their workshops were generally organized around an acknowledged master and carried out all the successive stages of the commission. Yet they did not in general confine their activities to painting alone, as Huizinga emphasized:

> As all art was more or less applied art...the great masters in the service of the courts of Flanders, of Berry, or of Burgundy...did not confine themselves to painting pictures and to illuminating manuscripts; they were not above colouring statues, paintings shields and staining banners, or designing costumes for tournaments and ceremonies.[43]

An excellent example is Melchior Broederlam, who worked on the automata of the chateau of Hesdin, the carriage of the duchess of Burgundy and even the decoration of the Burgundian fleet at L'Ecluse (Sluis) in 1387. One of the best-known names is that of Jean Pucelle, a painter who is revealed by the *Bréviaire de Belleville* (1323–6) in the role of *chef d'atelier*, distributing the work between the other painters (Mahiet, Ancelot and Chevrier), and paying them:

> [33] Mahiet. J. Pucelle a baillié XX and III sols VI deniers. [62] Ancelot pro I p[ecia]. [268] J. Chevrier pro I p[ecia]. [300] J. Chevrier pro I p[ecia].[44]

> ([33] Mahiet. J. Pucelle has lent XX and III sols VI deniers. [62] Ancelot for I p[ecia]. [268] J. Chevrier for I p[ecia]. [300] J. Chevrier for I p[ecia])

We may also cite Jean of Bruges, the king's painter; and Jacquemart de Hesdin (died *c.*1409), who worked for the duc de Berry in Bourges from at least 1384. A sketchbook in his hand survives, dating from the first decade of the fifteenth century: it consists of six boxwood leaves, washed with white gesso, bearing drawings done with a stylus (metalpoint); we may note the potential relationship with engraving.[45]

For the most part, however, the names of the artists remain unknown, in which case it is customary to attribute the manuscripts to different workshops on the basis of stylistic elements, as in the case of the workshops of the *Heures* of the maréchal de Boucicaut (*c.*1410), or the *Heures de Rohan* (*c.*1420), or the *Breviary of the Duke of Bedford* (*c.*1430). Other major workshops were those of the 'Master of Jouvenel des Ursins', those gravitating round the court of Anjou and the 'Master of Jean de Wavrin' (from the name of this councillor of Philip the Good). The proliferation of workshops and attributions testifies to the increased demand coming from court circles. Though Paris was the main European centre of production,[46] the 'Burgundians' were also extremely influential, and artists now readily moved from one court to another. The three brothers Paul, Jean and Hermann de Limbourg, originally from Nimègue, were the painters of the sumptuous *Très riches heures* of the duc de Berry. They were in the service of Duke Philip of Burgundy from 1402, then joined that of his brother of Berry, before all three died in 1416; Jean Columbe, born in Bourges around 1450, completed the *Très riches heures*, left unfinished, in 1485–9. The workshop seems to have been directed by the eldest brother, Paul de Limbourg. The three brothers are also famous for having offered the duke a counterfeit book, which was only of a piece of wood painted to look like a book, with no leaves or anything written in it (*'un livre contrefait d'une pièce de bois blanc paincte en semblance d'un livre où il n'y a nul feuillet ne rien escript...'*).

Also employed by the dukes of Burgundy was Loyset Liédet in Hesdin and Bruges. Simon Marmion was the son of Jehan Marmion, painter in Valenciennes and creator of the *Retable* of Saint-Bertin (*c.*1454–9), donated by Guillaume Fillastre to the powerful abbey of St Omer.[47] Michel Clauwet, another son of Valenciennes, was the ancestor of the Clouet, painters of Francis I and his successors.[48] However, the disappearance of the princely dynasties and the great families in their orbit was accompanied by a drastic falling off in commissions and a decline in the activities of copying and painting de luxe manuscripts throughout the region.

Conversely, Poitou and even more Touraine benefited from the shift of the political axis of the kingdom and the establishment of the Orléans dynasty.[49] Charles VII (died 1461) had to have himself pro-claimed king at Mehun-sur-Yèvre, and he was the 'King of Bourges', whose territories formed a compact block in Touraine, Poitou and Berry. The royal administration was organized around Bourges and Poitiers, both university towns. Then, as the military situation improved, the 'residence towns', hence also the centres of book pro-duction, reflected the ramifications of royal genealogy: Louis XI was in Tours and Plessis, but he installed his queen, Charlotte of Savoy, and his children at Amboise and it was here that he founded the Order of Saint Michael (1469), to rival the Burgundian Order of the Golden Fleece. The queen entrusted a *Vita Christi* in twenty-five quires to 'Thibault Bredinc, bookseller residing in Tours' to be copied, illuminated and bound.[50] Charles VIII was born at Amboise, where he undertook an extensive rebuilding of the chateau, assembled a large part of his Italian booty, and died after an accident in 1498.

The Orléans remained at Blois from the time of its acquisition by Louis of Orléans, in 1392. After Louis' assassination at the instiga-tion of the duke of Burgundy (1407), his widow Valentina Visconti also settled in Blois. Charles of Orléans went there on his return from captivity; he rebuilt the chateau (1443–57) and made it the seat of a brilliant court. It was at Blois that the future Louis XII was born, and he made the town the capital of his kingdom; the Estates General met there in 1506. All the great lords and crown officials then settled in the region. The court of Louise of Savoy was in Amboise, birth-place of Francis I, and, as is well known, the library of the Orléans, in the chateau of Blois, formed a part of the original French Bibliothèque royale. Of the major artists working within the orbit of the court and specializing in manuscripts, the most important is Jehan Fouquet, born in Tours *c.*1425, probably a pupil of the Limbourg brothers in Bourges, then of Haincelin of Haguenau in Paris.[51] Fouquet, attached first to the court of Charles VII, then to that of Louis XI, was described in 1475 as 'painter of the king'. He painted portraits of persons of high rank and religious paintings (the *Pietà* of Nouans), too; he also worked on the decor of festivals and on monumental projects (the tomb of Louis XI at Notre-Dame of Cléry), as well as manuscripts intended for the king, the princes and the dignitaries of the court. Among the most important of the latter was Etienne Chevalier, owner of some magnificent manuscripts. His grandfather Pierre had been valet de chambre of Charles V (1373), and his great-uncle Etienne was director of the lazar house of the duke of Orléans and secretary to the king (1423). He himself, notary and secretary to the king (1442), ended his career as treasurer of France and member of the Grand Conseil. A protégé of the favourite, Agnès Sorrel, he was an executor of her will (1450). We observe here, one last time, and in spectacular fashion in the case of the Chevalier family, the crucial and very modern theme of advancement through writing, through administrative specialization and through the service of the powerful.

PART II

The Age of Start-ups

The study of the humanities will be a powerful source of light for this new type of bookseller coming from Germany like a Trojan horse to spread to every part of the civilized world. It is generally said that it was in the region of Mainz that there lived this John, surnamed Gutenberg, who, first of all men, devized the art of printing, whereby, without use of reed or quill pen, but by means of metallic letters, books are made swiftly, accurately and elegantly...The invention of Gutenberg...has given us letters thanks to which everything that is said or thought can immediately be written, rewritten and handed down to posterity.

Guillaume Fichet, 1471

4

The Development and Logics
of Innovation

∽

Femme je suis, pauvrette et ancienne
Qui rien ne sait. Oncque lettres ne lus.
Au moustier vois, dont suis paroissienne
Paradis peint, où sont harpes and luths
Et un enfer, où damnés sont bouillus.
L'un me fait peur; et l'autre joie et liesse.

(Woman I am, poor and old/Who knows nothing. Nor ever learned to read./In church, where I am a parishioner I see/A painted Paradise, where there are harps and lutes/And a hell, where the damned are boiled./The one makes me afraid, the other joyful and happy.)

François Villon, *Grand Testament*

At a time of expansion that was at its height between the eleventh and thirteenth centuries, and of an increase in the demand for intellectual education and books, technological development provided Western society with the means to respond to these new needs, for a while. Though the first revolution of the book came in the mid fifteenth century, with Gutenberg's invention, the importance of the changes before this has led to the hypothesis of a 'scribal Renaissance', characterized by the increased production and much wider dissemination of books, a shift in intellectual curiosity and artistic forms and a first phase of technical innovation. These changes went hand in hand with a period of – uneven – economic and demographic growth. For the first time in European history, densities of sixty inhabitants per square kilometre were found over wide areas (in particular the old Low Countries), while urban networks grew denser, long-distance trade expanded and the more distant exploration of the 'Indies' began. The rise of capitalism accompanied these developments; it made available to the technicians and inventors the funds that were necessary if they were to persevere with their work and exploit its results.

For the historian, technological innovation is not the result of a single development. A certain problem (in our case, that of the multiplication of images and then of texts) gives rise to a number of experiments in all sorts of directions. Gradually, the most effective processes come to the fore, according to a standardized sequence: at each stage, various possibilities open up, more or less effective at the technical level and more or less viable at the economic level, and each choice made alters the range of future possibilities. Innovation involves not isolated inventions, but wider systems. The 'Gutenberg system' concerned, obviously, the press, the standardization of characters and their mass production, but also the paper, the manufacturing technology in printing (perfecting all the elements constituting a coherent whole, the ink, the material), the manufacturing practices and, over the long term, a whole new global 'economy', that of the printed word.

At the technological level, the changes were carried out by very small groups of inventors and technicians, but also financiers. The research, which was often long-drawn-out and always uncertain, was financed by capitalists who operated in the sphere of venture capital, as with the start-ups of the early twenty-first century. These capitalists sometimes exploited the enterprises established in this way, and some even specialized in the new sector of the 'book trade'. This is why certain phenomena that tend to be underestimated are so important, like family relationships and the journeys of individuals or small groups. The history of innovation requires a micro-sociology of the initiating and promoting circles, which is largely beyond our grasp for the fifteenth century. Finally, the success of an innovation was ultimately dependent on the market: the product had to be distributed and welcomed by the 'consumers' of the day. On the one hand, the new product had to satisfy a need; on the other, inventors worked on what they reckoned would be useful and profitable, which explains why analogous technical problems were simultaneously posed in different places by different researchers. Over time, the trend was for standardization: manufacturing processes converged at a certain level, which achieved a form of economic and technical equilibrium and facilitated the rationalization of the market.

Paper and Papermaking

The first major innovation concerned the support, that is, the paper, and transference phenomena played the principal role in its spread in the West. The invention and above all dissemination of paper are one of the main indicators of the changing conditions from the twelfth century.

Chinese paper

Paper was a Chinese invention dating back to the second century BC.[1] The raw material varied: hemp, mulberry (mostly in Japan), rattan, rice straw and above all bamboo. The bamboo was first cut, peeled and chopped up into bundles; it was then successively soaked, washed and pounded to make a paste. The mixture was allowed to ferment, then washed, before being strained through a 'mould', leaving behind the paste of the future leaf, which was then dried in the open air. The mould was initially made of a piece of cloth stretched over a frame, and the mixture poured over it with a ladle. With the rigid mould, a network of thin strips of bamboo, the operation was reversed: the mould was dipped into the vat to 'raise' the leaf. The composition of the paste was also gradually improved: a coating of starch rendered the leaves impermeable to ink, and they were sometimes coloured.

The use of paper should be distinguished from its manufacture. Paper was known in Samarkand in the fifth century, long before it was manufactured there, and it was used in Korea around 600, in Japan from 610 and in India in the seventh century. Paper documents have survived for the Mediterranean region from before the Arab conquest, but only sporadically. Tradition has it that it was Chinese prisoners who transmitted the manufacturing process after the Battle of Talas (Artlakh), near the Talas River (Aoulle-Ata) in 751.[2] Further west, paper was first manufactured in Samarkand (751), then in Baghdad (793), the Yemen, Syria and Egypt (beginning of the tenth century). The caliph Haroun al-Rashid (died 809) imposed its use on the chancellery of Baghdad because it was more difficult to forge than parchment. In the ninth century it was in general use throughout the Muslim world, though parchment was also used, in particular for languages other than Arabic, and sometimes also even papyrus. Further west the new support first appeared in the frontier zones, which acted as areas of exchange and transfer that were favourable to innovation: from Egypt paper passed to North Africa, Sicily and Arabo-Muslim Spain (Jativá, eleventh century). The first paper documents to appear in the West are the acts of the Norman chancellery in Sicily at the end of the eleventh century, followed by notarial registers in Genoa in the twelfth century. Little is known about the methods by which paper was manufactured in the Arab world; the paste was usually prepared from hemp or macerated and pounded rags. Arab paper was whiter and smoother than Western paper and it had no watermark.

Paper and papermaking in Christian Europe (thirteenth to fifteenth centuries)

In the West, paper first spread in Italy, the peninsula being open both to the Byzantine and to the Arabo-Muslim worlds. There were paper mills in Foligno, near Amalfi, in 1256, then in Fabriano, near Ancona. This town saw major technical innovations, not only in the form of paper mills but also in the use of brass wire for the moulds, the normalization of the watermark and the development of sizing with gelatin.[3] Two other important areas of production were Liguria and the environs of Lake Garda; Spain, the south of France (Toulouse and the Languedoc), then Avignon, and later Champagne (1340), the Île-de-France, Comté (modern Franche-Comté), etc., all developed in their turn. Lastly, in the late fourteenth and early fifteenth centuries, paper mills appeared in Nuremberg (1390), Ravensburg (1393), Basel (1430), Alsace (Strasbourg, 1431), Chemnitz and the lower Rhine Valley.

The speed with which this innovation spread is striking testimony to the strength of the demand, which parchment alone could no longer satisfy, and which cried out for a drastic reduction in production costs. The techniques that were developed in the West, first in Fabriano and then in the papermaking centres of France and later Nuremberg, made it possible to rationalize production and reduce costs. In essence, the process involved stripping the fibre of its cellulose, then reconstituting it in the form of leaves. The raw material, the cellulose, was obtained from undyed rags of linen or hemp, which were first washed, then soaked and fermented. A hydraulic wheel driving pestles reduced the material to a sodden mass; this was the process of 'crushing', which was done in mortars and produced a sort of pulp, which was subsequently diluted with water and then heated. Two operatives then worked in tandem. The first (the vatman) dipped the mould into the mix: the mould was a wooden frame fitted with a sieve of brass wires to allow the water to drain through, with a movable frame above, the thickness of which depended on the desired thickness of the leaf – this was the 'raising' process. The mesh of the sieve left a mark which was visible when held up to the light: the chain lines, the laid lines and soon the watermark, the first known example of which dates to 1282.[4] In the Middle Ages the mould, hence the leaf, measured on average 30 by 42 centimetres. The second operative (the coucher) slid the leaf over a felt. Finally, the pile of leaves and felts was placed under a press to extract the water. Each leaf was then hung on a line and dried during a series of successive operations, before being sized (to make it impermeable), burnished and polished. The pile was then counted into 'quires' and 'reams' and prepared for dispatch. We should note the technical proximity between paper manufacture and metallurgy, as wires had to be drawn to make the sieves; these techniques were significantly improved in Nuremberg in the first third of the fifteenth century.[5]

Thanks to the watermarks and to the study of provenances, we can tell that paper was soon the subject of a considerable long-distance trade. 'Pot' watermarks, for example, originating in Champagne, are found on a large number of manuscripts and incunabula. Further, Western capitalism, always seeking increased productivity, promoted improvements in the manufacturing process (process innovation), which meant that, by the fourteenth century, paper made in the West was being exported to the Arabo-Muslim world. Paper was a much cheaper support, which could be produced more quickly and in much larger quantities than parchment and, though initially relatively expensive, the price steadily fell. The new support was also better suited than parchment to the applications of typographical technology. It triumphed in the West in the fourteenth century for all everyday written matter and for an increasing proportion of the production of manuscript books: administrative or notarial registers, accounts, common or less expensive manuscripts, and so on.

This increasingly widespread use led to the appearance of what Marshall McLuhan, with his ear for a telling phrase, called 'paper empires'. Thanks to its cheapness, paper made possible a rapid growth of written matter, an increasingly effective management of global society through writing, recording, etc., and the associated development of a political structure that was modern, that is, based on writing and on 'graphic reason' (Jack Goody). Let us take as an ideal-type example the oldest paper document preserved in Germany, an account book from the Tyrol for the years 1299–1304, an object that is 'modern' in a number of different ways: its content relates to the administrative rationality then being developed, as it is a fragment of ducal accounting; it was also an item in a series, which is why it was written on a support of little value – which encourages us to engage in a sort of archaeology of administration and its practices; and, lastly, it illustrates a process of general political change, as the Duchy of Tyrol was then evolving into a principality administered according to the categories of modern rationality.[6] This same geographical area, Central Europe between the Rhine, the Alps and the Elbe, was soon to play a crucial role in Gutenberg's discovery and the early growth of typographical presses. The first paper mill known in this region was the *Hadermühle* built by Ulman Stromer (died 1407) on an arm of the River Pegnitz, at Nuremberg (1390); it produced poor-quality paper for packaging until 1452, paper that, if stuck together in several layers, could be made into card, which was soon used for the manufacture of playing cards, subsequently produced in large quantities with the aid of xylography.

Xylography

A world of images

The Far Eastern tradition distinguishes between stamping and xylography.[7] Epigraphy was the first means by which texts were disseminated in Imperial China and it encouraged the development of stamping: a thin, moistened sheet of paper was placed on a stone, and then inked with a tampon. It touched the parts of the paper not pushed in, allowing the original incised text to appear 'in negative' and in white (on a black background). This technique of facsimile could only develop once paper was in common use. The first known example is the *Hot Springs Inscription* discovered at Lishan, which pre-dates 653, but the technique had already been in use for many centuries. Some stamped inscriptions involved longer pieces of text and needed several successive leaves.

Xylography, meanwhile, developed from the engraved seals used to print pious images or formulas in seventh-century India. It was Buddhism, especially Tantric Buddhism, which created the demand. Dedicatory or votive inscriptions and magic formulas have been preserved, and then, from the ninth century, secular texts. Once established in China, the process was used in similar ways to stamping, so that the printing, done without a press, could be repeated as often as necessary to produce thousands, even tens of thousands, of copies (the absence of a machine meant that the woodblocks could be preserved and reused as desired without wearing out). Further, xylography was well suited to the reproduction of the very large number of

Chinese characters, though another process was also known, using small wooden blocks in whatever combination was needed, as with the rolls of the *Thousand Buddhas* (eighth century). The technology passed from China to Korea and then to Japan. Having suppressed a rebellion by some Buddhist monks (764–70), the Empress Shôtoku had a million paper scrolls printed bearing short Buddhist prayers (*Dharani*), kept in ten temples in the capital of Nara.[8] Xylography appeared in the West in the last third of the fourteenth century: the drawing was transferred on to a wooden block, and the engraving then done with a chisel. Two triangular grooves made the part that was to be inked stand proud. The engraver cut with the grain of the wood (*bois de fil*). The parts not meant to be printed were then cut out (*taille d'épargne* – literally 'saving cut'). The picture was transferred to the support (paper, no longer parchment) by the exercise of pressure on the back of the leaf, which had first been moistened. The pressure was applied either by a brush, a frotton (a ball made of horsehair moulded with strong glue and wrapped in cloth) or some other device. The ink used for this process was water-based, which produced brownish colours, a technique that allowed printing only on one side of the paper. The press was not used until later (around 1470); it required a much blacker, fatty, ink, and it had the disadvantage of wearing the plate down, making it more difficult to preserve. From the beginning of the fifteenth century, the technique of engraving on copper, or intaglio, was also known, first in Germany, then in Italy and the Low Countries: the *Passion of Berlin*, a copperplate engraving dated 1446, is the oldest known example of an image on the theme of the Passion. This technique was much less common and its use for printed matter made difficult by the fact that the two processes of typography and intaglio were incompatible. In some cases, for example for the Florentine edition of Dante of 1481, the difficulty was got round by gluing the engravings on copper into the text.

The beginnings of xylography in the West were described by Cennino Cennini around 1400, initially in connection with the impression of designs on cloth.[9] The 'bois Protat', the oldest woodblock known in France, dates from the 1380s and depicts a fragment of a Crucifixion scene, probably used to decorate altar cloths. In Germany, the xylographic incunabula date from the first decades of the fifteenth century: the *Christ on the Cross* of Munich, of 1410–20, reveals the intimacy of the piety and the special relationship to death. The *St Christopher* (at the Buxheim Charterhouse) is an image printed on Nuremberg paper and sold to pilgrims (1423). In Italy, the Ravenna library has a collection of forty-nine xylographic images, almost all figures of saints or scenes of the Passion. The engravings, of which the oldest date from the end of the fourteenth century, come from workshops located in Venice and the Veneto (Padua, Verona) and northern and central Italy (Prato), though with some also from France, the Low Countries and Germany (Swabia, Cologne). They are often the work of artisans from Northern Europe, either Germans or Flemings: engravers (with a very varied terminology) are referred to in Cologne and Mainz around 1400; a decree of the *Signoria* in Venice prohibited the import of images, to protect local craftsmen from dangerously strong competition from other centres of production.

The typology of subject matter provides the most fruitful approach to the identification of the customers for these images and the practices associated with them: Schreiber organized his *Manuel de l'amateur de la gravure sur bois et sur métal au XVe siècle* on the basis of a classification by genres, in which religious themes predominate.[10] We may, however, observe some more specific preferences: the theme of death is relatively better represented in Germany, for example,[11] with the image of skeletons emerging from the tomb and dancing to the sound of the flute being played by a corpse. In this case the content is associated with a form of social critique – death conquers all, whatever the qualities of each.[12] Not every image was pious, however, and we should note the large-scale production of playing cards, which had appeared in China under the Tang dynasty (618–907) and may have reached the West via the Silk Road. Some twenty years after the death of Marignolli, to whom we will return, the Signoria of Florence prohibited card games (1377), followed by Paris (1378), Ratisbon, Constance (1379) and Nuremberg (1380); the outcry only testifies to the speed with which card games had spread over a wide area. In 1381, however, Nuremberg softened its stance, partly because it had recognized the ineffectiveness of the ban, but also because a significant market seemed to be opening up for the manufacture of playing cards. As we have seen, Ulman Stromer had produced card in his mill of the *Hadermühle*, and gone on to use this support for the mass production of playing cards, with which he soon flooded Europe. Playing cards were also printed in Limoges at the end of the fourteenth century, and above all in Lyon in the fifteenth century, where a certain Jean Du Boys, '*tailleur de molles de cartes*' (carver of moulds for cards) and '*fayseur de cartes*' (maker of cards) is documented (*c.*1481); another '*feiseur des molles des cartes*', Pierre de Lan, is mentioned *c.*1493, and, a little later, Jean de Dale.[13] Other images of secular subjects are much rarer; they include the representation of a 'carrack' (a ship) preserved in Ravenna but apparently of Venetian origin, and the *Nine Knights* in Metz.[14]

A mass production

The wide dissemination of images was primarily linked to the shift of religious sentiment towards the individual piety and mysticism of the *devotio moderna*, and the geography of the two phenomena is similar. While figurative representations, with or without an accompanying text, were part of the public sphere, in particular in the iconography of churches (windows and sculptures), the printed image was now also an item of private consumption. Pictures were used as decoration, hung on walls, but they are also found on the inside covers of some bindings, even inside a manuscript or printed work.[15] The ordinariness of the object explains its poor survival rate, in that it consisted of a single leaf of paper, or even several in the case of xylographic booklets, but to which no commercial value was attached.

Xylographic images and booklets were published, in particular, on the occasion of pilgrimages, such as those of Saint-Servatius at Maastricht, Aachen, and Kornelimünster, events that might attract huge crowds (146,000 pilgrims to Aachen in 1496!), and were precursors of a true mass market. The pilgrims were offered not only images but mirrors and also badges cast in metal, and commercial companies were created to exploit these opportunities. The Gutenberg dossier provides one example,[16] but the most richly documented case in the case of xylography is that of the pious images printed in Padua in 1440–1.[17] According to a manufacturing contract dated 21 October 1440, Jakobus, a German established in the town as a finisher of parchment, undertook to produce printed and coloured images on white paper for a certain Cornelio de Flandria, for the sum of twenty Venetian ducats. The job was to be done very quickly, as the contract ran only until mid-January 1441, and penalties were stipulated in case of delay. An amendment of 23 October specified the quantity of paper necessary, the prices (according to the different formats) and the terms of payment: it has been calculated that the contract was for 3,000 images, plus 250 copies of a *Passion* in eight or ten leaves, and a very large number of a *Credo* (possibly 10,000 copies), all in barely twelve weeks.

The speed of the operation assumes both a substantial productive capacity and a skilled staff, especially when we remember that the images had to be coloured after printing. The subjects were exclusively religious: the Trinity, the life of the Virgin (for which the frescoes of Giotto in Padua may have served as model), scenes from the life of Christ (Nativity, Last Supper, Crucifixion, etc.) and figures of saints (Anne, Christopher, Peter, Augustine, Martin, etc.). In the case of the *Passion*, the contract specified delivery of 2,500 leaves; it is possible to deduce a print run as there survives in Berlin a xylo-graphed *Passion* with eighteen images on nine leaves, an impression which needed the use of a press.[18] This may be a copy corresponding to the contract of 1440, the blocks for which were re-used several years later. Some woodblocks are also found in an edition of the pseudo-Bonaventura in Italian made in Venice in 1487, on the presses of 'Hieronymous de Sanctis et Cornelio', probably the 'Cornelio de Flandria' of 1440. Many xylographic works preserved in Ravenna (*Biblioteca Classense*) can be attributed to the Master of the *Passion* of Berlin, whose subjects overlap with some of those mentioned in the Padua contract.[19] A last example illustrating the mass production of xylographic images: the shroud of St Veronica is a frequent theme in both painting and illumination, including in Books of Hours, and was also the subject of a number of engravings. We know that Stanislaus Polonus and Mainard Ungut printed 50,000 copies of *Veronica* in Seville in 1493.

On the basis of these observations and drawing on the iconology of Panofsky, Rudolf Schenda, in an article with a radically new per-spective, tried not to oppose the written word and the image, in the traditional fashion, with the image seen as the 'book of the poor', but rather to connect them as having both been created on the basis of combinations of signs. The very widespread diffusion of images then emerges as a highly effective factor for mass acculturation through a form of printed material and reproduction, affecting townspeople in particular but also pilgrims. In which case, the image and learning how to read it ('iconization') become the first vehicle of acculturation through the written word.[20]

The image and the text

To combine an image and a text (usually very brief) was not, of course, new; it already happened in China, but also in the West in those 'talking books', mural paintings, miniatures, even sculptures, in which the figurative representation was accompanied by a caption. Like a work of literature, a work of art was not valuable in itself, but for the instruction or the example it offered and which needed to be explained. Rudolf Schenda emphasizes that the picture cannot be considered as the 'book of the poor' or of those who could not read. On the one hand, when Gregory the Great (died 604) suggested that pictures were the 'books of the laity', he was stating the obvious at a time (the sixth century) when the book was almost exclusively an affair of the Church and the clergy. On the other hand, to read images and to identify the persons and understand their relationships, as well as the scene represented, demanded a certain level of education on the part of the observer. To make images 'talk' by the addition of captions made the task of identifying and deciphering easier. Thus, around 1200, the portals of the baptistery in Parma are illustrated by the themes of the Tree of Life and the Genealogy of Christ in which the different persons are identified by phylacteries. The same method was adopted in altarpieces and paintings, too, where the text was some-times not placed in phylacteries but in the lower register of the image – as for example in the *Annunciation* of Giovanni di Paolo in 1445.[21] And the same system is found, lastly, in many iconographical cycles illustrating a particular theme: the altarpiece of Heinrich Fullmauer at Gotha provides a particularly striking example, though later, with its 144 panels depicting biblical scenes around the Crucifixion, each panel surmounted by a commentary placed in a cartouche.

By the 1420s the Buxheim *St Christopher* included a short text.[22] In addition to pious images (*The Seven Capital Sins and the Devil*, the *Memento Mori* skeleton, etc.), sometimes with a mnemonic func-tion (the *Ten Commandments*), there also survive calendars and fragments of booklets showing the alphabet, so serving as a teaching aid, and even the woodblocks themselves – though examples of the latter are relatively late. However, while the technique of *taille d'épargne* meant that image and text could easily be combined, the alphabetic system, unlike the Chinese ideograms, necessitated a sig-nificant increase in the number of signs to be reproduced, which made engraving unsuitable for lengthy texts.

In each case, the xylographic booklets that appeared in the fif-teenth century were made by combining a number of xylographed leaves (up to twenty or twenty-five), with image and text, to form a cycle. The most common titles catered for individual piety, with the *Speculum humanae salvationis* (*Mirror of Redemption*), the *Illustrated Apocalypse* and the *Biblia pauperum* (*Bible of the Poor*). The text of the *Ars moriendi*, probably written on the occasion of the Council of Constance, was meant to aid the dying person represented in the image to withstand the temptations arising during his or her agony: doubt about the truths of religion (absence of faith), anxiety at the thought of one's sins (despair), regret for earthly possessions (avarice), refusal of suffering (impatience) and pride in one's virtues (vanity). The texts were either in Latin or in the vernacular, which reveals the existence of two separate markets, inadequately recognized by the usual educated clergy/uneducated laity dichotomy. This title disap-peared in the 1530s, to be replaced by the treatises of Clichtove (*De Doctrina moriendi opusculum*) and Erasmus (*De Preparatione ad mortem*), then by certain emblems and collections of emblems.

Other small xylographic works were in the nature of teaching manuals and reproduced the alphabet, the Latin manual (*Ars minor*) attributed to Donatus or little booklets of arithmetic. The *Abecedarium* of Augsburg is a piece of engraved wood dating from 1481, which comes from the Benedictine Abbey of Saints Ulrich and Afra: it bears the letters of the alphabet followed by a short sentence in German: 'Great labour and great bitterness, art cannot be sweet, so be ready to learn'. The copy of the booklet of Fridericus Gerhart (1455–64) dating from the years 1471–82, today preserved in Bamberg, contains a multiplication table, then a currency converter and a conversion table for measures; it is a practical document, aimed primarily at merchants and craftsmen, but which could also be used in the town's little schools. Lastly, calendars were sometimes produced in booklet form, and the genre illustrates the emergence of a particular type of bestseller: Johann von Gmunden, canon of St Stephen of Vienna, professor of astronomy and future chancellor of the university, compiled a calendar in 1439 which was reproduced in xylographic form around 1470.[23] Each day is indicated by the name of the saint, and the standardized indications (A...g) make it possible to locate Sundays or work out the date of Easter. Johann Müller (Johannes Regiomontanus) was the author, in Nuremberg, *c*.1472, of a calendar that was very widely circulated in the form of xylographic or printed booklets.[24]

Xylographic images and booklets were printed on paper, usually using a frotton and on one side of the leaf only, but sometimes using a press and on both sides (opisthographic impression). The format was folio and the most common arrangement was inspired by that of the corresponding manuscripts: two columns to a page, the upper part reserved for the illustration.[25] In the booklets, the leaves bear sets of figures separated by architectural motifs (columns and arches). The persons portrayed are identified by phylacteries, and texts of a few lines are engraved at the head and the foot of the image.

The distribution and reception of the xylographic engravings and booklets is very poorly documented. The first area of production was localized in Germany and the old Low Countries, and they were sold on the occasion of a pilgrimage, in a monastery, in front of the church door, even in towns during markets and fairs. The *Chronicle of Cologne* reports that, in 1499, 'printing had a prefiguration, with the Donatus...printed in Holland' before Gutenberg, a claim confirmed, as we will see, by other texts. The associated practices can be grouped into four types: assisting the work of preaching; sustaining individual piety and meditation; serving as a teaching aid, for example in the schools of the Brothers of the Common Life; as a work of reference or aide-memoire, as in the case of calendars and, more generally, practical booklets of every sort. Once again, with these new documents, a significantly larger sector of the population acquired a degree of familiarity with the world of graphic signs, and the viewers, those who looked at the pictures and who potentially read the accompanying text, now, with engravings and booklets, did so not only in the public but also in the private sphere. When the image took the form of an object capable of material appropriation, we are no longer in the world of the 'reading of the poor', even if the greater openness remained limited: the engraved or copied texts were aimed at a literate clientele, even a well-educated one if they were in Latin, despite the probable survival of the practice of 'commented' reading. The customers primarily consisted, therefore, of clergy and monks, persons attached to the noble courts and some of the 'bourgeoisie' and of the ordinary inhabitants of the towns. Lastly, we need to remember that, as regards 'consumption', there was no clear break between xylography and typography using movable characters; not only did a number of technical innovations appear before the latter but, conversely, the xylographic booklet did not disappear until long after.

Punches, Forms and Moulds

The last major technique pre-existing the invention of Gutenberg, and which would play a crucial role in the 'book-system', is that of impression. It had been known since antiquity: one need only think of the seals with which the potters of the Roman world identified their products (sigillated pottery), or the different moulding techniques which made possible, for example, the mass production of oil lamps, even minting. In China, impression was the basic technique for the reproduction of texts, whether by stamping or by the use of engraved seals bearing identifying references or incantatory formulas. In the West, it was, of course, the technique first used for xylography.

Towards Europe: the Mongol connection

China had been reproducing texts since the eighth century, either by engraving on wood or by movable characters carved in terracotta or in wood (eleventh century). This has given rise to the hypothesis that the invention of printing was transmitted to, or more likely inspired in, the West by Chinese or Uyghur objects.[26] By the thirteenth century the West had embarked on a critical phase of geographical expansion. The German push to the east led to the occupation of Prussia by the

Teutonic Knights (1283) and subsequent colonization of the Baltic and Eastern Europe, while the route to the steppes was opened up. But it was in the south that events were most pivotal: the Crusaders seized Constantinople in 1204 and the Latin emperors reigned there until 1261. The uncle of Marco Polo, Marco 'the Elder', had settled in Constantinople and his trading house had a branch in the Crimea (at Soldani/Sudak). At this same period, the Mongols of Genghis Khan took Peking (1215), Bukhara and Samarkand (1220), Moscow (1238) and Kiev (1240), reaching Germany and Hungary in 1241. Most importantly, the 'Mongol peace' established throughout the continent in the fourteenth century made possible the expansion of trade via the Silk Road and the oasis of Turfan:

> The free circulation of merchandise and men explains the extraordinary economic and cultural growth experienced in all the countries crossed by the great caravan routes...For the first time in history, China, Iran and the West came into real contact...A unique moment...when there were colonies of Italian merchants in Tabriz, Astrakhan, Karakoram and Peking, Chinese junks in the ports of the Persian Gulf, merchants from Novgorod in Alexandria and Shiraz, and Armenians in all the caravan towns from the Danube to the Pacific.[27]

Many anonymous travellers followed these routes – merchants, craftsmen, religious, official envoys, and so on. The Franciscan John of Piano Carpino, sent to Mongolia by the pope in 1245, met two Europeans in Karakorum, a woman called Paquette, from Metz, and the Parisian goldsmith, Guillaume Boucher. Eight years later, in 1253, William of Rubruck, a Franciscan from St Omer, left Constantinople for Karakoram as ambassador of St Louis to the Great Khan; he described the Chinese money printed on cotton cloth, also the different scripts and the 'letters hung up' in the temples – in other words, engraved votive inscriptions. John of Montecorvino, another missionary, lived in Peking from 1294 to 1328; he had pious xylographic images printed to be handed out to local people (1305).

Historians have focused less on Marco Polo's account, which is distinctly vague, than on other texts, for example that of a German Franciscan, Odoric of Pordenone (died 1331), who travelled to China, returned via Outer Tibet, and is supposed to have brought Chinese paper money to the West. Another Franciscan, Marignolli, professor of law at Bologna, was also sent with several brethren to China by Benedict XII (1338). They reached Qanbalik (Peking) in 1342, by way of Constantinople and Tana (Azov), returning in 1345 through Ceylon, Ormuz and then Baghdad, Jerusalem and Cyprus. Marignolli was in Avignon in 1353, and met Charles IV of Luxembourg in 1355 during his coronation in Rome. While there, he also met Ulrich Stromer the Younger, a financier sent by his city of Nuremberg to represent it at the coronation. Marignolli then followed the emperor to Prague: he was the crucial intermediary in the project of technological transfer which introduced both the use of punches and the manufacture of playing cards into Prague and Nuremberg.[28] Later, in 1437, another celebrated figure was also in Constantinople, in the person of Nicholas of Cusa (1401–64), who, according to Albert Kapr, may have learned while there about certain Far Eastern technical processes. Thus, there are numerous groups of intermediaries or persons through whom techniques might have been transferred to the West. Nevertheless, though the hypothesis of a transfer has been explored at length, it must be recognized that there is to this day no tangible evidence confirming it. Further, the Western technology, that of typography with movable metal characters, was completely different from the Chinese technology, and both financial capital and the market played a role in the West that had no equivalent in the Far East.

Siderurgy and metallurgy

Capitalism was once again crucial to innovation, driven by spectacular developments in the technologies of siderurgy and metallurgy in the West from the twelfth and thirteenth centuries. It was necessary for the ore to be extracted and purified and for the techniques for working it to be improved, but equally necessary for the capital to be found that would make it possible to carry out increasingly complex processes and respond to an ever-expanding demand. Mining had traditionally been in the hands of groups of independent workers who exploited the ore close to the surface, but once it became necessary to dig deeper, larger capital sums and new techniques were needed, not only for the mining itself but to finance the pumps, ventilation and transport. The area of greatest innovation was concentrated in the Hartz and in Thuringia, the Tyrol, Bohemia and Lower Hungary, Silesia and for a while also Sweden, whether in the case of iron, silver, copper, gold or salt. The capitalists gradually took over the mining operations in Central Europe, which they reorganized and developed:[29] it was the merchants of Augsburg, above all the Fuggers, who controlled the mines of Bohemia, Hungary and the Tyrol, and the former free workers became their employees. Governments played a part: the mining companies were generally divided into shares (the *Kuxen*), and the territorial princes participated as owners of the subsoil. The success and the administrative modernity of states such as Brunswick, the county of Mansfeld and the states of Thuringia and Bohemia was due to the new wealth acquired by this means. In the sixteenth century, conversely, declining revenues and American competition forced the capitalists into retreat, though they retained a degree of control over manufacture and distribution.

The techniques for obtaining iron and other metals were greatly improved by the use of hydraulic energy and the transformation of the kilns. Hydraulic piles driving bellows and hammers spread from the eleventh and twelfth centuries in Germany, the old Low Countries (Liège) and in eastern France.[30] The thirteenth century saw the introduction of the walled kiln, and the late fourteenth century that of the blast furnace, which made it possible to produce liquid pig iron. Cast iron was an alloy of iron and carbon, which could be cast or was refined (by eliminating some or all of the carbon) to obtain iron. Other improvements concerned the techniques for the separation and fusion of the metals: in silver metallurgy, the process of liquation, perfected in the mid-fifteenth century, allowed easier separation of the lead from the silver and copper. The forge hammer became much heavier (the tilt hammer) and the manufacture of moulded objects benefited from the improvements in the alloy process: the composition of the alloy had to be such as to allow fusion to take place, but solidification had to happen fairly quickly. Together, these techniques made it possible to procure a wide range of objects (conduits, plaques, pipes and cannon, anchors, etc.), while other major advances were made in Germany, as with hydraulic wire drawing, used in paper mills.

Metal was used in the manufacture of guns, in clockmaking and in the textile industry, and eventually in engraving and typography. At every level, the sector was one of the most crucial from the perspective not only of innovation but also of capitalistic structures. And the changes affected consumers, too. In Nuremberg, around Lyon, and in Brescia metal objects in everyday use were manufactured for a wider market, ironmongery, chests, locks and keys, pins, razors, nails, horseshoes, bits and a variety of tools. In other words, the transformation of the media system came about in an environment itself undergoing profound change, whether in the new developments in capitalism, technological innovation or the remodelling of models of consumption.

Letters with spurs and punches

According to Wolfgang von Stromer, Prague and Bohemia were central to the process of transfer and innovation which made

Gutenberg's invention possible. The castle of Karlstein, south of the capital, was the power base of the emperor Charles IV of Luxembourg. Its pictorial decoration was inspired by Marignolli's *Chronicle of Bohemia*; the imperial genealogy was the work of the painter Nicolas Wurmser, a native of Strasbourg whose family was close to that of the Heilmann, future financiers of Gutenberg. In 1360, Wurmser was succeeded by Sebald Weinschröter, originally from Nuremberg, and with him we are back once again in the Stromer circle. The ceiling of the Karlstein chapel was 'decorated with thousands of tiny convex mirrors and [its] walls [were] encrusted with polished semiprecious stones', on a stamped background. The decoration of the surrounds and the background was achieved by the use of designs printed with a punch, and combining the imperial eagle, the lion of Bohemia and the letter K (for Karolus). Let us anticipate here to observe that mirrors, gems and punches are three elements we will encounter again in the research of Gutenberg in Strasbourg. Karlstein was visited by numerous envoys and ambassadors, including the Stromer: Friedrich Stromer, related through his sister to the Schatz of Prague, and in the service of the Luxembourg, was even appointed lay administrator of the castle.

Another innovation was provided by sigillography. The technique of the impression of the seal, usually on wax, achieved using a matrix struck with a hollow design (*en creux*) and in reverse, has several points in common with that of typography. The seal of Rudolf IV, of 1362, bears an 'archydux' legend whose Gothic letters have postiche spurs. Closer examination shows that the letters with a complex design are based on simpler letters to which a projection has been added, making it possible, to choose an obvious example, to turn ſ into *f*. This practice meant punches could be made much more rapidly, hence speeded up the work of engraving. It presupposes, however, total mastery both of a technique of engraving so precise that it bears comparison with goldsmithing and of the smelting of the alloys:

> A careful examination of these letters with added spurs...makes it clear that this practice was borne of the need to rationalize the extremely demanding and difficult work of the engravers of letters and punches. In fact, the engraver need only reproduce the letters of relatively simple shape...then, on the original or a copy, add a spur [to] obtain [a more complex letter]. (Wolfgang von Stromer)

And it seems indeed to have been from Karlstein, Prague (with the mint) and Nuremberg (first known example, in 1395) that the use of letters with such projections spread. They were a huge success;

Figure 4.1 The aesthetic of the 'letters with secants' was extremely success-ful, and they were used not only in calligraphy but also in the decorative ele-ments of some remarkable buildings. Cistercian abbey of Alcobaça, Portugal.

initially used for gold plate, reliquaries, tomb slabs cast in bronze, belt buckles and even for the casting of bells and cannon, they are also found in handwritten texts and in epigraphy.

The technology of the punch developed further when, two genera-tions later (1433), in Nuremberg, the Dominican Konrad Forster struck short texts on bindings using metal punches, employing to do this alphabets composed of letters with spurs and engraved by Hensel Sigerstorfer. A total of eighty-five manuscripts with bindings deco-rated by Forster in intaglio or in relief have been identified. The rich and powerful cities of Bohemia, southern Germany and the Rhineland were in constant contact. In that same year, 1433, Gutenberg was working in Strasbourg on three technical problems, the polishing of precious stones, the manufacture of pilgrim mirrors and a third, not specified by the sources, but which had to do with the reproduction of texts. A binding decorated with texts printed with punches is known for Strasbourg in 1439; it was probably the work of Hans Ross, an engraver of punches for binding and possibly a collaborator of Gutenberg. Not only was the latter undoubtedly familiar with the technique of printing texts with a punch, but two of the five *42-line Bibles* which have preserved their original binding were decorated in Mainz using punches similar to those of Forster, bearing the same signs and in the same body – the engravers of punches who worked for Gutenberg had learned from Forster's achievements.[31]

In the last analysis, whether the precise technical filiation postulated by Wolfgang von Stromer between Prague, Nuremberg, Strasbourg and Mainz existed or not is of limited significance. The point is, there was innovation everywhere, in which metallurgy was crucial, and, in the favourable conditions of Central Europe, craftsmen were working on the same problems and in the same technical areas. The role of the merchants and investors was fundamental, both in financing the research and in exploiting, where appropriate, the results. Their power enabled them to make decisive interventions at the political level, as in the case of the Fugger: Jacob the Rich was established not only in Augsburg but in Venice, Rome and Antwerp; he was involved in the exploitation of metals in the Tyrol and in huge banking operations, and he put 540,000 florins at the disposal of Charles the Great to ensure his election to the empire (1519). Finally, and anticipating, we should remember the possible connection between the world of the technicians of printing and that of the great explorers: it seems likely that one of the first printer-booksellers of Flanders, Thierry (Dirk) Martens of Alost and Antwerp, was one and the same person as the Teodorico Aleman who, in 1477, obtained a royal privilege for the import of books into Spain. Christopher Columbus was received on the same day as he was, at the royal court of Spain, when he was described as '*mercader de libros de estampa*' (merchant of printed books), perhaps as one of his representatives in the Peninsula...[32]

From Prague to Avignon, Haarlem and Strasbourg

In the first half of the fifteenth century, the pivotal invention was, in the nice phrase of Henri-Jean Martin, 'in the air'. In Bohemia, southern Germany (Nuremberg, Constance), the Rhine Valley, Holland (Haarlem) and Avignon, groups of inventors and entrepreneurs were working on a wide range of technical problems: papermaking, the manufacture of mirrors, the polishing of precious stones, firearms technology, improvements to the stamping of bindings and the search for a new way of reproducing texts in large numbers.[33]

Procopius Waldvogel de Braganciis (*Pragensis*, that is, from Prague) came from a family of metallurgists established in Prague since the 1360s. In the wake of the troubles in Bohemia, he left Prague for Nuremberg, Lucerne (1439), possibly Constance,[34] and then Avignon (1444–6).[35] Little is known about him: married to a woman called Anne, he was a fine technician, skilled in the work of smelting and metallurgy. In Avignon, he initially lodged with a compatriot, a native of Koblenz, Gerard Ferrosse (*Yzsenrosse* = Eisenro, the Iron Horse). Ferrosse too was a specialized technician, a locksmith, clockmaker and firearms manufacturer – he was described as *magister bombardarum et colobrinarum* (master of bombards and culverins). A first venture is documented in 1444, when Waldvogel and Ferrosse made contact with a Jewish moneylender, David Caderousse, their sleeping partner. On 4 July they sold a collection of tools used for 'artificial writing' to a student from Dax, Manaldus Vitalis, namely two alphabets of steel, two 'forms' (*formas*) of iron, a metal screw, forty-eight 'forms' in tin and various other 'forms' 'concerning the art of writing'. A second contract, drawn up on 26 August of the same year, is evidence of the difficulties the inventors had encountered: they were unable to repay Caderousse and the society was dissolved. Waldvogel paid Ferrosse thirty florins in final settlement, and the latter undertook not to practise or disseminate his art in Avignon itself or within twelve leagues of the town.

Waldvogel then made contact with a rich Avignon bourgeois, Georges de La Jardina, who wanted to obtain a set of writing tools and learn the corresponding technology, all within the space of a month, to which Waldvogel agreed. One clause guaranteed secrecy on the part of La Jardina. In 1445 Waldvogel rented a house, but he was still in financial difficulties. Meanwhile, others were trying to exploit the techniques he had taught them: Vitalis had linked up with two associates originally from the south-west to this end. When one of them, Coselhac, left Avignon, he sold the tools in his possession to Vitalis for the sum of twelve florins, namely instruments and tools in iron, copper, lead, tin, etc., but also in wood, all for the purpose of 'artificial writing'. Another deal was agreed on 10 March 1446: Waldvogel would provide Caderousse with twenty-seven Hebrew letters in metal and tools of wood, tin and iron, all, once again, to enable 'artificial writing' (*ad scribendum artificialiter*). The equipment was to be delivered quickly and, in return, Caderousse would reveal to his partner certain processes for the dyeing of cloth. A few months later, probably in early summer 1446, Waldvogel left Avignon and all trace of him is lost.

What exactly was the technique Waldvogel had developed? In the absence of any system of legal protection, it was in the interests of partners to guard the secrecy of the process of which they had knowledge, and the highly evasive nature of the documentary records means that we are reduced to hypotheses. Further, the techniques were too recent for a specialized vocabulary to have developed and the meaning of many of the terms used is unclear. Audin believed that the first contract of 1444 referred to a collection of punches (two 'alphabets of steel'), a system of screw pressing and, perhaps, sets of matrices-blocks making it possible to print short texts by juxtaposition of the marks of the punches, previously inked.[36] If this was the case, it was possible to reproduce the texts, but composition with movable letters, crux of Gutenberg's invention, had not emerged. Further, none of the surviving contracts mentions purchases of parchment or paper or the manufacture of ink, which leaves open even the question of reproduction: if the hypothesis of the matrices-blocks fails to hold up and, consequently, there was no reproduction of one text in many copies, what we have is a technique analogous to that of Forster and based on the use of punches alone.

Proto-typographical techniques also emerged in the old Low Countries. The invention is traditionally attributed to Laurens Janszoon Coster, of Haarlem,[37] but we should primarily refer to the books *jetés en mole* mentioned in the *Memorials* of Jean Le Robert, Abbot of Saint-Aubert of Cambrai, in 1446 and 1451:

Item pour 1 Doctrinal getté en molle envoyet querre à Bruges par Marquet, 1 escripvain de Vallenciennes, ou mois de janvier XLV pour Jaquet, XX s.t. S'en heult Sandrins 1 pareil que l'église paia…

   Item, envoiet Arras 1 Doctrinal pour apprendre led. dampt Grard, qui fu accatez a Vallenciennes, et estoit jettez en molle, et cousta XXIII gros. Se me renvoia led. Doctrinal le jour de Toussains l'an LI, disant qu'il ne falloit rien estoit tout faulx. S'en avoit accaté IX patars en papier.[38]

(Item for 1 Doctrinal 'thrown by mould' sent to Bruges by Marquet, a scribe of Valenciennes, in the month of January XLV [old style] for Jaquet, XX sous tournois. Sandrins sent 1 similar which the Church paid for…Item, sent [to] Arras 1 Doctrinal to teach the said lord G[i]rard, which was bought in Valenciennes, and was 'thrown by mould', and cost XXIV *gros*. He sent me the said Doctrinal on All Saints Day in the year LI, saying it was [worth] nothing and all false. He had bought for it IX *patars* of paper.)

The expression *jetés en mole* does not yet refer, in these Cambrai documents, to typography in movable characters. It is also found, along with other Latin or French formulas, in the probate inventories of the canons of Cambrai. The vocabulary is once again vague, as was inevitable during the emergence of a new technology, and we find in the course of these texts three different formulas: first, books written by hand, *ad manum*; then, books in a mould or in forms, moulded books, thrown in a mould, *in mola* and *cum formis*; lastly, books printed, properly speaking, *impressus, in impressura*. Lothar Wolf, Lehmann-Haupt, and Audin take '*mole*' as indicating a xylographic technique or impression by pieces of metal; the term was already used with this meaning in the fourteenth century. Prosper Marchand had already, in the mid-eighteenth century, opted for this classic schema of technical filiation:

> These first impressions...being made only with the aid of blocks of wood such as I have just described, were much less true impressions than simple engravings, very similar to our images carved in wood or, better, to the famous prints of China and Japan...Only able to serve for one new impression of the same work, and uselessly filling whole shops, they soon became a burden by their huge number; and printing only on one side of the paper, the two white sides of which it was then necessary to stick one against the other in order to conceal this flaw, they necessarily caused both double trouble and double cost, only to produce after all a pretty imperfect book.[39]

Hélène Servant has added to the dossier the text of the will of canon Servais Le Roy, of Valenciennes, in 1473, which has the peculiarity of being partly translated into Latin: *en maulle* corresponds to *in mola* and *faitte en maulle* is rendered by *factam cum formis*. In which case, 'mould' is equivalent to 'form', which might indicate either a xylographic technique or a metallographic technique using page-blocks. There also survive a number of examples of prototypographies made in the old Low Countries using techniques of which the details remain unknown, but in a timeframe which overlaps in part with that of typography with movable characters.[40] Audin has therefore suggested a schema of technological development which may have corresponded to the technology employed by Waldvogel in Avignon:

> They carved punches with letters in relief and in reverse at the end of a thin rod of steel. These punches were pressed in succession in their order so as to form words and phrases in a plate of casting sand, clay or copper. In this way, lines and pages struck 'in hollow' [intaglio] were bit by bit formed. An alloy of lead, tin and antimony was poured into this matrix of lead. They got, on release from the mould, a block of metal which, in principle, must have had the same properties as the xylographic block. The saving of time obtained in this way was

considerable, but the result was poor: the moulded block had imperfections due primarily to faults in the alignment of the letters. (Marius Audin)

Another procedure consisted of printing directly with punches (as for stamped bindings), but the technological limit was quickly reached and it remained impossible to carve in metal the quantity of punches needed to print texts of any length.

In sum, typography with movable letters was a wholly original invention in the link between the metalwork, the breaking down of the text by the movable characters and the use of the press for printing. Reconstructions of the filiations, in particular from xylography to typography with movable letters, cannot fully account for the process of invention itself. This is not to say that, among the proto-typographical techniques that may have existed, xylography did not play a role. 'Some engravers in the old Low Countries carved in beech wood letters or groups of letters in relief, which could be assembled to compose short texts – this was "*xylotypie*"', suggests Audin – and, as we have seen, the process was already known to the Chinese. Specklin wrote, in his *Universal Chronicle*, of the beginnings of printing in Strasbourg:[41]

> I saw the first press [of Mentelin] and also the characters: they had been engraved in wood, as well as words or syllables; they were holed, they were strung on a thread with the aid of a needle, then they were laid out on the lines. It is a pity that such a practice was allowed to disappear, the very first of its kind in the whole world.

Gutenberg may have met the future Alsatian proto-typographer Johann Mentelin (*c*.1410–78) in Strasbourg, as the latter, a native of Sélestat, acquired burgess rights there in 1447 and had probably regularly lived in the town before that date. The fact remains, it was impossible to print by the xylotype method works of any length, as was, notably, the first known book of Mentelin, the *49-line Bible* of 1460. The crucial invention remained to be perfected.

5

Gutenberg and the Invention of Printing

Ars imprimendi libros his temporibus in Germania primum inventa est: quam alii repertam asserunt Gutenbergo Argentino, alii a quodam alio nomine Fusto. Qua certe nulla in mundo dignior, nulla laudabilior aut utilior sive divinior aut sanctior esse potuit.[1]

Historical Portrait of a City

A frontier town

Despite everything that has been said, the person primarily responsible for the invention of typography with movable characters can with some confidence be identified as Johann (or Henne) Genfleisch zur Laden, called Gutenberg, from the name of the house in Mainz where he was born (*Zum guten Berge* = at the beautiful mountain), some time between 1394 and 1400.[2] With Mainz, we are once again in a frontier region, the town having been founded in 38 BC by the Romans, on the Rhine, opposite its confluence with the Main and the Germanic territories. It was a powerful stronghold, held by two of the eight legions responsible for controlling the *limes*, but it was also a hub for trade with the Germanic peoples of the right bank – a bridge was built and a small fort erected at its outlet (*Castellum Mattiacorum*, today Kastel). This centre of power and trade was also one of the first Christian towns in the West. Christianity arrived from the East and first reached the ports, in Gaul, Marseille and its hinterland, before spreading along the principal trade and communication routes, the Rhône (Lyon), the Saône and the Moselle (Metz,

Trier), as far as the Rhine. Irenaeus mentions a bishop in Mainz before 202.

Both strategic military base and pole of exchanges and acculturation, Mainz was marked by its early history for many years to come. It became a centre of mission, hence acculturation by the written word, when the pope appointed as its archbishop Boniface, the apostle of Germany (746), and gave him the task of organizing the new Church. The province of Mainz included much of central Germany. From the end of the tenth century, the archbishop-primate was also chancellor of the Holy Roman Empire. In the thirteenth century Mainz was one of the principal towns of Germany, the only one to share with Rome the title of 'Holy See' (*sancta sedum Moguntiae*), and the 'golden crown' or 'diadem' of the Holy Empire. The power of the primate was confirmed by the Golden Bull of Charles IV (1356), which regulated the imperial election; first among the electors, he was seen as the 'kingmaker'. In Mainz itself and in its province, the archbishop was effectively the secular lord.

The political situation in these rapidly developing cities gradually became more complicated. The chief players in the politics of Mainz were the archbishop, often a member of the family of Nassau, and his entourage (the *familia*), the chapter, the urban patriciate and the masters of the guilds; the vast majority of the population was excluded. The patriciate consisted in principle of only twenty-eight families, which had exclusive right to the offices granted by the archbishop, and also a monopoly of the trade in cloth and precious metals and money-changing, the latter exercised through the society of Companions of the Mint (*Hausgenoss en auf der Münze*). The town and its elites controlled traffic on the Rhine and the Main, dominated an extremely rich hinterland and benefited from the presence of an important court, not to speak of the numerous prelates who passed through. From the twelfth century, however, the growing power and wealth of the towns was reflected in their desire for independence from their traditional lords: in Cologne the burgesses united against the archbishop, in Worms they drove the bishop out in 1174, and Spier, from 1198, was governed by a Council. It was the same in Mainz, but here the archbishop was able to remain master of the town, and the struggle focused on control of the Council and the municipal administration (the magistracy), including the appointment of the burgomaster; the representatives of the archbishop were excluded (1332), leaving the patriciate and the members of the guild to oppose each other.

These struggles were intensified by the serious difficulties the town faced in the fourteenth century: Mainz, which had between 20,000 and 25,000 inhabitants in *c*.1300, had no more than 5,000–10,000 by 1500. In 1411, bankruptcy was declared and the financial crisis degenerated into a political crisis. In 1428–9, a revolt against the patriciate led to the institution by the guilds of a Council of Ten, which embarked on radical reforms before being forced to compromise with the patricians, the town's principal creditors. But some of them had left Mainz, among them the Gutenbergs, who had settled in Strasbourg. In 1437, the budgetary deficit reached 200,000 florins and the Jews were expelled the following year. There was a new crisis in 1444–6, which established guild control: every Council member must be a member of a guild, and the patriciate lost its old political role. The initiator of this reform was the syndic (municipal legal advisor) Dr Konrad Humery, who would later be one of Gutenberg's backers. The financial difficulties were so acute, however, that, in 1446, the municipal council contemplated mortgaging the town to the capitalists of Frankfurt. These multiple crises ended in the return of the prince, a return made easier by the disastrous foreign policy choices made by Mainz, which had succeeded in alienating both the emperor and the pope. In 1462, the archbishop appointed by the pope, Adolf of Nassau, seized the city by surprise, abolished its privileges and installed an administration dependent on him alone as absolute prince. Mainz now resembled a 'residence town', characteristic of early modern Germany.

Clergy and patricians

In and around Mainz, the networks of merchants and financiers intersected with those of the clergy and prelates. Gutenberg was born around 1397 in the house that belonged to his family, the Genfleisch. They had been part of the urban patriciate for some two centuries, they were associates of the Mint and their marriage policy had connected them to most of the other families of note: the zur Laden, zum Gelthus, zum Fürstenberg, zum Jungen, zum Blashof, zur Jungen Aben, zum Silberberg, zum Eselweck, zum Rafit, zum Vitztum and zum Molsberg, not forgetting the Bechtermünze.... They were all rich merchants, who owned rural properties (in particular at Eltville, *Alta Villa*), benefited from the monopoly of the cloth trade, controlled the Mint and held decision-making positions in the municipal administration or service of the archbishop. They invested freely in annuities on the towns, in Mainz itself, but also in the region (Fritzlar) and as far afield as Strasbourg. Family ties and business interests were intertwined: Gutenberg's father, Friele Genfleisch, merchant and capitalist, Companion of the Mint, took as his second wife, in 1386, Else

Wittich, also from an active family of merchants. Her grandfather, Werner Wittich, had himself married Ennelin zum Fürstenberg, whose family was already related to the Genfleisch. These familial solidarities were crucial and among Gutenberg's relatives was also Arnold Gelthus, to whom he appealed for money before turning to Fust. But his parents had been too deeply implicated on the side of the patricians and had to leave Mainz during the crisis of 1411, possibly for Eltville.

As seat of the primate, Mainz was inevitably a city of transit or residence for a large number of prelates, benefice-holders and persons of note, and it was in constant contact with both Rome and the Imperial Court. These connections played a major role, but one we are left to infer, in the early dissemination of printing. In 1417, the prior of the Benedictine monastery of St Victor of Weisenau was Antonius de Bercka (died 1435), former physician to the Emperor Sigismund and dean of the university of Erfurt. Bercka bequeathed his library of 633 volumes to Erfurt, where he founded the Collegium Amplonianum. Many clergy of St Victor had close contacts with the Roman Curia: Goswin Mule, from Karden, on the Moselle, was prior of St Victor (1451), *scriptor* in the pontifical administration, then *collector* of the pontifical chamber, and close to the pope; Cyriacus Leckstein, canon, then prior in his turn, held several posts in the Curia; Wigand Menckler of Homburg was in the service of Nicholas of Cusa (1431), visited Rome in 1440 before becoming schoolmaster at St Victor and was also an associate of Cardinal Carvajal; August Bensheim, another client of Carvajal, succeeded him at St Victor in 1456.[3] The Benedictines of St James of Mainz (St Jakob) were also committed to the reform of the Church and they commissioned the edition of the second *Benedictine Psalter* (1459). Adrian, a monk at St James, worked as a typographic corrector for Fust and Schoeffer and was himself the owner of a very large library (which included a *42–line Bible* on parchment and a *Catholicon*).

At the heart of these networks was Nicholas of Cusa: born to a rich family of Kues,[4] on the Moselle, and probably a former pupil of the Brothers of the Common Life, he had studied at Heidelberg, Padua and Cologne.[5] At the Council of Basel he took the side of the pope, and he is next heard of in Constantinople, in 1437, preparing for the Council of Ferrara-Florence; he was also frequently in Mainz. Made cardinal in 1448, he was itinerant legate in Germany, Bohemia and the Low Countries before being made Bishop of Brixen, in the Tyrol, high in the Trent Valley (1452). He was close to Aeneas Silvius Piccolomini (1405–64) and lived mostly in Rome after the latter's election as pope with the name Pius II (1458). In that year Cusa founded a hospice in Bernkastel, under the rule of the congregation of Windesheim, and in 1461 instituted a scholarship (*Bursa cusana*) to accommodate in Deventer twenty poor students from the Moselle region. His library is preserved in Bernkastel; it consists of some 270 manuscripts from the ninth to the fifteenth centuries, but he may also have bought a copy of the *Catholicon* in 1460. With Nicholas of Cusa, we are in a milieu which unquestionably played a role in the early spread of printing.[6] Soon after his appointment to Brixen, he wrote from Bruneck (Tyrol) to Heinrich Brack, prior of St James of Mainz, instructing him to have prepared, within the month, 2,000 copies of a letter of indulgences for Frankfurt. The vocabulary of the letter is problematic: the word used is *expressio*, not the more usual *publicatio*, which refers to the act of orally 'publishing' something, for example from a pulpit. *Expressio* thus suggests a new process, alluding to the physical process of 'pressing': the word was used to describe the impression of a seal, and it is found with this meaning in Angelo Ambrogini, also known as Politien (*excudo formis, exprimo formis*), in Marsilio Ficino and in the correspondence of Amerbach. The large number of copies and the shortness of the time allowed for their production strengthens the hypothesis that the letter of indulgences of 1452 was printed – but no copy is known to have survived.[7] A statement by Giovanni Andrea de Bussi dating from 1470 suggests that the cardinal was also responsible for the arrival of the first Italian printers, Sweynheym and Pannartz, in Subiaco, *c*.1465.

On the middle Rhine

We know almost nothing about the childhood or education of Gutenberg. We know that Mainz was well endowed with educational institutions, tutors, 'Latin schools' teaching reading and writing and monastic schools in the first half of the fifteenth century. The Genfleisch had especially close ties with St Victor, which some family members had entered, and which was home to a fraternity which Gutenberg would later join. Founded in 1392 following the crisis in Prague, Erfurt was the university of choice for the young men of Mainz. Two of Gutenberg's relatives appear in its matriculation registers for 1417 and a certain Johannes de Alta Villa, who has been identified with Gutenberg, was registered there the following year. He passed the baccalaureate in 1419–20.[8] Gutenberg's own name appears only in chronicles of a much later date (seventeenth century), in connection with his father's succession (1419–20).[9] It is possible that he was apprenticed as a young man to a goldsmith, but there is no trace of his name in the guild lists of Mainz, and the fact that he later employed goldsmiths suggests that he may never fully have mastered these techniques. Other documents referring to him concern annuities on the city from 1427, but without further details.[10] Gutenberg was then personally caught up in the political struggles: the Council wanted to tax the patricians to reduce the town's debt, and it prohibited them from leaving Mainz for ten years. Some of them left, notwithstanding, including Gutenberg, probably by 1428. On 28 March 1430, the archbishop, who had intervened in the hope of fostering an agreement, notified them of the order to return to Mainz; the name of Gutenberg appears in the document, showing that he himself was then established in another city, probably Strasbourg. When he refused, Mainz suspended payments of an annuity due to him.

> It had been specified in the acknowledgement of the debt that the loan contracted by Mainz was to be guaranteed by all the citizens: so if the town ceased to pay the annuity, Gutenberg could demand payment from any of his co-citizens.[11]

Gutenberg's mother died in 1433, at which point he either returned himself or sent a representative to Mainz.[12] He alone of his family bore the surname *Hof zum guten Berge*, a property he may have inherited at this point. In 1434, his brother Friele was in Eltville, where he, in his turn, may have come into some family property.

Strasbourg

Gutenberg is known to have been in Strasbourg in March 1434, and he remained there for a decade. He never acquired full citizenship but was listed, in 1444, with his associate Andreas Heilmann, as a member of the guild of goldsmiths. He was also incorporated into the patrician category of the *Nachconstofler*, unique to Strasbourg.

A metropolis in the Rhine Valley

Strasbourg, in the province of Mainz, was one of the principal towns in the middle Rhine in the first half of the fifteenth century, and an economic, religious, political and intellectual centre of the first order. The city had developed in a similar manner to Mainz, with the same cast of actors, but at a higher level.[13] After a period of rapid growth in the thirteenth century Strasbourg had freed itself from the tutelage of the bishop in 1262, but here, too, the fourteenth century proved a more difficult period. The Council was dominated by the burgesses

Figure 5.1 Strasbourg (in Latin, *Argentina*), a Free Imperial City and true capital of the valley of the middle Rhine, received Gutenberg when he was forced to leave Mainz; it is very likely, therefore, that it was here that printing was definitively perfected. This view of the city, taken from the *Chronicle of Nuremberg* of Hartmann Schedel (Nuremberg, Anton Koberger, 1493), is remarkable for the modernity of its page layout: note the printed foliation and running head, also the spire of the Cathedral as if shooting up from the illustration in the inside margin of the text. Municipal Library of Valenciennes.

and the crafts. The guilds were extremely powerful, the most important of them being the Échasse, which brought together the painters on wood, cloth and metal, the glass workers, saddlers and makers of bows, crossbows and breastplates, then the goldsmiths (1362), the woodcarvers (1427), and finally the binders and printers (after 1470). A fair town since 1336 and a frontier town controlling the Rhine bridge (the customs house was built in 1358), Strasbourg was a commercial and financial centre, but also a town of remarkable intellectual and artistic dynamism. In the mid fourteenth century, the town's principal banker was Rulmann Merswin: a merchant and money-lender to the bishop, Merswin had agents in Bruges and collected the taxes levied in Germany on behalf of the Avignon popes. Under the influence of Tauler, he abandoned his commercial concerns in 1347 and went on to compose mystical texts. At a later date a certain Friedrich von Seckingen, with his son Johann, had business dealings with Milan (bank of Mayno) and Nuremberg (Peter Steinberger).

There was regular contact between Mainz and Strasbourg, two towns only some 200 kilometres apart, so there is nothing particularly surprising about Gutenberg's decision to settle in Alsace to pursue his affairs. The availability of capital in the town was a factor favourable to innovation and enterprise; the Seckingen were behind Gutenberg's backers.

So it was in Alsace that Gutenberg carried out his research and made his first forays into technical spheres. His work may have earned him enough to live off and the death of his mother Else Wittich probably brought him some capital (1433), but it was nevertheless necessary for him to approach investors able to provide him with the funds he needed to finance his activities. These capitalists engaged, at high risk, in what we would today call Research and Development: this is the meaning of the German *Aventur*, which is found, with a slippage of sense, in the English 'merchant adventurer' and the French *grosse aventure*. In Avignon, in Strasbourg and later in Mainz such men financed the development of a new technology without any way of knowing whether the research or the experiments would ever succeed, even less whether they would result in a viable product, likely to find a market. It was this system, which resembles that of the modern start-up, that financed a variety of projects: improving the techniques needed for the reproduction of texts, but also for papermaking, the manufacture of mirrors and the working of precious stones.[14]

The market was central to any such system: for production to be possible, it was necessary to commit the capital required to perfect the manufacturing processes, obtain the raw materials and pay the workers. It was equally necessary, at a later stage, to have access to efficient networks of correspondents and a grasp of trading practices. Finance was not only needed for the development of the process; it was necessary to be able to exploit it by maintaining, in the case of printing, the first typographic workshops, sometimes over the long term. Here, too, it was merchant bankers who committed themselves to the new medium, in some cases even specializing in it. These great financiers were also actively involved in operations conducted by the towns, the Church and the princely courts, though not to the exclusion of other activities – far from it: many of them had artistic, intellectual and even spiritual interests, as we have seen in the case of Rulmann Merswin. In fact it was probably inevitable that the geographical distribution of the small group of what Wolfgang von Stromer called 'Archimedean inventors' then active in Europe – like that of the small group of artists – would essentially replicate both the economic and the political geography, with the emphasis on the wealthiest, most active and best-situated centres. This was the case with towns like Prague and Nuremberg, with Constance at the time of the Council, with the various towns of the middle Rhine, with Avignon – and with Strasbourg.

Contracts and processes (1434–44)

Let us examine the dossier for Gutenberg's stay in Strasbourg, on which much work has been done, here simply to recapitulate the main points.[15] The first piece of evidence concerns the visit to Strasbourg of Niklaus von Wörstadt, town clerk and head of the guilds of Mainz, in 1434. Gutenberg had him arrested, as responsible on behalf of the town of Mainz for the annuity he was owed (310 florins), payment of which had been suspended. The burgomaster of Strasbourg intervened, von Wörstadt was set free and the debt was repaid, though the payment was made to Klaus Vitztum, Gutenberg's brother-in-law. For Gutenberg, the operation was advantageous at all levels: he had ensured, by his understanding, the goodwill of the burgomaster of Strasbourg, settled the situation as regards Mainz to his own benefit and at the same time recovered a large sum of money.[16] He was at this point established close to St Arbogast, a suburb some 2 kilometres from the city walls and dependent on Saint-Thomas. Two years later a certain Ennelin zu der Yserin Tür (Ennelin of the Iron Gate), from a patrician family, instituted proceedings against Gutenberg for breach of promise. As Gutenberg does not appear in the lists of burgesses, we may presume that no marriage took place. That same year, 1436, the goldsmith Hans Dünne left his natal town of Frankfurt for Strasbourg; he will reappear as one of the witnesses at the trial of 1439.[17]

Gutenberg was at this point working on the technology of the cutting and polishing of precious stones, which, before 1436, he taught to Andreas Dritzehn, himself a member of a family linked to the magistracy. A number of contracts were concluded, notably in 1438 with Hans Riffe, a wealthy member of the patriciate and prefect of Lichtenau, for a society to manufacture mirrors intended for the pilgrimage to Aachen. At this pilgrimage, which took place every seven years, four relics were presented to the believers: the robe of Mary, the swaddling clothes and the loin cloth of Christ and the cloth on which the head of St John the Baptist had been placed. Large numbers of mirrors were sold on this occasion; they enabled pilgrims to catch the image of the relics, despite the distance and the crowd, and so benefit from their miraculous power. At the technical level, this demanded a mastery of metalworking, both for polishing the mirrors and for the surrounds in which they were set. This was mass production: it has been estimated that the society established in Strasbourg produced between 30,000 and 40,000 items in 1437–8. Several features bring us close, indirectly, to typography with movable characters: at the trial in 1439 Hans Dünne declared that he had earned 100 florins for having delivered material relating to the 'press' that may have been used for this object – and Ritter emphasizes the size of this sum, equivalent to the cost of 'eleven oxen'. When Andreas Dritzehn got wind of the operation, he asked to join, as did Andreas Heilmann: they each paid eighty florins in apprenticeship fees and worked for the society, Riffe being the principal sleeping partner and Guttenberg the technician. It was laid down that 50 per cent of the profits would go to Riffe, 25 per cent to Gutenberg and 12.5 per cent to each of the others.

Manufacture of the mirrors began in 1438, only for the associates to learn that the next pilgrimage had been postponed to 1440, perhaps due to plague. So, in the autumn of 1438, a new contract was signed for five years: Dritzehn and Heilmann would pay a further 420 florins jointly and themselves work in the enterprise; Gutenberg and Riffe engaged to provide a similar sum of money. The available capital would be of the order of 1,300–1,500 florins, a very large sum, and Dritzehn, who was convinced of their eventual success, borrowed so as to be able to advance his share. The text of the contract uses the terms *Afentur* and *Kunst* ('adventure' and 'art'), and the records of the subsequent trial mention lead, a vice, a form and a press. This press, with its four principal parts, was installed in the house of Dritzehn. It seems possible, therefore, that Gutenberg was at this point, on the basis of his experience with the mirrors, actively researching into the techniques of casting and pressing which would be used in printing. Nevertheless, the hypothesis of a slow development process seems more probable, given that typography with movable characters proved a highly complex technology, in not only its conception but also the manufacturing processes necessary to make it work.

As always, the prospects envisaged by the financiers were a good deal more favourable than the hard reality. Dritzehn was convinced, according to 'Bärbel', one of the witnesses in 1439, that he would recover his costs a hundredfold within a year,[18] but he died, probably of plague, on Christmas Day 1438, even before this second contract could come into effect. His two brothers, Georg and Klaus, approached Gutenberg to ask either that they take his place in the business or that they were reimbursed for his contribution. Meanwhile, perhaps because they wished to avoid the contagion, Gutenberg and Heilmann sent their servant, Beildeck, to Dritzehn's house to dismantle the press, but they were too late. Gutenberg also instigated a search for the 'forms' in the houses both of Dritzehn and Heilmann and destroyed them at St Arbogast. No fewer than thirty-three witnesses were called at the trial of 1439, and the depositions of fifteen survive: the judgment of 12 December was favourable to Gutenberg, who was required to pay the plaintiff only fifteen florins. The affair of the mirrors, settled at last, provided him with new resources, which enabled him to settle in the town, near to St Thomas, possibly to escape the Armagnac bands then threatening the countryside. He was even in a position to act as security for Hans Karle the elder with the chapter of St Thomas, for the sum of 100 livres (1441). The following year he borrowed eighty livres at 5 per cent from the same chapter, evidence both of his creditworthiness and of certain financial needs, perhaps to pursue new research.[19] A surviving register records that he was taxed on 2,000 litres of wine cellared every year for two persons, himself and probably his servant Lorenz Heilbeck, whose wife was his housekeeper. Lastly, in 1444, Gutenberg is documented in Strasbourg for the last time: a member of the guild of goldsmiths, he paid the tax for the defence against the Armagnacs (on a capital of between 400 and 800 florins), but after the wine tax paid on 12 March 1444 we lose track of him again for four years.

It is possible that Gutenberg remained in Strasbourg after 1444, but more likely that he travelled, perhaps to Lichtenau (to stay with Riffe), Basel, Avignon or the Low Countries (Haarlem). It seems unlikely that he returned to Mainz, as the political crisis was once again acute. However the death of his brother Friele in 1447 made him head of the family and may mark the date of his return, which had taken place by the autumn of 1448. In Strasbourg, in 1444, Gutenberg's financial situation seems to have been healthy, but it remains unclear whether or not he had printed minor pieces, now lost, in the Alsatian capital. In 1446, the records of a trial concerning the Dritzehn brothers mention a library of theirs, which Francis Ritter believed might have included some copies of the first attempts at printing.[20] Though Wimpheling (1450–1528), in his *Epitoma rerum Germanicarum* (1505), declared that printing was invented in Strasbourg, we do not know the precise nature of a technology and a practice that must necessarily have taken a long time to perfect, and in which someone such as Mentelin may also have been involved. The fact remains, no printed item that can be dated to the Strasbourg years has been discovered, which means that the definitive invention of typography with movable letters seems more likely to have happened in Mainz.

The Return to Mainz

In search of capital

When we rediscover Gutenberg in Mainz (October 1448), it is in connection with a loan of 150 florins at 5 per cent, which Arnold Gelthus zum Echzeller sought on his behalf from Reynhard Brumbern zum Bangarten and Henchin Rodenstein.[21] Gelthus was guarantee for the loan, while Gutenberg, who had apparently already resumed his work, agreed to pay the interest and reimburse the capital at the end of the term. He was probably obtaining credit locally through one of his rich relatives, with a view to establishing the first printing house in Mainz; it may have begun to operate in 1449. We know nothing about his way of life or other activities at this crucial period. But the sum of 150 florins was not enough and he had to turn to other investors (end 1449–50) to procure the funds for the 'work of books' (*das Werk der Bücher*), in the event, to the Fust.

The Fust were a family of entrepreneurs and goldsmiths from Frankfurt, which the grandfather of Johann had left to settle in Mainz. Nikolaus Fust, the father, was a judge (1438–41) and a member of the municipal government (1444). He had two sons: Johann Fust, born around 1400, and the younger son Jakob, a future burgomaster of the city. Johann was active in finance, in precious metals and later in printing, and also in the casting of cannon. He died of the plague during a business trip to Paris in 1466. It seems likely that the financiers only got involved at the time of the first attempts, perhaps the *27-line Donatus* and the calendars.[22] Persuaded of the potential of the invention, Fust borrowed funds himself so as to be able to advance 800 florins to Gutenberg, so that he could 'finish his work' (*damit er das werck volnbrengen solt*). The security consisted of the tools manufactured with the aid of this sum. But it was still not enough, and two years later Fust advanced a further 800 florins, though no contract for this second transaction has survived. It seems likely that each of these investments responded to the need not only to enlarge the original workshop but also to finance the major undertaking represented by the *42-line Bible* – the masterstroke that would establish the new technology. Work on the *Bible* began in 1451 and would last for four years.

The first printed material

As far as we can tell, therefore, Gutenberg began to print in Mainz in 1449, though the 'first great European book' remains the *42-line*

Bible of 1455. In the intervening years, Gutenberg and his associates supported themselves by printing minor items, but while we know what sort of texts these were, the chronology remains unclear. They are identified by their typographic characters, of which the oldest were large gothic letters (known as 'DK-type').[23] They were minor works: a *Last Judgement* (*Sybillenbuch oder Fragment von Weltgericht*) appears to have been printed in 1452–3, probably by Gutenberg. This was a German text, written in Thuringia around 1360 and widely circulated in manuscript form in the fifteenth century.[24] Gutenberg also produced several (perhaps three) editions of the *Donatus*, a very popular manual of Latin instruction, using question and answer; the earliest, in particular the *27-line Donatus*, are believed to date from the years 1453–4.[25] A third genre consisted of calendars, of which the earliest seems to be the *Calendar of the Turks* (*Türkenkalender*), of around December 1454, one year after the fall of Constantinople. As will be apparent, these were all slight works, which could be produced quickly, demanded little in the way of investment in material or money (typographic characters or supplies of paper) and were cheap, hence relatively easy to distribute. For Gutenberg, as for his financial backers, this type of product made it possible to keep the business ticking over while in the process of perfecting their technology. However, these documents of little or no value have not survived well and it is likely that other publications have disappeared altogether. The *Last Judgement* is known only through a fragment discovered in Mainz in 1892 in a book binding, while the only known example of the *Türkenkalender*, that in the Munich Library, comes from the collection of the Augsburg humanist Konrad Peutinger (1465–1547).[26]

Gutenberg and his associates also prepared letters of indulgences (*Ablassbrief*). These were formularies, a type of product for which printing was obviously ideally suited. In exchange for each gift, the ecclesiastical authority issued a personal certificate, so it was necessary to have stocks of pre-printed forms ready, usually on parchment, which were then completed simply by adding the date and the name of the beneficiary. As we have seen, the letter of indulgences for Frankfurt of 1452 was probably printed; if so, it was one of the first – if not the first – printed items of which we have indirect evidence. But the first printed item that can be dated precisely is the so-called *31-line Letter*, the revenues from which were intended to finance the war against the Turks and the defence of Cyprus (1454–5).[27] Another letter, this one *30-line*, was almost contemporaneous. These publications have variants, most interestingly in the date: in some copies the date 1454 has been replaced by 1455, to produce a stock of formularies for the following year. It has been calculated on the basis of the large number of surviving copies that the print run must have been considerable, perhaps several thousand.

At the same time as these minor printed pieces, Gutenberg and his associates were doing work of a quite different order, pursuing their grand project, intended to demonstrate once and for all the superiority of printing and, of course, to make a large profit: an edition of the Bible, which demanded both heavy financial investment and many years of work. In October 1454, Gutenberg and Fust were at the Frankfurt fair, where they circulated the first specimen quires. A letter from Piccolomini, then bishop of Siena, informed Cardinal Carjaval that quires of the Bible had circulated at this fair. A second letter, of 12 March 1455, confirmed this:

> Everything that has been written to me about that remarkable man whom I met in Frankfurt is quite true. I did not see complete Bibles but sections in fives of various books thereof, the text of which was absolutely free from error and printed with extreme elegance and accuracy. Your Eminence would have read them easily and without the aid of spectacles. I learned from many witnesses that 158 copies have been completed, although some asserted that total was 180. While I am not altogether sure about the actual number, I have no doubt, if people are to be believed, about the perfection of the volumes.[28]

In any event, all the copies were sold before the work was completed, so Piccolomini was doubtful whether Carjaval would be able to acquire one, as he wished. It may be that the two different figures for print runs mentioned in the Italian cardinal's letter reflect an increase decided on by the printers as the work progressed, to meet a much larger demand than expected.

A modern fable: the inventor and the financier

In the meantime, however, the situation between Gutenberg and Fust had changed, as each seems to have been working independently in two separate workshops during the winter of 1454–5. This would explain the concomitance of the two editions of the letter of indulgences for the defence of Cyprus known as the *31-line* and *30-line*, of which the second, with characters slightly different from those of the *42-line Bible*, came not from the workshop of Gutenberg but from that of Fust and Schoeffer.[29]

In fact Fust started legal proceedings against his associate, probably early in 1455, over a matter about which we are informed by a notarized act of 6 November 1456.[30] Fust swore on oath that he had

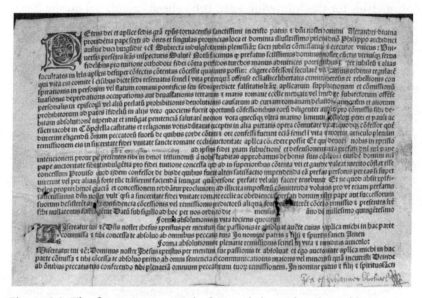

Figure 5.2 The first printers mainly financed themselves by 'jobbing printing', for which the model was provided by letters of indulgences. These were pre-printed formularies, sometimes run off by the thousand, which only needed the handwritten addition of the name of the beneficiary. The letter shown is an indulgence of the Bishop of Tournai dated 1500. The relatively commonplace nature of these minor items explains their poor survival rate. Municipal Library of Valenciennes.

lent Gutenberg 1,600 florins, to obtain which he had himself been obliged to borrow, and he demanded repayment of 2,020 florins, representing the capital and interest; he claimed that Gutenberg had used part of this sum for other projects than those of the company – probably to print on his own account. The judgment was evenly balanced, but Gutenberg was nevertheless required to reimburse between 1,000 and 1,250 florins, and probably to return to Fust some of the equipment (typographic fonts and presses) as well as part of the work in progress. The date is significant: the invention had been perfected and the major operation of the Bible completed, from which large returns were expected in the immediate future. We should remember that Tritheim, reporting Schoeffer's claims in the *Annales Hirsaugienses*, speaks of an expenditure of more than 4,000 florins committed for the Bible even before the third quire had been completed. It could be that Fust initiated the break-up, speculating that by demanding a repayment it was impossible for his partner to make, he would be able to seize the security (the equipment in the printing works) and use it on his own account. Conversely, Gutenberg may have intended to reimburse him with his share of the income from the *42-line Bible* and continue to run the workshop on his own.

> It is possible that Fust was able to seize one press or two, as well as the beginning of the composition of the Psalter. Gutenberg certainly kept the material acquired with the credit of Gelthus, hence probably one press and his first work, the Donatus. It remains unclear whether he was also in a position to free himself from a part of his security, the characters of the *42-line Bible*. What is clear is that this character was no longer used after 1455, either by Gutenberg or by the printing shop of Fust and that it [would not be] used again until after the death of Gutenberg. (Sabina Wagner)

The two Mainz workshops

Once again, the exact sequence of events is unclear and the historian has to be content with the most probable scenario. I have relied, in addition to the rare archival sources, mainly on studies of the surviving copies of the earliest printed works produced by the Mainz presses. The Bible project was of long standing and Gutenberg and Fust seem first to have envisaged a *40-line Bible* in a large character similar to the DK-type,[31] before abandoning this idea in favour of casting new, smaller characters and switching to a *42-line Bible*. The chief advantage was the possibility of limiting costs, as the volume to be printed would be smaller, so need less paper and less time. Conversely, if this hypothesis is correct, the sums necessary for the metallurgical work would be proportionately greater, but this would be capital investment, as the fonts would be retained, their value entered into the stocklist and they could be re-used. However that may be, the *42-line Bible*, in two volumes, probably came out in 1455. It has been shown that the simultaneous presence of four presses would have been necessary to print it, and that six compositors and a dozen press operators must have worked in the printing house. The print run was 180 copies, fifty of them on vellum.

This hypothetical reconstruction of events suggests that Gutenberg had retained some of his equipment (including his first characters) and that he continued to work in Mainz after the break with Fust. He was still in the town in 1457, when he was cited as witness in a legal document, but he suspended repayment of a debt to St Thomas of Strasbourg in 1458, which suggests he was then in financial difficulties. This may be connected to the project for the *Mainz Psalter*, for which new technical processes had been devised. Gutenberg approached another financier, Konrad Humery, who, on the printer's death, would receive his equipment (including the fonts for the Bible), later resold to Schoeffer. In fact a number of editions using the DK-type and datable to 1456 or later have been attributed to the printing house of Gutenberg, though his name does not appear on any book; they are for the most part minor publications, of which often only fragments survive: a bull of Calixtus III for the crusade (1456), a calendar for 1457,[32] an *Astronomical Calendar* for 1457–8, a list of ecclesiastical provinces,[33] a small prayer text, etc. Several more important titles may also be linked to Gutenberg: the *36-line Bible*, the *Catholicon* of Balbus and the *Mainz Psalter*.

The dossier for the *36-line Bible* is one of the fullest and most complex relating to Gutenberg. The characters are close to DK-type, but examination of the watermarks suggests that some or most of the work of printing was carried out not in Mainz but in Bamberg, and using a *42-line Bible* as exemplar.[34] Paulus Paulirinius, in Prague, refers to an edition of the *Bible* produced in Bamberg. Further, the DK-type characters disappear from Mainz just at the time that Albrecht Pfister, former secretary of the bishop of Bamberg, Georg I von Schaumberg (appointed 18 May 1459), began to use them for several publications, including the *Ackermann von Böhmen* of *c*.1460. Lastly, the incomplete (a single leaf!) example of the *36-line Bible* preserved in Paris bears a handwritten date of 1461. It remains unclear whether Gutenberg had moved his workshop from Mainz to Bamberg, opened another workshop in the latter town, sold a typographic font or sent some of his workers to Bamberg to trade on their expertise (Johann Neumeister, Berthold Ruppel, Konrad Zeninger, Johann Beckenhaub and above all Heinrich Keffer). Given the shortness of the timescale, Pfister seems initially to have played the role of local investor rather than printer; he could have familiarized himself with the technology during the printing of the *36-line Bible* before setting up his own workshop. However, his products are of significantly lower quality than the *Bible*. Others may also have been involved, in the person of capitalists of Frankfurt constituting the 'Community of the Books' (*Gemeinschaft der Bücher*), among them the brothers Peter and Nikolaus Ugelheimer: the latter was living in Mainz in the 1440s, while the former is found as an associate of Nicolas Jenson in Venice at a later date. Lastly, the bishop of Bamberg himself pledged 523 *livres* from the episcopal treasury (2 December 1459) and he later gave the Franciscans of Coburg the only known copy of the *36-line Bible* printed on parchment (1463); it is possible, therefore, that he had been financially involved in the operation.[35]

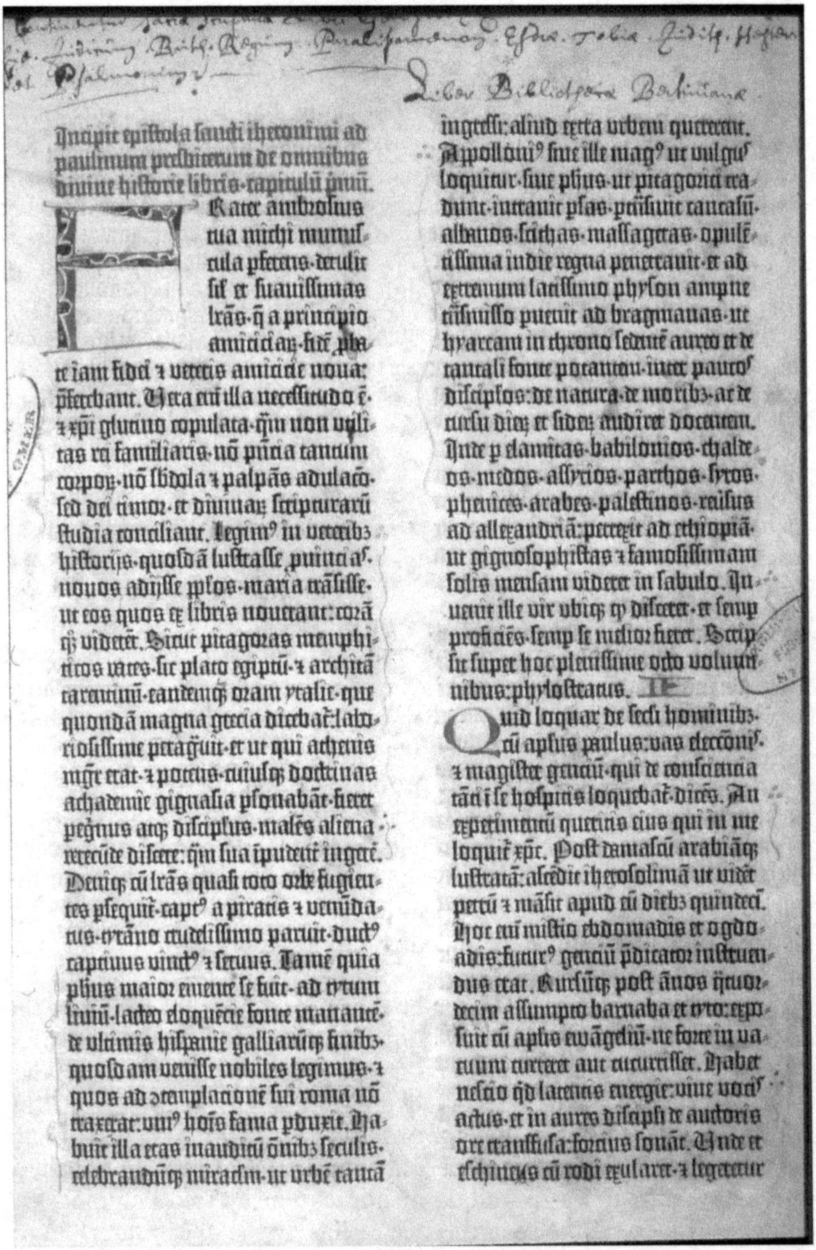

Figure 5.3 The 'first great European book' is the *42-line Bible*, which emerged from the presses of Gutenberg in Mainz in 1455. The impression is in two columns, abbreviated characters are relatively numerous and the decoration of the ornamented letters was still done manually. The copy shown here is from the ancient and very rich library of the Benedictines of St Bertin, near Saint-Omer. Library of Saint-Omer.

The other two dossiers, that for the *Catholicon*, a dictionary compiled by the Genoese Dominican Giovanni Balbi in 1286, and that for the *Mainz Psalter*, relate to the finalization of new technical research, and may explain the financial difficulties of Gutenberg while also revealing other business dealings, in particular with Eltville. Let us look first at the *Catholicon*: study of the slight variants in the text shows that it was printed using a composition consisting not of movable characters but taking the form of pairs of lines cast in blocks of two, using a technique prefiguring that of stereotypy.[36] In one case, the correction of an error has necessitated switching two blocks of two lines, which have been confused. At the technical level it involved metal strips cast on the basis of the original typographic form, with a wire at the ends to hold the lines together. A small body was used to produce a denser text, with a rotunda character close to, but not identical with, that of the *Rationale* of Guillelmus Durand produced on 6 October 1459 by the presses of Fust and Shoeffer. Why would a printing house take on the cost of manufacturing a duplicate font? There must have been two rival workshops in Mainz, a hypothesis confirmed by the fact that the materials of the *Catholicon* are found in large part in the *Vocabularius ex quo* printed by the Bechtermünze brothers at Eltville in 1467. Other analogous impressions may have come from Eltville in the 1460s, including some that mix characters from the *Catholicon* with others probably belonging to the workshop of Gutenberg (DK-type). The *Catholicon* had required considerable capital and long preparation but its dating is problematic. Though all the copies were printed from one single composition, study of the paper shows that the dates of printing ranged from 1460 to 1472.[37] A copy now in Gotha has an old binding, coming from a Leipzig workshop, and bears an *ex libris* with the date of 1465. The process of impression by two-line blocks meant it was possible to retain the composition of the work without undue expense, while retaining access to the fonts; later printings could be made from time to time, to revive the market. Other small impressions in quarto from the 1460s conform to this model: the *Summa de articulis fidei* of Thomas Aquinas in thirty-four or thirty-six lines and the *Tractatus* of Matthew of Cracow also use a technique of impression by two-line blocks.[38] Sabina Wagner thinks that the perfecting of the specific technique used to print the *Catholicon*, which may have taken several years, explains Gutenberg's money problems around 1458, when he must have been receiving financial support from Konrad Humery.

Other technical innovations on which Gutenberg may have worked were applied to the *Mainz Psalter*: new typographic fonts and, in particular, extremely thin metal plates (clichés) making it possible to print initials painted in two colours (three with the text in black). The decorated initials in red and blue were made by impression on metal, a highly complex operation in that the two parts composing the letter had to be taken apart and inked separately to obtain the two different colours and print the page at one go.[39] The volume also has red initials of smaller size within the text. The *Mainz Psalter* is the first printed book to bear a date, and also the first where the new technique is explicitly named, with the formula 'ingenious invention of printing and producing letters' (*adventia artificiosa imprimendi ac caracterizandi*).[40] But the preparation of the work and the manufacture of the blocks for the initials had consumed much time and considerable capital. We know that Gutenberg had faced a difficult financial situation in 1457–8, which has been related to the refining of the technology of the *Catholicon*, but which may also be due to the preparation of the equipment for the *Psalter*. In fact the typographic material seems to be that of Gutenberg and it is possible that the investment needed to perfect this extremely difficult technique exceeded his means. However that may be, the work appeared, perhaps as a result of a new legal ruling, with the address of Fust and Schoeffer.

The years 1459–62 were very difficult for Mainz, and culminated in the seizure of the town by Archbishop Adolf of Nassau (28 October 1462). Gutenberg's workers scattered in every direction and it is possible that he himself took refuge with his niece Else, widow of Henne Humbrecht, in Frankfurt. However, it seems more likely that he retreated for a while to Eltville and continued to print there. In this little town on the banks of the Rhine he would have encountered the husband of his deceased niece Odilgen, Johann Sorgenloch Genfleisch, and also Jakob Sorgenloch Genfleisch, son-in-law of Heinrich Bechtermünze. The latter, together with his brother Nikolaus, founded a printing house at Eltville around 1465 and published two editions of a *Vocabularius ex quo* with types cast on the model of those of the *Catholicon*.[41] The archbishop himself lived in Eltville, where he probably met the inventor, whom he appointed to his court (*Hofmann*) in 1465. Gutenberg was then able to return to Mainz. A member of the fraternity of St Victor, he died on 26 February 1468 in the house *zum Algesheimer* and, according to Adam Gelthus,[42] was buried in the church of the Franciscans (destroyed in 1742). On 28 February, Humery asked to be allowed to take possession of the equipment in the workshop, including some of the characters of the *42-line Bible*; he was authorized to do this by the archbishop, on condition he used it exclusively in Mainz, but he seems to have sold it to Peter Schoeffer soon after.[43]

6

Innovation

∽

Because, while it is true that people have always engraved on wood, stone and on metals, it is no less the case that, to engrave on wood for the purpose of printing, it was necessary to conceive of arranging the characters and the words from right to left, like those of oriental languages; of not engraving them *en creux* [intaglio], as in inscriptions, but of carving them *en relief*, as on coins and medals; of colouring them with an ink that was a thick and viscous but not too runny; of placing over them dampened paper or parchment to receive the impression; of then sliding them into a press capable of printing them; in a word, of acting in a way that meant they could be printed alone and clearly, on paper or on parchment, and be read there in their proper order.

Prosper Marchand

Techniques: Process Innovation

In the invention of Gutenberg, the key innovation was associated with the practice of impression: it involved composing a text by assembling 'prisms each bearing a letter engraved in relief' (Marius Audin). The decisive invention was linked to the use of metal, and its successive stages required the input of several technicians – though we are here in the realms of conjecture: Gutenberg for the overall conception and perfecting of the press, Johann Fust and Peter Schoeffer for the metallurgical techniques, and even the French Nicolas Jenson.

Composition

The central component of the invention consisted of the typographic characters (the alphabetical types) drawn in reverse and cast in mirror image in multiple copies by means of the casting instrument. The filiation, nevertheless, remains uncertain: as well as xylotype, the chronology of the different techniques of proto-typography overlaps in part, as we have seen, with that of typography. In typography with movable characters, the design of the character is first engraved in relief and in reverse, in the form of a punch, a familiar tool of goldsmiths: 'the punch was used in the Late Empire to strike in intaglio the bezel of the rings used as a seal' (Marius Audin). Similarly, the ancient world was familiar with the use of the matrix to cast seals, as well as that of the dies designed to strike coins and medals, and even some book bindings. The ancients had also mastered the technique of pouring metal into a mould, for the casting of coins, etc. These techniques, which seem to have been to some extent lost for part of the Middle Ages, were rediscovered in the thirteenth century. As regards printing, the crucial idea was to connect punch and casting: the punch was driven with a hammer into a matrix of copper, which was then placed in the casting instrument, making it possible to produce large numbers of types that were standardized, that is, aligned on the same plane and of the same height. This schema has been described by the phrase 'pyramid multiplication': starting from the alphabetical letters breaking down the text into a very small number of units, punches were engraved, with which as many matrixes as desired could be struck. These matrixes each made it possible to produce the types in large numbers, with which texts could be printed afresh in multiple copies. The last stage of the multiplication was that of the readers. At every level, the principle was that of linear analysis and alphabetical logic: a reduced number of elements made it possible to multiply their potency in an infinite number of combinations or copies.

> The alphabet only truly came into its own when Western Europe learned to reproduce the forms of letters thanks to movable type (Eric Havelock).

It is hardly surprising that the discovery and perfecting of the process should have taken several years, in Strasbourg and in Mainz, in the 1440s and even later.

Typographical analysis and the press

It is possible that sand moulds were used initially, made with the aid of wooden punches, but the decisive breakthrough came with the switch to metal. The casting instrument was a small device that was easy to manipulate: the matrix was inserted at one end and could be changed quickly, while at the other end was the channel into which the molten metal was poured. The combination of a fixed part and a movable part suited the variability in the size of the letters (between *i* and *m*, for example). The device was encased in wood to protect the operator from the heat. The type, once cast, was extracted with a hook. It still needed some reworking by hand, separating from the tail, and then polishing. When the impression was done with a press, the plane of the assembled types had to be perfect. As it was difficult to ensure by eye alone that the types were absolutely regular, it is possible, as suggested by Marius Audin, that

> Gutenberg [was first] led to assemble his 'punches' in whole lines, then in pages – the page of the first printed booklets was very small – which meant it was no longer necessary to 'strike' the matrix, but only to 'pour' it round punches.

It took a long time to perfect the combination of the different metals and alloys, the usual mix for the types being one that combined lead, tin and antimony in precise proportions determined by the conditions of manufacture. The composition of the fonts was always much greater than the number of letters in the alphabet, owing to the need to distinguish lower case and capitals and to anticipate all the special characters: diacritic marks preventing confusion between certain words (for example, *a* and *à* in French), more or less developed abbreviations, paragraph marks (¶), ligatures, and so on, as well as punctuation. Study of the early characters has revealed that they have a *biseau de pied* and a hole or nick 'made individually after casting'. The hole may have allowed a thread to be passed through the characters to hold the composition in place, or to raise the letters that were to appear in another colour (e.g., to change from red to black).[1] The ink used consisted of a mixture of turpentine, walnut oil and lampblack, reduced by boiling, which made a thick ink which did not run on the forme. Recent research has shown that the inks used in the very early days of printing contained significant quantities of lead and copper, whereas all trace of metals disappears after 1473. Some craftsmen made a speciality of ink manufacture, like Antoine Vincent in Lyon in 1515.

The principle of the press had been known since antiquity, with presses being used for oil, fruit (Egypt in the third millennium BC) and, above all, grapes. They may have been employed for the decoration of medieval cloth and, as we have seen, the first paper presses appeared on the Pegnitz in Nuremberg around 1390. The press of Gutenberg was built in Strasbourg by the wood turner Konrad Saspach, who probably later worked for Mentelin: the forme constituted by the typographic characters was placed on the carriage. This was slid under the cradle (the bed) and placed by hand under the platen, a rectangular block of copper. The size of the platen varied, but it was usually half the size of the forme; it was the platen which, moving on a vertical axis, 'fell' on the inked forme and produced the impression on the leaf, which had previously been dampened. It was actioned vertically by a screw with a large enough thread to reduce friction and overheating, and pierced by a hole through which passed the bar (lever). The press thus combined vertical and horizontal movement, and its efficiency lay in the gradualness and above all the evenness of the pressure exercised on the forme. The stability of the vertical frame was assured by the cheeks, the crosspieces and the crown, and the machine was often anchored to the ceiling of the room to prevent it twisting or shifting about in use.

It seems to be agreed that the press of Gutenberg represented an intermediate stage before the development of the double-pull press, probably in Rome in the 1470s.[2] Despite a number of minor improvements, this technique remained in use until the Industrial Revolution (*c*.1800). Lastly, the press was a machine held together by pegs, so it could be dismantled, which enabled some printers to practise their trade in an itinerant fashion or to settle temporarily in a given town on the occasion of a special commission.

Sales and circulation of the 'hardware'

The first printers were careful to preserve the secrecy of the processes they developed, their knowledge, before 1462, a precious safeguard when there was no protection by a patents system. Secrecy was guarded all the more carefully in view of the huge capital committed, especially to develop the types, but it was also necessary to pay workers and technicians, assemble the raw material (paper) and have access to distribution networks before there was any prospect of covering the costs. In the early days, the craftsmen made their own equipment and a sector specializing in the manufacture of printing material was slow to develop. In Strasbourg, Mentelin began as an illuminator and notary to the bishopric, before turning, perhaps at

the request of Bishop Ruprecht, to typography in 1458. The first
book known to have emerged from his presses is the great two-
volume *49-line Bible* of 1460–1. It was probably Mentelin himself
who designed and made the characters he used, from the *49-line Bible*
to the *City of God* of 1467. However, due to the absence of sources,
the manufacture and sale of the typographic presses during the *ancien
régime* has been little studied. One of the earliest known instances
dates from 1472, when the Benedictine Abbey of Saints Ulrich and
Afra in Augsburg bought several assembled presses and fonts from a
printer of that town in order to establish a printing workshop within
the confines of the monastery.

   We are better informed about the circulation of typographic fonts,
thanks to work on material bibliography.[3] The fonts represented
the main capital of a workshop and it is partly through their identification that certain unsigned impressions are attributed to Gutenberg.
The role of the specialists in engraving and casting was crucial in the
early spread of printing, as is shown by the example of Jenson.
The English proto-typographer Caxton bought his first typefaces
in 1471–2 from Johann Veldener in Cologne, before establishing a
press in Bruges in 1473, which he then moved to Westminster in
1476. Veldener came from the diocese of Würzburg and had first
worked as a draughtsman, engraver and typefounder before becoming the proto-typographer of Louvain in 1474–5. Johannes de
Westfalia was in Cologne in 1473, having returned from Venice with
Italian typographic fonts; he settled first in Alost (1473), then moved
to Louvain (1474), from which the competition then drove Veldener
to Utrecht.[4]

Practices

An essential aspect of the invention was the development of the pro-
tocols of manufacture. The work involved two operations, composition and impression, depicted in several printer's marks, the most
famous being that of the 'Ascensian press'.[5]

Composition

Composition is the term used for the process that consists, on the
basis of the text, of aligning the characters and constructing the
typographic formes preparatory to printing. The workers who carried
out this process were the compositors.[6] First, however, came the
'software': the initial problem for the master printer was finding a

text to reproduce. If the press was located in an important town, home of intellectuals who might be prepared to work on texts, the printer had a head start. In Venice, Basel, Cologne, Paris and even Louvain, there were authors and scholars living close to the great printing workshops, who were capable of correcting manuscripts – Froben in Basel, Aldus Manutius in Venice. The presence in Lyon of a number of physicians meant that some printers turned to them in order to publish this or that specialized treatise. When Johann Trechsel embarked on an edition of the works of Avicenna with a commentary by Jacques Despars, he procured the manuscript through the intermediary of the doctor Ponceau (1498–9), physician to Charles VIII.[7] Some Lyon physicians also acted as translators: Jean de La Fontaine, a small printer-bookseller active between 1488 and 1493, specialized in texts in the vernacular. In 1491, he published *La Cirurgie du très fameux et excellent philosophe docteur en médecine maistre Alenfranc de la cité de Millan* [*The Surgery of the highly renowned and excellent philosopher doctor in medicine master Alenfranc of the city of Milan*], a text translated into French by Guillaume Yvoire, 'surgeon practising in Lyon'. Nicolas Panis was a master of arts and doctor of medicine and it was he who prepared the French translation of the *Chirurgia* [*Surgery*] of Guy de Chauliac, printed by Marcus Reinhart in 1478.[8] For the first time, xylography made it possible to reproduce pictures of surgical instruments, and the page layout of the manuscripts was strictly adhered to.

Another prominent figure in the little group of physicians gravitating around the printing workshops was Jehan Thibaud. Born in Evreux, Dr Thibaud became scientific editor and corrector for the *Mesue (pseudo-Mesue)* and the *Matthaeus Silvaticus*, printed by Huss and Syber in 1478. It was in his house that Syber settled and established his workshop when newly arrived from Basel, and the contract specifies that, in compensation for the inconvenience this entailed, the printer would provide the doctor with one copy of each title emerging from his presses. Thibaud accommodated another professional of the book, in the person of Hervé Bésine, corrector of printing in 1493, then bookseller.[9] A last example, Hieronimo Ferrara, was a Spanish physician resident in the rue Neuve from 1493 to 1499.[10] He seems to have been the partner of Nicolaus Wolf, engraver and typefounder, with whom he rented part of a house; it is possible that the physician helped the craftsman on his arrival in Lyon, enabling him gradually to expand his business. Though no doubt interested in the work they were offered at the intellectual level, these physicians also found it an additional source of income – like one of their famous successors, Dr François Rabelais, anonymous author of the *Pantagruel* of 1532.

Good manuscripts were few and far between, even more so the skills needed to edit them. Texts circulated among a network of correspondents, scholars and professionals in the printing business, and everyone was on the lookout for them. On 18 February 1478, the burgomaster of Lübeck wrote to Mentelin and his son-in-law Rusch asking them to return a manuscript of Vincent of Beauvais that belonged to the Dominicans of Lübeck, which they had been given so they could prepare an edition.[11] The manuscript was to be returned with, 'as was the custom, a copy of the printed work'. The correspondence of Amerbach illustrates the problems associated with the transmission of manuscripts: Rusch, who was in contact with certain humanists, provided Amerbach with the titles and even the manuscripts of works to be published. In the case of contemporaries, the author might be present in person, like Niccolò Perotti for his *Rudimenta grammatices* printed by Sweynheym and Pannartz in Rome in 1473. The manuscript, happily preserved, is the autograph of Perotti.[12] For the new edition of the *Adages* (1508), Aldus collaborated closely with Erasmus, who edited it as the printing progressed. Another example is the *Commentarii linguae graecae* of Budé, printed by Bade in 1529, to which the author made major handwritten additions, on his own copy, an edition of which came out in 1548, before the copy was returned to the heirs.[13]

The connections between the circle of book professionals and that of humanist scholars formed one of the great strengths of the Parisian printers at the beginning of the sixteenth century. Even so, the copy itself might be faulty, as Du Bartas explained in *La Sepmaine* in 1578:

> Having been constrained to have this book transcribed in haste by different writers and each of them having retained his usual orthography, it happened that the printer, who used this copy, has written the same word sometimes in the old and sometimes in the new fashion, and sometimes adopted a totally distorted orthography.[14]

Once the text had been chosen it had to be carefully calibrated to determine 'the length of the copy so as to...predict the exact number of pages'.[15] This is well illustrated by the manuscript of the *City of God*, copied around 1460, probably with a view to the edition printed by Sweynheym and Pannartz in Subiaco. The text was first copied; it was then subject to a careful philological revision and the results recorded on the manuscript, which was used for the composition strictly speaking.[16] Study of the Italian *exemplaria* shows that the manuscripts were marked up to guide the work of a compositor: calibration of the text, organization of the subdivisions corresponding to the pages of the printed work. The manuscript also bears notes indicating the point the compositors had reached, perhaps used to determine their pay. They enable us to get a clear picture of how the work was done in the shop of these two printers, so we know, for example, that work on the *City of God* continued, on a single press, every day except Sunday until 12 June 1467. Some of the Subiaco *exemplaria* had been divided between several compositors, which presupposes a very careful preparation of the job to establish the beginning and end of each quire.[17] The calibration also made it possible to estimate exactly how much paper the impression would need. Examination of the *49-line Bible* printed by Mentelin in 1460–1 reveals that it had been composed on the basis of a copy of the *42-line Bible*.[18]

The manuscript, or copy of an earlier edition, was removed from its binding and its leaves placed in order on a support, the visorium, above the case – a flat, open box, sloping slightly forwards and divided into compartments in which the fonts were placed. The compositor stood to 'lift' the characters letter by letter with tweezers and arrange them, line by line, in a composing stick, with a strip which had previously been justified, that is, set to a length so that the successive lines would form a homogeneous block. The composing stick could hold one or several lines. The words were separated by spaces,[19] and, to ensure the justification, the whole unit had to be calibrated and locked up by adjusting the spaces and the word forms (abbreviations, etc.). As the end of the page or quire approached, the compositor would increase the number of, or, on the contrary, extend, the abbreviations, so as to avoid blank spaces. Then the operative:

> placed his composing stick on the case…he took the line between the thumb and index finger of each hand and placed it in the lower part of the galley, a sort of wooden oblong tray with the capacity of a page.[20]

The composed page was tied up (the 'knot') and placed on a page carrier to be taken close to the press. The most difficult part of the compositor's task was the process of raising the letter without error and placing it the right way round in the composing stick. Analysis of this problem led to an increasing rationalization of the movements, described by the printer Fertel in Saint-Omer in 1723: the nick made it possible to speed up the work, the fingers 'feeling' while the eye was busy elsewhere.

In composing, you have to work as skilfully with your eyes as with your hands, and the best way to be skilful is to look at each letter you wish to take hold of as you put out your hand to lift it; so you never take hold of another than the one on which you have fixed your eyes. You have to take the letter by the head, and look at the nick, in order to place it immediately in the composing stick without turning it round several times between your fingers, or in the composing stick, to find the side with the nick, as many journeymen do; because this bad habit leads to a great loss of time.[21]

The next stage, once a sufficient number of pages had been prepared, and depending on the available fonts, was imposition. The leaf of paper, less often parchment, to be printed was folded to form a quire, and the smaller the format, the more the number of folds. For the text to run continuously, the compositions of the successive pages had to be placed in the correct order, which was not the order of the pages: their arrangement was determined by the structure of the quires.[22] For example, in a quarto, where the leaf was folded twice, it was necessary to compose at the same time pages 1, 8, 4 and 5 (recto), then 2, 7, 3 and 6 (verso), the imposition being symmetrical on each side of the fold. The pages were placed by the compositor in a rectangular frame (the chase), locked into place by wooden reglets assuring the margins, then fastened together by a system of quoins. The term 'typographic form' describes the whole batch of pages assembled in a chase and serving to print a leaf on one side, and it was this complex operation which was called the imposition. Imperfections and even errors of composition and imposition were common, especially in the early years and in the less well-endowed workshops, where it was necessary to work more rapidly or where no one was available for an accurate correction of the text.[23]

Printing brought a major change as compared with transmission by manuscript, in that the exemplar was systematically reproduced. In theory, all the copies were now not only easy to read but alike, and there were no longer variant copies. Nevertheless, as the printing process was technically highly complex, the composition of a given edition was not always homogeneous: variants are found in the *42-line Bible*, with the text changing slightly from one batch of copies to another. This was a common phenomenon, for a number of reasons, chief of which was the difficulty of making accurate corrections to a faulty imposition. Where the corrections were minor, they were made during the course of the impression: they affected only part of the print run and resulted in variant printings which sometimes themselves introduced new errors. In the specialized vocabulary, the word used for these is 'states'; Jeanne Veyrin-Forrer suggests

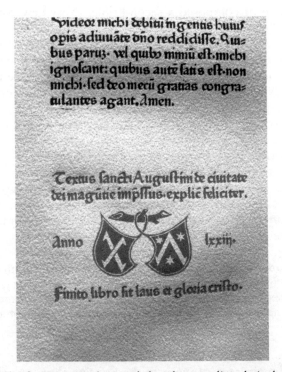

Figure 6.1 The first typographic workshop known directly is that of Johann Fust and Peter Schoeffer, successors to Gutenberg in Mainz: explicit printed in red in the Latin *City of God*, published by Peter Schoeffer in 1473, with a note of the date (*anno LXXIII*) and a xylographed typographic mark (the two shields hanging from a branch). Municipal Library of Valenciennes.

that the state should be defined by the printed leaf (which means that the combination of states can vary from one copy to another). In spite of the care taken by the printers, modern investigative methods sometimes make it possible to find variants that were previously extremely difficult to spot.[24] 'Cancels' constituted a specific category of corrections, and their use persisted into the nineteenth century; they were used for corrections important enough to necessitate abandoning one or more leaves, which were cut out and replaced by new ones, attached to the stubs. One of the earliest examples is found in the 1472 printing of the *Catholicon* of Balbus (Balbi).[25]

Another possible reason for variants came when the demand proved greater than expected and it was decided during the course of imposition to increase the print run, so leaves already printed might have to be composed a second time. Every new composition, however accurate, inevitably introduced variations, if only at the level of the line cut-offs and abbreviations. The same thing could happen when a new edition of a successful text was produced at speed, which was quite common at a time when neither the available equipment nor the possibilities of distribution made large print runs an easy option. One particular instance was when there was a change of title (alone, or sometimes with a few of the introductory pages) in order to shift the tail end of an edition some years after its first appearance, or after the title had been sold to another bookseller. In some incunabula, the errors have simply been corrected by pen in the copies affected, but it became the custom, in the case of corrections it had not been possible to make before printing, to collect them in the form of an erratum inserted at the end of the volume. Some errata confirm the presence of different states within the edition:

> There follow the said errata... And first, it should be noted that all the books of this impression are not subject to the present errata, because some were corrected almost at the beginning of the impression, others towards the middle, others towards the end, and others not at all.[26]

Impression

The second main area of work in the printing shop was that of the presses – though Audin emphasizes that a press was not absolutely essential, in that the itinerant printers who circulated from one town to another and produced minor works were able to manage using only a frotton. The care with which the press was prepared determined the quality of the work:

> Before printing, the pressman gets things under way, which essentially consists of adjusting and locking up the forme on the press bed and making register by ensuring the disposition of the margins and the placing of the two pins on the tympan. He must also stick a leaf of guide paper to the tympan, moisten the tympan, cut the frisket,[27] and ensure the evenness of the pressure exercised by the platen on the forme. (Jeanne Veyrin-Forrer)

Before the press started to roll, everything had to be in place, from the reams of dampened paper to the receptacle in which the ink would be brayed, which was positioned behind the press. Finally, the printing proper could begin, an operation which required the presence of two workers (pressmen): the feeder inked the forme with the ink balls, then placed the clean leaf on the tympan and lowered the frisket. The leaf was precisely placed thanks to the 'points', which were:

> two pins included in the forme which pierced holes in the leaf of paper making it possible, at the second pull, to position exactly the colour or the verso of the leaf.

The carriage was slid in by hand, until the press was improved by the addition of a windlass, then a rack and pinion (*crémaillère*). The pressman then pulled on the bar and the platen dropped on the screw. The exact details of the working methods in Gutenberg's day may remain unclear, but their development had benefited from the trial runs made on smaller printing jobs, such as indulgences. Larger works were probably at first printed one page at a time, as was still the case in Alost in 1473:

> The leaves were cut in two before being printed [and] the impression...was done...in four pulls; they printed page by page and in the normal order of pagination. This was hardly a technique with a high output, and the rate of production was very slow...The press was small...the platen could not exceed 16 by 10 centimetres [and] Martens printed only one page in two days.[28]

Then, when the size of the platen allowed, half-leaves were printed, the pressure remaining insufficient to print whole leaves. The carriage was pushed in halfway and the first half of the leaf printed, then the platen was lifted, the carriage pushed fully in, and the second half printed. This process assumes that the double-pull press had been perfected, which had not at first been the case. Once all the leaves had been printed on one side, the other side – that is, the verso – was printed, an operation which had to be performed fairly quickly (within seventy-two hours) to avoid the paper drying out and shrinking.

The impression was further complicated by the need to pull sets of proofs so that any necessary corrections could be made to the composition. For each leaf, therefore, a first 'proof' was printed, on which errors were recorded according to a code standardized by the sixteenth century. The corrector, the master printer, a scholar (for example Josse Bade for Trechsel), and even the author himself, reread the page before handing the proofs to the compositor; the *Chronique de Saxe*, printed in Mainz in 1492, has a page layout so complex that it must have been read by someone who was familiar with the text. Each proof, corresponding to one forme, had to be corrected at once, then printed, before the characters were redistributed to print the next page. The forme had to be washed after the proofs had been printed, the screws loosened and the corrections made, then the spaces calibrated once again – which is why it was important to have a specialized corrector or, better still, the author in the workshop or close at hand. It was common practice in the sixteenth century (in the workshop of Plantin, for example) for the proof to be read aloud, the corrector checking the text against the manuscript; this was another possible source of errors, if only at the level of spelling.[29] Typographic corrections were distinguished from authorial corrections, which were less frequent, except in the case of the humanist printers. Lastly, corrections might need to be made not only to the text itself but also to the running heads, pagination and so on. It was usual for two sets of proofs to be pulled, a number that increased to three in the eighteenth century. A last check was made as the print run started; nevertheless, corrections could still be made on the press (on the bed), though these had to be strictly limited so as not to upset the justification, which explains occasional differences from one state to another.

Authors and printers frequently disagreed over who was responsible for errors – which they all, of course, deplored. Germain de Brie, in 1526, thought it was hardly for him as author to make the corrections himself; he had provided a clean copy of the text of his translation of the *Letters* of St John Chrysostom, and thought that should be enough:

> I did not care to disturb my repose to devote myself to this devouring and unworthy labour of correcting characters, believing I had done enough if I had supplied an accurate exemplar.

A quarter of a century later Joachim du Bellay, also addressing the reader, blamed the printer for the faults found in the sonnet sequence *Olive*:

> If you find a few errors in the impression, you should not blame me, who put my faith in others. For the labour of correction is such, especially with a new work, that all the eyes of Argus would not be enough to spot the mistakes found in it.

At the end of the sixteenth century Étienne Pasquier returned to the difficulty of corrections, and above all to the sense of the dignity of the author and his work, whereas the typographer was on the 'mechanical' side. Nothing could be expected of the compositor, the corrector claimed skills he did not possess, and when the proofs were finally ready to be passed to the author, either he was nowhere to be seen, or he couldn't find the time to read them or correct them with the necessary care...[30]

Organizational innovation

Within the space of a few decades a whole new sector had appeared and expanded. The problems posed were not only of a technical nature. They also concerned the organization of the printing shops and distribution, the structure of the potential markets and the relationships with financiers. Our information is in general incomplete and, worse, indirect: the sources consist of the surviving copies rather than documentary records, which are sadly rare. Further, the innovation of Gutenberg was not only a matter of the technology but also of workshop organization and the refinement of manufacturing processes that made it possible, in only a few years, to print a perfect edition of a text as long as that of the Bible. What I will here call the 'typographical protocol' was gradually developed on the basis of the experience acquired through the production of short printed pieces; the *42-line Bible* was proof positive that printing made it possible to produce in bulk true masterpieces, in a material form as perfect as that of manuscripts.

The activities of the workroom were organized round the quire system. With manuscripts, the copy was made sequentially, page by page, until there were enough pages to form a quire. It was possible, of course, to imagine printing one page after another, a procedure which would complicate and slow down the work. Fairly quickly, therefore, and to the extent that the size of the platen allowed, the impression was done in half-leaves. Each leaf had to go under the press twice (for the recto and the verso), and provision had to be made for the proofs. But there were not enough fonts, and even carriages, which were very heavy, to print long texts in sequence. It was necessary to proceed by blocks of text: the compositors washed the formes and dismantled the composition of what had just been printed (this was distribution) so as to have enough characters available to continue their work. The aim, therefore, was to re-use the available fonts continuously and as rapidly as possible, until the whole book had been printed. The fewer characters available, the more often it was necessary to repeat the composition/impression/distribution cycle, which formed the first stage of manufacture. If the number of fonts was relatively small, this cyclical system encouraged the choice of larger formats, in folio and in quarto, easily the most numerous in the fifteenth century. This choice did not mean that the quires had to be only of a few leaves: in the *42-line Bible*, the bibliographical format was in folio, but each quire has had five leaves inserted. Each quire therefore had twenty pages, which meant the bound volume could be more solid. Investment in new fonts was financially justified by the reduction in the frequency of the successive production cycles and by the greater flexibility of the work.

The distribution of the characters was a lengthy operation: the worker washed the forme to remove the ink, placed it on two boards, then loosened it and redistributed the characters between the cases. Part of the composition was kept from one page to the next, for example the running title: this was the 'skeleton'. A composition that had already been printed was never kept, which meant that, if a second edition was projected, or if it was decided to increase the print run during production, it had to be composed afresh. It sometimes happened that the printing was ready, but some accident made it necessary to replace a leaf in a copy. It was probably in Mainz itself that someone copied, extremely carefully, by hand, meticulously adhering to the format of the two printed pages, the leaf of the *42-line Bible* that has been inserted into the copy belonging to St Bertin of Saint-Omer. The leaf must have been badly printed, lost or spoiled, so it had to be replaced by recopying the text, but this was done with such care that it is difficult to spot the difference.[31] The rhythm of work had to be maintained, and the manufacturing cycles had to follow one another speedily, so as not unnecessarily to immobilize the capital represented by the typographic material.

Another problem was that of coordinating work between the different parts of the shop devoted to composition and to the presses; the former was slower than the presses, which could 'roll' at a faster rate, especially if there were several of them. This meant that it was often worth dividing the composition between several workers. The *Explanatio super Psalmos* of St Augustine was a large folio of 418 pages (209 leaves), of which 1,325 copies were printed in 1528. Study of the quires shows that a system of simultaneous composition had been adopted:

If the composition had here followed the order of the copy, the nine first pages of each quire would have to have been composed before a forme could be delivered to the pressmen [they printed by half-sheets]. The process would have immobilised many characters and the composition of a whole quire (eight formes) would have represented for one compositor at least two weeks' work, whereas the pressmen could easily have printed the 5300 leaves corresponding to that single quire in four days. It is clear that they proceeded differently...

Several workmen must have shared the composition according to the marking up of the copy, itself probably inspired by the edition produced in Basel by Johann Amerbach thirty years earlier...the calibration...could not be perfect: it is significant that the number of lines of the Parisian edition varies according to the page from 65 to 67, with a measurable impact of some 7 millimetres in the height, just as the spacing varies between words, revealing the adjustments required by the division of the composition 'by formes'. The repetition of characteristic initial letters in the first half of several quires, initial letters which could not normally be reused in continuous composition, strengthens this hypothesis...

At least ten months would have been necessary for this job, but with continuous composition, that is, with one compositor working in the sequential order of the text, it would probably have needed twice as long and the pressmen who, according to the terms of their contract, should also have worked without stopping would have been idle a good part of the time....[32]

It is easy to understand why the ideal plan was generally not adhered to, while interruptions and disputes were the cause of many mistakes.

Once a leaf had been through the press, it had to be dried. The leaves were hung up on cords, then piled flat. When all the leaves of the book had been printed, they were gathered, that is, taken up one after the other in signature order (see pages 210–11) to form the successive copies. Each copy was collated, folded in two and stored, before being sold (these were the 'copies in leaves', or *'en blanc'*). These operations were performed in tiny and extremely cluttered spaces, which further increased the risk of mistakes. Binding, during which the quires were sewn, was usually carried out by an independent craftsman until the industrial age, and on the instructions of the owner of the volume. Schoeffer in Mainz and, above all, Koberger in Nuremberg, who often bound volumes before offering them for sale, are the most famous counter-examples.[33]

The invention of editorial policy

The first type of innovation concerned procedure: Fust and Schoeffer's series of publications started brilliantly with the Benedictine Psalter known as the *Mainz Psalter*, completed on 14 August 1457; as we have seen, this typographical masterpiece may have marked a turning point in the career of Gutenberg and in his relations with Fust. The operation was repeated for the second Benedictine Psalter (1459), which was also in three colours, and of which only thirteen examples printed on parchment survive.[34] In this case, too, the initials and decorations of metal were disassembled and then inked separately (in red and blue), which meant they need only be passed under the press once with the text in black; this was too complex and too onerous a procedure to continue in regular use. Generally speaking, Fust and Schoeffer, then Schoeffer alone, were adept at exploiting their skills: their technical and financial means, together with the location of their workshop in Mainz, allowed them, in particular, to dominate the production of missals not only for the archbishopric but also for more distant dioceses. Their print shop in Mainz produced in succession the missals of Breslau (1483, *c.*1488 and 1499), Cracow, Roskilde and the Danish mission, Meissen (1485) and Gnesen and Cracow. A new *Mainz Missal* was printed in 1493.[35]

Their product was innovatory, too. The *Rationale* of Guillelmus Durand was a treatise on the Roman liturgy written in the thirteenth century. Printed by Fust and Schoeffer in 1459,[36] it was the first book to use a new character, probably designed by Schoeffer, which made it easier, by a new page layout, to solve the problems posed by a lengthy text: its small size made it possible to change to sixty lines to the page in two columns, and to print the whole text in a single volume. It was the same with the edition of the *48-line Bible* completed on 14 August 1462: the character, probably engraved by Schoeffer, enabled the book to be printed in 962 pages, a significantly fewer number than that of the *42-line Bible* (1,280 pages), though more than that of the Bible of Mentelin in Strasbourg (850 pages).[37] Printers were now in competition and, for those with access to the indispensable fonts, the ability to reduce the number of pages while retaining legibility was important because it allowed them to produce a more manageable object while at the same time reducing manufacturing costs. The colophon of the *48-line Bible* is famous for its reference to the printing workshop and for the use of a specific vocabulary to describe the typographical technology:

> This book was made in the city of Mainz by the artful invention of printing or of tracing characters without the labour of a pen, and it was completed for the glory of God, by Johann Fust, citizen, and Peter Schoeffer of Gernsheim, clerk of this same diocese, in the year of our Lord 1462, on the Eve of the Feast of the Assumption of the Virgin Mary.

There was also innovation in the content. Once the technology and practice of printing had been perfected, the two partners adopted a systematic and sustained policy of publishing the essentials of every contemporary library of any importance: the Latin classics (Cicero) but above all, for a clerical clientele, the great juridical treatises and the principal patristic texts. These were usually beautifully produced and costly works, of which many copies were printed on parchment and illuminated. In 1465, the edition of the *De Officiis* of Cicero further innovated by its inclusion of several Greek letters in the body of the text; its success justified a reprint as early as 1466. And additional Mainz publications constituted a sort of catalogue of the classics: the *Letters* (*Epistolae*) of St Jerome was a sumptuous edition in two colours published in 1470.[38] The page layout was based on that of the *Bible* of 1462, but the care put into its production made it possible to move from fifty-five to fifty-six lines on the page. The magnitude of the capital needed for this massive work explains the publication of a special prospectus designed to encourage sales.[39] Three years later, in 1473, another classic of Christian literature appeared, St Augustine's *City of God*;[40] this was followed in 1474 by a contemporary text, the *Exposition of the Psalter* of Torquemada, which was so successful that it was reprinted three times in 1476 and 1478.

Also found in any large library were texts of canon law. In this case, the series of great treatises began in 1460 with the *Constitutiones* of Clement V, with commentary by Johannes Andreae. For the first time, the arrangement of the printed page reproduced that of the university manuscripts which combined text and commentary: the text was printed with the character that would be used for the *48-line Bible*, the commentary with the font employed the previous year for the *Rationale*. This arrangement was in future systematically adopted for the great treatises combining text and gloss.[41] The series of classics of canon law in monumental folio editions continued with the *Sixth Book of Decretals* of Boniface VIII (1465),[42] reprinted in 1470, 1473 and 1476, and then the *Decretum* of Gratian, founding text of canon law (1472). This was printed in two colours, adding another layer of complexity.[43] The founding text for legal studies in Bologna and Paris, the *Decretals* of Gregory IX, was published by Schoeffer in 1473, using the same arrangement,[44] and it was accompanied by the *Institutes* of Justinian, printed with the commentary of Accursius in 1468, 1472 and 1476.[45]

These works of reference had the twin advantages of being relatively expensive – hence ensuring substantial cash returns – and almost certain to sell. However, especially from the 1480s, the competition intensified while the market began to show signs of saturation. A change of direction was called for. Schoeffer adapted his editorial policy by aiming at a wider public, though without abandoning a high-quality material form. The model was the first printed herbal (1484), in Latin and illustrated. The book has a spectacular title page: the title (*Herbarius*) was followed by the place of printing (*Maguntie impressus*) and the date, the whole surmounting the typographic mark printed in red. The increasingly fierce competition favoured a policy of traceability and visibility, which included highlighting a prestigious manufacturer's mark, regarded as a guarantee of quality. The success of the *Herbarius* led Schoeffer to repeat the operation in 1485, with the *Gart der Gesundheit* (*Garden of Health*), the first handbook in German listing medicinal plants; it, too, was illustrated, with 378 original woodcuts.[46] This was the model for a new product, the practical manual, that is, a work in the vernacular, accurate, beautifully printed and lavishly illustrated, destined to be added as a handbook to the libraries of large numbers of readers interested in medical practice. The editor seems to have been Canon Bernhard von Breydenbach, the author Dr Johann Wonnecke of Caub and the illustrator Erhard Reuwich – to all of whom we will return. It was in continuance of this policy that, around 1487, Schoeffer published a cookbook (*Küchenmeisterei*),[47] and then, in 1492, the *Chronicles of Saxony* attributed to Konrad Botho.[48] The latter is remarkable for its vast iconographical programme, reminiscent in its organization of the *Nuremberg Chronicle*. This reorientation of editorial policy is strikingly demonstrated by the fact that, of all the books published by Fust and Schoeffer, only eighteen are not in Latin, but sixteen of these were published after 1480.

It was only natural that the largest printing workshop in Mainz should be commissioned to produce a number of more ephemeral and occasional printed pieces by the various administrations; a total of 128 titles of this type are known. This sector was not strictly speaking market driven, as the works were often commissions, hence works for which the risk of being sold at a loss was small; throughout the whole of the '*ancien régime* book system', even in the nineteenth century, jobbing printing of this type made a crucial contribution to the financial equilibrium of the majority of typographic workshops. Added to which, these more ephemeral pieces, with limited print runs, did not tie up the equipment for too long, and it was easier for them to be fitted into a work schedule which was extremely complex, as we have seen. Further, they were sometimes used to experiment with innovations that were later put to use in 'proper' books; it was in this way that Fust and Schoeffer created the first printed title page for a bull of crusade dated 1463.

The nature of the various occasional publications and hack print jobs was linked to the location of the workshop in Mainz: letters of indulgences, like that of Peraudi against the Turks (1488),[49] pontifical declarations and bulls, official publications of the archiepiscopal chancellery, the landgrave of Hesse, the count of Nassau-Dillenberg, and even the emperor (the workshop had a privilege for imperial edicts in the sixteenth century). Innovation here, however, was primarily in the sphere of mediatization and publicity, in that certain items might have a polemical dimension, as in the case of the proclamation of the archbishop of Mainz against the town of Erfurt (1480). Those in power sought to use the printed word to win over public opinion, so we see the very modern phenomenon – destined to a great future – of the formation of a sphere of public opinion around the media system. It was not of course a question of influencing the mass of the population: the distribution of these items, single leaves printed in quite small numbers (100 and 104 in the Erfurt affair), took the form of sending copies to prominent persons believed to be in a position to affect a decision.[50] This public sphere in which the media played a role appeared for the first time in 1461–2, when Fust and Schoeffer printed several pontifical briefs, bulls and other pieces relating to the deposition of Archbishop Diether von Isenburg in favour of Adolf of Nassau, including the latter's manifesto (1462) and the two letters of his opponent to the Imperial Diet and Pius II.[51]

The Society of the Workshops

The processes involved in printing a text, especially one of some length, were extremely complicated, which meant that procedural innovation had to be complemented by very specific organizational innovation if it was to result in a viable structure. The working practices that were to decide the way that printing operated throughout the typographic *ancien régime* – that is, until the Industrial Revolution – were quickly established. The emergence of this sector was accompanied by the organization of relationships that were themselves new between the different categories of workers involved.

Capital and labour

With printing, we have a system of manufacturing production in which the role of the capitalist became much more important than in the manuscript age. The investors, who at first often belonged to the world of merchant bankers, financed the research of the inventors without necessarily playing a part in the productive process. Their involvement at this level was encouraged at a later stage, however, not so much by a desire to exploit the workshop as by the need to distribute its products. The sales structures then in existence were totally unsuited to the printed works then being produced in ever larger numbers. The specialized book trade and the network of bookshops were slow to develop, which meant that, in effect, the only persons with the means to distribute printed matter were the merchant bankers whose speciality this type of operation was. The network of correspondents with whom they normally worked enabled them to sell throughout what was sometimes a very wide geographical area and to be sure of being paid. This was the case with Fust in Mainz and with Buyer in Lyon. The networks of the latter extended from Lyon to Paris, Avignon, Toulouse, and even into Spain; in Avignon, his correspondents were the binders Alain and Joachim of Rome, who also dealt in books. Also in Avignon was Girardan Ludovici, who represented several German printers and bookshops.[52]

Nevertheless, specialization developed at an early stage. Once a book business reached a certain size, the investor was able to concentrate on this field and take control of an enterprise combining production and distribution. Some, like Fust, printed and distributed the products of fellow printers as well as their own. Others, like Koberger, established a vertically integrated business, controlling all the stages of production and distribution, from the manufacture of the support, that is, paper, to the binding of copies and their distribution, by way of illustration and printing. Others confined themselves to finance and distribution, in the style of the modern publisher.[53] Antoine Vérard was initially head of a workshop of copyists serving a wealthy clientele, who later turned to printing (1485), beginning by employing Jean Du Pré for a *Decameron* of Boccaccio:[54]

> To assure the quality of the de luxe printed publications in which he specialised, he had the wood blocks carved and commissioned the fonts of which he remained the owner – but he did not print himself; he entrusted this work to craftsmen selected from among the best in the capital.[55]

On occasion Vérard had special sumptuously illuminated pages made in his own workshop to be inserted into copies intended for connoisseurs.

In Augsburg, the bookseller Johann Rynmann had access to substantial capital and perhaps sold printing equipment as well as books. He supported Heinrich Gran when he was newly settled in Haguenau and, through his commissions, enabled him to develop his business (1498). Rynmann ordered publications from workshops in Augsburg itself, but also from Nuremberg, Pforzheim, Strasbourg, Basel and even Venice, a town in constant commercial contact with Augsburg.[56] Overall, however, too few documents survive for it to be possible to establish in any detail for the fifteenth century the financial conditions in which books were manufactured. Most are contracts fixing the terms of agreement between booksellers, printer-booksellers or printers for a specific title. The correspondence of professionals in the business (Amerbach) and of authors (Erasmus) offers another very rich source. A number of contracts show how the investor established his control over the whole manufacturing process. When, in 1511, the Parisian Jean Petit decided to produce an edition of the *Sermons* of Raulin, he divided the work between several workshops to save time and increase the print run. Galliot Du Pré, another great Parisian bookseller, adopted a similar policy. In some cases, specific guarantees were sought by the sleeping partner, who wished not to immobilize his capital for too long a period of time: the contract would stipulate that the printer, especially if his was a small workshop, would not undertake any other work until he had finished the job in question. Lastly, the articulation of capital and labour needed the labour force to be as stable as possible, so as not to interrupt the manufacturing process.

Of course, several investors, not always resident in the same town, might join together for a particular venture. Such companies were made necessary less by the size of the investment needed than by the desire to spread the financial risk and facilitate distribution. This was the case, for example, with the edition of Caesar's *Commentaries* in Spanish printed in Paris in 1548, in a print run of 2,550. The productive capacity of centres like Paris and Lyon allowed them to dominate external markets, in this case that for books in Spanish, but it was also necessary to be able to sell at a distance and have access to the networks indispensable for channelling payments in return. The contract for the *Commentaries* was between a Parisian bookseller, Jacques Dupuis, and his colleague of Antwerp, Arnold Birckman; the Low Countries were then under Spanish rule and Antwerp was the financial capital of Europe, a commercial centre of the first importance and also a major typographic centre. The model in this case was an earlier Spanish edition and the manufacturing process lasted five or six months. A final operating model, illustrated by a Parisian contract of 1554, was more evenly balanced: the bookseller and the printer wanted to share the risks and collaborated on a book of which they planned to print 975 copies; these would be divided between them, each then disposing of his share on his own account. In a sense, the labour was here treated as its equivalent in capital.[57]

'Mr Son-in-law'

In a situation in which both governments and guilds were gradually tightening their grip, the career of Peter Schoeffer illustrates a route to social promotion and access to the status of master which remained common throughout the *ancien régime*. The Fust were persons of importance, close to the archbishop – Jakob Fuchs, the younger brother of the printer, was lynched by the mob in 1462 precisely because he was suspected of having, as burgomaster, assisted the primate's return. With Schoeffer, we are in a different world. He was the son of a peasant from Gernsheim, a little market town on the Rhine, where he was born some time in the 1420s.[58] Nothing is known of his childhood; Schoeffer was a common name in Gernsheim, where the young boy must have acquired his first schooling before moving, perhaps to Mainz, to complete his education, in particular in writing and calligraphy. He is next heard of in 1444, when he, like so many others, matriculated in Erfurt, and then in 1449 in Paris, where he stated in the colophon of a manuscript that he worked as a copyist and master of writing.[59] His name appears in 1450 in a list of *bacchalarii*, which, according to the university regulations, means he must then have been at least twenty years old and lived in the town for at least four years, that is, since 1446. The time spent in Paris as a young man was crucial to his career: it was here that he became familiar with the little world of the book, and he was in regular contact with the local bookshops, including that of André Le Musnier; it was also here that he acquired a training in calligraphy, that is, writing itself, the use of colours and also of decorations and the design of initials.

The work of the first printers was more a matter of reproduction than creation from scratch and Schoeffer's first skill was as a designer of letters.[60] It is possible that, having returned to Mainz in the years 1452–5, he worked as a journeyman with Gutenberg, where he would inevitably have encountered Johann Fust. According to Lehmann-Haupt, however, he returned from Paris only in 1455. However that may be, the colophon of the *Mainz Psalter* describes him in 1457 as an associate of Fust.[61] These were years of crisis between the inventor and his financier, who had grasped the huge potential of the new technology. It seems most likely that Fust, wishing to establish a workshop independently of Gutenberg, recognized in the young Schoeffer a craftsman able to perform, to his benefit, what we would today call a transfer of technology. The *Annals of Hirsau* make Schoeffer out to be the adopted son of Gutenberg, which is unlikely, but the *Breviarium historiae Francorum* of Johann Schoeffer suggests, in 1515, that Schoeffer had made crucial improvements to the invention of Gutenberg and Fust.[62] Some of the letters of the *Psalter* are directly inspired by his calligraphy, as were some of the engraved initials of the *Chronecen der Sassen*.[63] Though it is impossible to be more specific about his contribution to the typographic technology, we should remember, lastly, the tradition reported by Prosper Marchand that makes him the creator of the crucial metallurgical process combining punch, matrix, mould and character:

> But Schoeffer, a clever man and an astute and inventive mind, devoted much thought to this subject on his own account; he mulled it over, in all its aspects, until he had the idea of cutting punches, striking matrices and manufacturing and justifying moulds and in this way casting movable and separate letters with which he could at will compose the words, the lines and the whole pages he needed.[64]

Peter Schoeffer eventually married his master's daughter, Christine Fust, probably in 1462, thus inaugurating what was one of the most common routes to social promotion in the small world of the book until the nineteenth century. While, in 1462, the colophons present him as a simple clerk of the city and archbishopric, in two of the Ciceros of 1465 and 1466 he is described by Fust as *puer meus*, 'my son'. After Fust's death, in 1466, his widow married the printer Conrad Henli. She died in 1473, the year when, as a result, Schoeffer inherited through his wife her father's printing workshop; his brother-in-law Johann renounced his share of the inheritance in favour of his sister in 1476. The couple had four children, three of whom were active in the world of the book: Gratian was a printer in Oestrich; Peter II practised successively in Mainz, Worms, Strasbourg, Basel and Venice and is known to have been interested in the printing of music; Johann succeeded his father in Mainz, having worked with him from the 1490s; almost nothing is known of the fourth son, Ludwig. In becoming 'Mr Son-in-law', to use the expression of Jean-Yves Mollier, Schoeffer had traded his technical knowledge for spectacular social promotion: a judge in Mainz from at least 1489 and possessed of a considerable fortune which, in 1496, included three properties in Mainz and one in Frankfurt. He died during the winter of 1502–3.

The professions: crafts and status

The new crafts associated with printing were not immediately assimilated into the old guild structure, especially as some towns, such as

Lyon, were keen to liberalize the establishment of new printing shops. In other places, access to a mastership was still theoretically dependent on the university, though in reality free, and the route to advancement open – as the example of Schoeffer shows. The transition from the status of journeyman to that of master may have been made easier, in the early days, by the secrecy maintained with regard to printing. It was the first journeymen of Gutenberg who, from 1462, left Mainz and introduced the new art into a number of towns. And other persons, who had not initially intended to enter the book trades, were able to seize the opportunities offered and find success. A good example of this, as well as of the role played by capitalists who were also scholars and collectors, is Nicolas Jenson.[65]

Born in Sommevoire, a village in Champagne near Vassy, Jenson was probably educated in Troyes before becoming a *garçon* in the Mint at Tours. In 1458, aged about thirty, he was sent to Mainz by Charles VII to learn about the early printing. After the king's death, however, his successor, Louis XI, took no further interest in the project and Jenson seems to have remained in Germany, where he worked with Fust on improvements to the technology of cutting punches and typefaces. It is possible that he, like others, abandoned the town in 1462, perhaps to work in Cologne with Zell, before leaving with Sweynheym and Pannartz for Italy (1464). He was soon in Venice, where he initially worked with Johannes de Spira, the proto-typographer of the city (1469), probably as an engraver and caster. He continued to operate on his own after his master's death (1470), while the latter's business was taken over by his brother Wendelin. Jenson's success came with his employment of new fonts when, around 1475, he involved a number of capitalists in his business, which operated under the name of 'Nicolaus Jenson et socii' (Nicolas Jenson and partners); they were Paula, widow of Johannes de Spira, Peter Ugelheimer and Johann Rauchfas. Ugelheimer, descended from a family of merchants from Frankfurt am Main, had settled in Venice after the death of his father; Rauchfas had been an employee and then partner in the Frankfurt firm of Stallburg und Bromm (1474).

On 1 June 1480, when the company had come to the end of its term, it was extended and enlarged; it now consisted of Jenson, Ugelheimer, Johann Manthen,[66] Kaspar von Dinslaken and 'two Italians who, with Johann Manthen, represented [the bookseller] Johannes de Colonia' (Haebler), together with Paula and her two children. The company was now known as 'Johannes de Colonia, Nicolaus Jenson and partners', and the capital was in the region of 10,000 ducats. Jenson had correspondents or agents in several Italian towns and he maintained close relations with Lyon, where his son was living in 1480. He himself died in September of that year, in Venice, where he had been made a count palatine by the pope. Three crucial factors had contributed to his success. First, in Mainz, as a young man, he had made himself one of the most skilled technicians in the field of metallurgy. Then, having decided not to return to France, he had chosen to settle in Venice, the most dynamic town in Europe as regards the printing sector from 1470. And, finally, he had gradually abandoned the 'mechanical' in favour of commerce, where the possibilities of enrichment were greater; as he had lived in Germany, it had been easy for him to integrate into the little world of the Germans in Venice, some of whom were capitalists on a large scale.

Gradually, however, the sociological make-up of the sector contracted. It became increasingly difficult for a former workman to change his status, except through marriage to the widow or daughter of a master printer. The impossibility of procuring sufficient capital was the root cause of the problems encountered by Gutenberg and by numerous other printers of the period, such as Johann Neumeister. At the same time, regulation of the book trades both by local administrations and the guild system became tighter; marriage became one of the main routes to promotion within the sector.

Meanwhile, there was a polarization between a majority of very small printing shops, even those restricted to a single family (with only one working press), and a tiny minority of larger printing houses, benefiting from the trend for consolidation visible at an early date, and which between them accounted for an increasing proportion of production – Koberger with his twenty-four presses offers the best-known example. The working conditions were clearly different in each case. The workshop with a single press required the presence of at least three workers, a compositor (who might be the master) and two pressmen, to which we should sometimes add the foreman (in charge of the workshop) and one or more correctors responsible for preparing the texts and correcting the proofs. The work in a printing shop was extremely arduous, with a twelve-hour day or even longer, and a constant struggle on the part of the master to fix the workforce and control their activities. The normal practice seems to have been to allocate a particular job to a group of journeymen and apprentices who were paid by the day, on condition they maintained a minimum rate of production. The norm established for the compositors varied according to the difficulty of the text and its page layout. For the pressmen, the ratio between the number of formes and the size of the print run remained more or less constant, so as to allow a maximum intensity of labour. The standard number of leaves to be printed per day seems enormous: at the end of the sixteenth century the basic print run was 1,500 copies and each press should produce up to 3,350 leaves (on one side only), 2,650 in Paris, that is, 3,000 leaves for twelve hours of work, approximately one leaf every fifteen seconds without interruption. It was possible, therefore, to combine for one leaf the work of composition (two formes) and that of impression (1,500 copies twice). The majority of the workers were paid by the piece, only the most highly qualified receiving a decent wage based on the basis of time worked.

The developing tension between the low wages and the consciousness of workers who did not regard themselves as belonging to the 'mechanical arts', and who tried to organize to strengthen their position, explains why printing was the first sector in France to be hit by serious strikes, initially in Lyon, in 1539. The journeymen were subjected to increasing pressure from the masters to accept lower wages, while at the same time forced to compete with an increasing number of apprentices, who constituted a virtually free workforce. They stopped work in an organized action and the conflict gradually spread to the Parisian printing shops. It was not until 1541 that the strike was ended by a royal decree that was largely favourable to the masters, 'limiting' the working day to the hours between five in the morning and eight at night and prohibiting work on feast days. The crisis persisted, nevertheless, reaching a new peak in 1571–2. The Edict of Gaillon (1571) repeated the clauses favourable to the masters and introduced guild regulation into printing: workers could not leave a workshop without obtaining written permission, and only those who could claim three years' apprenticeship could become journeymen. The continued unrest eventually forced a declaration from the king that was on some points more sympathetic to the demands of the workers (1572).[67] But by now the professional landscape had been transformed and the simple printer was increasingly a craftsman working on the orders of a bookseller, or even of a capitalist investor, and subordinated to their interests.

Lastly, the invention and spread of printing did not lead to the immediate disappearance or redeployment of the specialists working on manuscripts – the copiers, designers, painters and even less the binders. Some painting workshops were established close to the first printing shops, their main business being the illumination of the latter's products: of the seventy-three surviving copies of the *Decretum* of Gratian published by Fust and Schoeffer in Mainz in 1472, at least ten were illuminated in a specialized workshop in that town, known as the workshop of the *Mainzer Riesenbibel*. Further, some collections of models used by the painters to decorate manuscripts are known that are more or less contemporary with the appearance of printing. One of them, today in Göttingen, was used for the adornment of certain copies of the *42-line Bible*. Peter Schoeffer started out as a calligrapher and copyist and it was as a designer of characters that he was first employed by Gutenberg and Fust. The Benedictine Leonhard Wagner, born near Augsburg *c.*1450, was a famous calligrapher and master of writing who worked in the scriptorium of Saints Ulrich and Afra; the fifty-plus manuscripts attributed to him include the *Proba centum scripturarum una cum manu exaratum*, the masterpiece of a man who was described as the 'eighth wonder of the world', in which he offered perfect samples of 100 different scripts.

In Florence and Naples, as in Avignon, Paris and Lyon, a whole community of specialists was still employed in the copying of manuscripts in the last decades of the fifteenth century, many of them from northern France, the old Low Countries or the towns of Germany. The presence of 'calligraphers from Mainz' is recorded in Foligno in 1463. This survival was due in part to the continued demand, as manuscripts were still commissioned, but it was also because in the fifteenth century and even into the sixteenth a printed book was not yet a 'finished product'; it was still necessary to add a number of manuscript references, decorated initials, painted letters, running heads, rubrications, and so on. This particular demand was greater in those towns with resident wealthy clients, for whom each copy had to be as sumptuous an object as possible. For the elites, the manuscript on parchment remained the 'noble' book par excellence: Duke Federico of Urbino (1422–82) would have no printed book in his library, which thus consisted solely of manuscript volumes. And when printed books were commissioned, every effort was made to give them a form as close as possible to that of a manuscript. As far as we can tell, the collection in the Bibliotheca Corviniana in the castle of Buda contained almost no printed books, only particularly precious manuscripts.[68] The same applied even in the case of the family of Langeac, who commissioned an extremely beautiful Book of Hours, copied in Paris in 1464, which they used as a *livre de raison*, or family record book, until 1537:

Ces heures sont à noble et puissant seigneur messire Jaques, seigneur de Langhac, vicomte de la Mole, conseiller et chambellan du roy nostre Sire, et furent faictes et eschevées à Paris par Jehan Dubrueil, escripvain, le XXe jour de janvier l'an mil CCCCLXIIII.[69]

(These hours belong to the noble and powerful lord messire Jaques, seigneur of Langhac, vicomte de la Mole, councillor and chamberlain of our Lord King, and were made and completed in Paris by Jehan Dubrueil, scribe, on the 20th day of January in the year one thousand CCCCLXIIII.)

In Spain, the rapid growth of printing was accompanied in the sixteenth century by a parallel growth in the production of luxury manuscripts, in particular liturgical manuscripts using parchment from Segovia. The monastery of the Escorial was one of the principal centres of production. Nevertheless, there are numerous examples of craftsmen moving from one trade to the other, from copying to printing or to the production of printed books. We have already noted the example of Antoine Vérard, but the same was true of Mentelin in Strasbourg and of Albrecht Pfister in Bamberg. In Bruges, Colard Mansion probably also worked as a copyist before turning to printing, at which he was not notably successful.[70]

Production and distribution

One final point needs to be made regarding the financial conditions of printing. The history of the invention underlines the extent of its capital needs: metalworking was extremely onerous, the investment needed for a specific publication was heavy (purchase of paper, cost of characters, preparation of any illustrations, and specialized technicians were essential to carry out the work). Gutenberg had fallen prey to financiers and some of the most important printer-booksellers were forced at a very early stage to associate in order to divide up the work or assemble the funds to invest. The Parisian Josse Bade published twenty joint publications out of a total of 729 attributed to his workshop; the Parisian bibliography includes 1,453 editions published between 1531 and 1535, of which 491 were published jointly between a number of persons seeking to spread the cost while limiting the risks and facilitating distribution.[71] As the volume of production grew, the publication of a book became an increasingly complex accounting, industrial and commercial operation: it was necessary to assess the market and the competition, decide on the print run, establish a provisional budget, assemble the funds, ensure the availability of both the raw materials (especially the paper) and the personnel and organize the work of the print shop. But the problems did not end there; it was also necessary to sell the copies produced on favourable terms. This required access to specialized networks and, as we have seen, it was the merchant bankers who were the first to have mastered these; investing, ensuring the dispatch of products and controlling the financial returns was their speciality. Like Fust, Schoeffer remained a merchant capitalist, involved also in the trade in wax and in the exploitation of a mine near Wetzlar. In the case of printed matter, he initially relied on branches managed by men he himself employed, before changing to reliance on temporary depots in Frankfurt, Paris, Trier and possibly Cologne.[72] From these he distributed not only his own products, but also those of other printing houses of Strasbourg, Cologne, Basel, Louvain and Rome.

Various events demonstrate the very privileged position of Paris. It was during a business trip to the French capital that Fust died (1466); he was probably buried in St Victor.[73] Two years later Schoeffer returned to Paris, where he sold to the College of Autun, for fifteen gold écus, a copy of the *Secunda secundae* (part of the *Summa*) of Thomas Aquinas, an edition produced in his own workshop in 1467.[74] Also in 1474, with Conrad Henlif, he sold to St Victor a copy on vellum of the *Letters* of St Jerome, in return for twelve gold écus and the foundation of a mass for Fust. This was the Mainz edition of 1470, for which a publicity leaflet was printed.[75] There also survives a copy of the *Commentary* of Duns Scotus on Peter Lombard (*in quartum Sententiarum*), published in Strasbourg in 1474, which has at the end a manuscript receipt in the hand of Schoeffer: '*À Jean Henri, chantre de l'église de Paris, de la somme de trois écus pour prise de ce livre*' ('To Jean Henri, precentor of the church of Paris, of the sum of three écus for receipt of this book').[76] Also revealing is the case of Hermann de Staboën of Munster, who had lived in Paris as a bookseller since the 1470s, where he sold the titles of Peter Schoeffer. On his death in 1474 his goods were confiscated by *droit d'aubaine*, which provoked a complaint on the part of the university, as some of the books seized were the property of Heynlin. The size of the sum at issue, 2,425 gold écus (3,880 livres tournois), testifies to the precocious importance of the book trade between Germany and Paris. The dispute dragged on for years; a French merchant even had his stock seized during the process of transferring his business to Speyer. In the end, however, the royal treasury repaid the sum due.

In parallel with his business in Paris, Schoeffer exported eastwards, through Lubeck and the Baltic; he had contacts with Nuremberg and Heidelberg and is known to have attended the Frankfurt fairs. A copy of the *Decretum* of Gratian, preserved until 1945 in Königsberg, had a manuscript note in his hand, dated 1474, indicating that the book had been given to a Franciscan monastery in Prussia; the writing, close to the humanistic, was reproduced by the typography of Mainz, Cologne (Zell) and Nuremberg (Koberger). The case of the *Breslau Missal* sheds light on the organization of the financial and sales networks: 400 copies of the *Missal* were ordered from Schoeffer in 1482 by Wilhelm Ruscher of Nuremberg on the occasion of the Frankfurt fair. Those behind the order were the Fleischmann brothers, Blasius Krieg and Hans Kirchnerg, all merchants of Breslau. In the event, delivery was delayed and the work was not completed until 24 July 1483. This was a one-off network, in which local capitalists used a Nuremberg intermediary familiar with the Frankfurt fairs to make an approach to a manufacturer in Mainz.

Several of the factors employed in towns by the great printer booksellers entered the business on their own account, sometimes with the support of their employer, as shown by the example of Peter Metlinger in Augsburg. This former student of Basel, a bachelor of arts (1465) and later a student at Freiburg am Brisgau, joined the firm of Amerbach, for whom he was the Paris correspondent in the years from 1482. In Besançon, in 1487, Metlinger printed several titles with Amerbach's types, before publishing the *Coutumes générales de Bourgogne* in Dole (1490) and the *Privilegia ordinis cisterciensis* (1491), commissioned by Abbott Jean de Cirey, in Dijon.[77]

Another publishing venture about which we are particularly well informed, thanks to the exceptional nature of the surviving documentation, is that of the *Nuremberg Chronicle* (1493). In spite of his great wealth, Koberger associated for this financially very demanding enterprise with two Nuremberg investors, the merchant Sebald Scheyer, a member of the Great Council, and his brother-in-law Sebastian Kammermeister. The sales records of this company, which was founded in 1493 and wound up in 1509, reveal that they sold not only through networks of professionals, booksellers, binders, and so on, but also through large merchants, private persons and, lastly, the network of factors of the Fugger. They had dealings over a very wide area, the whole of Central Europe, from Paris and Lyon to Budapest and Cracow, from Genoa and Florence to Lübeck and Danzig.[78]

Schoeffer also developed certain marketing techniques, returning to an idea that he may first have tried out in Strasbourg.[79] A printed catalogue, a single leaf dating from 1469–70, has been preserved in the library of Hartmann Schedel. The twenty titles it lists were sold by an itinerant clerk who had travelled to Nuremberg, where he put up in the Inn of the Wild Man (*hospicio dicto zum wilden Mann*). As well as books printed by Schoeffer, the list includes titles printed in Cologne by Ulrich Zell, and the last line is a sort of proof of the character used for the Psalter ('*Hec est littera psalterii*').[80] Other 'tracts' of Schoeffer list only a single title: the *Letters* (*Epistolae*) of St Jerome of 1470, the *Gratian* of 1472 and the *Decretals* of 1473.

Here, too, the aim was to use the printed leaf to give an idea of the quality of the work and a specimen of the characters employed.[81] These various procedures would be taken up by the great printer-booksellers at the turn of the sixteenth century, including Koberger and Aldus Manutius. Though printed in Schoeffer's case, the catalogues were sometimes manuscript, as in Rome for the editions of Sweynheym and Pannartz sold in the shop of Pietro and Francisco dei Massimi.[82]

The bookshop strictly speaking, in the sense of the specialized retail trade in printed books, appeared only very gradually, even though Du Pré and Gérard jointly designated themselves 'merchant booksellers' as early as 1486, in the colophon of the French translation of the *City of God* they printed in Abbeville. However, it is the *Danse macabre des imprimeurs* which depicts a bookshop for the first time, around 1500:

Le mort:
Sus avant, vous irés après/ Maistre libraire, marchez avant.
Vous me regardez de bien près./Laissez voz livres maintenant.
Danser vous fault, a quel galant./ Mettez ici vostre pensée.
Comment vous reculez marchant./ Commencement n'est pas fusée.
Le libraire:
Me fault-il malgré moy danser?/ Je croy que ouy, mort me presse
Et me contrainct de me avancer./ N'est-ce pas dure destress?
Mes livres il fault que je laisse/ Et ma boutique désormais
Dont je pers toute liesses./ Tel est blecé qui n'en peult mais.[83]

(The dead man: Up and on, you will go next/Master bookseller. Walk on./You're looking at me from not far off./Leave your books now./You must dance, like any galant./Set your mind to this./How your steps go backward,/The beginning is not the end.
The bookseller: Must I dance against my will?/I think yes, death presses me/And forces me to go forward./Is this not harsh distress?/My books I have to leave/And my shop from now on./At which I lose all happiness./How wounded is he who can go no further.)

Nevertheless, the speed of distribution by the fifteenth century is surprising, testimony to the efficiency of these networks. I will quote only a handful of French examples. The library of the Arsenal has a superb copy on vellum of the *48-line Bible* printed by Fust and Schoeffer in 1462; it belonged to Jean de Wailly, Dean of Orléans between 1463 and 1479, and appears to have been brought to Paris even before the printing shop was established there.[84] Servais Le Roy, who died in 1473, was a metropolitan canon of Cambrai who, on his death, left several books, which included a Bible in two volumes, on parchment, '*faite en molle*', deposited in Dixmude. His colleague Canon Raoul Mortier, who died in 1480, owned a magnificent library which contained a 'Bible in two volumes printed in Mainz', valued at twelve livres; his inventory also includes a volume '*Albertus Magnis De misterio misse, en lettre molée*', valued at fifteen sous.[85] The library of the Benedictines of St Bertin is known to have acquired a copy of the *42-line Bible* at a very early date. In Tours in the fifteenth century, Brother Amand de Bresche owned Torquemada's *Exposition of the Psalter*, in the Mainz edition of 1478. Lastly, near Orléans, the provost of Boiscommun, at the very beginning of the sixteenth century, owned both a *Nuremberg Chronicle* and an exceptional copy of the *Apocalypse* of Dürer of 1498.[86]

The Invention of the Graphosphere

The rapid emergence of the new media, within the space of a few decades, can only be understood as marking the apogee of a series of much earlier advances, but it was also the cause of changes so profound that it may correctly be described as a 'revolution'. With Gutenberg, a new era began for the whole of Western society and the quotations given above show that contemporaries were quick to realize this. It was the beginning of a new age, of what Régis Debray called the 'graphosphere', in which the written word, print and mediatized signs became central to the functioning of global society.

The first changes were economic in nature: they concerned not only the printing workshops, but the manufacture of hardware (the typographical equipment) and consumables (ink, paper) and also distribution. The originality of the West lay primarily in the articulation of capitalism and technical development. Contrary to the situation in China, the printing sector did not initially emerge in Europe as an affair of the state, or even of the Church, and the 'commercial' dimension gradually became stronger in the case of the software, too. With printing, texts and information became 'commodities', and as such could be bought and sold. Functions and fluxes were superposed in the first geography of the book, as regards not only production (the printing towns) but also distribution (the book fairs and the new bookshops) and financial networks. The economy of printing had a supranational dimension from the start and it was in this context that competition, specialization and relocation developed; we should remember that, in the face of strikes by their journeymen, the masters

Figure 6.2 The first book printed outside Germany, the *De Oratore* of Cicero, was produced by Sweynheym and Pannartz in Subiaco in 1465. The impression is in Roman characters and the page layout illustrates the humanist doctrine of 'the text alone', without additions or commentary. It is a book intended for instruction, as shown by the wide margins reserved for the reader's handwritten notes. National Széchényi Library, Budapest.

of Lyon had already threatened to relocate and print elsewhere, in Vienne (Dauphiné) or even Geneva.

There were also major consequences for the economy of intellectual consumption and production. The transition to printing was accompanied by a corresponding reduction in the average price of books, which meant an expansion of the traditional public of reader-purchasers. The proliferation, on an unprecedented scale, of titles and copies led not so much to a change in reading practices as to a generalization of this change; most medieval reading had been intensive, that is, the reading and rereading *in extenso*, as it were a 'rumination' (*ruminatio*), of a limited number of books that were largely committed to memory. This practice did not disappear, persisting throughout the early modern period if not beyond, but it lost ground in favour of the more modern practice of extensive reading, that is, reading a wide range of texts and consulting selected passages or extracts, as Montaigne was soon to delight in doing, tucked away in his 'library'. It was no longer a question of authority, on the medieval model, but rather of an interiorized conversation with the community of great minds. Though it can neither be counted nor measured, silent reading undoubtedly rapidly gained ground at the expense of the oralized or murmured reading and letter-by-letter deciphering which had characterized the medieval *lectio*. With silent reading, abstraction also gained in importance, through the increasing dominance of the sense of sight as opposed to the senses of hearing and smell; and there was a similar shift from an auditory and muscular memory to a visual memory, opening up the possibility of an externalization of the reference.

The economy of the media impacted, in return, on that of the texts. By the fifteenth century, financial logic ruled, through market forces and the power of competition. The investments made by the printers or their financiers had to be repaid, though it was also necessary to avoid too heavy a dependence on credit. Gutenberg was the first to engage in the production of new 'pieces', indulgences, etc., which brought in the necessary cash and could be sold more easily and more widely. Similarly, Fust and Schoeffer were careful periodically to kick-start their business, to the point where they appear as the inventors of what was already called 'editorial policy'. The role of money became more visible when the limits of a particular market began to be felt and efforts were made to respond to the increasing inertia by some innovatory move: a reorientation of production, the commissioning of texts (such as translations) or the production of short pieces which had the virtue of not either tying up the presses for long periods or requiring exceptional capital, and which were assured of a rapid sale. We are not very far from Rabelais (1494–1555) and his decision to write *Pantagruel* in 1532, though without going so far as to publish it under his own name. In fact, to paraphrase Marshall McLuhan, we might propose as an axiom that, in the economy of the media, the mechanization of the process was also the 'commodification' of the content.

Not only did the economic imperative determine the writing of certain texts, but, with the large-scale mediatization by printing, the body of authors and their mediators became established as the court of approval and acceptance in the various sectors of intellectual production. It would not do for Dr Rabelais to be recognized as the author of a text far removed from the university canons or the sphere

nere aliquando reperitur.Carpere est particulatim rem decerpere:z diminuere:sicut lanã car / **Carpere.**
punt pectine:flo:es z poma summis digitulis.famam hominis occultis mo:fibus.z viam cre
bris et firmis passibus.p:op:ie autem equus fo:tis viam carpit dum vngulis dilacerat et di
spergit.vnde qui firmiter z audacter ingrediuntur viam carpũt . vnde est illud virgilianum in
disticho de balista latrone.Nocte dieq tuum carpe viato: iter.Hec sunt que ad p:imum lib:uz
annotanda duximus.

¶ P:osa p:ima lib:i secundi.

Ost hec paulisper obticuit: atqz
vbi attentionẽ meaz modesta ta /
citurnitate collegit: sic exo:sa est.
Pbi . Si penitus egritudinis tue
causas habitumqz cognoui: fortune p:io:is
affectu desiderioqz tabescis:ea tãtũ animi tui
statum (sicuti tibi fingis) mutata peruertit
¶ Jntelligo multifo:mes illius pdigũ fucos

¶ P:osa p:ima secundi lib:i.

 Sauccus
Thomas

Ost hec paulisper
Dic est secundus
liber Boe. de cõ
solatione philoso
pbie qui continua
tur ad lib:um p:e
cedẽtem in hunc modum. Post q̃
philosophia in p:imo lib:o inuesti
gauit causas radicales infirmita
tis Boe.in hoc secundo p:ocedit
ad eius curatione.P:imo adhibẽ
do sibi remedia leuia.Secũdo re
media validio:a in l.b:is cõsequẽ
tibus.hunc enim modum medicã
di philosophia p:omisit Boetio.

Et diuiditur iste liber in .xvi.partes: quia octo sunt p:ose et octo metra huius secundi. partes
n p:cessu patebũt.quid aũt in qualibet parte agitur sr̃ videbi:f . P:ima p:osa diuidi:. P:imo
ostendit Boe.quid pbia egerit post p:edicta z resumit vnam causam dolo:is Boe . Secun
do pbia ponit quendam effectum fo:tune. Tertio excusat se de quodam.Quarto tangit opo:
tunitatem medendi Boe.Quinto p:cedit ad leuia medicamenta eius.secunda ibi.Jntelligo.
tertia ibi.Sed et arbitro:.quarta ibi.Sed tp̃s est.quinta ibi.Quid est igitur o Boe.p:imo di
cit.Post hec que dicta sunt pbia obticuit.i.tacuit paulisper.i.modicum:atqz p:o z vbi.i.post q̃
collegit.i.intellexit meam attentionem.i.diligentiam modesta taciturnitate.i.temperato sile
tio:exo:sa est.i.incepit loqui sic:idest taliter.si p:o quia ego cognoui caulas:idest rationes ra
dicales:qz p:o z habitum.i.dispositionem tue egritudinis.i.infirmitatis:tu Boeti.tabescis:
id est tristaris affectu:qz p:o z desiderio p:io:is fo:tune que fuit tibi p:ospera:ea fo:tuna muta
ta.i.variata apud te peruertit.i.mutauit statum.i.dispositionem tui animi.i.tue mentis sicu
ti tu tibi fingis.¶ Nota qz pbia post p:edicta obticuit vt Boe.magis animo deliberato verba / **Taciturni**
pbie colligere posset z sibi respõderet: quia fm̃ Sene.in p:ouerbijs.Deliberare vtilia mo:a tu / **tatis bona**
tissima est.Deliberandum est diu quicquid faciédu:z est semel . Discute quid audias p:oba quid
credas:z ideo pbia obticuit tanq̃ lassata ex questionibus p:ius motis.vnde Seneca li.de vir
tutibus cardinalibus. Non semp in actu sie: sed iterdũ a animo tuo requie dato:vt redea illa sit
plena sapientia z virtute.¶ Nota de boc q̃ dicit taciturnitas. duplex est taciturnitas: queda / **Taciturni**
moderata. alia superflua. Moderata taciturnitas est quãdo tacetur cũ tacedũ est. de qua lodq̃ / **tas duplex**
Sene.in p:ouerbijs di.Tene semp vocis et silentij temperamentũ:tũ in hoc libentius te inci
be vt libentius audias q̃ loqueris.qui enim nescit tacere nescit loqui. Superflua taciturnitas
est quando tacetur cum loquendũ est.de qua poeta. Nam nimiũ tacuisse nocet.¶ No.qz Boe.
in statu miserie non erat magnanimus:qz habuit animũ peruersũ fo:tuna. Magnanimus / **Magnani**
ẽst est qui cõtra diffo:mes insultus fo:tune vnanimi mentis constantia militat.fm̃ Alb.super / **mus.**
p:mo lib.ethi.z Sene.p:ima ep̃la ad Lu.di. P:imũ argumentũ cõposite mentis cristino posse
cõsistere et secus mo:ari.¶ Nota qz pbia dicit fo:tunam esse mutatam circa Boeti.sicut ipse / **Fo:tuna**
fingit hoc dicente p tanto qz fm̃ rei veritate fo:tuna non erat circa ipsũ mutata sicut pbia in
fra p:obabit.¶ Jntelligo multi.Dic pbia ponit effectum fo:tune di.ego intelligo.i.cognosco
multifo:mes fucos.i.deceptiones illius p:odigij.i.fo:tnue:z consũ.i.tamdiu scz ipsa fo:tuna
exercet blandissimam familiaritatem cum his quos nititur.i.labo:at eludere id est decipere:

Figure 6.3 The aesthetic of the *Boethius* printed in Lyon by Jean de Vingle for Etienne Gaynard in 1499 was the very opposite of the example shown in figure 6.2: note the Gothic characters, but above all the combination, on the same page, of the text itself (in larger letters and in the centre of the page) and the commentaries of St Augustine and of Josse Bade in the form of marginal gloss. The volume has been rubricated by hand. Municipal Library of Valenciennes.

of medicine. Conversely, the strategic use of correspondences, dedica-
tions, prefaces and other texts included in the introductory pages of
an increasing number of books constructed a network of recognition
in which everyone wished to claim a place. Lastly, at a higher level,
there is the question of the extent to which the economy of the media
influenced not only the reception of a particular text as conforming
to the canons of a certain category of texts (for example, the scientific
canons), but also the very definition of these canons (in other words,
staying with this example, what counted as scientific).

In fact the relationship to knowledge itself was changed by the
irruption of the media. The traditional image was that of the text
inspired in the author by a higher power, but, with entry into the
graphosphere, this vision was undermined and the figure of God
tended to fade into the background, well behind the processes of
writing and reading. One of the first thinkers to have grasped the
scale of these changes and realized their consequences was Luther,
who systemized the principle of reference to 'Scripture alone'
(*Scriptura sola*) and, consequently, the reduced importance of other
forms of sacred communication. Printed books and the escalating
mass of information they contained made it possible to know everything there was in the world, as Ickelsamer wrote in his *Teütsche
grammatica*;[87] books were a site of experience, even of individual
experiences, and were increasingly constructed as an ensemble of ever
richer expert systems. This accumulation soon necessitated the construction of working tools adapted to an expanding documentation,
like bibliographies and catalogues. The printed book held out the
promise of the universal catalogue and knowledge, while the actors
in the graphosphere became by definition those of the intellectual
sphere itself.

PART III

The First Media Revolution

Just as Christ's apostles once went out into the world and announced the good news to all, in our day, the disciples of the holy art go into all the countries and their books are the heralds of the gospel and the preachers of the truth and of science.

Wimpfeling

7

Printing Conquers the World

Hoc est, quod semper gloriosa et coelo digna anima Nicolai Cusensis cardinalis Sti Petri ad Vincula peroptabat, ut haec sancta ars quae oriri tunc videbatur in Germania Romam deduceretur.

Andrea de Bussy (1470).[1]

Artem pressurae quamquam Moguncua finxit
E limo traxit Basilea tamen.[2]

The Spread of the Innovation

The apostles of Mainz

Within fifty years, Europe was covered with a network of 'printing towns', in which these new machines, the typographic presses perfected in Strasbourg and Mainz around 1450, 'rolled'. To the contemporaries of the Savoyard William Fichet, an entire new economic sector seemed 'to have come out of Germany like a Trojan horse to spread' across the land (1473), a little like the Apostles dispersing to spread the Good Word on the day after Pentecost. It was a phenomenon that seemed, a posteriori, so remarkable that it was put on the same plane as the collapse of the Byzantine Empire and the discovery of the New World, with which it brought the canonical chronology of the Middle Ages to an end. The equivalence was soon established: printing was modernity, and the geography of printing was the geography of a modernity whose space was conflated with that of Western Europe.

The invention of typography with movable characters spread in time and space according to specific logics and tempos which we are now better able to understand, thanks to older works and even more the databases now available.[3] Several interconnected factors determined the early geography of this expansion: the structures of production conformed to a reticulated organization and they obeyed imperatives of a cultural but also of an economic and political order. The spread of printing was soon a matter of concern to the Church and the political powers. Over time, more advanced spaces slowly split off from regulated spaces, and the relationship between the two constantly evolved. The key question is that of the tempos and logics according to which the transition from the invention to its dissemination (to innovation) operated, or, in the words of Henri-Jean Martin, how 'printing conquered the world'.

The paper valley

Printing was invented in the middle Rhine Valley, in Mainz and in Strasbourg. It was from this Western European heartland that it spread, as if in concentric circles, throughout the whole of the continent, and then the whole world. In the lead-up, the demographic dynamic which had characterized the first half of the fifteenth century and continued into the sixteenth had favoured certain regions. Some 150 years after the crises of the fourteenth century, the 'full world' of 1300 was found once again on the Rhine, in Flanders and in northern Italy, with average densities as high as sixty inhabitants per square kilometre.[4] Between thirty and thirty-five European towns are estimated to have had populations of more than 40,000 in 1500, added to which was a network of medium-sized and smaller towns, thicker on the ground in the more densely populated regions: over 30 per cent of the population lived in towns in the Low Countries and 25 per cent in northern Italy, but the figure was less than 10–15 per cent over most of the continent. For Pierre Chaunu, the numbers attained in northern and central Italy and the Rhine Valley marked a major turning point.[5] To call the Rhine Valley the 'paper valley' is to emphasize its role in the first great revolution in the media system.

In Mainz order was restored in 1462, when the town, now under the control of Adolf of Nassau, became the effective capital of a territorial principality. Nevertheless, it gradually lost its position in the world of the book. Until 1462 the economy of secrecy had prevailed, except as regards Strasbourg and Bamberg, but everything changed with the dispersal of Gutenberg's teams. Mainz then lost its dominance in the face of new and more powerful rivals: Nuremberg,

Table 7.1 Printed production (number of titles) in Mainz and Speyer in the fifteenth century

	<1471	1471–80	1481–90	1491–1500
Mainz	81	54	101	92
Fust and Schoeffer	30	52	95	41
Speyer	0	67	148	122
Drach	0	35	91	54

Cologne, Strasbourg, then the great foreign centres of Venice and Paris. The profession was no longer exercised in neutral conditions. The highest ecclesiastical authorities made their presence felt in a strengthening of censorship from 1485, as well as in a degree of distrust for the editorial forms aimed at a wide readership, in particular books in the vernacular.[6] At the same time, the printers had to face increasingly fierce competition, often locally. Peter Drach, established in Speyer in 1471, kept a representative in Mainz to oversee sales of his products, where his business soon prospered to the point where, by the 1470s, more titles were printed in Speyer than Mainz. The same happened with the printers of Augsburg. The foundation of a university in Mainz in 1477 made no real difference.

The first printers outside Mainz were Germans, most of them former journeymen of Gutenberg, and often itinerant. The two first towns in which presses appeared were Strasbourg (*c.*1458) and Bamberg (*c.*1459). After the siege of 1462, a number of typographers left to seek their fortune elsewhere. In the absence of documentary sources, we are often reduced to guesswork, but they included men like Ulrich Zell in Cologne (1464–5), Berthold Ruppel in Basel (1468),[7] Philip Kefer in Nuremberg (*c.*1469), Johann Neumeister in Foligno (1470) and even the Italian proto-typographers, together with Nicolas Jenson and possibly Johannes de Spira.[8] In introducing their technology, the Germans also disseminated a printing aesthetic: Gutenberg printed in gothic and he was imitated by all his successors until Adolf Rusch, in Strasbourg, in 1464. It was Rusch who was the first to use a character of humanistic inspiration, followed by Sweynheym and Pannartz in Subiaco (1465).

Uncertainty surrounds the career of Johann Mentelin, the proto-typographer of Strasbourg:[9] born in Sélestat *c.*1410, probably a former pupil of the parish school, he worked in Strasbourg as an illuminator and copyist in the entourage of Bishop Ruprecht. He may have been trained as a printer in one of several ways: by meeting

Gutenberg himself, by going to Mainz or from a craftsman from Mainz passing through Strasbourg. His first known title is the Latin Bible known as the *49-line* (before 1461). What is certain is that it was thanks to Mentelin that Strasbourg, the largest town in the middle Rhine, quickly emerged as a centre from which printing spread through apprenticeship networks. Mentelin probably employed as an illuminator Johann Bämler, who later worked as a printer in Augsburg. The brothers Günther and Johann Zainer, originally from Reutlingen, also worked for Mentelin: Günther settled in Augsburg, Johann was the proto-typographer of Ulm. Other printers passed through Strasbourg, including Mentelin's two sons-in-law, Rusch and Schott, and also Sixtus Riessinger, later known in Rome and Naples, and Thibaldus Schenkbecher, born in 1445 in Niederehnheim and established in Rome in the 1470s. It is thought that Heinrich Eggestein, another printer in Strasbourg (1466), learned his trade with Mentelin, but he also knew Gutenberg and may have lived in Mainz in the years 1455–9, that is, when Gutenberg was working in that town.

The dynamism of Strasbourg and its printers continued to attract new arrivals. They included the goldsmith Georg Husner, possibly from Mainz, who married in Strasbourg in 1470 and opened a work-shop (1473) in association with a clerk from Mainz, Johann Beckenhaub, himself later (1479) a printer in Wurzbourg. It was not only men and their skills that circulated, but also, as we have seen, the hardware, that is, the typographic characters and sometimes the engraved woodblocks: Leeu, a printer in Gouda (1477) and then Antwerp (1484), acquired some of his fonts in Venice and took over the xylographed plates of Heinrich Knoblochtzer in Strasbourg. The example of Strasbourg and Mentelin illustrates the crucial role played by the transfer of knowledge, to which should be added the solidarities of apprenticeship: the fact of having spent time in this town was a sort of guarantee of competence for craftsmen, who sometimes styled themselves 'de Argentina' (of Strasbourg) even if they had not been born in that town but only received their training there. Lastly, these professional solidarities frequently overlapped with family ties.

A quarter of a century later a new stage had been reached, and it was to the 'second-level' centres that craftsmen went to learn their trade, before leaving for new pastures. The first printer of Pilsen came from Bamberg. Similarly, Andreas Hess had worked for Lauer in Rome before founding the first Hungarian printing shop in Buda.[10] The scribe Matthias Moravus, originally from Olmütz, joined forces with Michael of Monaco (Michael von München) and set up as a printer in Genoa in 1474. Among those who trained with him was Johannes Bonus, who continued there for several months before moving to Savone, where he was the town's proto-typographer (1474). According to Haebler, Michael von München is the same as the Michael Schopf (Michele Scopo) of Munich who had learned printing with Zainer in Ulm – here we encounter the Strasbourg networks once again.[11] Moravus set up in Naples in 1475, with the assistance of Blaisus Romero, a Catalan monk. His business prospered until 1491, from which date his typographic material appears in editions of Meinard Ungut and Stanislaus Polonus in Seville, both of whom he had previously employed; the latter was clearly of Eastern European origin.[12] Other persons from Central or Eastern Europe are known to have worked in the printing sector. One of the best known is Johann Sensenschmidt, born in Eger (Cheb), on the borders of Bohemia, who, after a spell in Bamberg, established himself as the proto-typographer of Nuremberg, probably in association with Johann Kefer, himself a former resident of Mainz (1469). Another 'Pole' working in Naples at the same time as Moravus was Johann Adam 'de Polonia' (1478). And, lastly, Pierre Hongre from Bartfeld became one of the principal printer-booksellers of Lyon from 1482.[13]

Pioneering circles

Let us try to model the process of innovation: as in all migration phenomena, two principal factors determined the transfers, namely, the degree of proximity and the size of the receiving communities.

It is clear that it was greater or lesser proximity that initially played the main role in the dissemination of the innovation, from a starting point in the Rhineland and central and southern Germany. After Mainz, Bamberg and Strasbourg, the first workshops were opened in Eltville (1464), Cologne, Basel, Nuremberg (*c*.1469) and Augsburg (leaving aside here the disputed case of Vienna). With some thirty workshops known, Cologne was the most important German printing town in the fifteenth century. But the process had already reached a number of Italian towns – Subiaco (1465), Rome (*c*.1467), Venice (*c*.1469), Foligno and Trevi (1470), and lastly Milan and Naples (*c*.1470) – as well as Paris. The first book printed by Gering, Crantz and Friburger in Paris dates from 1470. A calculation of the rank correlation between date of appearance of the printing shop and relative distance from Mainz gives a positive result of 0.71; in other words, proximity explains nearly three-quarters of the first spread of presses.[14]

Superimposed on this was the influence of a number of 'transmitter' milieus, chief of which was the Church. The role of the prelates in the establishment of printing in Strasbourg and Bamberg has

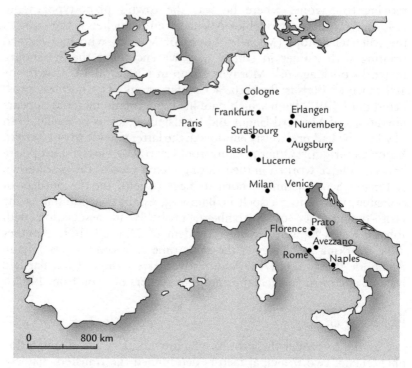

Map 7.1 The spread of printing in Europe, 1452–1470

already been noted. In Italy the chief innovators were found among the humanist prelates, often attached to the pontifical court or administration. Two members of the Sacred College played a decisive role in the transfer of technology. The links to Mainz and the Rhineland of the first of these, Nicolas de Cusa, are well known, but the cardinal died a little too early, at Todi, in 1464. The second was Juan de Torquemada (1388–1468), a Dominican, former student in Paris and defender of the prerogatives of the papacy at the councils of Constance, Basel and Florence. Made cardinal in 1439, Torquemada was apostolic protonotary and commendatory abbot of Santa Scholastica in Subiaco (1455), which received a number of foreign monks, many of them Germans. It was he who brought the two clerks Conrad Sweynheym and Arnold Pannartz to Subiaco,[15] the former from the Frankfurt region,[16] the latter from Cologne (1465–7). This pair may have printed a Donatus as early as 1464, but the first book printed outside Germany and surviving today is the Latin edition of Lactantius completed in Subiaco on 30 October 1465. It was followed (or preceded by a few weeks) by a *De Oratore* of Cicero, of which 275 copies were printed, and a *De Civitate Dei*.[17] Contrary to the German practice, these three editions were all printed in roman (*Antiqua*), perhaps due to the collaboration of Jenson. We should note in passing that Subiaco had a library and a specialized infrastructure, which, with the presence of copyists, may have simplified the transfer process.

In Rome the years 1464–6 were decisive. The eternal city had recovered its position as capital of Christendom only in 1420, with the definitive return of the pope, but there followed a period marked by a huge programme of reconstruction. The population rose from 20,000 (1450) to 55,000 inhabitants (1526), there was a building boom and trade of every sort rapidly expanded. The pontifical court and administration, the academy and the university, then the Greek college (1513), the library,[18] and the residence or temporary presence of many educated prelates combined to make Rome a cultural centre of the first order. An early attempt to introduce printing is known only through the archival sources: a company was set up some time before autumn 1466, perhaps as early as 1464, consisting of the apostolic notary Domenico da Lucca (then Simone di Niccolò of Lucca, alias Simone Cardella), Enrico di Ulrico Gallus Teuthonicus (Henry, son of Ulrich Han) and Clemente Donati of Urbino.[19] Cardella was a familiar of the Curia, to which he was attached as a merchant. Ulrich Han came from Ingolstadt and had spent some time in Vienna, where he had acquired burgess rights (and where he may have printed in 1462), before moving to Italy. He, too, soon gained entry to the pontifical court. This company may have been permitted to print one or more titles, but no copies have survived.[20]

Cardinal Torquemada was probably instrumental in the arrival of Han in Rome *c.*1464–6 to print his *Meditationes*; this was a commentary on the life of Jesus, illustrated with thirty-one engravings based on the frescoes the cardinal had had painted in Santa Maria sopra Minerva.[21] It was the first illustrated book (1467) after those of Pfister in Bamberg. Until 1471, Han was assisted by Giovanni Antonio Campano (1429–77), former professor of rhetoric at Perugia, then successively bishop of Crotone and of Teramo, who acted as proofreader and wrote a number of prefaces for editions of the classics. From 1471 to 1474, Han was still associated with Simone Cardella, though he later worked on his own. The sources show that, in 1474, he sought permission to sell books from a 'bench' in front of his workshop. In spite of the financial difficulties consequent on his separation from Cardella, Han published, in 1475, an important *Missale Romanum*, reprinted the following year in an edition in which he included printed music. He died in Rome in 1479.

By the end of 1467, however, Sweynheym and Pannartz had also moved their presses, and gradually their stock of books, to Rome, where they were established in a house belonging to the brothers Pietro and Francesco dei Massimi, between the place Navone and the Campo dei Fiori (where they had a moneylenders' bench). In November, Leonardo Dati, bishop of Massa, noted in his copy of St Augustine that he:

> had bought it for himself and for George, his nephew, with his own money, from those Germans established in Rome and who produce many books not by copying them, but by printing them [*non scribere sed formare solent*].[22]

It is likely that Santa Scholastica kept a share of the income from the sale of these copies. We may also note the presence in Rome in 1465 of another person who played a role in the early days of typography: Sixtus Riessinger, whom we have already encountered and who probably worked for some time with Han. In that same year, 1465, Adam Rot, a clerk of the diocese of Metz, received a canonry: he may have worked with Sweynheym and Pannartz before he, too, set up as an independent printer in 1471.

The second innovatory milieu that played a decisive role in the establishment of the very first presses was the university, itself closely associated with the Church. Many of the first typographers were university graduates, beginning with Gutenberg. The part they played is particularly clear in the case of Paris, the most important printing town in France. The city showed every a priori favourable indicator: it was the largest city in Europe demographically speaking (225,000 inhabitants in 1500) and it was the main economic, political (even though the monarchy remained itinerant) and intellectual centre in the kingdom. Printed books appeared in Paris at a very early date: in 1458, the king had sent Nicolas Jenson to Mainz to learn the secrets of the technology practised there, and Fust and Schoeffer were soon selling some of their books in Paris. But it was personal ties that were decisive in this case, and printing was introduced into the capital through individual networks of masters and students.

William Fichet was one of the first key players, in the 1460s. Born in 1433 in Faucigny, a student in Avignon, then Paris, and *socius* of the Sorbonne in 1461, he was rector of the university (1467) and doctor of theology (1468). Sent on a mission to Milan in 1469–70, he discovered Italian humanism, probably met Cardinal Bessarion, and returned convinced of the importance of printing. Alongside him was Johann Heynlin of Stein (Johannes de Lapide),[23] a former student at Erfurt, Leipzig and Louvain, who had arrived in Paris in 1453 and entered the college of Sorbonne.[24] He spent some time in Basel (1464–6), where he was dean of the faculty of arts, but perhaps also went to Mainz. It was in Basel that he met two young students, Ulrich Gering from Constance, and Michael Friburger from Colmar. He recruited them during the course of a second journey (1469–70), together with a compatriot from Stein, Martin Crantz. The first press was established by Heynlin in the college he directed, the Sorbonne, with Fichet responsible for the editorial programme and Gering, Crantz and Friburger supervising the operation of the workshop. The enterprise began with the *Epistolae* of Gasparin of Bergamo, whose manuscript had been transmitted to Fichet by Heynlin:

Like the sun, you spread the light of science across the world/
O Paris, royal city, mother of the muses./Accept it now for its merits/
This near divine art of writing invented by Germany.[25]

This was a milieu close to the Carthusians; Heynlin eventually retired to the Charterhouse of Basel, where he died in 1496. Among his Parisian students was none other than Johann Amerbach, who, after some years spent in Venice and Nuremberg, had settled in Basel, where he opened a printing house (1477) which was soon one of the most important in the town.[26] It is probable that connections between students also explain the appearance of printing in Lyon, through Barthélemy Buyer, the young merchant and 'artist'.

'Business' circles constituted the third group that was highly influential in the early spread of printing, and Buyer in Lyon is a case in point.[27] Having emerged from a difficult period, this town was experiencing rapid growth: from some 15,000 inhabitants in 1444, the population rose to perhaps 45,000 by 1515 and it continued to increase until the middle of the sixteenth century. Three events made Lyon one of the trading and artistic capitals of the Renaissance from the 1460s. The first was the confirmation of the four great annual fairs by Louis XI (1463); this was followed by the establishment in Lyon of the Florentine 'factors' working in France; and, lastly, with the beginning of the Italian wars, Lyon was the obvious support base for the forces engaged in the peninsula, and thus the scene of repeated visits by the court and constant diplomatic activity. The Buyer were one of the principal trading families in the town and they consolidated their rise by periods of study in Avignon and Paris. The father, Pierre Buyer, a graduate in law, apparently enjoyed considerable wealth and was head of the consulate of Lyon. The eldest son, Jacques, was a bachelor of both canon and civil law; the younger

son, Barthélemy, bachelor of arts, married the daughter of the notary
Claude Dalmès and was himself also later a consul. It was he who
financed the first printing house in Lyon, established in his house and
directed by Guillaume Le Roy of Liège (1473). The scale of his affairs
was such that he could bequeath 2,000 livres tournois to the collegiate church of Saint-Nizier to build his chapel.

The dynamism of this sector is illustrated by the proportion of
immigrants, especially German, in the Lyon book trade: of forty-
seven persons included in the prosopography of the 'men of the book'
of fifteenth-century Lyon, twenty-one are Germans and only nineteen
are French, with seven from elsewhere (Italy, Spain, Flanders and
Dalmatia).[28] In fact the local market was of only secondary importance for the town; the Lyonnais acted as intermediaries for the
Germans and the Venetians with regard to the south of France and
the Iberian Peninsula, while their own production was primarily
directed at the export market, in particular illustrated printed works
in the vernacular. Buyer's strength lay in his trading network, which
extended not only to Avignon (1481), Toulouse, Languedoc and
Spain (by 1477), but also Paris (where his representative was Nicolas
Guillebaud) and Italy (Venice and Jenson). When the town of Lyon
had to pay a large sum to Paris in 1482 and its representative was
unable to come up with the necessary cash, the consuls naturally
turned to their colleague to ask *'qu'il face délivrer par l'ome qu'il a
oudit Paris, vendant pour lu de livres, la somme qui sera nécessaire'*
('That he should have delivered through the man he has in the said
Paris, selling books for him, the sum that shall be necessary').

The workshops and shops in Lyon of men like Buyer or the Huss
gave employment to a whole group of cultural intermediaries, authors,
translators, adapters and artists, who kept the presses rolling. It was
in Lyon, in 1476, that the first printed book in French appeared, in
the form of the *Golden Legend* of Jacobus de Voragine, and also a
small abridged Bible (*Old Testament*) in the vernacular. The Lyonnais
Julien Macho translated the *Miroir de la rédemption de l'humain
lignaige*, which Martin Huss of Württemberg, who had settled in
Lyon in 1478, would make the first illustrated printed book in French.

Another region where merchants played a decisive role was England
and the old Low Countries, and its products were similar in many
ways to those of Lyon. William Caxton, born in Kent around 1420,
was a merchant and mercer, established on his own account in 1441,
and a regular traveller to the Low Countries.[29] He is documented in
Bruges, entrepôt for English wool, where he was governor of the
'English Nation' in 1462. He also worked at this period as a translator, copyist and dealer in manuscripts. In 1471 he was in Cologne,

where he probably established the first printing house and bought a press and fonts from Veldener, which he then moved to Bruges. It was here, in 1472–3, that he brought out the *History of Troy*, the first book printed in English, before, three years later, founding the first English printing workshop in Westminster.[30] He was primarily employed by court circles and published no fewer than ninety-six titles, mostly in English or French.

Ranking the Cities

The early days of printing

A statistical analysis enables us to identify the conditions favourable to innovation. As we have seen, calculation of the coefficients of the rank correlation confirms the importance of spatial proximity for the early spread of printing, but shows also that this changed after some two decades. If we confine ourselves to the seventeen towns which had a printing press before 1471 and consider population levels, we see that Mainz, the earliest printing town, is only in twelfth place. Conversely, the most populous town in Europe, Paris, was sixteenth in date order (1470). Overall, therefore, there is no correlation between date of appearance of printing and size of population; it was geographical proximity that mattered most, together with personal ties. The index improves if we take account of the volume of production before 1471, rather than the date of appearance of printing: the population/production correlation coefficient becomes positive, though remaining weak ($r = 0.39$). And it is only logical, lastly, that the results should be better for the correlation between the precocity of appearance of printing and the volume of production measured by number of titles ($r = 0.75$). Twenty years later, *c*.1480, it was the objective circumstances of growth that were playing an increasingly decisive role.

The end of the fifteenth century: factors of attraction

The calculations of Philippe Nieto for printed production in the years 1495–9 allow us to review the position at the end of the fifteenth century. The most important urban centre of production was now Paris, which was also the largest city in Europe, followed by Venice, another exceptionally large town. Cities like Florence, Rome, Lyon, Bologna and London each had more than 50,000 inhabitants and were amongst the most active centres of book production. Unlike the period before 1471, the correlation between demography and printed

Table 7.2 The main printing towns in Europe (until 1470)

Towns	Population in 1500	Printed in	Titles <1471	P	D	T	Km	d2	d2	d2	d2
Mainz	6,000	1454	81	12	1	3	1	121	81	4	0
Strasbourg	20,000	1458?	35	9	2	4	3	49	25	4	1
Bamberg	7,000	1459	10	11	3	8	5	64	9	25	4
Eltville	+	1464	4	15	4	10	2	121	25	36	4
Cologne	45,000	±1465	99	6	5	1	4	1	25	16	1
Subiaco	+	1465	3	15	6	11	16	81	16	25	100
Rome	55,000	1467	92	5	7	2	15	4	9	25	64
Basel	10,000	±1468	2	10	8	12	7	4	4	16	1
Augsburg	30,000	1468	13	8	8	6	8	0	4	4	0
Venice	100,000	1468	27	3	10	5	12	49	4	25	4
Nuremberg	38,000	1469	12	7	10	7	6	9	0	9	16
Foligno	++	1470	1	13	12	13	13	1	0	1	1
Trevi	++	1470	1	13	12	13	13	1	0	1	1
Milan	100,000	±1470	1	3	12	13	11	81	100	1	1
Naples	125,000	±1470	9	2	12	9	17	100	49	9	25
Paris	225,000	1470	1	1	12	13	10	121	144	1	4
Beromünster	+	1470	1	15	12	13	9	9	4	1	9
								816	499	203	236

First column: printing towns (in chronological order); second column: population estimate for 1500 (according to P. Bairoch et al.); third column: date of appearance of printing.

P: ranking according to population; D: ranking according to date of appearance of printing; T: ranking according to number of titles published before 1471 (according to ISTC); Km: ranking according to distance from Mainz.

+: ranking order for places too small for their population to be known.

d2: columns giving the figures used for the calculation of the correlation $r = 1 - \dfrac{6 \sum d^2}{n(n^2 - 1)}$

production (by number of titles) is positive, but the coefficient remains relatively weak (0.46). Further, some of the earliest towns to have had presses have disappeared from the list, beginning with Mainz, but including Bamberg, the small Italian centres (Subiaco, Foligno, and Trevi) and Beromünster.

The networks were increasingly structured according to the objective importance of the various towns, but also by the trend for specialization and the search for economies of scale. Italy is a case in point: the first presses began to roll in Subiaco in 1465, but printing reached Rome the following year, with Ulrich Han, who was soon joined by Sweynheym and Pannartz. The advantages of location in a major centre also explain why, in 1473, Johannes de Westfalia, the first printer in Flanders, moved his workshop from Alost to Louvain. The large cities dominated because they provided these early craftsmen with a larger market but also because they were administrative centres. This is clearest in the case of Venice: a political capital, it was one of the largest cities in Europe, with some 100,000 inhabitants in 1475, and it controlled financial and mercantile circuits extending throughout the whole of Europe and as far as the trade routes of the Eastern Mediterranean, and even beyond – at precisely the time that so much intellectual and cultural energy was focused on the rediscovery of classical Greek culture.[31] Printing was introduced into Venice in 1468 by Johannes de Spira, with the *Letters* (*Epistolae familiares*) of Cicero. In spite of a crisis of overproduction after 1472, the city was the second largest centre of printing in the world at the end of the fifteenth century: of some 30,000 incunabula, 3,500 are of Venetian origin – the *Clavis* of Borsa lists 271 printers or printer-booksellers operating in Venice before 1501.[32] Its success was aided by the fact that the authorities were quick to appreciate the potential economic benefits printing might bring: it was the Venetian Senate which, in 1469, granted the first known privilege to a bookseller. The city printed for the whole of the Adriatic and the Eastern Mediterranean, in Latin, but above all in Greek, even in Glagolitic.[33]

We should note, nevertheless, some very marked discrepancies between population and production, of which the most striking example is Leipzig: this was a small town (about 10,000 inhabitants), where printing appeared relatively late (1481), but which came third in the list of European centres in terms of output – an unlikely result in every respect. We may also note the very high ranking of some quite small towns, such as Basel and Deventer: in the latter case the school of the Brothers of the Common Life was famous, the young Erasmus studied there from 1478 to 1484 and Alexander Hegius became its director in 1483; whereas Basel, city of the Council, was a university and artistic centre and controlled the routes between the Rhine Valley and Northern Italy via the Lötschberg, the Simplon and the Gothard, even the Splügen. Sometimes it was too much competition within the principal town that caused printers to leave: when Koelhoff the Elder settled in Cologne in 1472 he was well supplied with capital and his arrival led to the departure of several other printers, including Schilling for Basel and Veldener for Louvain.[34]

Conversely, some of the biggest towns in Europe appear fairly low down in the list as regards their printed production. The most striking case is that of Naples, probably the second largest city in Western Europe around 1500, with some 125,000 inhabitants but with a printed output less than half that of Basel, which had a population only a tenth of its size. Prague had 70,000 inhabitants but printing appeared there only in 1487 and its output remained small (fourteen titles in the years 1495–9). The competition of the powerful German centres nearby explains why the printing workshops of Prague specialized in titles in the vernacular, Czech, which were not printed anywhere else and which had a regional market. At the other end of Europe the *reconquista* had been completed in Granada, abandoned by the last Nasrid Sultan in 1492; the first presses rolled in this large city (70,000 inhabitants) four years later, but production remained minimal (three titles). Towns such as Lisbon (65,000 inhabitants) and Palermo (55,000 inhabitants) were in a similar situation, while Marseille (45,000 inhabitants) had no printing workshop before the end of the sixteenth century.

These figures prompt three observations. First, they reflect the shift of Europe's centre of gravity to the north-west, with the large southern cities now ranked relatively low in relation to their population: Naples, Palermo, Lisbon, Granada and even Valencia and Seville. Second, we should note the peripheral location of the four most active centres (Paris, Venice, Leipzig and Lyon), which, as it were, framed a sprinkling of secondary centres. All four of these cities were particularly active in trade and distribution. Paris benefited from its exceptionally large population and from the presence of the university and the royal administration, and it was by far the most important printing city in France. Venice was the principal point of transit between Europe and the central and eastern Mediterranean and between Central Europe and Italy (by the Brenner and the valley of Trent); it was the most important commercial centre in the world. Leipzig was secondary at the demographic level, but a town of the first importance thanks to its fairs and the control its merchants had established over trade routes with the East; its university had also benefited from the decadence of Prague.[35] Lyon was in an analogous

Table 7.3 The twenty largest towns in Europe for printed production, 1495–1499

	Population	Number of titles	P	T	d	d^2
Paris	225,000	212	1	1	0	0
Venice	100,000	166	2	2	0	0
Milan	100,000	42	2	9	−7	49
Florence	55,000	62	4	5	−1	1
Rome	55,000	45	4	7	−3	9
Lyon	50,000	77	6	4	2	4
Bologna	50,000	30	6	12	−6	36
London	50,000	16	6	18	−12	144
Brescia	49,000	19	9	17	−8	64
Cologne	45,000	47	10	6	4	16
Nuremberg	38,000	29	11	13	−2	4
Augsburg	30,000	34	12	11	1	1
Antwerp	30,000	20	12	16	−4	16
Strasbourg	20,000	36	14	10	4	16
Pavia	16,000	23	15	15	0	0
Speyer	13,000	16	16	18	−2	4
Leipzig	10,000	83	17	3	14	196
Basel	10,000	27	17	14	3	9
Deventer	7,000	45	19	7	12	144
Westminster	5,000?	16	20	18	2	4
						717

situation: it controlled journeys between France and Italy and many large Italian firms had branches there; its printers and booksellers had succeeded in rivalling Paris in certain very specific areas; they sold throughout the whole of the south of the kingdom and their market extended into the Iberian Peninsula.

Some of the functions fulfilled by particular towns were favourable to printing presses, in particular, management functions in the religious sphere (seat of a bishopric or archbishopric, the presence of major religious houses, etc.), the intellectual sphere (schools, universities and colleges) or the political sphere. The role of the universities can hardly be overestimated: Paris and Cologne had major universities, Leipzig had been a university town since 1409, Basel since 1459; and, lastly, in the Italian peninsula, two thirds of the towns with a printing house before 1475 also had universities – the relationship between the university and the new art of typography seems to have been grasped very early in Italy.[36]

This very clearly structured geography was nevertheless riddled with contradictory phenomena. Most notable of these was the

Map 7.2 The twenty main centres of printing between 1495 and 1499 (by number of titles, not including placards and anopisthographic leaflets)

itinerant printer, caught between commission and the market, who remained a common figure. Johann Neumeister of Treisa (north of Marburg), another former student at Erfurt (1454), was probably a typographer in Mainz, perhaps even with Gutenberg.[37] He may have worked in the first printing house in Bamberg, but in any case left Mainz after the troubles of 1462. En route for Italy he probably stopped in Basel and possibly also in Rome, but he reappears in 1469 in Foligno, seat of a bishopric and an important fair town.[38] His establishment, as the town's proto-typographer, in the house of Emiliano of Orfinis, master of the Papal Mint, was financed by Emiliano and his brother Marietto. Neumeister went on to print what might be called a forgery of the Cicero of Sweynheym and Pannartz (1469), a Leonardo Bruni (1470) and, most notably, the first edition of the *Divine Comedy* of Dante (11 April 1472); a merchant of Trevi, Evangelista Angelini, was also involved in the latter operation. These three titles are significant in their 'modern' orientation, in a way that prefigures a 'national' market. It is possible that Neumeister worked with Stephanus of Moguntia and Crafto, two other Germans later found in Perugia in 1477.[39]

But problems arose in Foligno, too, and after a period of imprisonment for debt Neumeister left Italy and returned to Mainz, where he opened a workshop (1479). Peregrinations such as these facilitated the transfer of technology and innovation. Neumeister may have used Roman typographic material in Foligno, and he was the first to introduce book illustration into Mainz, using, for his *Meditations* of Torquemada, a technique of relief engraving (*en épargne*) on tin of Italian origin.[40] His magnificent *Ritual of Mainz* (*Agenda Moguntinensis*) of 1480, printed in red and black and illustrated with an engraving on metal, was a commission from the primate.[41] A highly skilled technician, always concerned about the quality of his products, Neumeister lacked the financial means he needed. He was once again unable to make ends meet and, in 1481, left for France, probably stopping in Basel and Lyon. Lyon and the south-west were in constant commercial contact and Neumeister is next documented in the rich episcopal city of Albi, in 1482. Here, as in Foligno, he introduced printing and produced another edition of his illustrated *Meditations* of Torquemada, a *Breviary* and a *Roman Missal* (1482), together with a small Cicero, and possibly also a *Trial of Belial*. The *Missal* is in two colours and is evidence of the technical research he had carried out in order to reproduce the musical staves. Lastly, he settled in Lyon, probably summoned by the archbishop, Charles of Bourbon (1482–3), where he printed a new *Roman Missal* commissioned by the cardinal-primate (1487); he also worked on the *Breviary* of Vienne on behalf of the archbishop-count Angelo Catone. But he was unable to maintain his independence and ended his troubled career working as a journeyman in various workshops in Lyon, even though the presses were experiencing a period of great prosperity and specialized technicians were in great demand. Neumeister died in Lyon around 1512.[42]

The distribution of presses

A map of the distribution of printing workshops active in the fifteenth century presents a false image, however, inasmuch as it is cumulative. The maps of Lucien Febvre and Henri-Jean Martin in fact mask two separate phenomena: on the one hand, the establishment of a workshop in a particular town on a temporary basis, for example, Subiaco and Beromünister; on the other hand, the gradual concentration of the network into a smaller group of more important and more active towns. These opposing trends reflect a conflict between the laws of demand and of the market. A printer might be attracted to a town by the custom of a person of importance, such as a prince or bishop, but, if the market was insufficient, be obliged to move on within a few years. Printing probably appeared in Albi in 1475, with the 'workshop of Aeneas Sylvius', while Neumeister settled there in 1481. In both cases the business was only temporary, and once Neumeister had left for Lyon there was no printing in Albi for almost two centuries:

> Printing in Albi was too heavily dependent on demand. What might be called editorial policy was dominated by the ecclesiastical cadres, the bishop and his entourage, who managed to procure, for a while, workshops which provided them – they themselves, the lower clergy and the faithful in their charge – with the reference books, educational books, and meditational books they needed. Added to which, Albi was well placed on the routes between the Auvergne, Lyon, Toulouse and Spain used by merchants, students, lay and ecclesiastical, and those summoned for trial. This assured a market for its books for a while, but was not enough to maintain over the long term an activity which was taken over by true commercial printing and bookselling enterprises. In the last phase of his episcopate, Louis of Amboise resorted to the services of a company in Lyon to publish his synodal statutes and a confessional; his successors turned to booksellers in the Lyonais, Auvergne and eventually the Toulousain, until printing was reintroduced into Albi in 1670.[43]

Similar examples were found all over Europe. If we confine ourselves to France, we may quote the presses of Chablis, Cluny and even Dijon. There was printing in Brittany, at Loudéac and Tréguier, in the 1490s, but printing works soon disappeared from the province. In the first half of the sixteenth century, when printing spread throughout Brittany, it originated from Nantes, Rennes and Caen, even Rouen. The determining factors interacted in paradoxical fashion, for example if a printing shop was close to a centre that was too large for there to be any chance of competing with success. This was probably the case with Chartres and even with a number of towns in the old Low Countries, such as Lille, where both the competition and the ease with which printed matter could be procured were such that it hardly seemed worth establishing a local press. In the end, the law of an integrated market prevailed: if we compare the map of active printing workshops in Europe at the turn of the sixteenth century with that of towns which had had at least one press since 1450, we observe both the concentration to the benefit of the major centres and the persistence of the most favoured regions, the Rhineland, but above all southern Germany, central Italy and the Low Countries.

Map 7.3 Towns with at least one printing workshop between 1452 and 1501

Map 7.4 Workshops active in 1500

The concentration was further strengthened by changes within the sector: the great bookshops and printer-booksellers were increasingly dominant, while the network of specialized traders, the retailers, organized themselves and spread, which was another factor encouraging concentration.

Printing spread fairly rapidly, but unevenly, throughout Central, Eastern and South-eastern Europe in the fifteenth and sixteenth centuries. The construction of territorial states gradually engaging in a process of political modernization was dependent on a religious identity (with the cities of Gnesen/Gniezno in Poland, or Gran/Esztergom in Hungary),[44] but it was also evident in the rise of political capitals, often tantamount to 'residence towns', and the presence of what might be called 'territorial universities': Vienna, Prague and Cracow, even Pressburg/Bratislava.[45] These were all centres where university, religious and political institutions provided work for the presses, even if permanent establishments were still a thing of the future. To the south, Italy was the first intermediary for the Illyrian coasts and beyond, but the Ottoman advance, marked by the fall of Constantinople (1453), introduced a barrier across Central and South-eastern Europe that lasted for centuries. Buda was without a printing press, except sporadically from 1473, and the new technology was only established in Vienna on a long-term basis in 1482, with Stefan Koblinger. The position of Vienna seemed to deteriorate around 1500, while the collapse of the kingdom of Hungary after the Battle of Mohács (1526) reduced the Habsburg capital to a frontier town. In 1529, the Turks were before Vienna, in 1532 before Graz...

The Adriatic was a Venetian lake and it was to Venice that many prelates turned to commission books and to which printers came to learn their craft. Erhardt Ratdolt, who published the Zagreb *Breviary* in 1484 for Bishop Osvát,[46] had already printed the *Breviary* of Esztergom, in 1480. In Dalmatia printing was at first only intermittent, with workshops associated with the Church: the first known was in Kosinje, in 1471, but the most important was the workshop of Zengg/Senj in 1494. Nevertheless, these were all sporadic attempts, considerably impeded by the difficulty of procuring the hardware, that is, the typographic fonts for Slav – the Glagolitic fonts were designed and engraved in Venice. The first book printed was the *Glagolitic Missal* of Blać Baromic and his partners, in Zengg in 1494.[47] When Prince Ivan Crnojević, a former ally of Skanderbeg against Venice, settled in Cetinje, near Lake Scutari, a first principality of Montenegro (Crna Gora) began to emerge, to which the metropolitan seat was also transferred.[48] Tradition has it that Crnojević sent the monk Makarios to Venice to learn about printing and to procure fonts. Georg, son of Ivan, who had married into a family from the Venetian patriciate, had a Glagolitic missal printed in Venice in 1494, perhaps a second missal the same year and a psalter in 1495. However, in 1496, he had to abandon Montenegro and take refuge in Venice. Early in the sixteenth century, around 1508–10, Makarios reached Wallachia, where he worked under the protection of the war lord Barraba, and from here Slavonic and later Greek books were distributed throughout the Balkans. If we except the workshops established in the Jewish and Armenian communities of the Ottoman towns, printing reappeared only gradually in the zones on the western

Figure 7.1 The *Histories* of Herodotus, in the Latin translation of Laurent Valla, published in 1494 in Venice by Johannes and Gregorius de Gregoriis, of Forlivio. The page layout is that of the Italian Renaissance, with a magnificent border on a black background. Beginning the volume is a xylographed illustration: a servant crowns the author as he writes (note the depiction of the *studiolo*). National Széchényi Library, Budapest.

frontier – Carniola, Croatia and some of the Slav countries of the south as far as Belgrade (1552),[49] and also in Transylvania (in 1529 at Hermannstadt/Sibiu).[50]

The spread of the typographic technology was effectively a non-event in the Ottoman Empire: the book par excellence was the Koran and its language, Arabic, was a sacred language, which disallowed any mechanical method of reproduction, while the powerful guilds of copyists and illuminators opposed the spread of a technology that might represent competition.[51] It was non-Muslim minorities, accordingly, and primarily the Jews, who were usually responsible for the introduction of printing with movable characters in the eastern Mediterranean. Almost until the end of the eighteenth century, all printed production in Greek came from Western presses, in the first place from Venice for 'scholarly' items and for a certain type of 'popular' publication,[52] from the borders of Russia (Vilnius and Leontopolis/Lemberg), in the second half of the sixteenth century, and then from Vienna,[53] and even Budapest. Further East, if we except Constantinople, the first presses rolled in 1563 at Safed (Zefat), near St John of Acre, in the workshop of the Ashkenazi brothers.

In the East, printing was primarily an affair of the Church and of government, in a region that was peripheral in relation to the heartland of the invention and also generally less open to a civilization of the book. The law of demand was more important than the law of the market. The role of government was still pivotal when Peter the Great decided to open the Russian Empire to the West, founding his capital of St Petersburg and organizing, round the Imperial Academy, the dissemination and then production of printed material in Russia. Conversely, even if, for the Church, printing was primarily seen as a means of evangelizing the New World, market forces very quickly played a determining role in the new European colonies: printing was established in Mexico in the decade after 1530, there was a paper manufactory in Mexico c.1580 and the second 'printing town' of the Americas was Lima, in 1584. The dominance of market forces was even more marked in the English colonies of North America.

Conjunctures and Specializations: The Market and Innovation

The geography of production

The geographical distribution of the workshops only partially coincided with that of printed production, measured by number of titles.

Division into chronological bands brings out the dominance of the two main centres of production, Italy and Germany, but it also reveals competition from new regions, the most dynamic of which was France.[54] And although Italian production was still dominant, its lead was reduced, falling from 46 per cent of the total before 1482 to 34 per cent after that. The dynamics, too, were less favourable: the growth rate in Italy at this same period was 263 per cent, as against 321 per cent in Germany and 454 per cent in the Low Countries. While Germany was close to retaining its earlier relative position, the shift was clearly in favour of France, where production rose from 7 to 19 per cent of the total, that is, a growth rate of over 900 per cent. Though the actual figures are far smaller (352 titles published after 1480), Great Britain, too, was characterized by rapid development, production increasing almost eightfold. The third most dynamic region was Spain, where production grew more than tenfold: from 83 titles before 1481 (1.4 per cent) to 867 between 1481 and 1500 (4 per cent of the total).

These figures reveal a phenomenon of great significance: not only was printing experiencing a notably dynamic phase in the fifteenth century, with a constantly accelerating output, but the years between 1480 and 1500 saw a shift in the geography of the book trade and the emergence of more autonomous national markets. The reasons for this were of two main types. First, the increase in the number of titles and the opening up of the market was dependent on distribution within narrower geographical areas: as competition increased, efforts were made to produce locally to avoid slow, risky and always expensive journeys. The reduction in the average price of books strengthened this trend, making the extra costs proportionally heavier. The German practice of the 'barter bookshop' (*Tauschhandel*) was a response to these imperatives: booksellers (we would today speak of publishers) engaged in reciprocal exchanges of some of their titles; this, at the level of the geography of the book, assumed a combination of dispersed producers and the existence of a venue for meetings and trade – this was the fair, where they could meet in principle twice a year, either in Frankfurt or, increasingly, in Leipzig. In sum, it was competition and market equilibrium over time that lay behind the increasing 'nationalization' of the geography of the new media.

Surprisingly, we have no statistics for the numbers of books printed by content so we are reduced to a few snapshots. I will confine myself here to two types, Books of Hours and law books. The former were small volumes, often in quarto, on vellum or on paper and illustrated with series of woodcuts. Though Roman Books of Hours were first produced by Jenson in Venice (1474) – this may be a case of a transfer

Table 7.4 Evolution of printed production by major regions (number of titles)

	Total	Germany	Italy	France	Low Countries	Others
<1481	5,869	2,049	2,693	431	377	319
%	100	35	46	7	6	5
1481–1500	20,567	6,585	7,075	3,911	1,711	1,285
%	100	32	34	19	8	6
Growth rate	350	321	263	907	454	403

between France and Italy – the specialized Parisian workshops soon became dominant. In 1494, of twenty-six editions, eleven were from Paris, where workshops like that of Philippe Pigouchet were very active in this sector. Among other centres of production were northern France and a number of towns in North-west Europe, corresponding to the old distribution of the *devotio moderna* – Leiden and Antwerp, Westminster, etc., which is hardly surprising when we remember that Books of Hours represented an appropriation by the laity of a certain type of religious reading. The concentration of their production, like that of missals, was encouraged by the fact that their purchasers chose the workshops with the best equipment (the woodblocks!), hence those best able to provide a particularly elegant type of book. It was a workshop in Troyes which published, in 1494, the *Heures à l'usage d'Autun*, while those of the diocese of Angers were the work, in the years 1488–90, of Bouyer and Bellescullée in Poitiers.[55] The Hours remained a speciality of the bookshops of Paris and Rouen in the sixteenth century: of 1,585 editions known for the years 1480–1599, 1,400 came from the Parisian presses and, in 1545, a certain Guillaume Godard, printer bookseller between 1510 and 1553, had some 150,000 copies of Hours in his shop.[56]

Another sector of the book trade in which the 'classics' of late medieval libraries featured strongly was law,[57] and, as the example of Fust and Schoeffer reveals, this was one of the very first areas to which printers turned to broaden an output initially almost exclusively dominated by religious books:

The main features of legal book production, which persisted for more than a century, were…very pronounced from the start. On the one hand, canon law benefited from larger print runs, and hence a potentially wider distribution, than Roman law. On the other, texts…from before the fifteenth century seem to have been printed in larger numbers than contemporary texts. Italian production, with Venice in the lead,

Table 7.5 Editions of Books of Hours (number of titles)

<1476	1476–80	1481–85	1486–90	1491–95	1496–1500
8	16	26	77	108	177
100	200	325	963	1,350	2,212

Source: ISTC. The second line shows the growth index of each chronological band in relation to the period before 1476.

was overwhelmingly predominant, followed by Germany and, well behind, France.[58]

Measured by number of titles, the legal sector accounted for between 7 and 8 per cent of production of incunabula, but in terms of volume of work and commercial value it was much more important, given that these were big works at the material level. Nevertheless, the sector was too specialized to support a sustained expansion: the production of legal texts accelerated between 1460 and 1500, but at a slightly lower rate than that of scholarly Latin books (+57 per cent as against +103 per cent). One edition followed another, each of them, given the length of the texts to be published, representing a heavy investment. Nevertheless, there was increasing competition in this area, too. One single year, 1476, saw the publication of no fewer than three editions of the Decretals of Boniface VIII, four of the *Clementines* and six of the *Institutes*! Saturation threatened and there was a shift of emphasis from the basic texts to more contemporary juridical treatises, then to other areas. Production of the classics of canon law was dominated by German centres and, in the case of Roman law and more recent treatises, by Italy. Study of the surviving copies shows that the principal market was provided by Germany, which absorbed a large part of the Italian production, whereas Italy remained relatively impermeable to anything published elsewhere. The concentration of legal production increased even further in Venice at the end of the fifteenth century; its main rival was Lyon, where the printers were also searching for niche markets that would enable them to expand their businesses in spite of Parisian competition, and where they benefited from the growth of the educated French market around 1500.

The example of law illustrates once again how market dynamics was the main factor explaining innovation and its adjustments within a European zone structured by competition. Pierre Aquilon's study of the editions of the *Works* of Gerson demonstrates this well: of the 150 surviving copies of the first edition (Cologne, 1483–4), most are found in the German-speaking countries. A total of 321 copies of the second edition, published in Strasbourg (1488), survive, again in Germany, but also in Spain, Poland and above all Italy. The next edition was published in Basel (1489); 212 copies survive, innovatory in the use of characters with a smaller body, hence a reduction in the sale price. Next came an edition published in Nuremberg (1489), of which 208 copies survive, most of them in the southern countries. Last was an edition produced in Strasbourg (1494), of which we have 362 copies; it was modelled on the Basel edition and distributed in peripheral zones, England, Austria, Hungary and Poland, but also Switzerland. Innovation can be observed, both in the content of the texts and in the material form given to them, as well as in the organization of a more or less geographically oriented distribution.

The vernacular

The tendency to segment into large markets was reinforced by the increase in the number of books published in the vernacular, a sector inaugurated by translations of the Bible. Though we should not forget that the volume of production differed significantly from one zone to another, for example from Italy to Great Britain, the distribution by languages was proportionately fairly similar in the three principal European markets: Italy, Germany and France between them accounted for 86 per cent of production measured in numbers of titles and the proportion in Latin was in each case between 72 and 75 per cent. Conversely, the vernacular dominated in the smaller markets of Portugal, Spain, Bohemia and Great Britain.[59] This is easily explained: the printers in these areas, who were both marginal in relation to the epicentre of the Rhineland and dependent as regards book production, lacked the means to compete with the great German, Venetian or Parisian printing houses in the case of publications in Latin, such as the Bible, patristic texts, legal collections, etc. Conversely, the market in the vernacular was of little interest to the great entrepreneurs if it involved an external geo-linguistic space. Florence, which was one of the ten largest European printing towns in 1500, was a special case. Here, the distribution of printing by language was reversed as compared with all the other centres, that is, about 78 per cent was in Italian, 20 per cent in Latin and the rest in Greek. This unique situation may be attributed to a political setting inclined, with the Medici, towards humanism and modernity and based on a close relationship between the prince and the educated elites.[60]

Bohemia was another special case: at the level of book culture, the kingdom was heir to a prestigious tradition but the troubles

Figure 7.2 The production of small and beautifully illustrated Books of Hours was a speciality of Parisian printers and booksellers in the late fifteenth and early sixteenth centuries. Shown here are the *Hours for the Use of Rome*, printed by Philippe Pigouchet for Simon Vostre in 1498. The central engraving (the *Adoration of the Shepherds*) still has an architectural frame of Gothic inspiration (note the French captions), the margins are decorated by combinations of small woodblocks, sometimes with a phylactery (the Delphic Sybil in the lower right-hand corner), the impression was done on vellum and the painted decoration is manuscript. Municipal Library of Valenciennes.

Table 7.6 Production of incunabula (number of editions)

	Italy	Germany	France	Low Countries	Bohemia	Total
Vernacular	2,321	2,380	1,321	538	33	5693
Latin etc.	7,930	6,623	3,516	1,535	5	19,609
Total	10,251	9,003	4,837	2,073	38	26,202

Source: ISTC.

associated with the Hussite movement had a twofold impact. Bohemia was in ruins, but Czech literature was based on and essentially linked to writing in the vernacular. Printing appeared first in Pilsen, in the reign of the Utraquist king, George of Podebrady (1458–71), with the eponymous workshop of the *Chronika Tranjanska* (*Chronicle of Troy*) of Guido de Colonna.[61] The first presses appeared in Prague in 1487, with the printer Jonata Vikohevo, and two other printing centres existed, in Winterberg/Vimperk (1484) and Kuttenberg/Kutná Hora (1489). Of the thirty-eight incunabula known for Bohemia, thirty-three are in the Czech language. This high ratio is characteristic of a limited market but it is also a sign of the high level of literacy in the Czech countryside and of the role of books in the vernacular in promoting a collective identity. We may cite in particular the superb Kuttenberg Bible (1499), an edition of the Bible in Czech with xylographed illustrations.

Yet another special case was that of the old Low Countries, deeply permeated by written civilization, where printing probably appeared, with xylotypy, even before Gutenberg. Printing in the vernacular (in Flemish) reached a level close to that of the other main regions (*c.*25 per cent of titles) but the nature of the output, which included many items of relatively low value, such as calendars, Donatus, manuals of piety, etc., probably meant a poor survival rate, so the proportion in the vernacular may be an underestimate. Analysis of the figures for the different printing towns reveals a regional specialization: the south (Alost, Brussels, Louvain etc.) was oriented towards editions of the classics in Latin whereas, in the north (Antwerp, Delft, Gouda, etc.), the vernacular was more important. With the great centres we are closer to the international bookselling model: in Deventer, the main regional centre, 7 per cent of books printed were in the vernacular (forty-four out of 580 titles) and in Louvain, the second largest centre, it was less than 8 per cent (twenty-one out of 243 titles). We have already noted the role of this area – between Cologne

Figure 7.3 A very rare example of a printed incunabulum in glagolitic, this missal was printed in red and black at Zengg (Croatia) in 1494. The canon Blać Baromić oversaw the printing, for which the special fonts had been ordered from Venice. National Széchényi Library, Budapest.

and the North Sea – in the transfer of the technology to England, and many titles in English were produced in Bruges and even more in Antwerp. Once established in Westminster, Caxton made the fact that he published in English a marketing tool he could skilfully exploit. It was he, for example, who took the initiative in getting a Latin epitaph composed and placed on Chaucer's tomb in Westminster Abbey, not far from his own shop. He then, in 1477, published the first edition of the *Canterbury Tales* with, the year after, the edition of Boethius translated by Chaucer.

Of the main areas of production, we may note Germany's advance in output in the vernacular. German had already been very present as a written language in the age of the manuscript and the proportion of books in German in relation to total production before 1481 came close to 22 per cent, compared with 16 per cent in Italy and France. The modernity of the market was probably a factor, but also the

Table 7.7 Production of incunabula: number of editions before 1481

	Italy	Germany	France	Low Countries	Bohemia	Total
Vernacular	433	448	70	74	4	1,029
Latin etc.	2,260	1,601	361	303	3	4,528
Total	2,693	2,049	431	377	7	5,557

Source: ISTC.

Table 7.8 Production of incunabula (number of editions), 1481–1500

	Italy	Germany	France	Low Countries	Bohemia	Total
Vernacular	1,888	1,932	1,251	464	29	5,564
Latin etc.	5,670	5,022	3,155	1,232	2	15,081
Total	7,558	6,954	4,406	1,696	31	20,645

Source: ISTC.

density of the printing towns, which increased the proportional importance of the local and regional market. With 20 per cent of titles in the vernacular, the Low Countries was in an intermediate position, but with a significantly lower level of production.

A similar calculation for the two decades 1481–1500 gives very different results: German production in the vernacular has once again increased, reaching nearly 28 per cent, a proportion still slightly higher than that of Italy (25 per cent). France, however, has made spectacular progress, with over 28 per cent for the vernacular over the whole period, over 30 per cent in the years 1486–90. Paradoxically, this may relate to the extreme concentration of printing houses in Paris and Lyon, that is, in two very large cities where the number of lay readers was proportionately much greater. We should take account also of a language policy which promoted French as the language of culture and administration, formalized by the legislative measures taken in the first half of the sixteenth century (Ordinance of Villers-Cotterêts).

Translations and translators

The integration of book production and distribution was initially made possible by the existence of an international written language, Latin. Though its exclusivity may have been diminishing, three-quarters of printed book production in the fifteenth century was still in Latin. However, as the different vernacular languages acquired a new importance, this changed. One of the ways in which a form of integration was restored was through a significant increase in the number of translations. A simple sounding in the *ISTC* produces a corpus of 1,198 titles published in a language other than the original (less than 5 per cent of the total number of titles). At first sight the situation is not what one might expect, as the proportion of translations in relation to total production decreased after 1480 (from 5.2 to 4 per cent); this is because about half the corpus (567 titles) consisted of translations into Latin either of 'scholarly' works (from Greek into Latin) or, on the contrary, of works originally published in the vernacular, which it was hoped would be made accessible to a wider readership thanks to Latin. The other, slightly smaller, half of the corpus, a total of 538 titles, was mainly made up of translations into the various vernacular languages. Circumstances favoured this latter sector, as its share of the corpus of translations rose from 40 to 52 per cent between one period and the next; contingency calculation confirms the over-representation of Latin in the first period and that of the modern languages in the second.

The situation with regard to the modern languages is revealing: up to 1481 German dominated (fifty-one translations into German of a total of 121). After that, things changed: the number of translations into German may almost have doubled (+ 198 per cent) but the increase was 262 per cent in the case of Italian, and there was a fivefold increase in translations into French. In fact the first language of translation in these two decades was French, with 112 titles, compared with 101 for German and ninety-seven for Italian. The Spanish market was also rapidly expanding, though more slowly: there were no translations into Spanish before 1481 and forty-six after, but we need also to take account of translations into Catalan, of which there were three before 1481 and twenty-one after; for the peninsula as a whole (without Portugal), this amounts to sixty-seven translations into the vernacular – equivalent to two thirds of the Italian figure. If we add the forty translations into English recorded for the period, what stands out most is the growth of increasingly dynamic secondary markets as compared to Germany and Italy, with France and Spain leading the field.

In fact translation took several very different forms. As well as scholarly translation, primarily from Greek into Latin, there was translation into Latin of works it was hoped might enlarge their potential readership by this means; and yet a third form, an opposite process of translation into the vernacular of works it was hoped would sell more widely within a given linguistic space. The example of the *Narrenschiff* (*The Ship of Fools*) of Sebastian Brant combines these three types: it was first published in German, then very quickly

Table 7.9 Number of translations printed in the fifteenth century (number of titles)

	<1481	1481–1500	Total
Total translations	304	831	1,135
Into Latin	183	400	583
Other languages	121	431	552
Total production	5,869	19,965	

Source: ISTC.[62]

translated into Latin and finally into a number of other vernacular languages. The author himself emphasized the exceptional nature of this process:

> I recently described the fools in a poem in the vernacular,/ This work of mine enjoyed great success./
> When we made the ship of the Narragonians [the fools],/
> We did it in a German parlance,/ A strange thing to the scholars...[63]

The translator, Jakob Locher 'Philomusus', listed all the various peoples who might get to know the text thanks to Latin, while also relating Brant's original choice to the desire to give German as a written language a status comparable to that of Italian and so introduce the muses and humanism to the banks of the Rhine:

> By this choice of writing, our most amiable master Sebastian Brant, doctor of law and poet of the first order, spread it among a large number of persons, for the common good of humanity, by using the vernacular language, having copied the Florentine Dante and French Petrarch, those heroic poets, who composed admirable poems in their Etruscan language. But as the *Narragonia*, or the *Ship of fools* (which we may justly describe as a satire) is necessary to all peoples, I regard it as worthwhile for me to transpose it into a poem in Latin, so that it will be useful to all the nations who have no knowledge of our language. These are the Gauls, the Ausonians,[64] the Iberians, the Pannonians, and lastly the Greeks who cannot read and reread this type of poem without difficulty...

The *Ship of Fools* was retranslated from Latin into other modern languages, French, English and Flemish. Let us leave aside the problem of the transition from one version to another – the translation was not always faithful, there were some adjustments of the text and the illustrations – to emphasize another point: the increasing importance of national markets inevitably structured round a community of

Figure 7.4 The *Letters* (*Epistolae*) of Marsilius Ficinus, printed in Venice in 1495, is a model example of the Italian Renaissance, with a first page within a spectacular archaizing engraved border. The work is dedicated to Giuliano de Medici. Municipal Library of Tours.

language was a factor clearly favouring the market in translation in itself. We observe the appearance of a new type of professional grouping specializing in this field. It is illustrated in Lyon by the Augustinian Julien Macho, but we may also cite Jakob Locher in Basel, Heinrich Steinhöwel in Ulm and Guillaume Tardif, reader to Charles VIII of France. This further complicated the typology of the authorial function, as well as the definition of the text itself, inasmuch as the work of the translator was also original and as the translation was often accompanied by some rewriting, which might or might not always be faithful to the original text. For the translator, it also meant assuming a place in the community of the educated that was structured round the media, and the relationship between original and translation was sometimes distorted as a result. So it was the community established round the printed work which made the latter agent of its own legitimacy.

The geography of translation is also significant. A survey of the translations of *Aesop* (fifty-three editions) highlights the role of a few major centres: Augsburg, where the printers took care to distinguish themselves from their Nuremberg neighbours by exploring new directions, followed a path similar to that taken by Lyon, a town which had to face competition from Paris and even Italy. Venice was in the second rank of centres of production. Then, in both Germany and Italy, there were a number of towns with workshops that produced one or sometimes several editions of Aesop in Italian: Milan, but also Brescia, Bologna, Florence, Verona, Naples and others, and in Germany Magdeburg, Basel, Strasbourg and Cologne. Lastly, there were the subordinate markets, which naturally turned to translating the principal classics into the vernacular: England, with Westminster and London, and the old Low Countries, with Antwerp and Delft, but also Bohemia (Prague) and Spain (Zaragoza, Burgos and Seville).

The role of a minority: the Jews

Printing in Hebrew, lastly, had its own specific geography, primarily correlated, as one would expect, with that of the Jewish communities. The first problem it faced was that of the fonts: to print in Hebrew meant having access to specialized equipment, hence a large enough market to justify the investment in it. In Mantua, Avraham ben Šelomoh Conat worked alone, possibly from 1474,[65] on a *Josipon* (*History of the Jews*) in quarto, then on a work of rhetoric.[66] There was printing in Hebrew in 1475 in Reggio Calabria, almost certainly also in Rome, while Conat associated with Avraham Yedidyah ha-Ezrahi, of Cologne, on the *Perouch ha-Torah*, commenting on the

Figure 7.5 *The Ship of Fools*, written by the Strasbourg physician Sebastian Brant, was one of the first success stories of the book trade: first published in German (*das Narrenschiff*) in Basel, it was next translated into Latin (*Stultifera navis*) and French, then into other vernacular languages. It consisted of a collection of short moral pieces describing the human condition, each illustrated by a xylograph. The series begins with the celebrated 'Bibliomaniac', the fool who collected books that he never did anything but dust: 'I open the dance of fools/Because all around me/I accumulate the books/That I do not understand/And that I never read'. The proliferation of books thanks to printing posed in new terms the question of the justification of reading, hence also the question of censorship.

Pentateuch (1475–6) and on several other titles. The *Psalms* came out in Bologna in 1477,[67] and printing in Hebrew was introduced into Naples by two emigrants from southern Germany, Joseph ben Jacob Ashkenazi and his son Azriel Gunzenhauser.[68] Their most notable product was an edition of the *Psalms* (1487), with a text revised by Jacob Landau, probably an emigrant from that town. There was then a flourishing trade between Naples and Spain. According to Moshe Catane, there was printing in Hebrew in Montalban (near Téruel), at very much the same time as in Italy, while the first Portuguese-printed output emerged from Hebraic workshops: at Faro (1487), then Lisbon (1489), with a commentary on the *Pentateuch*; the press was established in the house of the scholar Eliezer Toledano.[69] The expulsion of the Jews from Spain in 1492 brought a particularly brilliant chapter in the history of Hebraic printing to an abrupt end.

But the earliest centre of production was a small town in northern Italy and it was Ashkenazy from the Rhineland who played the principal role. A certain Moses is known to have been in Speyer and his son, also named Moses, was in Fürth in the mid-fifteenth century. The expulsion of the Jews from Bavaria (1455) may have driven him to seek refuge in Italy. His grandson, the physician and rabbi Israel Nathan ben Samuel, was the first to have engaged in printing. He was forced to leave Speyer around 1480 for Lombardy, where the Sforza encouraged the new arrivals to settle in Soncino, north of Piacenza (1483).[70] The Soncino (the Jews, as is well known, adopted toponyms as surnames) printed a variety of small texts: *Choice of Pearls* (1484), *Examination of the World* (1484), *Sentences of the Fathers* (*c*.1484) and, most notably, *Former Prophets* (1485) and *Later Prophets* (1486), before, in 1488, a complete Hebrew *Bible*. They were also the first to introduce vocalized characters into typography. In 1490–1, faced once again with growing tensions, the Soncino left their new home to settle as printers throughout the Mediterranean basin, successively in Brescia (1491), Pesaro and Naples (where they printed a folio Hebrew *Bible* around 1492), but also Salonika and Constantinople. Gerson Soncino, whose activities in Brescia mark the apogee of the dynasty, signed a *Pentateuch* with the formula 'Gershom, son of the scholar Rabbi Moses of Soncino, whose German surname is Mentzlan Schonzin' (1492): if *Schonzin* comes from the toponym Soncino, *Mentzlan* may be related to Mainz/ Mainzer and allude to the place where the family had done its apprenticeship in the typographic technology.[71] The same printing shop published a new *Hebraic Bible* in 1494.[72]

The Hebrew printing houses were all in touch with each other, at different levels: Haebler suggests that the printer Abraham ben Chajim, in Ferrara and then Bologna from 1477 to 1482, collaborated in the early days of the Soncino business. Ben Chajim himself came from a family of dyers (*tintori*) of Pesaro.[73] Itinerant correctors also worked in these different print shops, like Josef Chajim ben Aaron of Strasbourg, in Bologna in 1482. His brother, Gabriel ben Aaron, was in Soncino in 1484. In short, community was a major factor here, based primarily on confessional networks but also on solid and very active mercantile, familial and professional (apprenticeship) networks. The production of these various printing houses was primarily intended for the Jews themselves. After 1492, Hebraic printing also developed, on the model of the polyglot editions, in the centres of Western humanism in Italy and the Rhine Valley. It was through scholars in Rome and the Rhine Valley (Basel) that Reuchlin learned the language and philological critique of Hebrew; the role of the 'Reuchlin affair' in the early days of scholarly publishing in Hebrew in the West is well known.

This brief survey of the geography of the presses in the incunabulist age allows us to emphasize three main points.

First, at the end of the fifteenth century, some seventy-five European towns had a printing house. The geographical distribution of the presses then changed in response to two contradictory phenomena. At first the networks continued to expand, ever more widely, and the number of towns with one or more typographic workshops further increased. Within a generation, however, there was a trend for increasing concentration and the most important centres began to monopolize the activity. They constituted a sort of oligarchy dominating the sector and formed a network through the intermediary of the fair towns – chief of which in the sixteenth century was Frankfurt. The book trade had become a financially profitable business, its affairs were increasingly structured and, at the same time, the printing and bookselling business came to be dominated by veritable entrepreneurs, like Peter Schoeffer of Mainz, the Parisian Jean Petit and Anton Koberger of Nuremberg.

Second, we see in operation, through the prism of the typographic geography, the integration/differentiation pair round which the geography of modern Europe developed. This was not something set in stone, but a shifting reality, a space that was constructed and deconstructed from one period to the next, depending on circumstances, such as the supply–demand relationship or certain particularly significant events (wars, the sack of Rome in 1527, even the collapse of a kingdom in the process of rapid modernization, like Hungary after Mohàcs). It is possible to focus on the distribution of the presses because it is on this area that scholars have access to the most complete serial sources, but it can only be understood in conjunction with the other activities constitutive of the economy of the book: the geography of the workforce and of distribution, and networks of financing and payment.

Lastly, a crude typology of the printing towns and regions suggests a distinction between three principal groups.

The first is that of the multipolar spaces, chief among them Germany, where printing took place in a dense network of towns, some of which, like Nuremberg, Cologne and Leipzig, overshadowed the rest. The pattern was similar in northern Italy as far south as Tuscany, a region thickly scattered with printing towns, though with a very marked imbalance in favour of Venice. This pattern, in which the book business was decentralized and direction came from the fair towns, was most likely to escape political categories (as was decisively shown in Leipzig in 1767),[74] and to articulate with the economic and above all commercial geography. By contrast, we also observe a phenomenon of 'paradoxical openness', where the ease of circulation and the proximity of great urban centres prevented the development of the book trade in regions otherwise highly favourable. This was the case in northern France, where the only printing workshop in the fifteenth century was that of Jehan of Liège in Valenciennes, which was itself short-lived. Similarly, it has been suggested by Albert Labarre that the proximity of Paris, Rouen and the Low Countries explains the delay in the spread of presses in Picardy: there were no workshops permanently established in Amiens until 1609, in Beauvais before 1615 and in Saint-Quentin before 1627, and they were even later to appear in Laon, Soissons, Noyon and Abbeville (even though the latter had a workshop at a very early date).

The second group consists of the spaces dominated by a very small number of centres, even a single main centre, where the activity was most highly developed. The best example is France, though we might also quote England. Here the coincidence between the geography of the book and the political geography is clearest, while the centralizing tendency linked political and cultural categories increasingly closely: Frances I pursued a systematic policy of adding lustre to the monarchy through 'letters' from 1515. Conversely, the dialectic of centre and periphery operated everywhere in these areas; concentration increasingly favoured the towns which performed the superior functions of direction and representation, even though the process by which some areas became printing 'deserts' was, as Jean-Dominique Mellot has shown, much longer and more complex.[75]

The third group was that of those spaces more peripheral in relation to the Europe of printing. The technology spread in circles around the epicentre of the Rhine Valley, by means of a group of more active and more innovatory intermediaries. England was still for many generations a subordinate region which imported most of its books from the continent and where printers specialized in the production of vernacular literature. The situation was in some ways similar in Eastern Europe, which was very slow to catch up, as a consequence of the weakness of the political powers or, as in Hungary, of external events like the Ottoman invasion and the collapse of the kingdom. We might also quote the example of the Scandinavian countries.

In studying the geography of the presses, we remain at the level of hardware, which is the most obvious, but, as might be expected, it is at the level of software that the process of distancing and domination was most effective. It was extremely difficult to make up for a cumulative backwardness with regard to the new media. It was generally accompanied by a certain backwardness not only in the circulation of ideas but in the spheres of social and political modernization. In short, it was in principle a process of dis-equilibrium and domination to the benefit of the groups most advanced in the control and exploitation of the media – a process that resembles what I have suggested calling a form of 'communicational imperialism',[76] and which, in the early years of the twenty-first century, recent developments have shown to be one of the major factors in geo-political analyses. We encounter the problem of those who are 'poor' in education and information and who, as is well known, are present not only on the periphery but also, and with increasing visibility, at the heart of the most modern and most advanced countries.

8

The Nature of Text

∾

Now, all disciplines have been restored, languages revived...elegant and correct printed editions are available, the result of a divinely inspired invention of my time...the whole world is full of learned men, fine teachers, ample libraries...

Rabelais

Gutenberg and the first printers offered their readers a product as close as possible to the manuscript. The character used for the *42-line Bible* was based on textura and the page layout was the same as that of a monumental Bible; Gutenberg always tried to print his initial page in two colours (black and red) and the printed work, on leaving the printing workshop, still went next to that of the painters, decorators and rubricators. The continuity was all the clearer in that the most privileged readers still preferred the manuscript: from 1485, Antoine Vérard sometimes printed an edition with variants that might take the form of simple engravings, engravings illuminated by hand or paintings in place of engravings. When, in 1492–3, he published *Les paraboles de maitre Alain* in French, he produced a copy for the king, Charles VIII, in which the initial engraving of the scene of representation was not printed, but replaced by a sumptuous illumination.[1]

Soon, however, the dynamic of innovation radically changed the form of the object, for several interconnected reasons. The first two involved the producers. Under the pressure of competition the printers paid more attention to management issues. Their desire to contain expenses and reduce the cost price, hence sale price, gradually resulted in a standardization of the printed object, which further distanced it from the manuscript: limiting or even dispensing with the use of colours and manuscript additions, simplifying the typography, abandoning most of the abbreviations and ligatures, etc. On the other hand, in a competitive field, every printer tried to individualize his product and make it more attractive. This led to the appearance of the title page, which had not existed in the world of the manuscript, and which could be a showcase for promotional features such as the spectacular character of the font used or the 'mark' of the bookshop or printer. The desire for traceability on the part of the producer soon combined with the interests of authorities becoming more alert to the problems posed by the rapid increase in printed production; for them, the identification of those responsible for a publication – the printer and the bookseller, even the author – was an aid to control and, if necessary, prosecution. Lastly, we should not forget that research on the technology continued, and that this too could be a way of distinguishing between printers, for example for those who first succeeded in mastering the complex field of musical printing.[2]

Innovation was soon also prompted by the needs of the users, the buyers and the readers. Printed works were freely available, and this in itself led to the emergence of new practices in the spheres of storage, reading and consultation. As a result we see the emergence and spread of new features that served as navigational aids: foliation, then pagination, and the various systems of classification and indexing. The booksellers were quick to see the advantage of innovating in this area by offering purchasers the product best suited to whatever use they might intend. Title pages highlighted the advantages of this or that edition, for example the fact that it was new, better than its predecessor, contained additions, notes, an index, illustrations, etc. Reference to the author or, as appropriate, to secondary authors, commentators or translators served a similar purpose. In short, with printing, the book became a commodity, but this made it an object that was reactive between the world of the producers and that of the users. The product, as product, was a site of innovation, because it was the place where both the constraints and the dynamics driving the world of the producers encountered the world of the 'consumers', the readers. It was the operation of the market, combining product and demand, which ensured the articulation between 'commodity' and 'ferment' (or force for change) – not yet fully constructed by Febvre and Martin in their *L'Apparition du livre* (*The Coming of the Book*).

The Book System

Text space, book space, reading space

Without revisiting communication theory, it will be helpful to distinguish the most useful conceptual constructions available for the analysis of the printed object as support for the text. The *mise en page* or page layout designates the repetitive elements organizing the page of the volume: on the blank surface, the organization of the block or blocks of text, the presence or not of more or less developed elements forming the 'skeleton', any decoration, the illustrations and so on. We should note that, for the user (the reader) of a book in quires (a codex), the page layout was not constructed page by page, but in blocks of two pages visible at the same time (for a Western book, a verso on the left, a recto on the right). It was in this context that those who laid out the *Chronicle of Nuremberg* (1493) took care to ensure there was always a balance between text and illustration. This is particularly striking in the case of the view of Strasbourg at folios 139v–140r, of which it occupies the lower half, with the spire of the cathedral rising in the centre, in the inner margin of the text. The page layout might vary, of course, according to the type of page and its position in the volume: standard page of text, initial page, introductory page, title page, index, tables, etc. The arrangement chosen indicated the nature of the text presented: the concept of the *mise en page* was articulated with those of the *mise en livre* and the *mise en texte*, that is, the organization of the book and the structuring of the text, to construct an organized whole, the 'book system'.

The construction of the page layout continued at the level of the book, whether it comprised one or several volumes. The book functioned as a system of signs, in which the discursive signs, though the most visible and probably the most important, were by no means the only ones. We need to consider the format first, but also the choice of typography (character and body) and the internal organization of the text; here too the *mise en livre* was inseparable from the *mise en texte*. In the West, since the semiological revolution whose importance in the twelfth and thirteenth centuries has been emphasized, the theory of the text has the text functioning as a transparent system of signs, which can be used with a certain end in view: to obtain eternal salvation, entertainment and pleasure, knowledge, information, practical know-how or something quite different, and even, as was usually the case, a combination of several of these. The instrumentalization of the text supposes that it was in a sense objectivized: the *mise en texte* refers to the material elements present in the book

Figure 8.1 *The Chronicle of Nuremberg* begins with an index (*Tabula*) of the subjects addressed in the book, here arranged in alphabetical order: note the elegant page layout, in two columns, with a painted initial for each letter (the initial A has not been added) and letters of larger size for the sub-classifications (A, Ad, Af, Ag, etc.). The references are to the different leaves. At the beginning of the index, a few lines of text describe its use. With printing, the book became a machine with an apparatus that facilitated its use: the *Chronicle* shows how human memory was now externalized, the index enabling readers to find the passage they wanted quickly. Municipal Library of Valenciennes.

which define, extend and amplify this construction of the text as a certain text, belonging to a certain category of texts, endowed with certain characteristics and open to a certain type of use, even intended for a certain public.

The nature of the printed book as product meant that the text might also, by the fifteenth century, become a product. To a degree, with the manuscript, it was the book itself, by definition unique, which was where the text was created, and the copyist did not hesitate to adjust it, add to it or modify it more or less radically. With printing, however, and the multiplication of similar copies, the text was no longer the 'snug airtight inside of an interiority' (Jaques Derrida), whether of the author or of the copyist/author, because the latter was not the only person responsible for it (in communication theory, one would speak of the transmitter). Things happened quite differently: in a way, the text was a given, in this new manufactured object, the printed book. Conversely, however, all the actors in the book chain, from the initial investor to the reader at the end, now intervened. They, too, to varying degrees, helped to 'fabricate' the text, which its modern definition would in future place at the point where an uncertain balance was established between the already constructed and reproduced object and the object open to construction through its process of mediation.

Even if we leave aside the question of reading as practice, the construction of the text is also the product of a dialogue between the professionals and the public: the bookseller publishes (the word is significant) what he thinks likely to succeed. Further, some authors will angle their writing with the possibility of success in mind, as illustrated by the example of Rabelais and his *Pantagruel*. A graduate of Montpellier and a famous physician of the Hotel Dieu of Lyon (1532), Rabelais had published several scientific works before he observed, with amazement, the success at the fairs of a small popular volume of his, *Gargantua*. It was primarily for the money that he wrote a sequel, *Pantagruel*, published under a pseudonym by Claude Nourry – a not uninteresting choice given that it was a house specializing in the publication of leaflets and 'romances' for a mass readership.[3]

In the same vein, Rabelais quickly wrote an almanac, then the *Pantagruéline prognostication pour 1533*, before returning to the theme of *Gargantua* (1534). From the *Tiers livre* the text became less 'popular' and the author, writing under his own name, also included his title of 'doctor of medicine'. One might, therefore, risk the hypothesis that the 'popular market' of the historians of literature is at least in part the a posteriori result of project innovation on the part of certain bookseller-editors.[4] This example also suggests, however, that we cannot systematically conclude from the commercial orientation of the publication or even of the writing that a text will be pedestrian.

With the publicity brought by printing, the text too had a history. The example of Rabelais shows not only how the decision to write was made with reference to a certain readership and its expectations, but also how the change in the status of the text and in ways of reading it must be analysed in terms of responses to shifts in this same readership. The printed text was a *trifrons* (three-faced) entity: it enabled the author to represent and to manipulate the world (in Rabelais's case, to earn money); it was a tool of information and of communication, transmitting a certain content to successive readers (making them laugh, but also defending humanist positions); and, lastly, it created another complex of significations, more or less out of sync, resulting from its appropriation by each different reader. McLuhan explained the inevitable participation of the reader in the creation of the text by defining print as a 'hot' media, unlike television, to which the joint presence of images and sound gives a sort of hypnotic charge that makes it a 'cold' media. The analysis may be extended back in time, and the example of Rabelais shows how the use of the medium created a dynamic which also affected what the text, and its author, 'meant': the historical contextualization makes the text a palimpsest and Rabelais, little appreciated, even scorned, in the seventeenth and eighteenth centuries, would in the nineteenth century assume a place in the ranks of the classics of French national, and then world, literature.[5] The historian of the book, who knows that the text does not exist outside the object which is its support, must therefore try to analyse the features and the potentialities of this support.

We will return to the question of reproduction, in other words to the consequences of the multiplication of copies. With printing, the text no longer stood alone, surrounded as it was by an increasing number of extraneous elements, title page, introductory pages, running titles, tables and so on, which together constitute what is called the paratext – which might be more or less unwieldy, complicated, oriented or restrictive.[6] A number of other elements, which are not part of the text, nevertheless added significance to it at the level of discourse or, more often, of representation and symbolism. I have already discussed page layouts and the material form of the object (today, the difference between a quality newspaper and a tabloid is apparent at first glance), with features such as the format, choice of characters and a certain type of illustration more or less present. As a result, by changing form, even support (in the nineteenth and twentieth centuries, a novel would be published first in serial form, then as a printed volume, before being transposed on to a computerized support such as an e-book or digital library like *Gallica*), the text itself, as text, also changed its nature. We need, therefore, to analyse the categories which shaped this process of mediation: the use of the print media was accompanied by the appearance and then generalization of elements of presentation and framing which had not existed in the manuscript and which delivered the text to be read. In the end it could no longer be conceived without a number of component elements that would identify and fix it, even confine it within a particular possible reading. Meanwhile, the relationship between the object and the content remained open; for example, certain printers prioritized the material form over the quality of the content, or vice versa – the same phenomenon may already be observed in the copyists of the first half of the fifteenth century.

Organizing and designating

A number of elements appearing in printed volumes do not fall within the modern construction of the editorial field, but were intended to organize and simplify the task of manufacture: catchwords, signatures and register guided the work of the printer or binder and reveal the attention paid to what I have earlier called organizational innovation.[7] At the end of the quire, the 'reclamans', or catchword, recorded the first word of the following quire at the foot of the page. This made it easier, when the impression was completed, to arrange the quires in the correct order. The earliest known example is that of the *Tacitus* of Wendelin of Speyer, in Venice, around 1470; other examples are found in Italy up to 1480, and also a few in Germany. Manuscript catchwords appear in the *Speculum aureum* of Schoeffer in Mainz in 1474, and Johann Koelhoff in Cologne printed them the following year. Catchwords by leaves were an Italian practice which appeared in the fifteenth century, becoming general during the Reformation; they may also have facilitated reading, especially reading aloud.

The use of 'signatures' served a similar purpose: each quire was identified by a sign taken from a continuous series (very often alphabetic) and written in the lower right-hand margin, the successive pages of the quire being numbered in Roman figures (a^i, a^{ii}, a^{iii}, etc.). The aim was to avoid inverting the quires when the volume was assembled. The geographical distribution of this practice differs from that of catchwords. Pfister was already using manuscript signatures in Bamberg in 1460–1, and he may not have been the first, given that they were written on the outside corner of the leaf, so have often disappeared during rebinding. Johann Koelhoff in Cologne was apparently the first to print the signatures with the rest of the composition (1472), a practice which soon spread in Germany and elsewhere. French printers usually used the letters of the Latin alphabet (except *j*, *v* and *w*), first in lower case, then, if the work was too long, in capital letters; if necessary, they then resorted to combinations of the type *Aa*, then *AA*, *Aaa*, etc. Special signs (*, &, etc.) and vowels with tildes (*ã*, etc.) were used for the introductory or final quires. The list of quires was recapitulated in the 'register' at the end of a volume, primarily intended for the binder: it consisted of a list, arranged in columns, of the first words of each quire, then of each leaf (necessary if they were inserted), leaving a blank line when the quire changed. This practice appeared in Rome in 1469–70, and Gerard de Lisa explains, in the *Tesoro* of Brunetto Latini (Treviso, 1474):

> And know that the first quire [quinternio] has for name a, the second b, the third c, and so on up to the last, which has for name o. You will next find the number of the first leaf, then of the second and of the third, until the middle leaf of each quire...[8]

The register subsequently become the norm, eventually mutating into a working habit, especially in Italy: when Stephan Planck, in Rome, printed Petrus de Abano (*De Venenis*) in 1484, he made provision for a register, which was completely pointless given that there were only three quires to be printed. From 1475, the register was adopted in France and Spain, and then Germany – though it is possible that the German practice was a register on a loose leaf. Registers were particularly common in Nuremberg, but never found in Cologne: these particularisms can sometimes help to identify the possible origin of an otherwise silent impression. Haebler says that the printers of the *42-line* and *36-line* Bibles prepared a *Tabula rubricarum* which, in the majority of cases, has not survived (it indicated to the rubricator the leaves on which he was to work). This practice was still found in the earliest impressions in Strasbourg (with Mentelin) and Basel. In the fifteenth century the printer-booksellers found other ways of indicating the order of the quires and avoiding errors in their assembly. Apart from the signature, each leaf sometimes carried an abbreviated indicator of the work: for example, the letters 'R' or 'Ro' distinguished the *Hours of Rome*, while some printers recorded the number of quires on the title page itself (for example *viii.c.*, for '8 quires'). These practices were primarily useful, of course, if the content was neither foliated nor paginated. Once numbering became general it was less necessary to identify the quires, because the numerical sequence of the pages was, in principle, continuous. Nevertheless, the signature persisted throughout the '*ancien régime* book trade' and into the nineteenth century. These three first elements, catchword, signature and register, were of no concern to the reader of the volume, therefore, but only to the craftsmen who worked on it. This was not the case with the elements described below.

There had been no title page in medieval manuscripts in the West, so it was natural for the first printed works also to be without one. As we have seen, the name of Gutenberg does not appear on any volume, and books, like manuscripts, were referred to by their incipit. That of the *42-line Bible*, printed in red, announces the introductory text (incipit = here begins), in exactly the same way as in the great manuscript Bibles:

> Here begins the Letter of St Jerome to the priest Paul on all the books contained in the Holy Scripture. First chapter.

Most volumes, which were sold unbound, began with a simple blank leaf – hence the common French expression '*livres en blanc*' used to refer to them. Haebler estimated that a third of incunabula are without any specific indication, so the dating and identification of the workshops have to be based on analysis of the internal features of the text (appearance of contemporary persons...), the volume (identification of typographic characters, origin of the paper, etc.) or the exemplar (possible references to provenance). The *Mainz Psalter* (1457) has the first colophon, a brief final formula which, in principle but not invariably, identifies the text and records the date printing finished, the place of impression, the name of the printer or printers and sometimes also the typographic mark. In some cases the colophon also provides information about the circumstances in which the work had been carried out, whether testifying to a sentiment of piety or revealing a desire for publicity. It is in the colophon that, where appropriate, the privilege granted to the printer by the authorities first appears.

This display was systemized with the generalization of the title page.[9] In one edition of Virgil produced in 1500–1 the title page runs to eight lines, is printed in red and black and lists the various pieces comprising the volume (*Bucolics, Georgics, Aeneid, Opuscula*, and so on, with such and such a commentary and additions). The promotional intent is clear in the use of printing in two colours: this involved a first printing in red, cutting out in the frisket only the parts corresponding to the passages to be inked in this colour; the red composition was then replaced by quads, and inked in black. This was a far more complicated and tricky process than monochrome printing and it took significantly more time, if only because the page had to go under the press twice. The wording of the title page also includes phrases designed to 'hook' the customer: the author was 'very learned', the edition was as complete as possible (such and such 'has been added'). The typographic mark is that of Charles Debougnes, bookseller at Angers, with the formula *'Dieu gart le roy et la noble cité d'Angiers et l'université'* ('God preserve the King and the noble city of Angers and the university'). Finally, the address, appearing at the bottom of the page, also in red, states not only that the printer was Thielman Kerver in Paris (a guarantee of the technical quality of the printing), but also that the work was on sale in Angers at the bookshop of Jean Alexandre, *'à la chaussée Saint-Pierre'*.[10] In fact the whole history of the volume is here laid out: the bookseller of Angers, who worked with the university, had collaborated with Parisian colleagues in order to print Virgil's classic. Different title pages were run off for the copies destined for the Angers market and for those to be sold in Paris, in this case in the shops of Jean Petit and Johannes Confluentinus.

From the economy of the media to the organization of the literary sphere

Competition between printer-booksellers appeared at a very early date and its growth prompted specific editorial policies, as we have seen in the case of Fust and Schoeffer. Men like these soon realized the potential advantages of enabling the purchaser to identify their product: to know that a certain book came from a major workshop, such as that of Koberger, was a guarantee of quality and helped to attract potential buyers. The first typographic mark was that of Fust and Schoeffer, who were soon imitated by their peers (by 1483 in France). The majority of marks fall into one of three types: the arms or initials of the craftsman or craftsmen responsible for the edition; a 'canting' image (the galley of Galliot Du Pré); or a picture, probably reproducing the sign of the shop or building ('The savage man' of Pigouchet). The 'Dolphin' adopted by Aldus Manutius of Venice in 1502 (for the edition of the *Poetae christiani veteres*) was a mark recognized by humanists all over Europe. In Paris, from 1507, Josse Bade Ascensius, put as his mark at the beginning of his volumes a drawing of his workshop, in a frame repeating a Renaissance architectural motif (the 'Ascensian press'). The title of the volume and the name of the author were inserted above the image, that of the printer and the place and date of printing below – the press was symbolically placed at the centre of the design, just as the printing house and the bookshop were at the centre of the communication system organized by the Christian humanists of the early sixteenth century. The success of this mark, linked to the quality of Bade's work, made this a trademark guaranteeing the calibre both of the content and the form of the volumes. So powerful were these symbols that they were copied, pirated and even forged, as in the case of Aldus Manutius.

After the title the second main feature of the printed title page was the name of the author. For the majority of medieval manuscripts the author was unknown and, if his name was recorded, it was often by reference to authority (*auctoritas*) and to establish the conformity of a certain text in relation to the consecrated canon of knowledge – Aristotle, the Fathers of the Church, the great scholastic doctors.[11] This pattern was already being modified with Boccaccio and his *Life of Dante*, but more radical change came with printing; the pressure of competition now made it necessary to be distinctive and to publish new texts, as the traditional market gradually became saturated. Added to which, some authors realized that times were changing in their favour. The first of these was Erasmus, who cultivated his status as universally renowned author and spoke directly to a wide audience, in particular through his open letters.[12] The identity of the author was now a sort of complement to that of the text, and the promotional dimension was more overt: the title pages of the late fifteenth and early sixteenth centuries can be read as advertisements, sometimes lengthy, in which the printer-bookseller described everything that was to be found in the volume and, most notably, the identity and the quality of the various persons responsible for the edition.

A couple of examples show how developments in the media caused a major re-ordering of the literary sector. The title page of the edition of the *L'Arbre des batailles* published in Paris in 1493 still records only the contents of the volume ('The Tree of battles newly printed and corrected in Paris'), without any indication of the author, but adding that this edition, which was very recent, provided a carefully corrected text. The use of a xylographed decorated letter (*L*) showed this to be a work of high quality, which was confirmed by the spectacular typographic mark surmounting the name of the printer-bookseller. The near-contemporary example of Sebastian Brant sheds light on the process by which the system of modern mediatization was constructed, showing that the intellectual initiative had in part passed to the 'publisher', but also that the author was emerging as the key figure in the literary sphere as far as readers were concerned.

Brant, former pupil in the school of Sélestat, university student, then professor of law at Basel, was what would today be called a committed intellectual.[13] He frequented the shop of a new arrival, Johann Bergmann, a native of the Cologne region (Olpe) and probably also a former student. It was with him that, in 1494, Brant published his *Ship of Fools* (*das Narrenschiff*), a story in verse on the human condition, which was both satirical and moralizing. This bookseller was not without commercial nous, as he also produced that same year an illustrated edition of the *Letter* in which Christopher Columbus announced his discoveries (*De insulis nuper in Mare Indico repertis*). The *Ship* made Brant a celebrity, a change in status assisted by several factors: he was a master of the university and surrounded by his followers, but he also knew how to use typography for political propaganda ends. The decision to publish in the vernacular, at first sight surprising, enhanced his public persona. Meanwhile, the title page of the German editions of the *Ship* (1494) was different (it was blank) from that of the Latin edition (1497), which gave the name of the author.

The status of the author was in a paradoxical relationship with that of the text. On the one hand, the text was altered from one edition to another, sometimes quite drastically, without the author having given his consent. On the other hand, and conversely, the new consciousness among authors of their work and their dignity emerged when Brant complained about precisely these alterations; it was the book's success that made it vulnerable. Two chapters were added by him to the second Basel edition (1495) to pre-empt potential forgeries which would be to his disadvantage (the counterfeiters lacking access in the short run to the unpublished additions).[14] When Grüninger, in Strasbourg, 'expanded' the original *Ship* from 7,000 to some 11,000 verses in 1494, Brant complained about it in the third Basel edition (1499). The transition from one language to another was accompanied by further modifications: the order of the chapters in the Latin edition was different from that of the German editions, while the intertextuality led to changes in the content, biblical or classical quotations replacing the popular German idioms. The French translations by Pierre Rivière and Jean Drouyn differed substantially from the original and Drouyn's second translation (*La Grant nef des folz du monde*) of 1499 made yet more modifications by comparison with his first, as poetry replaced prose.

The Brant dossier also provides a particularly striking illustration of the new balance of power between bookseller and author. Antoine Vérard, in c.1500–3, published in Paris a text by a friend of Rivière, Jean Bouchet, with the title *Regnards traversans....* [15] Showing a remarkable lack of scruple, the great Parisian bookseller chose to attribute this book to the author of the *Ship of Fools*, Sebastian Brant, whose name he clearly thought would be more likely to make the book a success:

Les regnars traversant/les perilleuses voyes des/folles fiances du mode/ Composées par Sebastien brand, lequel composa la nef des folz/ dernierement Imprimée a Paris Et plusieurs choses co-/posées par autres facteurs...

(The Regnards crossing the perilous ways of the foolish beliefs of fashion./Composed by Sebastian Brant, who recently composed the ship of fools./Printed in Paris. And many things composed by other agents.)

In reality, the cheated young author had not really been in a position to stand up to Vérard, but he bemoaned his treatment in a passage in his *Epîtres morales et familières du traverseur* (Poitiers, 1545): Vérard, he said, had claimed the text was by Brant, a German who had never known French. This was all the more shocking in that the bookseller had essentially, despite adding several new passages, retained Bouchet's text. The case seems to have been taken before the Châtelet in Paris, where an agreement was finally reached – we may even detect a hint that the 'present' made by the bookseller to the author took the form of printed works:

Le premier fut les Regnards traversans/L'an mil cinq cens, qu'avois ving cinq ans/
Ou feu Vérard pour ma simple jeunesse/Changea le nom, ce fut a luy finesse/
L'intitulant au nom de monsieur Brand/Un Alemand en tout scavoir très-grand/
Qui ne sceut onc parler langue francoyse/Dont ie me teu, sans pour ce prendre noise/
Fors que marri ie fuz, dont ce Vérard /Y adiousta des choses d'un aultre art,/
Et qu'il laissa trèsgrant part de ma prose,/Qui m'est iniure, & a ce ie m'oppose/
Au chastellet, ou il me paciffia/Pour un présent le quel me dédia...[16]

(The first was the Regnards crossing/In 1500, when I was twenty-five/ The late Vérard in view of my simple youth/Changed the name, it was a ruse of his/Ascribing it to Monsieur Brand/A German, very great in all learning/Who could never speak French/Whereat I keep mum, for fear of attracting trouble/Except that I was cross, so this Vérard/

arranged things differently/And he left out a good part of my prose,/ which is an affront to me, and I oppose it/At the Chatelet, where he mollified me/with a present he dedicated to me...)

We may recall here that Vérard was always ready to put himself to the fore, substituting for the author in the canonical scene of the dedication of a copy to the king; the example of *Les paraboles de maitre Alain* referred to above is particularly striking, as it seems the author himself appears in the background of the picture, in conversation with an angel.

With printing, the figure of the famous author emerged at the beginning of the sixteenth century: the man whose name, as in the case of Erasmus, was a selling point in itself. This meant that booksellers were always ready to publish him, but that they were also strongly tempted to counterfeit him. In parallel, a network of scholarly sociability and recognition was constructed round the media and the book, into which it was necessary to be accepted in order to carve out a career. Printers and booksellers sometimes played the key role in these networks, as in the case of Aldus Manutius. Having arrived in Venice in 1490, Aldus quickly made contact with a student of Constantine Lascaris, Georgio Valla, professor of humanities in Venice. A group of humanists soon formed around him, including Angelo Politian, Pietro Bembo and Angelo Gabriel, and his house of Sant'Agostino became a meeting place for scholars and intellectuals, all the livelier in that events at the end of the century made Venice a safe haven in contemporary Italy. In 1502 the group formed themselves into an 'Aldine Academy', on the Florentine model, which acted as a social centre and office for correspondence. The colophon of the *Sophocles* of 1502 was the first to use the formula '*Venetiis in Aldi Romani Academia*' ('In Venice, at the Aldine Academy'), and a sheet printed in Greek lists the 'Statutes of the new Academy'. The notably vague aim was to promote the 'Greek heritage', but after only a few years the new institution fell into decay. Having on several occasions considered leaving Venice, Aldus sadly returned, in a preface of 1514, to the failure of his Hellenist dreams. He died the following year. We may think also of the correspondents of Erasmus and of his 'preferred' printing house, that of Johann Froben in Basel. And, lastly, we may remember the Parisian humanist printers of the early sixteenth century, and the innumerable prefaces published by Josse Bade.

In contrast to these examples, which highlight the role of the intermediary, whether bookseller or printer-bookseller, the example of the *Voyage to the Holy Land* illustrates the increased power of the author and the artist. In April 1483, the painter Ehrard Reuwich, of Utrecht, accompanied the dean of the chapter of Mainz, Bernhard von Breydenbach (died 1497), on a pilgrimage to the Holy Land. Having reached Venice in May, Breydenbach, his companions and their servants stayed with Ugelheimer, who, as we have seen, had interests in printing and bookselling. They then resumed their journey, during which Reuwich made a large number of sketches. They were used to illustrate the superb *Voyage to the Holy Land* (*Peregrinatio in terram sanctam*), published in Mainz in 1486 in Latin, soon followed by an edition in German.[17] The book begins with a full-page engraving, in the centre of which is a female figure surrounded by the arms of the three travellers, the author himself (Breydenbach), Johann von Solm and his vassal Philipp von Bicken – but the title of the work does not appear. As no other title of Reuwich is known, and as the characters are those of Schoeffer, we may reasonably assume that the printing was done in the latter's workshop, which must have been known to Breydenbach.

The printed *Peregrinatio* is a very modern object, in particular in the way the author and the artist had embarked on a speculative venture aimed at enthusiasts, a hypothesis supported by the existence of editions of the illustrations on vellum intended for very wealthy purchasers; one such is the spectacular *View of Venice* (1.60 metres long!) seized from the Vatican library in 1799 and today in Paris.[18] Other instances of similar ventures are known, notably that undertaken by Dürer with his *Apocalypse* of 1498. The *Peregrinatio* is modern also in its content (the genre of the travel story) and in the material form of the volume (the xylographs). It is modern, lastly, in the sustained nature of the editorial operation: initially published in Latin, for an international clerical readership, the soon completed German translation made it possible to expand the market to include readers who might not know Latin. As the same engravings were used for both editions the manufacturing costs were proportionately reduced. Two years later it was translated into Flemish, perhaps by Reuwich, and again printed in Mainz. The success of the *Peregrinatio* explains the speed with which it was counterfeited, in German by Sorg in Augsburg (1488), in Speyer by Drach (1490) and in Latin in the same town and same year. Other printers and booksellers financed translations into other languages. That into French was the work of Nicolas Le Huen and it was printed in Lyon by Topié and Heremberk in 1488 – Le Huen too had made the pilgrimage to Jerusalem.[19] A second edition was produced in 1489 by Gaspard Ortuin, again in Lyon, which was illustrated with the woodcuts of the first Mainz edition, apparently sold by Schoeffer to his Lyonais colleague. Two further translations appeared in 1498, in Czech (Pilsen) and Spanish (Zaragoza), and the success of the *Peregrinatio* continued into the early sixteenth century. Once again, the absence of any institutional protection of intellectual works explains the precocity and dynamism of the counterfeiting, which was itself made easier by political fragmentation. But this dynamism is also testimony to the dynamism of the sector and to the strength of the demand on the part of a now fairly wide readership.

Lastly, the case of the Hebraizing Johann Reuchlin illustrates how the social grouping of authors, scholars and 'men of the book' formed a pressure group in the early sixteenth century. At the heart of the dispute was the status of the Jewish religion: should books in Hebrew be destroyed, as was maintained against Reuchlin by the university of Cologne (1509)? The debate between him and Pfefferkorn was conducted through the medium of print until, in 1514, Reuchlin published in Tübingen, without the name of the printer, the letters of support addressed to him by numerous humanists, a book that was reprinted in Haguenau in 1518.[20] Through this means, printing allowed the emergence of a sort of prefiguration of the 'republic' of humanists and scholars as constitutive of 'reasonable' opinion and as players in the debate; they were the *viri clari*, or famous men. The advance of the Protestant Reformation after 1517 relegated the question of books in Hebrew to the backburner, while also leading to a hardening of positions on all sides. Leo X (the Florentine Giovanni de Medici, elected in 1513) condemned the *Augenspieghel* of Reuchlin in 1520, for reasons that were as much political as theological, but the author died the following year. In short, developments in the economy of the media constitute, for us, the first and principal factor that gave impetus to and re-ordered the literary sector in the early modern period.

The Meaning of the Text

Alongside the re-ordering of a literary sector that was increasingly closely linked to the publishing sector, the crucial developments, for the historian of the book, took place at the level of the media: how did the changes in the object and in the uses that might be made of it constrain and impel the definition and organization of the texts, their identification, and their possible utilization? Working on the text and increasing the complexity of its material presentation, systematically differentiating the components of the discourse (for example, a quotation in a common text),[21] and ranking the texts, hence also the books, in more or less complex hierarchized systems became, from the fifteenth century and especially in the sixteenth, the main tool for the organization and advancement of knowledge.

Coding and letters

Let us look first at the question of coding and the theory of communication, a subject which, in spite of its importance, remains practically unstudied in the history of the book. Communication theory analyses the transfer, between several participants, of an ensemble of signs themselves referring to a signification according to a certain code. This code, in part arbitrary, derives from the auditory (the sounds) or the optical. In the case of the book, a first encoding operation involves the transcription of the discourse by writing: in the alphabetic system, the analysis is made through a linear sequence of signs (the graphemes, here the letters) corresponding, in principle, not to the concepts, but to the minimal units of articulation (the phonemes). In reality, these units are not always minimal: in the Western alphabetic system, first used for Greek, certain letters refer to a compound sound (the Zeta, ζ, represents the sound *dz*; or Xi, ξ, the sound *ix*), and the same phenomenon may be observed in modern languages like French. Further, the written text is not, as is commonly believed, the transparent copy of the oral discourse (nor would this be the case if the discourse was recorded and reproduced by a phonographic process) – it creates a different object. Independently even of the grammatical structure of the discourse, which changes from the oral to the written, all sorts of significant elements are excluded from the written message which had been present in the spoken: the speed of diction, the tone employed and the facial expressions, and even gestures of the speaker.

Printing is part of a second encoding operation, which introduces a number of new distortions in relation to the original. It should be noted first that it is the alphabetic structure which supposes the construction of the semiotic triangle combining sound (the word, *vox*) and writing – unlike ideographic writings, which do not break down the sound and refer directly to the signified. The alphabet thus introduces a standardized coding system which offers the possibility, over the long term, of an increasingly abstract analysis of the text. Printing is a sort of first outcome of the logic of alphabetic coding, before digitalization and the reduction of the code to a matter of 0 and 1 took the formalization further.

Though printing does not reproduce an ideal manuscript text, it implicitly assumes the existence of such a text. As a result, the first

theoretical reference of printing is the manuscript because it materialized the trace of the discourse or the original thought. But handwriting has to respond to two contradictory objectives, speed of execution
and legibility. One of the consequences in the Middle Ages was the
proliferation of abbreviations: a sign might replace a syllable, for
example a tilde e (ē) for *est*, a '9' for the prefix *cum/com/con*, a
superscript 9 (^{9}) for the termination *us*, etc. The majority of these
abbreviations are common (*dñs = dominus*) and pose no problem for
the reader; indeed some have survived today: *&* for *and*, and in
French the circumflex (^) as evidence of a letter that has disappeared
(*forêt* for *forest*). However it could also happen that the sheer number
of abbreviations made both specialized and more common texts
extremely difficult to read.

With the advent of typography with movable characters, the logic
of pyramid multiplication would suppose limiting the maximum
number of signs so as not to engrave extra punches, cast unnecessary
signs or complicate the work of the compositors. It is more logical
to use only the three letters *e*, *s* and *t*, and not add a fourth sign, the
tilde e (for *est*). In practice this did not happen. Analysis of the *42-
line Bible* reveals that Gutenberg used a font of some 240 different
characters, which was extremely cumbersome. For certain types of
text, especially in the vernacular, the use of abbreviations was limited,
because the intended readership was not composed primarily of ecclesiastics, although there were always ligatures. If all the consequences
of the typographic process were not realized, it was due to the general
desire to conform as closely as possible to the manuscript model, for
reasons that were both theoretical (reference to the text and its visible
trace) and commercial (the habits of the readers). Nor should the role
of memory in the medieval tradition of intellectual labour be underestimated: when William of Occam was exiled to the Franciscans of
Munich, he had to appeal to his 'mnemonic library' to continue to
write. And, as was emphasized by Hugh of St Victor, it was not only
the layout of the page that was essential to the memorizing of large
numbers of extracts, but also the colour of the painted letters and
the decoration. The first printers probably had this in mind when,
once the presses had done their work, they sent the printed copies to
the workshops of rubrication and painting.

When we read books, it is very important in order to fix our memory
to try to imprint [on it] not only the number and the order of the
words, but also the colour, the form, the position and the placing of
the letters, the place where we saw the written [extract] and at what
point on the page, and the colours and the decoration.[22]

The students of today are not all that far removed from this practice when, revising for their exams, they memorize their course notes by highlighting passages in different colours.

Concern for the aesthetic of the letter and the written page also helps explain the persistence of the material forms from the manuscript to incunabula; the correspondence of Piccolomini shows the awareness of this aspect among scholars – and we know also that aesthetic reasons contributed to the initial rejection of typography with movable characters in China. The success of italic, especially that of Aldus, is surely evidence of the favoured status of the manuscript, the text of the author, in that the humanistic italic, slightly inclined towards the right, elegantly reproduced the handwriting of contemporary Italian scholars. The spectacular characters used in Paris for the title pages of *The Art of Chivalry according to Vegetius* and *La Mer des histoires* (*The Sea of Stories*), and in Nuremberg for the monumental *Chronicle* of 1493, as also in Augsburg for the sumptuous *Theuerdank*,[23] all testify to the importance of appearance, which might also sometimes have a political dimension. In the end, of course, the abbreviated characters were gradually abandoned so as to reduce the number of signs to be manipulated by the compositor, even if traces of the influence of the aesthetic of handwriting still survive in printing today: linked characters like fi, fl or the German ß (= ss). The canonization of the typographic forms was achieved in the two decades from 1520.

At the same time, the unwieldiness and above all the cost of the hardware (typefaces and fonts) encouraged concentration; only those with access to sufficient capital could invest in new fonts. The creation of specific typefaces for minority languages or writings (Greek, Czech, Glagolitic, etc.) was a further complication, and their rarity, when the decision was taken to publish in these languages, dictated variously clumsy processes of transliteration. The Hellenist Victor Berard described this phenomenon as late as the second half of the nineteenth century, in connection with *Macedonia* (*Makedonija*), a newspaper founded in 1865 in Constantinople, before returning to the problem of Albanian:

> Slavejkov included in his newspaper, alongside Bulgarian articles, articles written in Greek, or even articles in Slav, but in a Macedonian dialect and composed with Greek characters because many Bulgarians, in Macedonia, especially those of a certain age, did not know the Slav alphabet...
>
> The first and greatest difficulty was stabilising Albanian, a language not yet written in particular characters. The 'Albanophobes' had... adopted the Turkish alphabet, but [it] could not render exactly all the

inflections of Albanian speech. The bazaar and the clergy habitually used Greek letters to write most of the standard phrases...The Vlachs had dreamed up a new alphabet of thirty-five letters: the twenty-five Latin letters, plus ten modifications of these letters. Two years were spent in making alphabet books...grammars, dictionaries, textbooks...[24]

Consequently, though the choice and the composition of the fonts were primarily determined by the status of the text and of the written manuscript, the transition to print introduced numerous other filters and forms of coding in relation to the theoretical schema. Of course, the coding also functioned as an agent of cultural imperialism.

The choice of characters contributed to a second level in the construction of the code. It was first determined, in medieval fashion, by the nature of the text: gothic of large body (textura) for the Bible and the classics of the Church, bastarda for the vernacular, roman for the classics and humanistic texts. The first roman character, introduced by Rusch in Strasbourg in 1464, was a sort of intermediary character combining traditional gothic with a rounder form, which made it easier for the engraver and the typographic casting (similar to rotunda). We should also note, as a backdrop, the permanence of a geography of typographic forms which continued that of medieval writing practices: roman (Italy and the southern countries) as opposed to gothic (the Germanophone countries and Northern Europe), while the gothics of the Rhineland and above all Italy were 'rounder' than the German gothics. The most beautiful roman character was initially the *Antiqua* cut and cast by Jenson in Venice in 1470, which was immensely influential. Another famous creation, also in Venice, was the roman developed by Francesco Griffo for Aldus in 1496 – known as *Bembo*, after the first book to be printed using it. [25]

The character was part of the coding in that it also proclaimed the greater or lesser modernity of the book and the type of clients for whom it was intended. We know that the first Parisian printers began by publishing textbooks for the university in roman, but, this market being soon saturated, they set out to expand their clientele to include the urban bourgeoisie. This meant switching from gothic to the bastarda that was more familiar to the readers of 'romances'.[26] The promotional intent was even clearer in the case of the humanist printer-booksellers, in particular Aldus. His italic, also created by Griffo in 1499, was a superb character for which some 150 punches were cut, including more than sixty ligatures. The number of the latter shows that the aim was to reproduce the handwriting of the humanists; the design of the character and an aesthetic style of drawing was a way of exalting the status of the author, ancient or contemporary, and also that of the text and, indirectly, the printer and his circle. The Parisian dossier of the *grecs du roi* nicely illustrates this: Pierre du Châtel made a contract in 1540 with the engraver Claude Garamont for the manufacture of Greek punches, for which payment would be made by Robert Estienne. The design would reproduce the script of the Cretan calligrapher Angelo Vergecio, who worked on the Greek manuscripts kept at Fontainebleau. The font was of extreme complexity: not only were there variants for certain letters according to their position in the word (ß and γ, σ and ς, etc.), but also a very large number of ligatures (twenty-seven for the single initial γ). The first book printed with these magnificent fonts was the *Ecclesiastical History* of Eusebius of Caesarea (1544).

The practices and technical capacities of the different workshops imposed a set of imperatives on what might begin as free choices. The possibilities of the workshop were limited by the fonts it owned and by the financial circumstances of the edition: character and page layout determined how much money needed to be spent on the purchase of paper and on the composition, then the organization and speed of work in the printing shop. The choice of format varied from one region to another: we know, in particular, that in the sixteenth century the larger formats (folio), were proportionately more important in Germany than in Italy, whereas it was octavo (8vo) and, to a lesser degree, quarto (4to) in France. In Antwerp, where printing appeared in 1481, 7 per cent of production was in-folio between 1491 and 1500, compared with 28 per cent in Strasbourg and 47 per cent in Venice. Of 253 titles produced by the Antwerp presses of Mathias van der Goes and Gerhard Leeu, the smaller formats account for an unusually high proportion: thirty-one in octavo, a dozen in sextodecimo (16o) and even vincesimo-quarto (24o), all formats relatively rare for the incunabula age. And this choice was inevitably influenced by form and content, too: the relative importance of small formats in Antwerp was related to the numerical importance of works of piety and books of devotion.

Hierarchizing and marking

The framing of the text was determined by the *mise en pages*, or page layout, which might consist either of long lines or of columns, depending both on the format of the book (a small format was less suitable for columns, except if a very small typographic body was used) and on the nature of its contents.

The theory of the text made serious analysis of it possible. In the West, the first text to have been the subject of this was Scripture, but the procedures invented to present, read and interpret the Bible were gradually extended (and considerably developed) in the case of secular texts, especially from the sixteenth century. The page layout of the Bible traditionally took the form, which persists even to this day, of a two-column schema, and was based on the double paradigm of the original text and of its tradition. The page layout highlighted the different levels of text and the relationship between the text and its commentary or commentaries; the most common glosses were those of Walafrid Strabo (ninth century), Anselm of Laon (eleventh century) and Peter Lombard (twelfth century), together with the *Postilia* of the Franciscan Nicholas of Lyra,[27] which was repeated in many printed editions up to the end of the *ancien régime*.[28] The gloss of Walafrid Strabo was generally arranged round the principal text, in a smaller body and closer lineation, that of Anselm of Laon, by contrast, being interlinear. The desire to keep to these traditional schema, as in the monumental edition of the Bible published in Strasbourg by Rusch for Koberger *c.*1480, enormously complicated the layout of the pages and, more generally, the whole printing process.[29] In other cases the schema was simpler: the Mainz edition of the *City of God* of 1473 has text and commentary succeeding one another, according to the order of the chapters, each time repeating the incipit and each new chapter opening with a painted initial.

The page layout of the polyglot Bible takes this approach further but from a more philological perspective: the comparison of the different versions of the text made it possible to clarify the meaning and, it was hoped, get closer to the original, the Word of God. Lefèvre d'Étaples prepared his *Quintuplex Psalterium* (*Fivefold Psalter*) by study of the collections of St Germain-des-Prés and published it with Henri Estienne in 1509.[30] He constructed the page in four columns of the different Latin versions, to which he added his own version, in a fifth. Though he abandoned the doctrine of the fourfold meaning in favour of work on the text itself, Lefèvre stuck to the Latin translations and adaptations of texts which were themselves sometimes already translated, in particular into Greek (the *Septuagint*). The *Polyglot Psalter* of the Genoese Dominican Agostino Giustiniani (1470–1536) was published in 1516. It presented on two facing pages the Hebrew (Masoretic text), Greek, Arabic and Aramaic Targum versions, with Latin translations (except the Arabic), and, finally, the scholia drawn from the Midrash and the Kabbalistic traditions. But the first complete polyglot Bible is that of Cardinal Cisneros, printed in Alcala between 1514 and 1517.[31] The arrangement of the page shows that Hebrew was regarded as the founding language, which the others followed. In the case of the Holy Scriptures the genealogy of the text resulted in the construction of a genealogy of the languages in which Hebrew, language of the Creation and the only antediluvian language, was established as the most ancient.

The different composition procedures supported reading, facilitated the construction of the sentences and brought out the structure of the text, hence the argument of the author: separation of words (the norm in northern France by the eleventh century), codified use of precisely differentiated punctuation marks, introduction of capital letters to mark the beginning of sentences and use of numerous diacritical marks.[32] In the case of French these included accents, which made it possible to distinguish words that were spelled the same way but were very different in nature and meaning. Over and above these devices, three main factors combined to organize the text and present it to the reader: sequentialization, signalization and marking. Sequentialization distinguished the units of meaning presented on the page; it was first, in the fifteenth century, achieved by the text itself, but also by a number of specific signs. In the French that St Augustine published in Abbeville in 1486–7 each chapter is introduced by a summary of the contents. For example, for book 12:

Déclaration de ce livre. L'intention principal de monseigneur Saint Augustine en ce XII. Livre est de parler de la création du premier homme...

(Declaration of this book. The principal intention of Monseigneur St Augustine in this XII. Book is to speak of the creation of the first man...)

As we see, the beginning of the text guides how it should be read. Here, a passage is to be taken as an introduction, at least up to a certain point which marks the beginning of the first chapter:

Ce chapitre est par manière de prologue jusques où il dist: ce n'est mie chose convenable: ou le premier chapitre commence.

(This chapter is by way of prologue up to where it says...or the first chapter begins.)

Sequentialization was strengthened at the level of the secondary units of meaning by the use of pieds de mouche (¶), sometimes alternating blue and red. In the first Latin Bible edited by Jenson in Venice, in 1476, each book opens with a printed running head which made it easier to read discontinuously. The successive chapters are materialized by a line break, an order number in roman and a painted initial.

There is neither foliation nor pagination, but the quires are numbered. The sequentialization was systematized at the level of the sentence by the introduction of punctuation, which was gradually standardized. Lastly, the organization of the paragraphs, studied in detail by Henri-Jean Martin, was part of a certain lightening of the aesthetic of the printed page, as well as a desire to assist the identification of the successive sections of the text, and hence signpost its appropriation by the future reader.[33] It was Descartes who, in the first edition of his *Discourse on Method*, theorized the use of the paragraph as materializing through the layout of the pages a coherent unity of meaning and its development.

Signalization was designed simply to mark out a particular passage as important: the most frequent sign, carried over from manuscript practice, was the manicule, a hand with a finger pointing at the line to be emphasized; if the drawing included the sleeve, it was called a manchette, a term which, by extension, also indicated the notes placed in the margin of a text and either commenting on the passage opposite or briefly summarizing its contents. For certain specialized texts, however, the marginalia grew into a coherent series which surrounded the whole of the main text. This was the case, for example, with the edition of the *Supplementum chronicarum* published in Venice in 1492. According to the biblical schema, the history of the world was divided into six ages corresponding to the six days of Creation and the six ages of life, which were the subject of the engraved illustration on the title page at the beginning of the volume. The text itself was presented in successive paragraphs, separated by a blank line, each beginning with a painted initial. In the external margin two columns enabled the reader to follow the chronology, the first noting the date in relation to the birth of Christ, the second to the Creation of the world. The framing was completed by a printed running head for each of the eleven successive books and by foliation, also printed.[34] This example demonstrates in spectacular fashion how the systematic organization of the text on the page reflected the organization of the knowledge, and the unfolding of the universal history was represented according to a linear schema exactly as in a printed discourse.

Generally speaking, navigation of the text was made easier by the numbering of the leaves or pages, which already in effect existed with signatures. Though foliation was occasionally found in the manuscript age the practice was slow to be carried over into printing, and it was at first usually handwritten. It was customary to use Roman figures (Arabic figures were found only in Venice), sometimes in a larger body than that of the text, sometimes also with reference to the word 'folium'. Page numbering was virtually non-existent. The only example quoted by Haebler is that of Aldus, whose *Cornucopia* of 1499 was not only paginated but had its lines numbered, testimony to the need for precise reference to the text. The practice of number- ing the leaves responded to a change in reading practices: it was counting not for the sake of counting but to provide navigational tools, in other words to facilitate a potential extensive reading or to provide a homogeneous framework that made it possible to fix the text. Similarly, the fact of numbering the discrete units comprising the volume (leaves and pages) was linked to the development of modern navigational tools such as tables and index.

Recapitulating and indexing

The book in quires did not present the text in the linear manner of the roll, but in a discrete form, in successive sequences, each disposed on a page or double-page spread. This is not the place for a lengthy discussion of the tradition of navigational systems, whose premises, in the West, derived once again from work on the Bible. This had involved, in particular, placing the different passages of the Gospels side by side, on the model conceived by Eusebius of Caesarea in the fourth century. The work of the Parisian Dominicans extended and systematized this schema, focusing attention on the analysis of the words. Hugh of Saint-Cher (died 1263) specified the division of the Bible into chapters, a division first established by Stephen Langton, and drew up the table of the occurrences of the words, identifying them by an indication of the book and the chapter, then by a marker from *a* (beginning) to *g* (end), which made it possible to find them in the chapter:

> His aim was to base firmly on the foundation of truth all the words
> of the sacred text of the entire Scriptures, so that theological studies
> would be built with greater certainty on a text more certain of the
> letter.[35]

Though the *Vocabularium* of Papias (eleventh century) is the earli- est example of a list in abstract alphabetical order,[36] the medieval tradition preferred to adhere to the internal logic of the text and avoid an order which it saw as reflecting, in its arbitrariness, a form of disorder. Let us return to Schoeffer's Mainz edition of the *City of God*, of 1473: the commentary of Thomas Waleys and Nicholas Trivet is followed by an alphabetical table prepared by the Dominican Nicholas Cerseth. Each indexed word is followed by two numbers which refer not to the page on which it featured but to the book and the chapter in which it appeared in the main text or the commentary:

> This table notes for each word two numbers, of which the first gives the book and the second the chapter both of the book of St Augustine and of the said treatise...[37]

The organization was similar in the editions of the great scholastic treatises, for example in the *Summa theologica* of Thomas Aquinas published by Heinrich Gran in Haguenau in 1512 on behalf of Knobloch in Strasbourg. The treatise is divided into three parts (*partes*), and each part into subsections (*membra*), questions (*quaestiones*) and articles (*articuli*). The basic intellectual unit, the article, always begins with the same alternative formula: *utrum...an* (= either...or). The response is introduced by the formula *Videtur quod non* (= it does not seem that...) and the successive elements that follow by *praeterea* (= also). The author then examines the contrary arguments, introduced by *sed contra* (= but on the contrary...). Lastly, he gives his reply, introduced by *respondeo dicendum* (= I answer by saying that...) and subdivided according to the order of the objections (*ad primam, ad secundam*, etc.). In its typographic arrangement this Alsace edition follows very precisely the scholastic construction of the text: in each part the questions are numbered in roman characters, each introduced by a lettrine and by a capital with a larger body. The stages of the argument are emphasized by a typographical device and each point by a pied de mouche, with marginal notes facilitating identification of the matter in question. Lastly, the publication was completed not by an index, strictly speaking, but by an alphabetical table of the questions and articles compiled according to the internal structure of the text. The material organization of the volumes follows the intellectual organization of scholasticism, which obviated the need to introduce a navigational aid such as pagination.

The transition to a tracking system that referred not to the content but to the support came about only slowly, and marked a decisive step towards modernity. The *Nuremberg Chronicle* published by Koberger in 1493 was in every respect an exceptional book.[38] Not only did it begin with an index (*Registrum*) but this was introduced by a spectacular title page (see the capital R and the capital E!), whose xylographed characters copied the calligraphy of the imperial chancery. The text combined advertising and aesthetics: 'Index of this book of the Chronicles with drawings and images from the beginning of the world'. The alphabetical table that followed presented in two columns the names of places and persons, noting after each occurrence the subject of the passage referred to and giving opposite, in Roman numerals, an indication of the leaf (*charta foliorum*) to which the reader should refer. The use of a capital of a larger body emphasized the transition from one sub-letter of classification to the next (for example, from *Af* to *Ag*). The framing of the text in this book was not limited to the index: even to conceive of the latter assumed that the leaves or pages would be numbered, and each leaf consequently had the word 'Folium' printed in the top right-hand corner, followed by the number in Roman figures. Lastly, the printer has specified at the top of each page in a running title the age of the world in which the events described on the page took place (for example, *Sexta aetas mundi* = the sixth age of the world). In addition to its sumptuous illustrations, the page layout of the *Chronicle* distinguishes the different paragraphs, each introduced by a capital, with the hierarchy between those printed in black and those handwritten and rubricated. The same devices were repeated exactly in the German edition, with the engraved captions to the illustrations remaining in Latin.

The styles of image

Though it may sometimes be difficult to distinguish decoration from illustration, let us accept that the former describes all the graphic elements that are not primarily figurative, that are present in the volume and that contribute to its aesthetic, such as decorated letters and bands. The page layout left spaces for the insertion of hand-painted capital letters. In the *42-line Bible*, the *lettres d'attente* (small 'holding' letters telling the rubricator which letter to insert) were handwritten, but the printed 'holding' letter became the norm (as in the *Nuremberg Chronicle*). Above all, and at a very early stage, printers tried to mechanize the decoration, and the capital letters were inserted in the form of xylographed lettrines. As we have seen, Gutenberg's financial difficulties in the years from 1457 were probably related to the investment needed to perfect the technique of printing in two colours the large decorated letters of the Mainz Psalter. The other decorative elements found in books consisted of xylographed bands, sometimes achieved by combining a large number of small woodblocks (as in the Parisian Books of Hours), and also the typographic marks, some of which were of very high aesthetic quality. Lastly, the volumes were in some cases completed by hand after the impression itself. The role of the decoration was ambiguous in that it related to elements in principle independent of the text and whose signifier was therefore neutral. Nevertheless, the decoration also signified in itself as decoration, proclaiming a certain material quality or the intellectual orientation of the workshop: the decorative lexicon of the Renaissance was combined with the use of engraving on a black background to indicate the particular interest in antiquity of numerous Italian workshops, as with the Venetian *Herodotus* of 1494. In the case of Aldus, the absence of decoration on the title page and the choice of character referenced monumental epigraphy, while the superb 'Dolphin' mark was a sort of manifesto of the intellectual choices of the group of humanists gravitating round the workshop. The decoration also served, in short, as decor in the theatrical sense of the term.

The appearance of xylographed illustrations in typographic books was a logical development of the contemporary techniques used for xylographic booklets, but it seems also, by the 1460s, to characterize the precocious dialectic between the market and competition. In the face of the printers of Mainz Albrecht Pfister of Bamberg, perhaps with Gutenberg's help, looked for a different production model, aimed at a different readership. He struck out with the vernacular and was also the first to introduce printed illustrations into books. In 1461, his *Der Edelstein* (*The Jewel*) collected a group of fables written by the Bernese Dominican Ulrich Boner. This book, of which a number of earlier manuscripts survive, has 102 engravings illustrating the different fables.[39] In 1461–2, Pfister also produced the small in-folio *Ackermann von Böhmen* (*The Ploughman from Bohemia*), a text associated with early German humanism; attributed to Johann von Tepl (died c.1414), it tells the story of a peasant who puts Death on trial after the death of his wife.[40] The illustrations are full page, or in the upper register of the page or achieved by combining small woodblocks; the colouring was done by stencil. Also at this period Pfister printed an illustrated *Biblia pauperum*, in Latin and German, and the *Belial* of Jacobus de Teramo in an illustrated German version. Sadly, this highly innovative body of work aimed at a non-clerical readership has been very poorly preserved, as it consisted of small volumes that were not seen as possessing any particular value.

There were frequent and sustained connections between the wealthy towns of middle and southern Germany. The Pleydenwurff dynasty of painters originated in Bamberg; in c.1470–5, Cuntz Pleydenwurff painted a picture of Johannes Kapistran preaching on the cathedral hill. It was also the Pleydenwurff who founded the school of Nuremberg engravers. Hans Pleydenwurff (died 1472) was responsible, c.1457, for a portrait of Count Lowenstein, who is shown in strikingly realistic fashion as an old man, a book in his left hand.[41] In 1472, Michael Wolgemut (died 1519) married the widow of Hans, whose son Wilhelm (died 1494) was also a painter. The son and the father-in-law then ran the largest workshop of artists in Nuremberg; it was here that the young Dürer (he was born in 1471 and Koberger was his godfather) did his apprenticeship (1486–90) and they were responsible for the illustration of the *Chronicle* of 1493. By giving their name, the colophon of the Latin edition reveals the new importance of identifying the artists, from what might be called a 'promotional' perspective.

Dürer, first apprenticed as a goldsmith, then as a draughtsman and engraver, was the key figure in the transition from the German artistic model to humanism and in its wider geographical diffusion. After a period in Colmar with Schongauer (1490), he moved to Basel, where he worked for Sebastian Brant and Johann Bergmann on the illustration of the *Narrenschiff* – of the 112 engravings of the first edition (1494), seventy-three were his work.[42] He is next heard of in Venice, from which, two years later, he returned to Germany. His *Apocalypse* of 1498 demonstrates in spectacular fashion the radical change in the status of the artist, thanks to the media and to the distribution networks which accompanied their rise to fame:[43] the illustrations were given priority, with the engravings printed on the recto and the corresponding text on the verso, so that it was impossible to 'read' one while looking at the other. Two versions were produced, to maximize the potential market, the German edition repeating the text of Koberger's Bible (1483) and the Latin sticking to the Vulgate. This book, on which Dürer laboured for two years, was the first to be published by a named artist, in association with a professional publisher for the typographical sections. As the woodblocks were preserved, a second edition could appear in 1511, together with the *Great Passion* and the *Life of the Virgin*.

In the 1470s a number of craftsmen left Basel, where the competition had grown too fierce, for Lyon – and with them went the practice of including illustrations in printed books. The art of engraving was hardly new in Lyon, as the town was already a centre for the manufacture of playing cards, with specialized craftsmen, the 'cutters' or 'makers of moulds', often of German origin. Xylography followed the trade routes of the Rhine Valley; as we have seen, once established in Lyon, Matthias Huss commissioned Julien Macho to translate the *Spiegel menschlichen Behältnissen*, already published in Basel (1478). This *Miroir de la rédemption de l'humain lignage* was thus the first illustrated book printed in France, with blocks copied from the original.[44] German influence was a recurrent feature in Lyonnais illustration at this period, with plates either imported, or reproduced, more or less accurately – sometimes by inverting the design transferred on to the wood. The model for the *Aesop's Fables* (*Les Subtiles Fables D'Esope*) published by Huss in 1486 was again German.[45] This was a text that had circulated widely, initially in a translation by the physician Heinrich Steinhöwel, who then had a bilingual version printed in Ulm by Zainer in 1476–7. It was soon counterfeited in both Augsburg and Strasbourg.

Other schools of engraving developed in Italy, France and the Flemish countries. In Italy, where copper was used from preference, the favoured style was a form of line drawing and deployment of perspective within the scenographic cube, as for example in the title page of the Venetian *Herodotus* (1494), the illustrations of Boccaccio's *Famous Women* (1497) and, above all, the celebrated *Dream of Poliphili* published by Aldus in 1499. In Florence, Baldo Baldini (died 1487) illustrated *Alemanus*, the Dante of Nicolaus Laurentii (called Niccolo Tedesco: he came from Breslau), with a commentary by Christoforo Landini (1481); Botticelli (died 1510) may have been responsible for the preliminary drawings, now lost. In the 1480s, Paris achieved greater autonomy in the sphere of the printed image. It had a different style, some illuminators seeming to go back to xylography, whereas in Germany this would have been, rather, a new art. We may cite classics like the *Mer des hystoires* (Pierre Lerouge, 1488) or the different titles of Vérard. The latter, probably from Touraine, was himself a painter who turned to publishing and specialized in illustrated books. He assembled a unique collection of particularly beautiful xylographed plates which he used for successive titles:[46]

> By his choice of texts in French, by the care he lavished on the material quality of his publications, and by his ability to find and deploy illustrations, [he] sought to conquer...readers who were educated, wealthy, appreciative of a certain luxury, and open to a new beauty, that which was due simply to the blacks and whites of engraving on wood. It was this overall project which seemed to guide his activity...gave him a special place in the Parisian book market of his day, and brought to the fore a new type of actor: the editor who was identified with an editorial policy. (E. Toulet)

The principal speciality of the Parisian book trade in the late fifteenth and early sixteenth centuries was its famous beautifully illustrated and small format Books of Hours. The style was at first 'gothic' until, in 1508, the printer-bookseller Simon Vostre moved to another model, that of Hours '*à l'antique*' – so, within the illustration, too, we encounter the problematic of decoration.

Finally, the revival of the techniques of the image contributed to a change in the conditions of publication of scientific texts, but also in the construction of scientific knowledge itself. We may cite, for example, in the sphere of natural history, the herbarium of Leonhart Fuchs (1542),[47] the anatomy of Vesalius (1543)[48] and the geology of Agricola (1556).[49] With his *Historiae animalium* (*History of Animals*) published from 1551,[50] Konrad Gesner (1516–65) proposed to offer 'a complete library in a single book'. The structure of his work was based on a combination of elements placing the word and the printed discourse at the centre of the tools of knowledge: the list of authors, embryo of the specialized bibliography, made it possible to check the validity of the work. Series of tables established the concordance of the signifiers, that is, of the names of the animals in the different languages (Latin, Hebrew, the vernaculars). Lastly, Gesner offered veritable 'operating instructions' (*ordo capitum*) for the notes describing the different species: they followed a standard pattern, with subsections (*a*, *b*, *c*, etc.) each of which dealt with a specific topic – for example the method of reproduction of the species. Together with denomination, the key issue of zoology was that of the classification of species, which the author presented in his five successive volumes (viviparous quadrupeds, oviparous quadrupeds, birds, fish and snakes), each species classified alphabetically and illustrated with a xylograph. With Gesner, the classification of the printed descriptions reproduced that of the external world and the information was of value both in itself and as part of a systematically treated whole: the scientific discourse served as a model of objective reality, of which the printed text rendered both the organizational structure and the details. The world of animate creatures was brought together, classified and analysed in a book that was constructed as a mirror: the illustration enriched it as a system of signs that was part of a more all-encompassing system. Gesner's aim was encyclopedic, if we remember that he published a universal bibliography and an encyclopedia of zoology, and that he died before finishing his *Historia Plantarum* (*History of Plants*), intended to complete this whole.

The 'Book-Machine'

With the mechanization of the 'art of writing', the status and role of the media changed, slowly at first but nevertheless radically. The book now functioned like a data-processing 'machine' (that is, storing and delivering information) combining programme (the environment and the structuring of the book) and content (the text):

If I compare the book to a machine, it is because this word evokes the concept of a 'functional mechanism': an arrangement of parts whose interaction obtains a deliberately pursued result. And, in this sense, the book is certainly a machine intended to transmit a text-model by transforming it into a text-image reconfigured on a new support.[51]

As we have seen, in the medieval tradition, the text had not been recognized as text because the attention of the reader was focused on the signified, the spirit, which unquestionably took precedence over the letter. What mattered was the transmission of a certain message, which was, so to speak, independent of the discursive form it had been given: this was the project of Isidore of Seville when he embarked on his works of compilation intended to achieve a merger between the Hispano Roman archaizing culture and the Christian Gothic culture.[52] This is also what made his work so functionally important for the Carolingian Reformation, in that it postulated the existence of the possible relationship with antiquity and offered the means to achieve this, though the texts were lacking:

> It seems to have been rare, before the end of the Middle Ages, to have the historical or philological wish to leave or recover the work of an author in the exact form that he had wished to present it. According to a generally accepted idea, every piece of writing intended to instruct was perfectible, and ... there was no reason not to modify it in the taste of the day or improve it by completing it.[53]

A first revolution was that of semiology and the attention systematically paid by scholasticism to the sign as sign – that is, to the word as word. The literality of the discourse could be freshly interrogated, and scholars worked on the text and its component parts in order to determine its possible meaning. A second phenomenon followed in fourteenth-century Italy with the Renaissance, that is, with the attention paid to the texts of antiquity, which it was hoped to recover in their original purity, beyond the many works of compilation and commentary which had largely obscured them. The Italian humanists, familiars of various prelates, took advantage of their presence at the Council of Basel to scour the monastic libraries of southern Germany in search of manuscripts that might provide them with unknown texts of the classics. And, in the humanist manuscripts, the text was in future presented on its own, as if enshrined in a sumptuous writing and decoration.

Typography with movable characters added a new dimension to this quest. Several of the Aldus title pages bear only the short title of the work, in a typography based on Roman capitals which clearly

referenced ancient epigraphy. Statistical studies of the 'classical incunabula' will enable us to refine and deepen our discussion.[54] Finally,
the proliferation of printed books radically modified the category of
intertextuality and this change was itself connected to the change in
reading practices. A first indicator of the shift in the status of the
text and in the system of intertextuality was the appearance and systematization of the footnote.[55] More generally, however, the shift to
a form of extensive reading led inexorably to the decline of all that
had belonged to the traditional genre of compilation and summary.
Conversely, reflection on the texts identified them as objects, made
easier to navigate and utilize by, on the one hand libraries, on the
other works of bibliography – the first ideal type of the latter being
the *Bibliotheca* of Gesner. Other major consequences of the invention of typography with movable characters for the identification
of the modern text followed from the rise of the vernacular; these
texts were not generally glossed but taken as a whole, sufficient in
itself, while the affirmation of the function of the author tended in
the same direction.

Further, the printed book operated as an instrumentalized system
assuring interaction between the reader and the world: the book and
the text constituted a machine providing readers with a model on
which it might be possible to base their reasoning and their actions.
As we have seen, Christopher Columbus read Ptolemy, by way of
Pierre d'Ailly, and based his projected voyage on the Ptolemaic model
of the universe. We may also note the blank pages reserved by the
printer of the *Nuremberg Chronicle* under the running title of the
'Sixth age of the world', so as to allow each owner of the volume to
complete the Chronicle after 1493 with his or her own notes. With
Peter Bienewitz, called Apian (died 1552), the book became a calcu-
lating tool, rather in the style of the future movable book. The
Astronomicum caesareum (*Emperor's Astronomy*, 1540) offered a set
of engraved movable disks making it possible to identify and calculate
the movement of the stars,[56] on an analogous model to that of the
miniature globes (the terrestrial globe, the armillary sphere) and of
automata. It was through direct observation, but also through books,
that astronomers and cartographers constructed the new image of the
world, from Gemma Frisius and Copernicus to Mercator, Tycho
Brahe and Blaeu. We have here reached the apogee of the semiological
revolution begun with Aristotelianism: for centuries, the printed book
prevailed as the prime tool of rationality.

This same conception of the 'book-machine' was applied to the
world of the books themselves. Once writing was both the precondition and tool of knowledge, and once the book became the model of

the world, this model grew increasingly powerful as more books were published and their potential use became rationalized. It was from this perspective that, from 1545, Gesner published the first universal catalogue of books, recapitulating, under the title of *Bibliotheca universalis*, the intellectual production so far in existence – some 12,000 books by 3,000 authors.[57] The material form of the volume was extremely elegant, in its title page, in its roman character, in the near absence of abbreviations and in the standardized organization of the bibliographical notices, arranged alphabetically. All the references and navigational aids placed by the author round the notes were conceived for a modern practice of consultative reading. At the same time the great scholarly libraries, like those of Hernando Colón (Columbus) in Seville, Philip II in the Escorial and the king of France at Fontainebleau, were gradually established throughout Europe as the laboratories of modernity. The modern library, in which printed books were now in a majority, marked a new stage in the externalization.

> For a million years, human beings have one by one externalized their faculties, which has enabled them to decouple them (there is more memory in a library than in a brain)...writing 'externalizes' speech (materializes it and visualizes it), just as printing externalizes writing, the diary, the book, the screen, the journal, etc. To externalize is both to expel and to reincorporate differently. Once the anatomical evolution of mankind had ceased, the evolution of technical means took up the baton in the ongoing process of hominization, and the generation of our successive memory stores, from the volumen to the CD-ROM, follows the same path: gradual integration of functions, greater economy of means, dematerialization, etc. Thus, our organic faculties have one by one left us to settle in artifacts: today, celluloid sees, the magnetic tape speaks, the chip calculates, the keyboard draws and fantasizes.... (Régis Debray).

9

The Media Explosion

Indeed I disagree strongly with those who are unwilling that Holy Scripture, translated into the vulgar tongue, be read by the uneducated, as if Christ taught such intricate doctrines that they could be understood only by very few theologians, or as if the strength of the Christian religion consisted in men's ignorance of it...I would that even the lowliest women read the gospels and the Pauline epistles. And I would that they were translated into all languages so that they could be read and understood not only by the Scots and Irish but also by the Turks and Saracens...Would that the farmer sing some portion of them at the plough, the weaver hum some part of them to the movement of his shuttle, the traveller lighten the weariness of the journey with stories of this kind!

Erasmus, *Paraclesis*

A New Paradigm: Production and Reproduction

Production

The calculations made possible by the existence of the cumulative catalogues of old books, which are almost exhaustive for the fifteenth century, though not for after that, allow only partial conclusions, because we cannot consider the results in relation to the importance of the printed volumes (not all titles are equal) or the print runs. The general catalogue of incunabula (ISTC) lists some 27,000 editions published before 1501. This figure is very close to that proposed by Carla Bozzolo and her colleagues, who have estimated the total number of known fifteenth-century editions at between 27,000 and

29,000.[1] If we assume an average print run of 200, which is at the low end of the range, we arrive at a total of more than 5,000,000 copies put into circulation; if we put the average at 500 copies, the total would exceed 13,000,000 – perhaps 15,000,000 if we take into account that some titles have not survived and thus not been counted. On this hypothesis, we have a 6,000 per cent increase in relation to the manuscript age – and the sale price would inevitably have decreased in proportion:

> In the beginning, editions consisted of scarcely more than 100 to 200 copies: thus [that] of the Familiar Letters of Cicero printed in 1469 in Venice...was of only 100 copies; but already, after 1470, there were editions of between 200 and 300 copies. After 1480, the [figure] rapidly increased...Peter Schoeffer, in 1483, printed 400 copies of the Missal...of Breslau and editions of between 800 and 1000 copies were not uncommon towards the end of the century.[2]

Some printing houses specialized in large print runs. One of the most important of these was that of Koberger, with the German Bible of 1483, and even more the *Chronicle* of 1493, for which the print run for the Latin edition is estimated to have been 1,400 copies, plus 700 for the German. The conclusion is clear: within the space of some thirty to fifty years printing had made possible an unprecedented increase in the volume of written material in circulation. In the second half of the fifteenth century, and in its most advanced regions, European society was the first ever to have experienced the effects of what might be called a phenomenon of mass mediatization.

The process only accelerated in the sixteenth century. A global calculation of printed production may not be realistic for this period, but it has been estimated at between 300,000 and 400,000 titles, between 90,000 and 120,000 of them in Germany, with a total number of copies in circulation possibly as high as 400,000,000. On the basis of a random sample, Jean-François Gilmont has suggested a distribution of production as follows: 29 per cent in Germany, 26.5 per cent in France, 25 per cent in Italy. In France, Paris and Lyon respectively accounted for 60 and 30 per cent of total production, with some 35,000 titles in the case of the capital; these figures would put global production at only 225,000 titles. The trajectory was comparable in both cities, that is, a period of decline around 1522–5 (which may relate to the generally more difficult situation in the kingdom) with an apogee around 1530, when some 350 titles were published in Paris. The first world centre was Venice, with 45,000 titles for the century.

The nature of the subject matter radically changed in this same period. In 1502, of some 130 editions known for Paris, ninety-five (73 per cent) belonged to the religious sphere, consisting primarily of Books of Hours and liturgical volumes.[3] A generation later (1534) the situation had changed: of 335 editions, ninety-four (28 per cent) were religious, with fewer liturgical volumes (a score of titles) than full or partial editions of the Bible. Belles lettres and the classics (twenty editions of Cicero), rhetoric and grammar were on the increase. Erasmus, prince of the humanists, was represented by eighteen editions. In the case of one of the great Parisian bookshops, Galliot Du Pré, we know that a total of 350 titles were published between 1512 and 1560, of which 42 per cent were related to the law, 19–20 per cent history and literature and 9 per cent the classics, with only 6 per cent religious and 4 per cent the sciences. All over Europe it was editions of the classics (Cicero) and manuals of instruction that underpinned the increase. And Erasmus himself testifies to what had become a familiar type of behaviour, exploited by the printer-booksellers, especially the 'sect' of those not overly burdened with scruples:

> This is the principal modus operandi on which this sect relies: they attract people to the sermon and then they hold onto them; by parading the taste for languages and good literature, they win over the young and those who get great pleasure from this sort of study... The role of the printers in all this is surely by no means negligible.[4]

The problematic of 'publicity'

One of the most important consequences of the irruption of the new media was the invention of a paradigm that was, if not completely new, at least new in the terms in which it now appeared: 'publicity', alias the 'public sphere', or the 'public'.[5] True, the spread of 'bourgeois' modernity was very uneven. The reading public had first been visible in the towns, especially the largest and most active, when the rural world was still a world in which oral communication was paramount; the continued power of the latter would be revealed, much later, in a phenomenon like the Great Fear of 1789.[6] Nevertheless, in the towns the change was palpable: the civil and religious authorities now spoke to the people not only, as in the past, through criers, but through posters; let us remember the bishop of Mâcon who employed Neumeister to print the announcement of the appointment of the new archbishop of Lyon (1489) and had it posted all over the town.[7] Similarly, increasing numbers of single sheets and leaflets dealing with recent events such as battles and royal entries were published, some workshops making a speciality of them, as also of the texts of new regulations. On the first leaf of the *Ordonnances royales* printed in Toulouse in 1499, a naive xylograph shows Louis XII surrounded by civil officials and prelates to whom he is handing a document – possibly the very text of the *Ordonnances*.[8] This type of output became increasingly important. In 1540, for example, the Parisians Gilles Corrozet and Jean (III) Du Pré printed *La Triumphante et magnifique entrée* (of Charles V, the dauphin and the duc d'Orléans into Valenciennes on 21 January 1500), the *Double et copie d'une lettres envoyées d'Orléans* describing the entry of the emperor into this town the previous year and *L'Ordre tenu et gardé à l'entrée de très hault et très puissant prince Charles, Empereur tousjours Auguste, en la ville de Paris*.[9] These minor pieces – a poster, a few octavo or quarto pages – could be printed rapidly, without major investment, and distributed easily and quickly in the locality; in fact, as with Gutenberg and his indulgences, it was a way of keeping themselves in business. It is clear once again that the growth of the market and, in part, of product innovation also resulted from the editorial policies of the printers. It is hardly necessary to add that most of these pieces have not survived.

Some events were more promising, that is, more suitable for exploitation by the media. The year of the pontifical Jubilee of Sixtus IV, 1475, saw the appearance of a small book entitled the *Mirabilia Romae* (*Marvels of Rome*), which was published in Rome, Sant'Orso (by Johannes de Reno) and Treviso. Writing about the sack of Rome by the imperial armies in 1527, André Chastel has emphasized the novelty of the stir surrounding this event and spoken, with perhaps a little exaggeration, of 'public opinion' within the Christian world, of 'press', and even of 'journalism':

> Notable events have always had their popular expressions. But in the case of the capture and sack of Rome in May 1527, the press makes it possible to follow closely the reactions of public opinion within the Christian world. For more than thirty years, the Italian wars had seen the spread of posters bearing 'canards', sensational reports, generally untrue, called Flugblätter, which played a new role in public life... The statistics speak for themselves: if any single event was sensational at the time, the number of pamphlets and posters, followed by brief accounts, hastily printed in a number of languages, amply demonstrates that it was the events of May 1527...
>
> In fact, we have the impression of witnessing the birth of journalism with the appearance of novellas (*storie*), scandal sheets, and more or less fanciful commentaries. The *giudizio* was a short report of an event

that was instantly printed and sold in sheets on the public squares. Around 1527, these improvised newspapers enjoyed great success... Some of Aretinus letters, printed on unbound sheets to assure their rapid dissemination, were *giudizio*, or the beginnings of newspaper articles.[10] During the period of the sack, these 'special editions' flourished everywhere, and that was precisely when that master journalist discovered his vocation. His *giudizio* and *pronostici*, in great demand in high places, were quite simply buffoonish predictions, undisguised parodies of astrologic *pronosticationes*, accompanied by a readily discernible commentary of the current situation...A few years later... Aretinus...introduced the vendor of *storie* who calls out the 'headlines' of the day: 'News, news, wonderful news – the Turks at war in Hungary, the sermons of Brother Martin, the Council, news, news, events in England, the procession of the pope and the emperor, the circumcision of the Voievods, the sack of Rome, the siege of Florence, the meeting in Marseille and its results, news, news.'[11]

We see the emergence of a new economy, that of the 'real time' that made it possible to know (to see) what was happening, here and now, in the kingdom and in the wider world. The huge repercussions extended to the economy of the most contemporaneous information, with problematics which seem in some respects not so very different from one century to another. Among the major consequences of the rise of 'publicity' was also the appearance of 'great writers' (today we would speak of 'icons'...), beginning with Erasmus, though we might equally well cite Luther. Their fame made their writings valuable commodities in themselves, to the point where, as we have seen, they on occasion complained about this mediatization, as when one of their pieces was published without their consent. The crucial question quickly became knowing to what extent this newly available 'publicity' now affected politics itself.

The ambivalences of reproduction

Typography with movable characters introduced another problematic, increasingly present in modern times, that of reproduction.[12] With the proliferation of copies of one same edition, the question of the text and its reproduction was posed in different terms: it was easier for the text to be a subject of study, because it was open to a critique allowing the construction of its genealogy and thus the identification of the supposedly best version, which was confused with the original. Nevertheless, the discourse of the humanists was sometimes ambivalent with regard to the benefits of printing, hence reproduction, for philology.[13] True, the possibility of distribution in large numbers was the precondition for research, because each individual could work on one and the same version and the results would be comparable, so cumulative. But, for Erasmus, for example, this argument was more than counterbalanced by the impossibility of carrying out an external critique of a printed work: study of a manuscript allowed the philologist to distinguish the different hands, hence the successive strata of the text, and provided him with numerous pointers which standardization through printing eliminated. This had already been said, in effect, by Budé when, in his commentary on the *Pandects* (1508), he regretted his lack of access to the manuscripts that were indispensable to his work; collecting manuscripts, which he would soon do in his capacity as grand-master of the library of Fontainebleau, was the main means to make work on texts possible. At this level, printing, by increasing the number of copies, also increased the possibilities for working on them. Unfortunately, the greed of the printers too often meant that the quality of the text was for them a matter of secondary importance. As a result, not only did reproduction produce as many faulty editions as good ones, but the law of the market even contributed to an overall decline in quality. When he received a copy of Galen from Torresanus, Erasmus was dismayed by its poor quality:

> I am in torment at seeing such a great author edited at such great cost with so many faults, like most of the works which reach us today from Italy. See what the thirst for gold leads to! What sacrilege is committed for the sake of a few pieces of gold that could have been used to pay a skilled corrector.[14]

In fact the quality of the text was declining because the book had become a commodity, even though this status might have provided certain guarantees. The structure of the guilds and the attention they paid to the skill of the craftsmen and the quality of the products could have been influential in printing as in other fields. Yet Erasmus also complained that printing, a new activity, was not always incorporated into the guild structure and that the printers were able to produce and distribute a shoddy product. He did not, however, mention the possibility that competition might actually encourage high quality. In the end, reproduction strengthened the contrast between original and copy: the manuscript text, original, or at least closer to the original, had been transliterated in the form of a piece of print and lost, in the process, some of its power as mediating object, while the proliferation of the printed item by the hundred, even thousand, further relativized its value.

We also need to examine the consequences of reproduction from the standpoint of reception, especially in the case of religious books. The reception in bulk of a certain version of a text inevitably encouraged the formation of 'communities of readers' (Stanley Fish), for whom it was an identity-forming element. In some instances, like that of the Protestants and in particular the Calvinists, the reading of a key text, in this case the Bible, provided the community with a model for all other reading practices, while the opposition between Catholics and Protestants led to the opposition between two scriptural textual traditions: the Sixto-Clementine, fixed in 1590–2, became the version of reference for the Roman Church, which it remained until the Revolution in France. By contrast, the Protestant tradition prioritized the return to the text, hence to the original languages, here Hebrew and Greek, but it also made a priority of the transmission of the message to the largest number, hence translation into the vernacular – which culminated in a Protestant 'Vulgate'.

A second question arises not from the work of deconstruction/reconstruction of the text but from its dissemination and reception by a large population of readers. Printing was an effect of divine grace, but the potential risks posed by the circulation of the texts and the images in new circumstances were not immediately appreciated: the risks of a mediatization creating new and autonomous configurations in the minds of the readers (listeners, readers strictly speaking, even people who had heard talk of a phenomenon without themselves having direct knowledge of it). The 'event' became to some degree an effect of its own reception, in other words, a media construction. When, in 1517, Luther drew up his *95 Theses* against indulgences, he could not have imagined that printing would give the controversy it occasioned an impact so huge that it led to the disintegration of the Church to which he himself belonged. Similarly, when, on the night of 17–18 October 1534, some 'partisans' posted a copy of the *Placards against the mass* on the door of the king's chamber in Amboise, they had no idea that they would drive Francis I to adopt a new politics, that of contraction and repression: the first burning at the stake, of 'Berthelot Mylon, called the Paralytic', followed as early as 30 November. And again, when the bishop of Ypres, in 1640, published a lengthy and, it must be said, indigestible treatise in Latin on his reading of St Augustine, he could hardly have known that he was starting a controversy, Jansenism, which would not only intensify for more than 150 years but spill over from the sphere of religion and faith into that of politics. The media dimension was one of the most important elements in the affair of the *Provincial Letters* and the growth of the controversy.[15]

The 'media explosion', to use the expression of Paul Virilio, was first apparent in the impossibility of controlling the distribution of information and in the irrational reactions this very impossibility provoked. Further, if printing and the book trade had a potentially subversive, even scandalous, dimension, it was also because they made it possible for anyone and everyone to speak in public or be part of a public debate in place of the traditional mediators, the Church, the lay authorities and in particular the king. This theme joined up with that of the foundational category of time: the scandal of the *Placards* showed, in 1534, how the collectivization of time was brutally imposed, creating a sort of continuum for which no one was as yet prepared. Whereas traditional rural society lived in a time of which it had direct knowledge, that is, the natural time of the seasons and days and the religious time punctuated by local church bells, the modern 'typographic society' lived in a new time, that of immediacy and, in a way, of virtuality. It was his failure to grasp the scale of the change that caused Francis I to 'overreact' and, in January 1534, take measures to prohibit the printing of any new book in the kingdom before being forced, like many another after him, to retreat before the juggernaut of the omnipresent media. We may also note that Ferdinand I of Hapsburg, too, elected in Bohemia in 1526–7, shut down all printing workshops except in Prague in 1547, a measure quickly seen as unenforceable.

The paradigm of reproduction also played a major role with regard to a last global problematic, to which I have already referred, and which was itself destined to a great future: the development of modern scientific thinking and the place occupied in it by the image – or, more recently, imagery. Let us leave aside here the question of the relationship between the image and the text, a relationship that changed not only as a result of the technique of reproduction employed (wood or copper, relief carving (*taille d'épargne*) or intaglio (*taille douce*)) but was also affected by aesthetic criteria and, lastly, the discursive status of the image: illustrating the text by copying it or going beyond it by adding something else, visible along with it or separately. Reproduction, in the primary meaning of the word (representation), was central to the 'modern' scientific image because it appeared independent both of the gaze of the observer and of other intrusive phenomena capable of confusing it. The ideal was the objective reproduction of the world, which might serve as a model for identifying, listing, classifying and acting.

What was convoked to this end was an 'imaginary of transparency': a transparency both of the reality being analysed and reproduced and of the techniques and procedures employed to do this. In

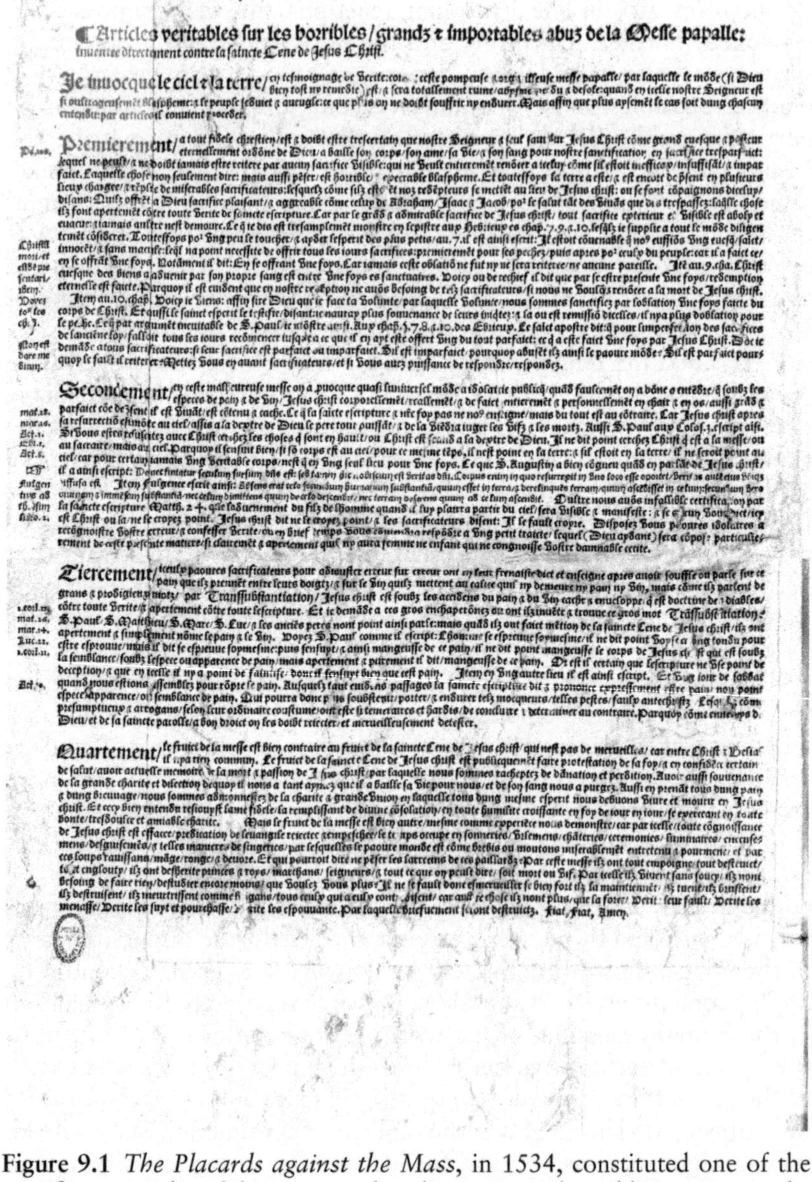
Articles veritables sur les horribles/grandz & importables abuz de la Messe papalle: inventee directement contre la saincte Cene de Jesus Christ.

Je invocque le ciel & la terre/

Premierement/

Secondement/

Tiercement/

Quartement/

Fiat, Fiat, Amen.

Figure 9.1 *The Placards against the Mass*, in 1534, constituted one of the very first examples of the process of mediatization. The publicity given to the text led Francis I to take drastic action, to the extent of briefly prohibiting printing anywhere in the kingdom. Museum of Printing, Lyon.

Figure 9.2 With the Zurich physician Conrad Gesner, we enter the virtual world: the printed book, even more the collection of books (the library), constituted an immensely powerful means of knowing and mastering the real world. Gesner, author of the first universal bibliography (*Bibliotheca bibliographica universalis*), also embarked on an inventory of the physical world with his *Historia animalium* (Zurich, 1551). Municipal Library of Valenciennes.

the case of scientific and technical images, printing introduced a logic of hyper-reality, that is, of a representation more 'true', because more potent, than the reality. Nevertheless, if the paper world, which was that of books, was more effective than the real world, it was para-doxically because it did not reproduce the latter exactly and because the reality presented by the images was in fact purged of non-relevant elements. This was the case, for example, with the medicinal plants reproduced in the early printed herbals (*Hortus sanitatis*), which it was vital to be able to identify with certainty so as to be able to use them in complete safety. The same observations may to some extent be made of the images of the technological world, whether in the case of identifying, on the basis of ancient texts, the machines of war or of the Roman poliorcetica, or of particularizing the devices used in the mining industries.[16] The effectiveness of the reproduction sometimes surpassed reality itself, as when Breydenbach and Reuwych represented the unicorn as one of the animals they had actually been able to see in the East, or when Dürer added an extra horn on the back of his rhinoceros. The proclaimed objectivity derived from virtuality, which did not detract in any way from its effectiveness, and the scientific image, which reproduced reality, was also part of the imaginary.

With the scientific and technical image the two acceptations of the word 'reproduction' came together: on the one hand, production of a reality 'more real' than reality itself; on the other hand, reproduction of this reproduction in hundreds or thousands of copies.

The Reformation and Printing

The Bible, a text

The first great printed book was the Latin Bible. It was only logical for the printers, whatever the difficulties, to begin with the text that was both most in demand and most spectacular, especially when we remember that this was Germany, which seems to have been relatively less well off than France in biblical manuscripts in the first half of the fifteenth century. The inventory of the Bibles preserved in Paris allows us to list and date the complete editions of the Bible in Latin:[17] the *42-line Bible* of Gutenberg was a huge undertaking and it was many years before a second edition appeared, that is, the *36-line Bible* printed partly in Bamberg in 1459–60. The Strasbourg edition of Mentelin followed soon after (before 1461), then that of Fust and Schoeffer, in Mainz, in 1462. It is significant that the largest workshops embarked as soon as possible on editions of the Latin Bible, for example the Basel printing houses of Bernhard Richel (*c*.1474), Johann Amerbach (1479) and Johann Froben (1491).

The Parisian collections contain evidence of eighty-six incunabula editions of the Bible in Latin, of which seven were published before 1471, thirty-six between 1471 and 1480, twenty-four between 1481 and 1490 and nineteen in the last decade of the fifteenth century. The peak period was therefore the 1470s, before a decline which drove booksellers to turn to new products. If we assume an average of 500 copies for each edition, we arrive at a total of more than 40,000 Latin Bibles put into circulation in less than fifty years. This number is all the more remarkable in that the Bible was often published in one or even two in-folio volumes, each comprising several hundred leaves. Certain workshops specialized in these, chief among them that of Koberger, whose first edition, repeating the version of 1462, appeared in 1475, to be followed by new editions in 1477, 1478 (two), 1479, 1480, 1482, 1485, 1487, 1493 and 1497. These dates of publication reveal the editorial policy of Koberger from 1477, with regular re-editions as and when stocks were exhausted.

Production peaked around 1480, after which the apparent saturation of the market forced the workshops to turn to some form of product innovation. New Nuremberg editions were now less frequent, but 1483 saw the appearance of the famous edition of the German Bible of Koberger, magnificently illustrated, to which I will return. The changing circumstances were accompanied by a change in the geography of production, which passed in part, around 1475–80, into the hands of great foreign printing houses. The first edition of the Latin Bible outside the German-speaking world was that produced in Rome by Sweynheym and Pannartz in 1471 – a very large in-folio volume of 628 leaves. It was followed by the editions of Johannes Petrus de Ferrariis in Piacenza in 1475, of Frantz Renner (of Heilbronn) and Nicolas of Frankfurt in Venice the same year and of Matthias Moravus in Naples in 1476. As we see, the vast majority of these early editions printed outside the German-speaking countries were the work of craftsmen of German origin: the transfer of techniques and production practices extended to editorial policies and choice of texts to be published, alike in Rome, Venice, Naples – and also Paris. In fact, it was once again the Mainz edition of 1462 which was the model for the German proto-typographers established in Paris, Gering, Crantz and Friburger, for their edition of 1476–7. The first Lyon printer to have published a Bible also came from an intermediary zone, Lorraine (Perrin Le Masson, alias Lathomus, in 1479), and all the others that have been identified are equally the work of Germans established on the banks of the Rhône – Marcus Reinhart and Nikolaus Philippi, Matthias Huss and Johann Syber.

The market and competition were once again central to product innovation, with the shift to the Bible in the vernacular. The European market for printed matter in the fifteenth century may have consisted largely of editions in Latin, but there was also a public of non-clerical readers for texts in the vernacular. There had already been a move to translate the Bible in the manuscript age in circles associated with religious reform or the *devotio moderna*, and also, especially in France, in those close to the royal court. The printing of Bibles in the vernacular began very early, the first German Bible (in old high German) being published by Mentelin in Strasbourg in 1466. However, its poor quality testifies to the difficulties encountered in an undertaking of a totally new type. The translator may have been Andreas Rüdiger, professor of theology at Leipzig. We may note in passing that Mentelin produced a number of other books aimed at a lay market: after the first German Bible, he printed two other major texts, the *Parzival* of Wolfram von Eschenbach and the *Der Junge Titurel* of Albrecht von Scharfenberg in 1477.[18] Also, Mentelin used a gothic font of small body for his German Bible, which enabled him to contain the text within the limits of a single in-folio volume, of 406 leaves in two columns and sixty-one lines to the page. The desire to limit costs is clear, with a view to facilitating distribution and producing a more manageable object.

Mentelin was followed, in 1470, by another Strasbourg printer, Heinrich Eggestein, with a quasi-counterfeit version of the Bible of 1466. Bibles subsequently became a speciality of the printing houses of Augsburg. Although this city was one of the largest in Germany at the time, its printers had to face fierce competition from their neighbours in Nuremberg, which led many of them to specialize in particular areas, in this case counterfeiting and books in the vernacular. A series of German editions of the Bible followed, from Jodocus Pflanzmann (*c.*1475), Günther Zainer (*c.*1475–6, then 1477) and Anton Sorg (1477 and 1480); we may recall here that Zainer had worked for a while in Strasbourg with Mentelin, suggesting the transmission of editorial policies from one town to another. Once again, however, the search for novelty drove printers to differentiate themselves, while at the same time reviving the market. Zainer innovated by establishing a better text than that used in Strasbourg and he inserted a beautiful historiated woodcut letter at the beginning of each book. The colophon emphasized the improvements he had made: this version was 'larger, clearer and more authentic' and the language used was superior. After Zainer's death (1478), the woodblocks were acquired by Sorg, who used them for his edition of 1480. In spite of the active censorship in Cologne, two editions were also printed in this town, perhaps by Bartholomäus von Unckel with the financial support of Koberger, in the years after 1478.[19]

The superb edition produced by Koberger in Nuremberg in 1483 combined innovations, for the most part following the text of the edition of Zainer, but re-using the 109 woodblocks of the Cologne editions of 1478.[20] The print run has been estimated at between 1,000 and 1,500 copies. The colophon emphasizes the improvements made both to the quality of the text and its presentation, hence its readability:

The text has been checked against the Latin, and it has been subdivided by the employment of punctuation, and it contains for the majority of the chapters and the psalms superscript titles specifying the content and the arguments. [Lastly, the edition comes] with beautiful illustrations explaining the stories.

The other editions in the vernacular (old high German) that were published before the version prepared by Luther at Wartburg in 1519 came from Strasbourg (1485), Augsburg (1487, 1490, 1507 and 1518) and Lübeck (1494, low German). The Reformation brought a new geography of production with a shift to Thuringia and the Saxony of Frederick the Wise (1463–1525).

In Italy the cultural transfer was again from Germany, as the first edition of the Bible in the vernacular was produced by Wendelin of Speyer in Venice in 1471, in a translation by Niccolo Malermi – and most of the editions of the Bible in Italian produced before 1501 came from Venice. We see once again the influence of the market and competition in the incunabula editions of the Bible in French, which initially emerged as a speciality of the printers not of Paris but of Lyon. The French *New Testament* came from the presses of Guillaume Le Roy, for Barthélemy Buyer, *c*.1476, followed two years later by the *Old Testament*, though in a translation not based on the original text but on the paraphrase of Petrus Comestor.[21] Different abbreviated editions of the Bible in French were also published in Lyon at this period, including the *Bible moralisée* of Martin Huss, *c*.1477. Paris took over from Lyon rather later, in 1488, with Antoine Vérard, but in a different context: Vérard had always specialized in books for court circles and the wealthy, at whom he aimed his first abbreviated Bible in French. He remained the chief supplier of 'the' Bible in French for many years to come, with the abbreviated edition of 1496 and the two-volume Bible of 1498–9, which was reprinted twice in the early sixteenth century (*c*.1505 and *c*.1517).

The *New Testament* came out in Czech soon after 1475, while the complete Bible appeared in the superb Prague edition of 1488. In Flemish it was the *Old Testament* that was published first (1477), the *New* only appearing much later (1522). We may also quote the first and very early Catalan version, published in Valencia in 1478. The wide dissemination of the Bible in the vernacular meant that the tradition of Holy Scripture was extremely influential in the construction of what would become the Europe of nationalities. And this Europe was further strengthened by the creation, with the Reformation, of territorial and sometimes national churches; the formation of the Anglican Church, for example, was based to a large extent on the vernacular, with not only the English Bible of Tyndale (1537) but also innumerable printed leaflets.

The traditional status of the text of the Scriptures as given in the Latin Vulgate was implicitly challenged from two directions: by the wider population, through translations, even adaptations, and by scholars and humanists, through reflection on the sources and new approaches to them. The problematic of the text and its analysis (philology) was first applied in the religious sphere. In his Latin commentary of the *Pandects* published by Josse Bade in Paris in 1508, and contrary to the tradition of Accursius, Guillaume Budé developed a systematic critique on the basis of the different versions to which he had access, in order to establish the best possible reading. This method was that of philology (*De Philologia*, 1532), which was subdivided into two branches, *philologia minor* dealing with profane texts, and *philologia major* dealing with Holy Scripture, the latter regarded as the keystone of knowledge. The editors first turned their attention to Greek, language of the New Testament, but also considered Hebrew, in spite of the difficulties, especially in the Rhine Valley.[22] Reuchlin had learned Hebrew in Italy; after the *De Verbo mirifico*, published by Amerbach in 1496, he produced a first Hebrew manual, the *Rudimenta linguae hebraicae*, in 1506.

After the *Quincuplex psalterium* of Lefèvre d'Étaples, initiatives came thick and fast, each more ambitious than the last. In 1516 Johann Froben, who had heard about the Polyglot Bible of Alcalá, published a *New Testament* in Greek, in Basel, with a facing Latin translation by Erasmus.[23] It owed its success to the latter's fame, but also to the novelty of his translation and the quality of the xylographic decoration by Urs Graf. Over 3,000 copies of the first two editions were printed in 1516 and 1519; the third edition appeared in 1522, and a fourth in 1527, to which the editor added the text of the Vulgate. As we have seen, however, the first true polyglot Bible was that of Cardinal Cisneros, archbishop of Toledo, printed in Alcalà in six volumes by Arnao Guillén de Brocar between 1514 and 1517 (the *Biblia complutense*).[24] Thanks to the scholars assembled by the cardinal it juxtaposed for the first time the Hebrew, the Latin, the Greek and, in this case, the Aramaic; the sixth volume consisted of a Hebrew dictionary and grammar, which provided, as it were, the tools for exegesis. Though the *Complutense* had a print run of 600, it never achieved the fame of the *New Testament* of Erasmus, but it was the basis for the work of Arias Montano, in Antwerp, for the *Biblia regia* of Plantin (1569–73).[25]

In Paris, Lefèvre d'Étaples published his first French translation of the New Testament with Simon de Colines in 1523 (this was also the first work the latter printed in the vernacular);[26] quickly examined by the Sorbonne, it was condemned in 1525. Philological study reached an apogee in 1529 with the creation of the College of Royal Readers, where the first chair was in Hebrew, while, in 1539, Robert Estienne was given the title of Royal Printer in Greek and Hebrew.[27] He embarked on a Hebrew Bible that same year, an in-quarto (4to) edition completed in 1544 – his first impression using Hebrew characters. Each book came out separately and the text was that of the 1488 edition of Soncino.[28] The enterprise was so successful that Estienne soon printed a version in sextodecimo (16mo). But the reaction of the Church and in particular the university of Paris became increasingly hostile with the advent of the Reformation, especially after the condemnation of the doctrines of Luther in 1521. In 1523, the Sorbonne declared that the new translations based on Hebrew or Greek were unnecessary and pernicious and that they should be excluded by the Church. When, in 1546, the Council of Trent decreed that every publication of scriptural texts should be submitted to the local Ordinary, the faculty of theology in Paris was able to condemn all the Latin editions of the Scriptures produced by Estienne since 1528: the condemnation, published in 1548, appeared in the first pontifical index of 1559. Two years later Estienne left Paris for Geneva; his Hebrew characters were acquired by the Parisian dynasty of Le Bé.

The project for a polyglot Bible was revived in the context of the Counter-Reformation with the *Biblia regia* of Plantin, for which the printer-bookseller was assured of the support of persons in high places, including Cardinal Granvelle and the private secretary of Philip II, Gabriel de Çayas. The *Biblia regia* offered versions of the text in five languages (Hebrew, the Latin of the Vulgate, Greek and its Latin translation, Syrian and Chaldean (Aramaic) and its Latin translation), completed once again by lexicons, grammars and historical commentaries. In 1573–4 Plantin printed an edition of the Hebrew Bible in small octavo (8vo), apparently intended to constitute, in conjunction with that of the New Testament in Greek and in Syriac, an edition of the sacred books in the oriental languages.[29]

The Reformation

The relationship between printing and the Reformation has generated an immense bibliography. There can be no question of recapitulating it here, except to emphasize that the theme of mediatization has a central place in this problematic, with regard not only to the Word of God, Scripture and its exegesis, but also to Grace, and even images and iconoclasm.[30]

Luther had once been an Augustinian at Erfurt, and then a student at Wittenberg, awarded a doctorate in 1512. He worked on the *Psalms* and the *Epistles* of Paul and, in 1512–13, developed his doctrine of Grace, which he refined in his teaching until 1518: man cannot justify himself by his acts or by his will; he is saved only by the unintelligible gift of the grace of God. The principle of indulgences and of all religion of contract was therefore to be condemned ('you cannot ride to heaven on parchment and wax', he wrote). On 31 October 1517, Luther attacked indulgences in his *95 Theses*, which he posted in manuscript on the door of the chapel of the Augustinians in Wittenberg. The *Theses* were quickly translated from the original Latin into German, then printed and widely disseminated, and they fed into the widespread criticism in Germany of the 'princes of Rome', that is, the princes of the Church. The controversy escalated, punctuated by university debates (*disputationes*) and printed publications, until the break with Rome (1519), excommunication (June 1520), publication of the *Address to the German Nobility*, the imperial ban and sanctuary in Wartburg, near Eisenach, under the protection of Duke Frederick the Wise (1521). It was here that Luther embarked on his translation of the *New Testament* into German. It was completed scarcely three months after the second edition of the translation of Erasmus, and published in September 1522 in Wittenberg, in an in-folio edition illustrated with engravings by Cranach; 2,000 copies were sold in the first few weeks, necessitating a reprint as early as December. Luther's complete translation of the Bible was published in 1534. The success of the Reformation from the point of view of the 'book trade' can be measured by the fact that, between 1522 and his death in 1546, 445 complete or partial editions of Luther's Bible were published, while catechisms and canticles were also widely circulated.

It may be impossible to establish a direct correlation between the invention of printing and the Reformation, but it is nevertheless clear that typography encouraged the fixing of texts, hence a hardening of positions, making conciliation more difficult, even giving its own dynamic to the polemic, which then acted in its turn as an echo chamber. Initially a religious issue, the Reformation became a political issue, and was soon also a publishing issue. The return to the text was central to Reformation thinking from the beginning, but its success was also due to its use of a concerted policy of mediatization. It was then the aspirations of a potentially sizeable public that made it possible for the media to develop its revolutionary impact, as Luther marvelled, with a perhaps assumed naiveté, in his famous letter to Leo X:

It is a mystery to me how my theses, more than my other writings and even those of other professors, were spread in so many places. They were meant exclusively for our...academic circle.[31]

In fact, it is still something of an open question how a message in Latin intended a priori for an audience of specialists so rapidly affected such a large number of readers. There existed, it is true, in Nuremberg, Augsburg, Basel and Leipzig a circle of cultivated readers interested in an issue debated in the sermons of many ecclesiastics. Pierre Chaunu has correctly emphasized that 'what happened in the sixteenth century came about in the area...of maximum cultural accumulation and sedimentation'.[32] The expectancy was there, and Luther's success cannot be understood without reference to the latent criticism of an omnipresent clergy; in Cologne, for example, a city of 30,000 inhabitants in 1400, there were no fewer than nineteen churches, 100 chapels and twenty-two monasteries (it has been estimated that one in nine inhabitants belonged to the clergy). Added to which, political divisions prevented the formation of any sort of German national church, and strengthened the subjection to Rome. The political position and interests of certain princes and magistrates, their power relations with the emperor and, lastly, the choices made by powerful foreigners, in particular the king of France – always keen to oppose the emperor – also played a role. The Reformers learned their lesson and their 'mediatic' choices were very quickly designed to appeal to the mass of the population, to whom of course one should preach the good word, but who should also be won over for political reasons – this was the invention of 'propaganda'.[33] Their thinking about language was characteristic: you should write in the language of the people and use only simple words, accessible to all. Luther theorized:

You must question the mother of the family at home, the children in the streets, the man of the people in the market, and hear out of their own mouth how they speak, then they will understand and they will realize that you are speaking to them in German.

If we turn our attention to England, we see that from propaganda to manipulation need not necessarily be a big step: when Thomas Cromwell, secretary to Henry VIII, organized the breakaway of the Anglican Church, he decided to have certain texts of Erasmus translated to make them accessible to the people. But the translation was far from faithful and there was no hesitation about opportunely misrepresenting the original text to make it conform more closely to the official anti-papist positions.[34]

Another innovation was the widespread use of printed matter of a modern type, single sheets and tracts (*Flugschriften*). These were short texts, in German, that recorded recent events with a polemical or parodic twist. The page layout was equally innovative and characteristic: the fonts were the standard gothic and images, even caricature, featured prominently. At the level of production and distribution, these publications had the dual advantage of being possible to prepare and print quickly and cheaply and of being easy for the partisans of one or the other camp to distribute outside professional circles, strictly speaking. The success of the Reformers also owed much to their excellent understanding of distribution, as when Johann Schabeller suggested, in inimitable style, to Guillaume Farel, then in Montbéliard, that he place his leaflets with mercers: 'But send them to some mercer, so he might acquire an appetite for selling books, and it might happen that bit by bit and in parallel he might earn something....'[35]

The flimsy nature of the object also made it easy to reproduce in large numbers: a successful text was very quickly taken up by other printing houses and the production/distribution network expanded in proportion. The multiplier continued to operate at the level of appropriation, which was on a very large scale, not only through individual reading but also through public readings, commentaries, and so on. The number of people affected was far in excess of the number of copies printed, especially as the sale price fell in line with the reduction in production costs. The figures are to some extent guesswork but it has been estimated that, between 1501 and 1530, some 8,000 pieces and pamphlets were published in Germany. The other parties seized on this weapon and a title like that of the *Zwölf Artikel* (*Twelve Articles*) of the rebellious peasants was quickly reprinted in fifteen towns. More than 300,000 copies of thirty writings of Luther were disseminated between 1517 and 1520,[36] and a correspondent wrote to Zwingli, from France, in 1520 that:

> [In Paris] no books are more avidly bought [than those of the Lutherans]. One bookshop has sold 1400 of them. Everywhere, people speak well of Luther.

Finally, the rapid increase in the production of Protestant printed matter was directly linked to the new geography of 'the book trade' in Germany. Leipzig and the publishing towns of Saxony (first Wittenberg, later Halle, etc.) were the chief centres of production for 'German books', as opposed to 'international books', the latter in Latin and chiefly published in the West (Frankfurt and its fairs), and which fell gradually into decline in the seventeenth century. In 1519, the principal Lutheran printer-bookseller was Melchior Lotter in Leipzig and Wittenberg, but others soon followed, such as Georg Rhau, publisher of Melanchthon's *Confessio Augustana* and later cantor at St Thomas of Leipzig. Other forms of propaganda existed alongside printing and engraving, like the portraits of Luther painted by Cranach and his workshop; these were widely disseminated, especially after 1521, in the form of paintings, but above all in the form of engravings: everybody could recognize the face of the Reformer or of the Duke of Saxony in this or that engraving or caricature. The fact that Dürer gave his support to Luther's theses, as also did a number of humanists such as Melanchthon, was another factor that played an important role.

The situation in Germany was complicated by the rupture and political rivalries. The Reformers had not intended to form a new Church but they were overtaken by events, from 1524–5, when Luther called on the princes to crush the rebellious peasants. In 1530 the Reichstag of Augsburg revealed, paradoxically, that the religious unity desired by Charles V was impossible, and the Protestants then organized themselves within the territorial frameworks of the different principalities, while also creating broader federative structures. Even after the death of Zwingli (1531), the Lutheran doctrine lost some of its universality, to the extent that it was now compromised by the princes or magistrates. The revival of Lutheranism would come from Calvinism.[37]

Regulation: Imposing Order on Books

The opening up through the media generated a ferment from which humanists and scholars benefited, but which was also accompanied by the affirmation of new reading practices and a new scale of values, following a radical re-ordering of the model of knowledge. In antiquity and the Middle Ages the world order was conceived as a concentric system, closed in on itself, in which, with Christianity, the successive circles of Creation were organized round the figure of God: it is he who is seen on the ceiling of the baptistery of Parma and in the magnificent engravings of the first leaves of the *Chronicle of Nuremberg*. The increased number of books and the changed status of the text represented a threat of dislocation; as today with the screen and the Internet, the system of knowledge seemed to be losing its cohesion in favour of a sort of potentially subversive chaos – it quickly came to seem even more necessary to regulate possible reading practices, and no longer only through the devices of the *mise en texte*.

Openness would force control, just as the fixing and diffusion of the model of the printed page imposed order on the words and the language while strengthening social 'policing' and recording. The possibilities opened up by the media led in the medium term to a process of closure and confinement: increasing deregulation had to be met by a new form of regulation.

The text and the norm

I will pass quickly over the first point, which I have discussed above. Printing was an extremely powerful tool for the definition and organization of the text as text. The standardized presentation of the book in quires related to the linear, analytical and hierarchized structure of thought: linear, because the reader necessarily followed the development, itself linear, of the discourse; analytical, because the analysis of the alphabetical system was continued in that of the discourse in sentences, paragraphs, chapters, parts, etc., made visible by the typographical arrangement and organized with the material structure of the volume in leaves and pages; hierarchized, because this analysis in smaller and smaller units substituted for the mnemotechnical reference a detailed and abstract scale of the components of the discourse. It was inevitable that this standardization would eventually lead to a standardization of grammar, orthography and the usages of the 'classical' language. Lastly, the proliferation of books entailed their classification according to an epistemological division that was itself more precise, between the knowledge regarded as fundamental and the knowledge considered more subsidiary – according to the image of the tree of knowledge.

As already stated, writing, and printing even more so, served as an aid to supervision and social control. A contrario, songs, cries and spontaneous manifestations were regarded as subversive and as such to be suppressed. In Valenciennes, in 1562, two heretics were condemned to be burned but the crowd freed them before the execution – and the scandal was first and foremost one of singing in public, in spite of the prohibitions posted throughout the town:

> We inform and advise you that both by the notices of our Lord the King and the proclamations made in this town it has been forbidden to each and every one to sing the Psalms of David in the streets and meeting places, yet it has come to the attention of MM the provost and jurors that Marie Massart, on the day of high feeling at the impending execution of their prisoners, allegedly came forward to put herself in the throng of singers in the marketplace and allegedly sang with the others in great contempt and as an affront to justice and gave

by these means comfort to the audacity of those who were preparing
the escape of the said two prisoners.[38]

Open-air preaching, in the countryside or at the city gates, was forbidden the following year and a notice posted to this effect.[39]

For printing also provided the authorities with the possibility of
fixing and above all disseminating normative and regulatory texts.
With Schoeffer and the first printers, legal publishing had initially
concentrated on 'scholarly' law and the great juridical collections and
their commentaries, all in Latin. In the sixteenth century the principal
printing houses in Lyon continued to work in this sector but there
was also, in parallel, a change of direction, with the rise of the history
of law (we may think of Cujas) and the publication of contemporary
regulation – in the vernacular. If we confine ourselves to France, in
the sphere of private law, custumals were the first texts to be systematically published, following the Ordinance of 1454 (Montils-lès-
Tours) imposing the committal of customs to writing. The first
Coutumier général, published in 1517, inaugurated a series which
culminated in 1724 with the *Nouveau coutumier général* of Bourdot
de Richebourg. From the point of view of the publishing economy
we should add a second category, that is, editions of private custumals, first in Maine and Anjou (by 1476), then gradually throughout the kingdom. This regulation was theorized by the French
monarchy in the ordinance of Villers-Cotterêts (1539). So alongside
private law there was now public law and affairs of state: the great
normative texts organizing the functioning of the kingdom came one
after the other throughout the sixteenth century, at a time when,
paradoxically, the monarchy was gradually losing the means to apply
them (ordinances of Villers-Cotterêts, Orléans, Moulins and Blois).
At the same time, the creation of the post of royal printers (1539)
made it possible eventually to grant them exclusive rights to publish
public documents. In fact the model for the policed society was provided by the court, and it was above all by the regulation of the new
media of printing that the court, in France, imposed its choices on
the rest of the social body. The 'book-machine' was succeeded by the
'king-machine' of the reign of Louis XIV.[40]

The proliferation of titles and copies also had the effect of encouraging the fixing of a standardized language. Italian was already the
language of Dante, the first edition of whose work was published in
1472 by Neumeister in Foligno. In England, Caxton was troubled
by the diversity of dialects, but effectively imposed the English of
London and the court by his publications. In Germany, the choice was
made by Luther, who wished to use printing to reach the maximum

number of people. In France, the situation was more complicated: on
the one hand, the vernacular was imposed by its use at court and by
the administration; on the other, language became a subject of debate
among humanists and writers as efforts were made to enrich French
to give it the status of language of culture, hitherto reserved for Latin.
When, in 1529, Geoffroy Tory published his *Champ Fleury*, he organized his thesis into three books; in the first of these he tried to 'put and
order the French language by certain rules of speaking elegantly into
a sound and more proper French language'.[41] In almost Rabelaisian
vein, he laid into those who corrupted and deformed French, the
'*escumeurs*' ('skimmers') of Latin, the '*plaisanteurs*' and the '*jargon-
neurs*' ('jokers' and 'jargonmongers'), then the 'forgers of words' and
the 'innovators'. He suggested making the language subject to rules so
that the 'speech and words were proper and acceptable in all reason
and all honour', to avoid excessively rapid changes. Tory explained
that he could have written his treatise in Latin but that:

> wishing in some small way to illumine our French language a little so
> that, alongside educated persons the common people may use it, I wish
> to write in French. I am sure that some tedious scoffer will soon say I
> want to pass as the author of something new...So I shall write in my
> own humble style and language learned from my mother...In that I
> may well seem a new man because no one has yet seen written instruc-
> tion in the French language in the manner and style of writing, but
> desiring in some small way to light up our language I am content to
> be the first little marker to stir some noble spirit who will go further,
> as the Greeks and Romans once did, to set out and arrange the French
> language with a certain norm for pronunciation and good speak-
> ing...Here I call to witness Latin poets and orators to show that we
> have a gift of grace in our fine French language.

The same argument was repeated and taken further by Du Bellay
in 1549 in his *Défense et illustration de la langue française*:[42] French,
he said, could not be described as barbaric; even if it was less rich
than Greek or Latin, it had already made considerable progress and
might one day, through the labours of writers, reach a comparable
peak of perfection. Du Bellay returned at several points in his text to
the decisive role he attributed to Francis I; French specificity appeared
above all in the cultural dimension of political action.

The drive for standardization was also applied to the aesthetic of
typography and here, too, Geoffroy Tory played a major role. Born
in Bourges, Tory had made two journeys to Italy before returning
and starting to teach in Paris, where he opened a bookshop and then
a printing house (1529). His *Champ Fleury* is a treatise

which contains the art and science of the due and proper proportion
of the Attic letters that are sometimes called antique letters, and popu-
larly Roman letters, proportioned according to the body and the
human face.

His aim was to define and improve the typographical vocabulary in
order to make it serve the public good and the glory of the mother-
land. The aesthetic context was defined as that of 'due proportion'
and symmetry and its status combined bibliographical reference and
geometric 'evidence'; its scale was provided by the human figure. At
the beginning was a table of the authorities, in this case the authors
and other 'honest persons' mentioned in the text. It was not an index,
as there was no system of reference making it possible to find the
various passages, but a simple alphabetical list consisting of the body
of leading authorities as determined by the author and as generally
accepted at the time. The choice of language, Latin or French, was
not consistent for each name but varied, presumably according to
custom and above all ease of pronunciation – Tory put Cicero in
Latin but Erasmus in French (Érasme) and he returned elsewhere in
the text to the question of French or foreign pronunciation.

The organization of the printed text continued with detailed
instructions regarding punctuation marks. Tory then moved to the
Hebrew and Greek letters and to the different categories of French
'letters': cadel initials at the beginning of a book, littera formata,
bastardas, etc., not forgetting flowered letters and even 'utopian'
letters, a paradoxical term for a sphere he was attempting to rationalize and standardize. We should note that he used the term 'Attic',
rather than 'ancient': the reference was to ancient Greece, to which
the kingdom of France was immediately related by this ideal genealogy, beyond a Roman intermediary he wished to deny. The geometri-
cal basis of the constructions was provided by the two letters *I* and
O, in which Tory also saw an echo of the legend of Io; the typographic aesthetic and its justifications had an obvious political dimension both in the choice of the vernacular and in the status accorded
to the Greek tradition. Lastly, research on the page layout was also
sustained in the body of the volume, in spite of its small format and
the need to incorporate numerous xylographs.

Controlling the media

Under this head we need to distinguish several different issues,
depending on whether the aim was to protect the economic interests
of the printers through the grant of an editorial privilege, to control
the content of the books through censorship or, later, to restrict the

number of those involved, in particular in printing, and thus reduce competition; or even, lastly, to address the problem of intellectual property and the rights of the author. In every case, however, what was involved was regulating printed output and confining it within the canon of the lawful uses to which alone it might be put. For the historian, there is also the question of the normative character of the regulatory text and its efficacy in reality.

The privilege was a title by which the government protected the interests of the printers by guaranteeing exclusive rights to a particular text to whoever had printed it or organized its printing: it was forbidden to publish, even import and sell, this text for a certain period of time, usually five or ten years, within the jurisdiction of the authority issuing the privilege. As we have seen, the first act of this type dates from 1469, when the Venetian Senate granted a privilege of five years to Johannes de Speyer for his edition of the works of Cicero. The aim was to protect the printer-bookseller who had committed the investment necessary to the publication, although we know that the nuncio constantly complained that the supervision exercised by the Serenissima was still insufficiently strict... In France, as elsewhere, to obtain a degree of protection one needed access to the highest circles of power. It was through the intermediary of Constantine Lascaris that Jacques Ponceau, physician to Charles VIII, obtained a privilege for five years for the edition of Avicenna published by Trechsel – and the letter from this great humanist was reproduced in the first volume.[43] According to the calculations of Elisabeth Armstrong, a total of 106 privileges were granted to booksellers by the Grand Chancellery of France between 1498 and 1526.[44]

The principal booksellers were quick to see the advantages of systematically seeking a privilege, the text of which they could include in the published volume. Thus the second part of the title of the *Champ Fleury* states, before the address, that 'this book is privileged for ten years by the King our Sire', under penalty for counterfeiters of a fine of 100 silver marks and confiscation of their entire stock; in addition, the complete text of the act signed at Chenonceaux was reproduced at the beginning of the volume. It was equally logical that as soon as privileges represented a negotiable value the principal printers working in foreign markets should aim, like the Giunti, to acquire numerous privileges for the various countries in which they hoped to distribute their books – in the case of the Giunti in Venice, Naples, Spain and France. Paradoxically, however, the increasing geographical integration of the states of Western Europe made privileges increasingly ineffective. The vast majority of French literature was counterfeited abroad in the eighteenth century, and sometimes reintroduced illegally as contraband into France itself. In Germany, it was the printers themselves who set out to organize the exclusion of forgeries from a rapidly expanding German-speaking market where political fragmentation made control impossible.[45] Conversely, the privilege system also tended to strengthen the position of the biggest printers and implicitly encourage them to stricter observance of the various measures taken to police books. The privilege system was here a factor favouring conservatism.

Alongside commercial protection, the key issue was control of content: doctrinal censorship (*censura*) was administered by the faculty of theology; religious censorship by the ecclesiastical authorities, pope, bishops or council; a third form of censorship, political, was the business of the secular authorities alone. Another distinction was between preventive censorship (applied to texts before publication) and repressive censorship (imposed after the event). It was the latter that was most effective, because it was applied after the copies had been printed, when distribution was prohibited or the books were seized. The threat lay heavy on whoever was responsible for the edition, the printer or the bookseller, and encouraged the habit of self-censorship. One last distinction, much more difficult to apply, related to the identification of the authority responsible for censorship – the Church and its representatives, the prince, the university, a sovereign court, etc. When Erasmus attacked those he called the 'monks', he meant by this term the doctors he accused of wishing to substitute their power for that of the prince. The problem was complicated by the fact that these 'monks' were not judicially dependent on the civil authorities and it was often difficult to know exactly who they were accountable to, even within the Church; the result was that 'these buffoons, trusting to this state of affairs', were 'as bold as can be'.[46]

With printing new measures began to be introduced when, in Germany, the publication of the German Bible of Cologne (1478) galvanized the university into seeking a brief from the pope authorizing it to censor books (preventive censure). In 1485 the archbishop of Mainz followed suit. Two bulls instituted prior censorship, the first in 1501 (*Inter multiplices*) and the second in 1515 (*Inter sollicitudines*); the latter, declaimed by Leo X at the Fifth Lateran Council, generalized the principle that all books published ought first be authorized by the Church.[47] Very soon after 1517, however, the booksellers sensed a commercial opportunity in the Reformation, and the very wide circulation of the first Lutheran texts owed much to the fact that German printers and booksellers were still prominent in the 'little world' of the book.[48] Luther's theses were condemned by the universities of Cologne and Louvain (1517), followed by Rome and Paris: with the bulls *Exurge Domine* (1520) and *Decet Romanum pontificem* (1521), Luther was excommunicated and his books condemned to be burnt. Most intellectuals agreed with Erasmus that some degree of control was necessary, if only to avoid scandals and defend the honour of those who had sometimes become public figures – the authors. Yet this was a double-edged weapon, which illustrated the paradox of censorship: Erasmus obtained an edict from the king prohibiting distribution of a book by Beda, but then grumbled that this prohibition had become a marketing tool and that the book had spread even more rapidly, if clandestinely, as a result. In fact repression and autos-da-fe often had unintended consequences and Erasmus emphasized that the success of the Reformers had been consolidated by the suppression of their books:

> The clamour has only brought fame to these books, which were previously known only to a very small number, and it has caused people to read them who had never intended to do so. This was all gain for the booksellers; the louder our people shouted, the more profitably they distributed their copies.[49]

In fact censorship was inextricably caught up in the new paradigm of publicity, which meant it was necessary to act with a degree of moderation, given that overall control of the media already seemed unattainable: when Erasmus told the pope, in 1523, that he wished that, 'if such a thing were possible...even permission for pamphlets would also be restricted', he was already implicitly doubting the feasibility of his proposal.[50]

But if Erasmus remained on the side of moderation, the hardening of opposing views on religious issues meant that, from the 1520s, censorship was increasingly conceived as an ensemble of repressive measures to be systematically organized and implemented. The spread of printed matter spurred the Sorbonne into publishing an Index of the books it prohibited (1452), a practice soon copied in Louvain (1546), then Portugal (1547), Venice (1549) and Spain (1551). The first Roman Index was issued by Paul IV in 1558; it included some 8,000 forbidden titles and a list of sixty-one printers whose entire production was prohibited. However, it was the Index of the Council of Trent (1564) that marked the decisive moment before, in 1571, the new Congregation of the Index was made responsible for maintaining the list. By the end of the sixteenth century it contained some 2,400 condemnations.

The rapid spread of Lutheranism and the 'scandals' which accompanied it prompted, at this same period, the development of true political censorship, the responsibility of governments. In France, Luther's writings were widely found in Paris in the 1520s, and also in many provincial towns (Meaux, Bordeaux, Grenoble, Lyon, Avignon, etc.). A royal mandate of 18 March 1521, confirmed by a decree of Parlement in June, prohibited the distribution of books dealing with theological issues if they had not first been approved by the faculty of theology in Paris; the university wasted little time before condemning Luther through 104 of his propositions time (5 April), a condemnation repeated by Parlement – and we may note that this decision was publicized in the traditional fashion, with a trumpet:

> In the said year 1521, Saturday, 3rd August, it was proclaimed with trumpet call at the crossroads of Paris that by order of the court of Parlement all booksellers, printers and any other persons having books by Luther, they should bring them to the said court within eight days on pain of a fine of 100 livres and imprisonment...[51]

Further controls followed: Parlement ordered the seizure of all the books of Luther and Melanchthon, which were to be examined and if necessary destroyed; translations of the Bible and Books of Hours were also targeted (1523). Unsurprisingly, the booksellers, who often had many copies of these suddenly forbidden titles in their possession, opposed these measures, but uncertainty reigned due largely to the position of Francis I. For example, the king intervened in 1526 to halt the proceedings against Erasmus and Lefèvre d'Étaples and to forbid the distribution of the book by Noël Bede, syndic of the faculty of theology. The Berquin affair, which dates from this period, reveals the struggle for power: Louis de Berquin, a Flemish gentleman born in 1490 and a former student at Orléans, translated Luther, Erasmus and Ulrich von Hutten and wrote a *Farce of the Théologastres*. Twice accused before Parlement, he escaped prosecution after the king intervened in his favour, but on the third occasion, this time in the king's absence, Berquin was condemned to death and executed as quickly as possible before the king's return (1529).[52] Two years later, Parlement instituted the visiting of bookshops to examine the books and if necessary make seizures.

The situation became even more difficult following the affair of the Placards (17–18 October 1534), after which seven executions were ordered in Paris by Parlement. Among those condemned were three men of the book, including Antoine Augereau. At the beginning of 1535, as we have seen, the king issued an edict forbidding printing in the kingdom, a measure soon withdrawn. The appearance in Basel in 1536 of Calvin's *Institutes of the Christian Religion*, in Latin, heightened the tension and the hardening of attitudes made things increasingly difficult for the printers close to humanism. When the *Institutes* was prohibited (1542), many booksellers and printers chose exile in Geneva; others were executed, beginning with Étienne Dolet (1546).[53] After the death of Francis I, the edict of Chateaubriand reorganized and extended the censorship of Protestant books (1551). In other countries, too, executions marked the high point of the repression, as in the case of William Tyndale, condemned to the stake at Vilvorde in 1536.

The situation was very different in Spain, where the Inquisition was given the prime role. Created at the beginning of the thirteenth century for the defence of the faith against heresy, the Inquisition was an institution which derogated from the power even of the Church. However, its influence had become negligible by the period of interest to us here except in Spain, where, in 1478, the Catholic Kings obtained a bull from the pope creating the Spanish Inquisition under their authority. The first inquisitor general was Torquemada (1485–94), and a special administration was established, with a supreme council and regional tribunals. Though initially preoccupied with overseeing the conversion of the Jews and Muslims, from 1492 the Inquisition exercised repressive censorship, then extended its activities to the Protestants. At the same time, the Pragmatic of Toledo (1502) reserved to the Catholic Kings the right to issue permits to print. From 1533–6 the Inquisition controlled the import of books into Spain. In 1551 it published a first Index, on the basis of that of Louvain, followed by a second in 1559, and then a General Index in 1583. This was a highly oppressive structure which, even in the case of authorized works, made the conditions of publication and the delays a disincentive for booksellers.

Control and censorship were not exclusive to the Catholic states and, as is well known, both Luther and Calvin favoured the policing of texts. For Luther, it was necessary to control the production and distribution of books because the majority of readers were not capable of his reading ethic – they read too much, too quickly, and without discernment. He developed (this was in 1520) a relatively traditional conception of the practice of reading. For him the doctors, including the theological doctors, were creatures of the universities, when the Holy Spirit alone 'made [a] doctor of Holy Scripture'. The only way to achieve this was through a form of intensive reading – reading and rereading the same texts, memorizing them and making them fully one's own. This was still a system of authorities, more reminiscent of medieval conceptions of reading than the modern choice made by the humanists of a sort of conversation with the texts and their authors:

As for books, you should reduce the number and choose the best, nor should you read many, but should read good things and read them often, and even if they are few, it is this that brings knowledge of Holy Scripture and piety at the same time. You should not even read the writings of all the Holy Fathers except for a while to be initiated, thanks to them, in Holy Scripture; I read them now only to look back at them; and I never embark on the Scriptures.[54]

Luther theorized an opposition between the mass of 'common people' (*gemein*) and a minority whose specialized education qualified them to guide and administer the Church. Cochlaeus even complained that:

Luther's New Testament has been so multiplied and so widely disseminated by the printers that even tailors and shoemakers...women and ignorant people, who have accepted this new Lutheran gospel and who can read a little German have studied it avidly as the source of all truth.

Not all the humanists welcomed the growth of a doctrine which saw in the sole text of Scripture the purpose of all things. But Calvin was no more in favour of letting everyone read what they wanted, even if it was Holy Scripture: you needed to be initiated into a proper understanding by those whom God had called on to instruct the rest. The censorship instituted in Geneva in 1539 required the deposition of one manuscript copy of the text for scrutiny, the prior authorization of the Council and observance of the legal deposition for the purpose of surveillance. Even if the enforcement of these measures was more desultory, they nevertheless resulted in a number of condemnations.

Printing and Governments

The power balance with regard to the media was unclear, even irrational. In France, the government responded to the media explosion by putting in place an administration for the book trade, but the relationship between the three competing powers, that is, the king, Parlement and the Church remained confused. Supervision was exercised through the identification of the editions and those responsible for them. Erasmus was already of the opinion that every publication should bear the name of the author and an indication of the place of publication and the printer. In a memorandum to the magistrates of Basel, he declared that the absence of these elements should be punished, particularly if false information had been given (*c*.1525).[55]

However, it was the Ordinance of Moulins (February 1566) which, in France, in its eighty-six articles, organized the whole of the printing and bookselling sector comprehensively and systematically. By making the possibility of printing a book dependent on obtaining a sealed privilege from the Grand Chancery (article 78), the Ordinance established the principles of the book trade in France throughout the *ancien régime*, by which the commercial protection provided by the privilege was coupled with a degree of control:

> We forbid every person whosoever to print or cause to be printed any books or tracts without our leave, permission and letters of privileges sent under our great seal, in which case we enjoin the printer to put and inscribe his name and address together with the said leave and privilege, this on pain of confiscation of property and corporal punishment.

Yet, at the same time, printing was instrumentalized in order to add lustre to a government long close to the humanist movement. When, in 1529, Frances I instituted the Royal readers, the future Collège de France, it was in opposition to the Sorbonne, and the first holder of the chair of Hebrew was Vatable, formerly of the 'Meaux group'. The young Calvin studied with them. Seven years later the edict of Montpellier forbade the sale of any book that had not been deposited in the Bibliothèque royale, but the aim was less that of control than of glorification; it was necessary to prevent editions from being lost in the absence of measures to preserve them. The sovereign was mindful of the quality of the printed works: Charles VIII had been the first to emphasize the exceptional success of the *Mer des histoires* printed by Pierre Lerouge for Vincent Commin in Paris in 1488–9 by making him the first recipient of the title of Royal printer. Francis I revived the title, granting it on a permanent basis to Robert (I) Estienne, 'printer of the king for Latin and Hebrew', then for Greek. The merging in 1544 of the library of Blois with that of Fontainebleau, which had been administered by Budé (died 1540) since the end of the 1520s, prefigured the future Bibliothèque royale and completed a project in which *les bonnes lettres*, printing and the graphic arts were all called on to glorify the monarchy and the kingdom.

Conclusion

꩜

It was [with the passage of the Cape of Good Hope] that the men of the most distant countries became necessary to each other...everywhere [they] exchanged their opinions, their laws, their customs, their cures, their illnesses, their virtues, and their vices...
Guillaume François Raynal, *Histoire des deux Indes* (1770)

In the space of three generations the social communication systems of Western societies had experienced an unprecedented transformation: typography with movable characters had everywhere prevailed, an entire new economic sector had emerged, new reading practices had been generalized and the categories of intellectual representation itself had been redefined. This was truly a revolution, in that one system of social communication had replaced another, while, at the same time, the conditions and practices of the reading and appropriation of texts had radically changed.

Chronologies

Let us look first at the chronology of this complex of phenomena. Printing appeared around 1450, but, for this process to be intelligible, the historian needs to adopt a more long-term approach.[1] The discovery was only made possible by a number of earlier developments, and in particular by a fundamental change in the economy of the manuscript. In the twelfth and thirteenth centuries market forces began to play an increasingly large role, totally transforming the earlier system of auto-production (a religious house creating its own library through copying). Writing and the associated techniques increasingly penetrated Western urban society, to which they offered new possibilities for growth, whether in the expansion of trade and the economy, the establishment of more modern political structures or even, soon, territorial expansion, with the beginning of the great voyages of discovery. Lastly, the invention of Gutenberg was only one of a whole range of diverse and innovative developments. It marked the apogee of a general opening up which had begun long before and it happened in the region of maximum innovatory sedimentation, that of the towns of the Rhineland and Central Europe.

But we need to examine the changes after the invention, too, and a historical approach brings out the importance of continuity. First, internal continuity: what was written on the new printed support, to use a modern term, was quite naturally – it might even be said inevitably – the old content. Continuity of form, too: the aim, initially, was to reproduce the form of the manuscript, whether in the case of the writing, the layout, the format or even the models of decoration and illustration. The possibilities presented by printing were slow to be identified and even slower to be explored and exploited – the genealogy of the title page is a good example. Innovation developed at the meeting point between the different actors comprising the literary sphere, who reorganized round the media. It came from the craftsmen who innovated to expand their businesses, but also from the consumers, or from certain categories among them, who changed both reading practices and categories of representation. And it came, lastly, from the authors, researchers and scholars. They were of very different types (authors, adapters, translators, correctors, etc.) and they, too, tried to position themselves as favourably as possible in a changing environment. The revolutionary effects of the media penetrated to the heart of the social configuration as a whole, to which they were constantly reacting.

In fact the study of the history of the media ends up displacing the very category of chronology, because it is the nature of the media as media that allows the articulation between continuity and rupture. Continuity, because the change was the inevitable consequence of what went before, but rupture, because the media and its environment led to major innovations in the ways it was used and in the representations that were associated with them.

Semiology and Virtuality

One of most important characteristics of the media was its presence at the confluence not only of material categories (technology, the economy, etc.), but also of cultural and intellectual categories. In the latter case the decisive innovation came much earlier than the invention of Gutenberg: the importance of the rereading of Aristotle by the scholastic doctors can hardly be exaggerated, in that it was the basis, over the very long term, of the system of modern thought. The construction of the sign as a transparent tool which was used to describe a particular reality (whose representation as such belongs to the sphere of philosophy) marked a decisive advance on three essential points relevant to the history of the media. The first was the spread of the practice of silent reading, which assumed full internalization of the logic of the semiotic triangle. The second is the idea of the arbitrary code, which led, for example, to the construction of new types of index and other systems of classification. Last, the principle of semiology facilitated not only the storage and treatment of information, but proved a particularly powerful aid to the growth of the intellectual tool constituted by virtuality. Almost no research has been done on this subject, although the construction of a 'paper world' on the basis of which experiences (including, at the literary level, the novel) and arguments were developed has been one of the key elements in modernity.

The possibility of constructing a virtual world was opened up by the new theory of the sign, but its development was hugely assisted by the technology of printing. Scholasticism still functioned as an intellectual technique characteristic of an environment poor in texts; it involved organizing the oral discourse so as to control it and encouraging memorization independently of the support. Everything changed with printing and its increasingly universal presence; not only did the transformation of reading practices accelerate (extensive reading), but it was no longer necessary to memorize in the same conditions, and even the very category of the text changed. A contrario, the massively increased power of the media meant that it related in new ways to the political configurations in the broad sense of the term. It posed, for example, the problem of the control of texts, but also of their more or less open circulation and its consequences. To develop the theory of a universal priesthood, based on open access to the Scriptures, was in itself revolutionary, because it challenged the definition of the first order of society, that of the *orantes*, those who prayed. The generalization of printing inevitably came to pose the question of literacy, and democracy itself would be understood as universal participation in the collective life by means of the media. In fact with printing the media became political, as would soon also be the case with the history of the book as a subject of research.

It should be added as a codicil that there is no 'instrumental history of thought' in itself (Alain de Liberá); but the genealogy of thought and the archaeology of knowledge can only develop by integrating these very 'instruments' which are a priori external to them and among which those relating to mediatization logically occupy first place. This articulation becomes all the more important when it itself reflects a cumulative process of externalization – the metaphor of the computer helps us to understand the phenomenon by the way it highlights the opposition between on the one hand hardware and consumables, and on the other software and information. Thought, too, operates as an interface and requires a certain lapse of time before it is able to absorb, integrate and go beyond the new information that is submitted to it. What has been called the 'media explosion' describes precisely this configuration, in which a collectivity is subject to the revolutionary consequences born of an increasingly large-scale and increasingly rapid growth and circulation of information, which it does not yet have the capacity to absorb. The effects of this are manifold, and I mention here only the instrumentalization of information and the integration of propaganda as a political weapon. Luther had already reproached Rome for its instrumentalization of words:

> The *administratio* is also one of these glosses, it establishes that someone may have, in addition to his bishopric, an abbey or an office and possess all this property provided he has no other title than that of administrator; because it is enough for Rome that the words change and not the reality.[2]

One of the questions in need of further research, consequently, is whether these phenomena are quantifiable and in what circumstances; we may assume that the bibliographical databases that are today being rapidly assembled will enable us to take the discussion further by measuring more precisely the volume and the distribution of the information available at each period.[3]

Product and Market

The study of the first 'media revolution' also brings into relief the huge importance of economic factors in the process of innovation, and this at two levels. The two principal actors behind the change have been identified as the capitalist investors and a public of 'new consumers'. With the former we are in Braudel's logic of capitalism. It was the capitalists who financed the technical research carried out in all sorts of different areas, and it was also they who, at a later stage, exploited the new processes that had been developed. In a relatively short time the capitalist investors brought the new sector of the 'book trade' into the modern system structured round the editorial function.[4] The profit motive determined not only the development of the innovation, but also the transition from process innovation (the invention of printing) to product innovation (new objects, then new contents).

So the business of a man like Melchior Lotter in Leipzig and Wittenberg may have owed as much to clearly perceived financial interests as to strictly religious preferences. The paradigm of 'money' and 'letters' may have been present from the beginnings of printing, but it should not therefore be understood as an antagonistic system, rather as, on the contrary, making it possible to connect the two. A second phenomenon appears in the background: 'business' functioned outside political categories and the geographical distribution of publishing and bookselling quickly expanded to include the whole of Western Europe. Here too, as sometimes today with the Internet, governments were alive to the consequences that followed from an omnipresent media, which they saw as escaping them and threatening chaos; some societies respond by allowing free play to the economic actors (England and the United Provinces), others not.

The consumers were the second main agents in the process of change. I have already described the role played by the interrelated concepts of the market and competition in innovation and in its differentiations, and I return to this point only to emphasize that the consumers – in this case, the readers – did not simply receive a certain innovation and adapt to it. Not only was the economy of consumption itself innovatory, but individual and collective practices should also be understood as innovatory, so that product innovation as practised by the printer-booksellers may be seen as resulting from the dynamic balance between producers and consumers of books and texts. Lastly, in the long term, one of the trends set in motion by the imperative of the market and the product was increasing concentration and globalization.

Gutenberg's Europe

Let us return, in conclusion, to my title, 'Gutenberg's Europe', and use to illustrate it an image famous in the little world of the historians of the book, that chosen by Prosper Marchand as frontispiece to his *Histoire de l'imprimerie*, published for the third jubilee of the invention (1740). It reveals the European dimension of the phenomenon, as well as the hierarchy of the process of transmission which had made possible its spread. The scholarly activity which developed round the media eventually culminated in this modern science, this *Wissenschaft*, for which Prosper Marchand's book was the model. Its geography was that of a Europe both 'international' – the Europe of the learned, the scholars, and the 'enlightened' men of the Republic of letters (itself structured round the written word) – and 'national', a Europe in which the media of print tends precisely to reinforce the enlarged solidarities of national frameworks. These tend in time to model themselves on the logic of nation-states, whose founding categories are those of a language and a 'culture' fundamentally linked to writing and the book.

'Gutenberg's Europe' is first the Europe in which Gutenberg lived, in other words the Europe of the first two thirds of the fifteenth century – it, too, of course, the product of an earlier history. But 'Gutenberg's Europe' is also the Europe created, over time, by Gutenberg, or rather by the effects of the medialogical revolution set in motion by the invention of typography with movable characters. In this sense modern Europe is Gutenberg's Europe, the Europe to which the medium of print gave its means of understanding, of action and of world domination (physical, intellectual, internal) and the impulse for its own organization (princely state, then nation-state). Its favoured organizing categories were cultural in nature, that is, political, first as regards the glory of the prince, later a shared language and culture. It is possible that by the same token the gradual expansion of the European model into a Western model extending to the whole world will combine with the transformations of the system of the 'globalized' media – and that 'Gutenberg's Europe' will disappear with the exclusivity of the civilization of the printed word. The expression 'Gutenberg's Europe' has allowed me to describe both the original connection (Europe and printing) and its possible future towards another media, other solidarities and no doubt another Europe.

Notes

⁂

Foreword

1. <http://www.enssib.fr>, then follow the book marks.
2. <http://www.ihmc.ens.fr/>.
3. <http://www.ephe.sorbonne.fr/enseignements/4livre.htm>.

Introduction: The Media and Change

1. *Trois révolutions, passim*; CNAM, *passim*; DEL, *passim*; Elizabeth Eisenstein, *The Printing Revolution in Early Modern Europe* (Cambridge, 1983); *Incunabula and Their Readers: Printing, Selling and Using Books in the 15th Century*, ed. Kristian Jensen (London, 2003).
2. Robert Marichal, 'L'écriture latine et la civilisation occidentale du Ier au XVIe siècle', reprinted in *Histoire et art de l'écriture* (Paris, 2005), pp. 650–700.
3. *La Cantilène de sainte Eulalie* (Valenciennes, 1990); at: <http://www-01.valenciennes.fr/bib/decouverte/histoire/cantilène/transcription.htm>.
4. The genealogy of the scripts is explained by Denis Muzerelle in the article 'Gothique' in DEL, 2.
5. Jacques Le Goff, *Les Intellectuels au Moyen Age*, 1st edn (Paris, 1957; reissued 1985), trans. Teresa Lavender Fagan as *Intellectuals in the Middle Ages* (Oxford, 1993); Alain de Libéra, *Penser au Moyen Age*, new edn (Paris, 1996).
6. See the map in Jean Delumeau, *La Civilisation de la Renaissance*, new edn (Paris, 1984), p. 71.
7. Marie-Thérèse Lorcin, *Société et cadre de vie en France, Angleterre et Bourgogne (1050–1250)* (Paris, 1985), p. 31.

8. Fernand Braudel, *Civilisation matérielle, économie et capitalisme, XVe–XVIIIe siècle*, 3 vols (Paris, 1979), vol. 3, p. 470; trans. Siân Reynolds as *The Perspective of the World* (London, 1984), pp. 15–16.

Chapter 1   The Preconditions for a New Economy of the Media

1. Fernand Braudel, *Civilisation matérielle, économie et capitalisme, XVe–XVIIIe siècle*, 3 vols (Paris, 1979), vol. 3, p. 472; trans. Siân Reynolds as *The Perspective of the World* (London, 1984).
2. *Histoire de la France urbaine*, vol. II: *La ville médiévale à la ville de la Renaissance*, ed. André Chedeville, Jacques Le Goff and Jacques Ross (Paris, 1980). Paul Bairoch, Jean Batou and Pierre Chèvre, *La Population des villes européennes, 800–1850: banque des données et analyse sommaire des résultats 800–1850 = The Population of European Cities: Data Bank and Short Summary of Results 800–1850* (Geneva, 1988). For the modern period, see Jan de Vries, *European Urbanization, 1500–1800* (London, 1984).
3. *Histoire de Chartres et du pays chartrain*, ed. André Chédeville (Toulouse, 1983).
4. *Memling und seine Zeit. Brügge und die Renaissance* (Stuttgart, 1998).
5. François Deshoulières, 'L'abbaye de Chezal-Benoît', in *Mém. Soc. Antiquaires du Centre*, 32 (1909), pp. 149–223; Catalogue ancien de la bibliothèque (1649) BnF, ms. lat. 13068.
6. Hippolyte Boyer, *History des imprimeurs et libraires de Bourges, suivi d'une Notice sur ses bibliothèques* (Bourges, 1854).
7. Paris, Arsenal, ms 3686 (CMEL, I, p. 167 and plate CXLVI).
8. Henri-Jean Martin, *History et pouvoirs de l'écrit* (Paris, 1988), trans. Lydia Cochrane as *The History and Power of Writing* (Chicago, 1994).
9. *Histoire de Valenciennes*, ed. Henri Platelle (Lille, 1982), p. 53; more generally, Harvey J. Graff (ed.), *Literacy and Social Development in the West: A Reader* (Cambridge, 1981).
10. *Florence et la Toscane, XIVe–XIXe siècles. Les dynamiques d'un Etat italien* (Rennes, 2004).
11. Brussels, Royal Museums of Fine Arts, Inv. 3637.
12. Bruges, Groeninge Museum.
13. Berlin, *Gemäldegallerie*, 1645 and 1645A.
14. AmValenciennes, AA 148.
15. Paris, Louvre Museum, Inv. 1444. The painting once belonged to Rubens.
16. Brunswick, Herzog Anton Ulrich Museum, Kupferstichkabinett.
17. Marie-Thérèse Lorcin, *Société et cadre de vie en France, Angleterre et Bourgogne (1050–1250)* (Paris, 1985), p. 317.

18. Gerhard Dohrn van Rossum, 'The diffusion of the public clocks in the cities of late medieval Europe, 1300–1500', in *La Ville et l'innovation en Europe, 14e–19e siècles*, ed. B. Lepetit and J. Hoock (Paris, 1987) pp. 29–43.

19. *Püchel von mein Geslecht und von Abentewer* (HAB, Cod. Guelf. 19 Aug. 4°).

20. Max Weber, *The Protestant Ethic and the Spirit of Capitalism* [1905], trans. Talcott Parsons (1930); Max Weber, *The City* [1921], trans. in *Economy and Society* (1922).

21. Michael T. Clanchy, 'Literate and illiterate; hearing and seeing: England, 1066–1307', in Graff (ed.), *Literacy and Social Development in the West*, pp. 14–45.

22. Donatella Nebbiai dalla Guarda, *La Bibliothèque de l'abbaye de Saint-Denis en France du IXe au XVIIIe siècle* (Paris, 1985).

23. Franz Buschholz, *Die Bibliothek der ehemaligen Kölner Kartause* (Cologne Bibliothekar Lehrinstitut, 1957) (typescript); Gérald Chaix, Réforme et contre-réforme catholiques: recherches sur la chartreuse de Cologne au XVIe siècle, thèse de IIIe cycle, Tours, 1981, 3 vols, typescript.

24. C. Lautier, 'Les arts libéraux de la librairie capitulaire de Chartres', in *Gesta* XXXVII-2 (1998): 211–16.

25. AdNord, 1G 780.

26. G. Ouy and V. Gerz von Buren, *Le Catalogue de la bibliothèque de l'abbaye de Saint-Victor de Paris de Claude de Grandru (1514)* (Paris, 1983); Alfred Franklin, *Les Anciennes bibliothèques de Paris* (Paris, 1867–73), 3 vols ('Histoire générale de Paris').

27. Kunstmuseum, Basel, Inv. 510; reproduced at: <http://www.kunstmuseumbasel.ch/de/collection.html>, signet 'Virtuelle Sammlung'.

28. Henri Pirenne, 'L'instruction des marchands aux Moyen Age', in *Annales d'histoire, économie et société*, 1 (1929), pp. 13–28.

29. Jean Favier, *Paris au XVe siècle* (Paris, 1974) ('Nouvelle histoire de Paris').

30. Richard and Mary Rouse, *Illiterati et Uxorati: Manuscripts and Their Makers. Commercial Book Producers in Medieval Paris, 1200–1500*, 2 vols (Turnhout, 2000).

31. Bologna, Bibl. univ., ms 1456 (Sorbelli 963), foline 4r.

32. BmCambrai, ms 620.

33. Jacques Verger, 'Les bibliothèques des universités et collèges du Midi', in *Livres et bibliothèques* (Toulouse, 1996), pp. 95–130.

34. Isabelle Chiavassa-Gouron, 'Les lectures des maîtres et étudiants du Collège de Navarre…(1380–1520)', in *Positions des thèses des élèves de l'École nationale des chartes* (Paris, 1985); Karine Rebmeister, 'La bibliothèque médiévale du collège des Cholets', ibid. (Paris, 2001). See also *HBF*, pp. 92–111 ('Les bibliothèques de collèges et d'universités'), pp. 112–23 ('La bibliothèque du collège du Sorbonne').

35. H. M. Vicaire, article 'Dominicans', *DEMA* (Paris, 1997).

36. P. Amargier, 'Le livre chez les prêcheurs dans la province de Provence au XIIIe siècle', in *Actes du 95e Congrès national des sociétés savantes*, I (Paris, 1970), esp. p. 414; Kenneth William Humphreys, 'Les bibliothèques des ordres mendiants', in *HBF*, pp. 125–45; A.-M. Genevois, J.-P. Genest and A. Chalandon, *Bibliothèques de manuscrits médiévaux en France* (Paris, 1987).

37. Nathalie Hurel, 'À propos de quelques manuscrits enluminés de la bibliothèque des dominicains d'Avignon (XIIIe–XVe siècle)', in *Livres et bibliothèques*, pp. 418–40.

38. Father Bernard Montagnes, OP, 'La bibliothèque de Saint-Maximin en 1508', in *Livres et bibliothèques*, pp. 241–59.

39. P. Pansier, *Histoire du livre et de l'imprimerie à Avignon du XIVe au XVIe siècle* (Avignon, 1922).

40. Frankfurt, Städel Museum (Dominikaneraltar).

41. Paris, Musée Jaquemart-André.

42. Their role would be essential in the sixteenth century in the sphere of cultural history: Sylvie Le Clech, *Chancellerie et culture au XVIe siècle: les Notaires et secrétaires du roi* (Toulouse, 1993).

43. *Schriftstücke*, 39.

44. With increasing complexity in the types of administrative documents: mandates, letters missive, letters close, letters patent, letters under seal (*lettres de sceau plaqué*), *lettres de cachet*, warrants, orders, bonds, and so on.

45. Françoise Autrand, 'Le service public', in *La France médiévale* (Paris, 1983), pp. 285–303.

46. Hélène Millet, *Les Chanoines du chapitre cathédral de Laon (1272–1412)* (Rome, 1982).

47. René Fédou, *Les Hommes de loi lyonnais à la fin du Moyen Age* (Paris, 1964).

48. Charles de la Roncière, 'De la ville à l'Etat régional: la constitution du territoire (XIVe–XVe siècle)', in *Florence et la Toscane*, pp. 15–38.

49. Pierre Bourdieu, *La Distinction: critique sociale du jugement*, 2nd edn (Paris, 1979) ('Le sens commun'), trans. Richard Nice as *Distinction: A Social Critique of the Judgement of Taste* (London, 1984).

50. Chantilly, Musée Condé, ms 65, reproduced at: <http://humanities .uchicago.edu/images/heures.html>. See also M. Meiss, *French Painting in the Time of Jean de Berry* (London, 1969).

51. Städel Museum, Frankfurt.

52. Bedford, who was regent of the kingdom, bought what remained of the library of Charles V after the death of Charles VI (1424), that is, 843 manuscripts.

53. Élisabeth Pellegrin, *La Bibliothèque des Visconti-Sforza, ducs de Milan* (Paris, 1955).

54. *Bibliotheca corviniana*, catalogue of exhibition, Budapest, 1990.

55. Frédéric Barbier, 'Représentation, contrôle, identité: les pouvoirs politiques et les bibliothèques centrales', in *Francia: Forschungen zur westeuropäischen Geschichte*, 26/2 (1999): 1–22, illustration; Patricia

Stirnemann, 'Les bibliothèques princières et privées aux XIIe et XIIIe siècles', in *HBF*, pp. 173–91, illustration; Geneviève Hasenohr, 'L'essor des bibliothèques privées aux XIVe et XVe siècles', ibid. pp. 215–63, illustration.

56. Jaques Monfrin, 'Humanisme et traduction au Moyen Age', in *JS* (1963), pp. 161–90.
57. BnF, ms fr. 1348 (*Charles V*, Paris, 1968, 198).
58. BnF, ms fr. 1950 (*Charles V*, 183).
59. *Charles V*, especially 168.
60. BnF, ms fr. 2813 (*Charles V*, 195); *Traduction et traducteur au Moyen Age*, ed. G. Contamine (Paris, 1989).
61. Patrick M. de Winter, *La Bibliothèque de Philippe le Hardi, duc de Bourgogne (1364–1404)* (Paris, 1985); Danielle Quéruel, ed., *Les Manuscrits de David Aubert, 'escripvain bourguignon'*, (Paris, 1999).
62. Ludwig Mohler, *Kardinal Bessarion als Theologe, Humanist und Staatsmann* (Paderborn, 1923); *Storia della cultura veneta*, 3 vols (Vicenza, 1980): vol. 1, pp. 252ff and n. 334.
63. *Le Livre voyageur. Constitution et dissémination des collections livresque dans l'Europe moderne (1450–1830)* (Paris, 2000).
64. Lord of Gruuthuse and Steenhuijs, c.1422–92. Councillor of Philip the Good, then of Charles the Rash, chamberlain of the duke, governor of Holland, Zeeland and Frisia, knight of the Order of the Golden Fleece (1461).
65. The Hague, Museum Meermanno, ms 10–B 23 (and *Charles V*, 168). Jean Bondol was also the author of the cartoons on which the Apocalypse Tapestry at Angers was based.

Chapter 2 The Economy of the Book

1. Robert Mandrou, *Introduction à la France moderne, 1500–1640. Essai de psychologie historique* (new edn, Paris, 1974) ('L'évolution de l'humanité'), pp. 76ff., trans. R. E. Hallmark as *Introduction to Modern France, 1500–1640: An Essay in Historical Psychology* (London, 1975).
2. Uwe Neddemeyer, *Von der Handschrift zum gedruckten Buch. Schriftlichkeit und Leseinteresse im Mittelalter und in der frühen Neuzeit. Quantitative und qualitative Aspekte* (Wiesbaden, 1998), 2 vols ('Buchwissenschaftliche Beiträge aus dem deutschen Bucharchiv München'); Carla Bozzolo, Dominique Coq and Ezio Ornato, 'La production du livre en quelques pays d'Europe occidentale aux XIVe et XVe siècles', in *Scrittura e civiltá*, 8 (1984): 131–60.
3. Jesús Alturo i Perucho, *Història del llibre manuscrit a Catalunya* (Barcelona, 2003) ('Textos i documents').
4. BnF, ms orient., arabe 4457.
5. *Tous les savoirs du monde* (Paris, 1996), pp. 136ff.
6. *Federico II. Immagine e potere* (Venice, 1995).

7. Umberto Eco, *Le Signe* (new edn, Paris, 1998) (French translation, adapted from *Il segno*, Milan, 1973).
8. Reprod.: <http://www.ipf.tuwien.ac.at/publications/ld_ch 96/>.
9. Germaine Aujac, *Claude Ptolémée astronome, astrologue, géographe* (Paris, 1993).
10. Etienne Gilson, *La Philosophie au Moyen Age*, 3rd edn (Paris, 1947); Alain de Libéra, *Penser au Moyen Age*, new edn (Paris, 1996).
11. Corinthians II: 3–6.
12. David R. Olson, *The World on Paper: The Conceptual and Cognitive Implications of Writing and Reading* (Cambridge, 1994).
13. Quoted by David Olson, ibid., p. 172.
14. *Pratiques de la culture écrite dans les universités du midi de la France*, ed. E. Ornato and N. Pons (Louvain-la-Neuve, 1995).
15. See the reproductions at <http://classes.bnf.fr/phebus/index.htm>.
16. Anne Lefèvre-Teillard, 'Le livre juridique manuscrit (XIe–XVe siècle)', in *HCL*, 1 (2005): 11–32, illustration.
17. *Dictionnaire des lettres françaises. Moyen Age*, new edn, ed. Geneviève Hasenohr et al. (Paris, 1992).
18. BnF ms fr. 117. Reproduction of the illuminations: <http://gallica.bnf.fr/Catalogue/noticesInd/MAN00805.htm>.
19. Ernest Langlois, *Les Manuscrits du* Roman de la rose: *description et classement* (Lille, 1910).
20. BnF ms fr. 380. The father of Guillaume Budé also owned a beautiful illuminated manuscript of the *Roman de la rose*, which can be dated to the thirteenth century and is almost certainly of Parisian provenance (Paris, Bibliothèque Ste-Geneviève ms 1126).
21. Johan Huizinga, *The Waning of the Middle Ages*, p. 118.
22. Berlin, Gemäldegalerie, 2142. (repr. <http://cgfa.sunsite.dk/paolo/p-paolo6.htm>). Another representation with the St Jerome of Ghirlandaio in 1494 (<http://www.wga.hu/frames-e.html?/bio/g/ghirland/domenico/biograph.html>).
23. *Mise en page, passim*.
24. Erwin Panofsky, *Gothic Architecture and Scholasticism* (New York, 1957) (the 'sensus communis').
25. The *ductus* was the movement of the pen in tracing a letter, and, by extension, the order of the elements constituting each letter as it was written, as well as the direction in which they were written.
26. *Mise en page, passim*.
27. Jean Vexin, 'La ponctuation aux XIIIe, XIVe et XVe siècles', in *Mise en page*, pp. 443–5, illustration.
28. The modern verses were introduced into his editions by Robert Estienne from 1551 to 1557. The Lyonnais printer-bookseller Jean Frellon inserted an indent at the beginning of the first line of each verse (1555).
29. BnF ms lat. 513 (and *Dieu en son royaume* (Paris, 1991), no. 77).
30. Serge Lusignan, 'Lire, indexer et gloser: Nicole Oresme et la *Politique d'Aristote*', in *L'Ecrit dans la société médiévale* (Mélanges Lucie Fossier) (Paris, 1991), pp. 167–81.

31. The running head, in the upper margin of each page, showed the title of the work, book or chapter, or even a brief note of the content of the page.
32. Danièle Jaquart and Charles Burnett, *Scientia in margine. Etudes sur les Marginalia dans les manuscrits scientifiques du Moyen Age à la Renaissance* (Geneva, 2005) (Hautes études médiévales et modernes, 88); see also p. 260.
33. M. A. and R. H. House, 'La naissance des index', in *HEF*, pp. 76–85.
34. BmValenciennes, ms 1–5, after the notice of Françoise Simeray, in *Livres parcours* (Valenciennes, 1995), p. 4; Reproduced, at: <http://www.ville-valenciennes.fr/bib/accueil/mani1-5.asp>.
35. Erwin Panofsky, *Studies in Iconography* [1937] (Oxford, 1972), pp. 26–7.
36. Erwin Panofsky, *Perspective as Symbolic Form* (New York, 1991), p. 44.
37. Pierre Francastel, *Peinture et société* (Paris, 1965), p. 133 ('idées/arts').
38. BrB, ms 9004.
39. Saint Augustine, *Confessions*, quoted by Alberto Manguel, *Une Histoire de la lecture*, trans. French (Arles, 2000), p. 61 ('Babel').

Chapter 3 The Birth of the Market

1. *Pragmatische Schriftlichkeit im Mittelalter: Erscheinungsformen und Erscheinungsstufen* (Munich, 1992).
2. *La Face cachée du livre médiéval. L'histoire du livre vue par Ezio Ornato* (Rome, 1997), p. 91.
3. Richard H. Rouse and Mary A. Rouse, 'The Book trade at the university of Paris, ca 1250–ca 1350', in *La Production du livre universitaire au Moyen Age: exemplar et pecia* (Paris, 1988), pp. 41–114; Jean Destrez, *La Pecia* (Paris, 1935).
4. *Chartularium Universitatis Parisiensis*, ed. H. Denifle and E. Chatelain (Paris, 1889–97), 4 vols, I, 462: AN M⁶⁸, no. 1; see also *Le Livre*, 419.
5. Louis Jacques Bataillon, 'Les textes théologiques et philologiques diffusés à Paris par *exemplar* et *pecia*', in *La Production du livre universitaire*, pp. 155–63. I here follow this contribution.
6. *La Mystique rhénane* (Paris, 1963), especially Philippe Dollinger, 'Strasbourg et Colmar, foyers de la mystique rhénane (XIIIe–XIVe siècles)', pp. 3–13.
7. F. Brunner, 'Maître Eckhart et la mystique allemande', in *Contemporary Philosophy: A New Survey*, 6, 1 (1990): 399–420.
8. Digitization of the manuscripts of the 'Rhenish mysticism' preserved in the national and university library, Strasbourg: <http://www-bnus.u-strasbg.fr/default-elibrairie.htm>.
9. H. B. Workman, *John Wycliff* (Oxford, 1926); K. B. McFarlane, *John Wycliffe and the Beginnings of English Nonconformity* (London, 1952).

10. The most important manuscript of Wycliffe preserved in England contains a collection of 243 sermons: Trinity College, Cambridge, ms B-16.2.

11. The modern edition is *The Holy Bible...Made from the Latin Vulgate by John Wycliffe and His Followers*, 4 vols (Oxford, 1850).

12. Mirjam Bohacová (ed.), *Česká kniha v proměnách staletí* [*The Czech Book over the Centuries*] (Prague, 1990).

13. I. Hlaváček, 'Zum böhmischen Bildungs-u. Bibliothekswesen der ersten Hälfte des 14. Jts.', in *Scientia und Ars im Hoch-u. Spätmittelalter* (Berlin and New York, 1994), vol. II, pp. 795–806.

14. Marie-Élisabeth Ducreux, 'Lire à en mourir: livres et lecteurs en Bohême au XVIIIe siècle', in *Les Usages de l'imprimé* (Paris, 1987), pp. 253–303.

15. *5e centenaire*.

16. Father De Backer, *Essai bibliographique sur le livre* De Imitatione Christi (Liège, 1864). The first French translation was published by Henricus Mayer in Toulouse in 1488.

17. Victor Leroquais, *Les Livres d'Heures manuscrits de la Bibliothèque nationale*, 3 vols (Paris, 1927–43); see also the article by Albert Labarre on the 'Hours' in the *Dictionnaire de théologie catholique*.

18. Le Livre dans la vie quotidienne, exhibition catalogue, Bibliothèque nationale (Paris, 1975), p. 81.

19. Chantilly, Musée Condé. Reproduced: <http://www.institut-de-france.fr/animations/berry/berry.swf>.

20. Johan Huizinga, *The Waning of the Middle Ages*, pp. 153ff. ('Religious Thought Crystallising into Images').

21. Paris, Arsenal, ms 5059 (CMEL, I, 171 and plate XXXII).

22. Paris, Arsenal, ms 2071 (CMEL, I, 143 and plate LVIII).

23. BnF ms fr. 246.

24. Paris, Arsenal, ms 2886 (CMEL, I, 151 and plate CXXXI).

25. BmBourges ms 4; reproduced at: <http://www.enluminures.culture.fr/documentation/enlumine/fr/>.

26. 'Dit du département des livres', ed. J. Engels, in *Vivarium* (1970), pp. 70–9.

27. C. P. Christianson, 'Evidence for the study of London's late medieval manuscript-book trade', in *Book Production and Publishing in Britain 1375–1475*, ed. J. Griffith and D. Pearsall (Cambridge, 1989), pp. 87–108.

28. Patrick de Winter, 'Copistes, éditeurs et enlumineurs de la fin du XIVe siècle: la production à Paris de manuscrits à miniatures', in *Actes du centième congrès national des sociétés savantes* (Paris, 1978), pp. 173–98.

29. Giessen, Universitätsbibliothek, ms 945.

30. Introduction to the facsimile of the *Roman de Fauvel*, BnF ms fr. 146.

31. BnF ms fr. 10132.

32. AN M^{68}, 20; BnF ms fr. 241; *Le Livre*, 426, 427.

33. *Le Livre*, 430.

34. Chantilly, Musée Condé 277 (CMEL, I, p. 21) for the first volume, and BnF ms fr. 9106 for the second. For Chantilly, notice in *Le Cabinet des livres. Manuscrits. Tome premier* (Paris, 1900), pp. 215ff.
35. Paris, Arsenal, ms 3483–94 (CMEL, I, p. 161).
36. *5e centenaire*, pp. 3ff.
37. Konrad Bürger, *Buchhändleranzeigen des 15. Jahrhunderts in getreuer Nachbildung* (Leipzig, 1907); Auguste Hanauer, 'Diebolt Lauber et les calligraphes de Haguenau au XIVe siècle', *Revue catholique d'Alsace*, 14 (1895): 411–27, 481–93, 563–76; Rudolf Kautzsch, 'Diebolt Lauber und seine Werkstatt in Hagenau', *Centralblatt für Bibliothekswesen*, 12 (1895): 1–112; W. Fechter, 'Der Kundenkreis des Diebold Lauber', *Centralblatt für Bibliothekswesen*, 55 (1938): 121ff.; Liselotte Saurma-Jeltsch, *Spätformen mitterlalterlicher Buchherstellung. Bilderhand-schriften aus der Werkstatt Diebold Laubers in Hagenau* (Wiesbaden, 2001). The Lauber catalogue is preserved in the university library of Heidelberg, Cod. Pal. Germ. 314, reproduced at: <http://www.ub.uni-heidelberg.de/helios/fachinfo/www/kunst/digi/lauber>.
38. Paris, Arsenal, ms 5070 (CMEL, I, p. 173 and Plate XCIV); *La Librairie des ducs de Bourgogne*, 1 (Turnhout, 2000), p. 61.
39. BnF ms fr.166.
40. Patrick M. de Winter, *La Bibliothèque de Phillippe le Hardi, duc de Bourgogne (1364–1404)* (Paris, 1985).
41. A. Sorbelli, *Storia della stampa in Bologna* (Bologna, 1929); G. Orlandelli, *Il Libro a Bologna dal 1300 al 1330* (Bologna, 1954).
42. Vespasiano da Bisticci, *Le Vite*, ed. A. Greco (Florence, 1971).
43. Huizinga, *Waning of the Middle Ages*, p. 248.
44. *Manuscrits à peintures du XIIIe au XVIe siècle* (Paris, 1955), no. 106. The numbers in square brackets indicate the leaves on which the various entries are found.
45. P.M.L., New York, inventory M 346 (and *Le Dessin français: chefs-d'oeuvre de la Pierpont Morgan Library* (Paris, Louvre, 1993). Other similar but extremely rare documents are known, of which the most famous is the 'Carnet de Villard de Honnecourt', an architect of the thirteenth century (ed. on CD-ROM by Roland Bech mann, BnF/Hexagramm 2).
46. Charles Sterling, *La Peinture médiévale à Paris, 1300–1500*, vol. 2 (Paris, 1990).
47. The duke's library had from him the *Pontifical de Sens* (Brussels, B.R., ms 9215), the *Grandes chroniques de France* (St Petersburg, Erm. 88) and the *Heures* of Philip the Good (Paris, BnF ms. n.a.f. 16428).
48. *Le Siècle d'or de la miniature flamande* (Brussels, 1959); Hélène Servant, *Artistes et gens de lettres à Valenciennes à la fin du Moyen Age (vers 1440–1507)* (Paris, 1998) ('Cahiers d'histoire du livre', 3).
49. Charles Sterling and Jean Porcher, *Musée des Beaux-Arts de Tours: l'art du Val-de-Loire, de Jean Fouquet à Jean Clouet, 1450–1540* (Paris, 1952).
50. *Le Livre*, pp. 435, 436.

51. *Jean Fouquet, peintre et enlumineur du XVe siècle*, ed. Françoise Avril (Paris, 2003). Reproduced at: <http://classes.bnf.fr/fouquet>.

Chapter 4 The Development and Logics of Innovation

1. Henri Alibaux, 'L'Invention du papier', in *Gut. Jb.* (1939), pp. 9–30; Dard Hunter, 'The papermaking moulds of Asia', in *Gut. Jb.* (1940), pp. 9–24.
2. *L'Art du livre arabe* (Paris, 2001), p. 38.
3. *Wolfgang v. Stromer*, 'Große Innovationen der Papierfabrikation in Spämittelalter und Frühneuzeit', in *Technikgeschichte*, 60/1 (1993): 1–6, illustration.
4. The laid lines (thick wires) run parallel to the shorter side, the finer and denser chain lines parallel to the longer side. Their arrangement in a copy of a particular book is an important indicator in determining the bibliographical format. The variability of the size of the leaves explains the variability of the physical formats (for example, an 8vo is larger or smaller according to the size of the leaf).
5. Giancarlo Castagnari, 'L'Arte della carta e il suo museo a Fabriano', in *Fonti e studi di storia dell'editoria* (Bologna, 1995), pp. 125–36; *Le Papier au Moyen Age: histoire et technique* (Turnhout, 1999); C.-M. Briquet, *Recherches sur les premiers papiers employés en Occident et en Orient du Xe au XIVe siècle* (Paris, 1886); C.-M. Briquet, *Les Filigranes*, new edn (Amsterdam, 1968), 4 vols.
6. *Schriftstücke*, 84.
7. CNAM, pp. 51–62.
8. Wolfgang von Stromer, 'Au berceau des médias de masse: l'invention de l'impression des textes et des images', in *Mélanges Aquilon*, pp. 9–24, illustration; CNAM, pp. 63–9.
9. Perhaps by the tenth century in Germany and the twelfth century in Italy. But, according to *Le Livre*, since antiquity.
10. Ludwig Wilhelm Schreiber, *Handbuch der Holz- u. Metallschnitte des XV. Jts.*, new edn (Stuttgart, 1969–76), 11 vols.
11. BSB, Cgm 281; *Thesaurus librorum*, no. 85; *Blockbücher*, no. 12.
12. *Blockbücher*, 29b.
13. *Villes d'imprimerie et moulins à papier du XIVe au XVIe siècle* (Brussels, 1976); Natalis Rondot, *Les Graveurs sur bois et les imprimeurs à Lyon au XVe siècle* (Lyon–Paris, 1896), pp. 128ff.; *Le Siècle d'or de l'imprimerie lyonnaise* (Paris, 1972), pp. 123ff.; CNAM, 49.
14. CNAM, 48.
15. Horst Appuhn and Christian von Heuisinger, 'Der Fund kleiner Andachtsbilder des 13. bis 17. Jahrhunderts im Kloster Wienhausen', in *Niederdeutsche Beiträge zur Kunstgeschichte*, 4 (1965): 157–238.
16. *Blockbücher*, 42c.

17. Leonhard Hoffmann, 'Druck von Bild und Schrift vor Gutenberg. Massenproduktion von Andachtsbildern in Padua 1440/41', in *Gut. Jb.* (2004), pp. 57–74, illustration.

18. We know from the inventory of the Abbess of Bethany, near Malines, that a press was used to print the engravings in 1465: W. L. Schreiber, 'Vorstufen der Typographie', in *Mainz 1900*, p. 30.

19. *Fifteenth century Italian woodcuts from Bibliotheca Classense in Ravenna* (Ravenna, 1989); *Xylografie italiane del Quattrocentro da Ravenna e di altri luoghi* (Ravenna, 1987).

20. Rudolf Schenda, 'La lecture des images et l'iconisation du peuple', trans. Frédéric Barbier, in *RFHL*, 114–15 (2002): 13–30, illustration.

21. Vatican Museum.

22. *Blockbücher des Mittelalters. Bilderfolgen als Lektüre* (Mainz, 1991); *5e centenaire*, pp. 78ff.

23. *Blockbücher*, 50.

24. *Blockbücher*, 49. *Regiomontanus* = of Königsberg (between Bamberg and Schweinfurt), his place of birth.

25. Elke Purpus, 'Die Vorläufer der Blockbücher der Apokalypse', in *Blockbücher*, pp. 99–180.

26. Jean-Pierre Drège, *L'Imprimerie chinoise s'est-elle transmise en Occident?* (Peking, 2005) (Publications de l'École française d'Extrême-Orient, 'Conférences académiques franco-chinoises'). It offers a critical approach to the work of Thomas F. Carter, *The Invention of Printing in China and its Spread Westward* (New York, no date).

27. Chantal Lemercier-Quelquejay, *La Paix mongole* (Paris, 1970), here p. 47 ('Questions d'histoire').

28. Wolfgang von Stromer, *Gutenberg's Secret. From Turfan to Karlstein*, ed. Dirk Reitz, trans. from German by Catherine Dyer and Philip Gilead (Geneva, 2000).

29. Fernand Braudel, *Civilisation matérielle, économie et capitalisme, XVe–XVIIIe siècle*, 3 vols (Paris, 1979), vol. 2, pp. 280ff., trans. Siân Reynolds as *The Wheels of Commerce*.

30. Bertrand Gille (ed.), *Histoire des techniques. Technique et civilisation. Technique et sciences* (Paris, 1978) ('Encyclopédie de la Pléiade').

31. Franz Falk, 'Der Stempeldruck vor Gutenberg und die Stempeldrucke in Deutschland', in *Festschrift zum funfhundertjährigen Geburtstage von Johan Gutenberg* (Mainz, 1900) ('Beiheft zum Centralblatt für Bibliothekswesen', 23); Ernst Kyriss, 'Schriftdruck vor Gutenberg', in *Gut. Jb.* (1942), pp. 40–8; Ernst Kyriss, 'Schriftdruck auf Einbänden des 15. Jahrhunderts', in *Gut. Jb.* (1950), pp. 88–96.

32. *5e centenaire*, pp. 107–8, 123–4.

33. Jean-François Belhoste, 'Les hommes du fer: réflexions sur l'émergence et la diffusion de l'innovation (XIVe–XVIIe siècle)', in *Le Technicien dans la cité en Europe occidentale, 1250–1650* (Rome, 2004), pp. 271–89.

34. It was in Constance, in the 1440s, that engravings on metal (copper) were used for the first time.

35. Abbé Requin, *L'Imprimerie à Avignon en 1444* (Paris, 1890) (review by K. Dziatzko in *Centrallblat für Bibliothekswesen*, 7 (1890), pp. 248–51); Abbé Requin, 'Origines de l'imprimerie en France', in *Journal de l'imprimerie et de la librairie* (28 February 1891); M. L. Du Hamel, *Les Origines de l'imprimerie à Avignon* (Paris, 1890); M. A. Claudin, 'Les origines de l'imprimerie en France: premiers essais à Avignon en 1444', in *Bulletin du bibliophile* (1898); Ritter, p. 489 (appendix X); P. Pansier, *Histoire du livre et de l'imprimerie à Avignon du XIVe au XVIe siècle* (Avignon, 1922).
36. Maurice Audin, *Histoire de l'imprimerie. Radioscopie d'une ère, de Gutenberg a l'informatique* (Paris, 1972) (with supplementary bibliography).
37. A. J. van der Aa, *Biographisch Woordenboek der Nederlanden... voortgezet van K. J. R. van Harderwijk*, III (Haarlem, 1858), pp. 760–4.
38. AdNord, 36 H 431*, fols 158, 161v (cf. Hélène Servant, *Artistes et gens de lettres à Valenciennes à la fin du Moyen Age (vers 1440–1507)* (Paris, 1998) ('Cahiers d'histoire du livre', 3), p. 258). *Gros* and *patars* are monetary units.
39. Marchand, pp. 15–17.
40. *5e centenaire*, pp. 66ff. An example of *Speculum* in Flemish preserved in the north of France (BmLille D–45) dates from the 1480s and was probably printed by a technique of block-pages.
41. Manuscript lost in Strasbourg in 1870, but which had been copied by Spach; quoted by Ritter, p. 27.

Chapter 5 Gutenberg and the Invention of Printing

1. '(1458) The art of printing was invented in those days for the first time in Germany; some attribute this discovery to the Strasbourger Gutenberg, others to a different person who bore the name of Fust. Nothing in the world could be more worthy, or more deserving of praise or more useful or even more divine or more holy': Jacobus Philippus de Bergamo, *Supplementum chronicarum* (Venice, 1492–3).
2. G. Baechtel, *Gutenberg et l'invention de l'imprimerie* (Paris, 1992); H. Widmann, *Der Gegenwärtige Stand der Gutenberg-Forschung* (Stuttgart, 1972); Albert Kapr, *Gutenberg* (Leipzig, 1977); Aloys Ruppel, *Johannes Gutenberg. Sein Leben und sein Werk*, 3rd edn (Niewkoop, 1967); Lotte Hellinga, 'Gutenberg et ses premiers successeurs', in *Trois révolutions*, pp. 19–34; *Mainz 2000*, passim. Website: <http://www. gutenberg.de/> (in German and English).
3. Karin Emmerich, 'St Viktor bei Mainz', in *Gut. Jb.* (2001), pp. 87–94.
4. Auj. Kues-Bernskastel. Vue de la bibliothèque fondée par Nicolas de Cues: <http://www.bernkastel.de/fr/images/bib1.jpg>.
5. Kurt Flasch, *Nikolaus von Kues* (Frankfurt am Main, 1998).

6. Karl-Michael Sprenger, '*Volumus tamen, quod expressio fiat ante finem mensis Maii presentis.* Sollte Gutenberg 1452 im Auftrag Nikolaus von Kues' Ablassbriefe drucken?', in *Gut. Jb.* (1999), pp. 42–57, illustration.
7. René Hoven, *Lexique de la prose latine de la Renaissance* (Leiden, 1994); Edoardo Barbieri, 'Contributi alla storia del lessico bibliografico', in *La Bibliofilia* (1999) (centenary number), pp. 267–81.
8. Stadtarchiv Erfurt, 1–1/X BXIII-46, vol. 1; *Mainz 2000*, GM 43.
9. *Mainz 2000*, GM 47.
10. *Mainz 2000*, pp. 120ff.
11. Ritter, p. 4.
12. *Mainz 2000*, GM 47b.
13. Georges Livet and Francis Rapp (eds), *Histoire de Strasbourg, II: des grandes invasions au XVIe* (Strasbourg, 1981).
14. Luigi Balsamo, 'Tecnologia e capitali nella storia del libro', in *Studi offerti a Roberto Ridolfi* (Florence, 1973), pp. 77–94.
15. The Strasbourg sources relating to Gutenberg are given in Johann Daniel Schoepflin, *Vindiciae typographicae* (Strasbourg, J. G. Bauer, 1760), 2 parts in one volume, quarto.
16. *Mainz 2000*, GM 56.
17. Ritter, p. 8.
18. Ritter, p. 17.
19. *Mainz 2000*, GM 60, 61.
20. Ritter, p. 16.
21. *Mainz 2000*, GM 129.
22. *Mainz 2000*, p. 130.
23. Donatus-Kalender type, or characters used for the printing of the *Donatus* manual and the calendars.
24. *Mainz 2000*, GM 132 and illustration p. 195.
25. *Mainz 2000*, GM 133–7 and illustration p. 196; *Buchkultur*, 40–1; *Le Livre*, 107.
26. *Thesaurus librorum*, 88.
27. Falk Eisermann, 'Hinter Decken versteckt', in *Gut. Jb.* (1999), pp. 58–74; *Mainz 2000*, GM 130; *Le Livre*, 108.
28. Vatican library, ottobr. lat. 347 (and Mainz 2000, GM 139).
29. *Mainz 2000*, pp. 194–5; *Wolfenbüttel 1972*, 2.
30. Rudolf Blum, *Der Prozess Fust gegen Gutenberg* (Wiesbaden, 1956) ('Beiträge zum Buch-und Bibliothekwesen', 2); *Mainz 2000*, in particular the comments of Sabina Wagner, p. 135.
31. A trial leaf of forty lines is preserved in Cracow.
32. *Mainz 2000*, GM 133, thus logically dating from 1456; the fragment, discovered in 1802 in Mainz, is preserved in the BnF.
33. Printed *c.*1457; the only known example, preserved in the Academy of Kiev, is today lost.
34. *Wolfenbüttel 1972* (21) attributes the first twelve leaves to Mainz, the rest to Bamberg.
35. *Mainz 2000*, pp. 200–201 and illustration p. 199; *Thesaurus librorum*, 90.

36. Paul Needham, 'Johann Gutenberg and the Catholicon Press', in *The Paper of the Bibliographical Society of America*, 76 (1982): 395–456; Lottie Hellinga, 'Analytical bibliography and the study of early printed books with a case study of the Mainz Catholicon', in *Gut. Jb.* (1989), pp. 47–96, illustration.

37. *Wolfenbüttel 1990*, especially the article of Martin Boghardt, pp. 24–44.

38. *Mainz 2000*, GM 156, 158.

39. As shown by examination of the surviving copies (no marks revealing a double impression, perfect justification). For Lehmann-Haupt, this is the natural procedure for a printer without experience of printing in several colours. The printing has been done by the page, not the leaf: the recto has not been printed with the preceding verso: Heinrich Wallau, 'Die zweifarbigen Initialen der Psalterdrucke von Johannes Fust und Peter Schoeffer', in *Mainz 1900*, pp. 261–304.

40. Hans Widmann, 'Die Übernahme antiker Fachausdrücke in die Sprache des Frühdrucks', in *Antike und Abendland: Beträge zum Verständnis Griechen und Römer und ihres Nachlebens*, XX (1974):179–90.

41. *Mainz 2000*, p. 139.

42. *Ad illustrissimum Bavariae ducem Philippum* (Peter Friedberg: Mainz, 1499).

43. *Wolfenbüttel 1972*, 4.

Chapter 6 Innovation

1. Maurice Audin, *Les Types lyonnais primitifs* (Paris, 1955).

2. Lotte Hellinga, 'Press and text in the first decades of printing', in *Libri, tipografi, biblioteche*, Mélanges Luigi Balsamo (Florence, 1997), pp. 1–23.

3. Konrad Haebler, *Typen repertorium der Wiegendrucke*, 4 vols (Halle–Leipzig–New York, 1905–10). The repertories are today accessible in part on the website: <http://www.ndl.go.jp/incunabula/e/font/font_01.html>.

4. Severin Corsten, *Die Anfänge des Kölner Buchdrucks* (Cologne, 1955); Rouzet, *passim*.

5. From the name of the Parisian printer Jodocus Badius Ascensius, who, from 1507, used a picture of his workshop as typographic mark on his title pages.

6. R. A. Sayce, *Compositorial Practices and the Localization of Printed Books, 1530–1800*, 2nd edn (Oxford, 1979).

7. Margaret Lane Ford, 'Author's autograph and printer's copy: Werner Rolewinck's *Paradisus conscientiae*', in *Incunabula: Studies in Fifteenth-century Printed Books Presented to Lotte Hellinga* (London, 1999), pp. 109–28.

8. *Livre appellé Guidon de la practique en cyrurgie*. The success of this treatise lasted for several generations, and the work went on being

printed, for example in Spanish in 1596: *Cirurgia de Guido de Cauliaco con la glosa de Falco* (Valencia, Pedro Patricio Mey, for Francisco Miguel, 1596).

9. AmLyon, CC. 4, fol. 30v°.
10. Ernest Wickersheimer, *Dictionnaire biographique des médicins en France au Moyen Âge*, 2 vols (Geneva, 1979), vol. 2, p. 509.
11. Ritter, p. 47.
12. Vatican Library, lat. 6737; reproduced in *Roma 1997*, p. 35.
13. Veyrin, p. 279.
14. Veyrin, p. 282.
15. Jean-François Gilmont, *Jean Calvin et le livre imprimé* (Geneva, 1997), p. 277.
16. Subiaco, Bibl. di Sta Scolastica, ms XLII. See also *Roma 1997, passim*.
17. *Roma 1997*, pp. 37ff.
18. Another example of a manuscript exemplar in *5e centenaire*, pp. 96ff.
19. With 'slugs', pieces of the composition less high than those to be inked (characters, punctuation, and so on), which thus marked the blanks and locked up the text.
20. Veyrin, p. 283.
21. Martin Dominique Fertel, *La Science pratique de l'imprimerie*...(À Saint-Omer, par Martin Dominique Fertel, imprimeur et marchand libraire, rue des Espeérs, à l'image de Saint-Bertin, 1723).
22. The quires might be simple (the number of folds determined by the format, or inserted one within the other, by whole leaves, by half-leaves (sextodecimo), even by thirds of leaf (duodecimo).
23. Annie Taurant-Boulicaut, '*Vacat nec vitio nec defectu*. Du blanc et de l'excès dans l'incunable', in *Mélanges Aquilon*, pp. 105–24, illustration.
24. *Wolfenbüttel 1990*, for example p. 30.
25. *Wolfenbüttel 1990*, p. 31.
26. Gratien Du Pont, *Controverses des sexes masculin et féminin* (Toulouse, 1534), quoted in Veyrin, p. 304.
27. 'Frame covered with paper dampened and cut, which was put on the tympan of the press and of the page to be printed' to protect the margins from ink: *Grande Encyclopedie*, XVIII, 184. The tympan was 'covered by the frisket, a new metal frame connected to the other end of the tympan and designed to protect the margins. To this end, the frisket was furnished with a sheet of vellum or thick paper in which the pressman cut windows corresponding to the spaces to be printed': ibid. Audin believed that the frisket dated only from 1572.
28. *5e centenaire*, pp. 105–6.
29. Nina Catach, *L'Orthographie française à l'époque de la Renaissance (auteurs, imprimeurs, ateliers de l'imprimerie)* (Geneva, 1968).
30. Veyrin, p. 298.
31. Frédéric Barbier, 'Saint-Bertin et Gutenberg', in *Mélanges Aquilon*, pp. 55–78, illustration.
32. Veyrin, p. 313.

33. Oscar Hase, *Die Koberger. Eine Darstellung des buchhändlerischen Geschäftsbetribes in der Zeit des Übergang vom Mittelalter zur Neuzeit*, 2nd edn (Leipzig, 1885).
34. *Mainz 2000*, GM 170b; *Thesaurus librorum*, 91.
35. *Mainz 2000*, GM 171, 172, 173 and illustration p. 223.
36. Ibid., GM 164.
37. Ibid., GM 163 and illustration 4 p. 216 for the typographic mark.
38. Ibid., GM 175 and illustration p. 367.
39. Ibid., GM 169.
40. Ibid., GM 174.
41. Ibid., GM 180.
42. Ibid., GM 181.
43. *Thesaurus librorum*, 96.
44. *Mainz 2000*, GM 182.
45. Ibid., GM 183.
46. Ibid., GM 193 and illustration p. 221.
47. Ibid., GM 194.
48. Ibid., GM 195 and illustration p. 231.
49. Ibid., GM 179.
50. Ibid., GM 188a–d, 189.
51. Ibid., GM 184–7; Lehmann-Haupt, pp. 6–11, 14, 15, 17.
52. P. Pansier, *Histoire du livre et de l'imprimerie à Avignon du XIVe au XVIe siècle* (Avignon, 1922).
53. Frédéric Barbier, 'Habermas et l'éditeur, ou Qu'est-ce que la médiatisation?', in *Buch-Kulturen*, Mélanges Wittmann (Wiesbaden, 2005), pp. 37–57.
54. John Macfarlane, *Antoine Vérard* (London, 1900), 1.
55. Febvre et Martin, p. 180.
56. G. W. Zapf, *Augsburgs Buchdrucker Geschichte* (Leipzig, 1968), 2 vols; Hans-Jörg Künast and Briggite Shürmann, 'Johannes Rynmann, Wolfgang Präunlein und Georg Willer: drei Augsburger Buchführer des 15. und 16. Jahrhunderts', in *Augsburger Buchdruck und Verlagswesen: von den Anfängen bis zur Gegenwart*, ed. Helmut Gier and Johannes Janota (Wiesbaden, 1997), pp. 23–9.
57. Other examples in Veyrin, pp. 311, 315.
58. Lehmann-Haupt, p. 2; Aloys Ruppel, *Peter Schoeffer aus Gernsheim* (Mainz, 1937).
59. Manuscript destroyed in Strasbourg in 1870, but a copy of the colophon survives in the *Vindiciae typographicae* of Schoepflin of 1760 (p. 31 and facsimile no. VII).
60. Lehmann-Haupt, pp. 23–4, 37ff.
61. Lehmann-Haupt, pp. 5, 1.
62. Marchand, p. 21.
63. Lehmann-Haupt, pp. 16–17.
64. Marchand, p. 19 and the detail of note *I*.
65. Henri Stein, 'L'origine champenoise de l'imprimeur Nicolas Jenson', in *BEC* (1887), pp. 566–79; Martin Lowry, *Nicholas Jenson and the Rise*

of Venetian Printing in Renaissance Europe (Oxford, 1991); Lotte Hellinga, 'Nicolas Jenson et les débuts de l'imprimerie à Mayence', in *Mélanges Aquilon*, pp. 25–53, illustration (but an error in the reading of the date); Haebler 1924, especially pp. 27ff.

66. Born in Gerresheim, near Düsseldorf, Manthen was a partner of Johannes de Colonia in 1474, who had himself married the widow of Johannes de Spira. The daughter of Paula and Johannes de Spira, Hieronyma, married Kaspar von Dinslaken in 1477. The company founded in 1480 was virtually a family affair. Haebler also points out that, in 1471 and 1472, Wendelin de Spira printed for the bookseller Johannes de Colonia.

67. Paul Méllottée, *Histoire économique de l'imprimerie*, I: *l'imprimerie sous l'Ancien Régime, 1439–1789* (Paris, 1905); Henri Hauser, *Ouvriers du temps passé* (Paris, 1917); Maurice Audin, 'Les grèves dans l'imprimerie à Lyon au XVIe siècle' in *Gut. Jb.* (1935), pp. 172–89; Paul Chauvet, *Les Ouvriers du livre en France, des origines à la Révolution de 1789* (Paris, 1959).

68. Csaba Csapodi and Klára Csapodi-Gárdonyi, *Bibliotheca Corviniana. Die Bibliothek des Königs Matthias Corvinus von Ungarn* (Budapest, 1969). Website: <http://www.corvina.oszk.hu/>.

69. BmLyon ms 5154, fol. 194.

70. Rouzet, pp. 136–9.

71. Annie Parent-Charon, 'Associations dans la librairie parisienne du XVIe siècle', in *L'Europe et le livre* (Paris, 1996), pp. 17–30.

72. *Mainz 2000*, p. 221.

73. Lehmann-Haupt, p. 5.

74. Reproduction of the receipt in Lehmann-Haupt, p. 19.

75. Alfred Franklin, *Les Anciennes bibliothèques de Paris*, 1 (Paris, 1867), p. 148; *Mainz 2000*, GM 169.

76. *Trésors de la bibliothèque de l'Arsenal* (Paris, 1980), 125.

77. *Le Livre en Franche-Comté* (Dole, 1983).

78. Peter Zahn, 'Die Endabrechnung über den Druck der Schedelschen Weltchronik (1493) vom 22. Juni 1509. Text und Analyse', in *Gut. Jb.* (1991), pp. 177–213.

79. By Mentelin in 1469: Ritter, p. 34.

80. *Thesaurus librorum*, 95; *Mainz 2000*, GM 167 and illustration p. 213.

81. *Mainz 2000*, GM 168, 169.

82. BSB Munich, Einbl. VII–1/2 (Rome, 1997, pp. 114, 73).

83. IB 41735. The growth of the bookshop network has been best studied in Italy: Angela Nuovo, *Il Commercio librario nell'Italia del Rinascimento*, 3rd edn (Milan, 2003).

84. Trésors de l'Arsenal, 124.

85. AdNord 4G–1407, 1467.

86. *Catalogues régionaux des incunables des bibliothèques publiques de France*, vol. 10, région Centre, re-ed. Pierre Aquilon (Paris, 1991), 133, 663.

87. Valentin Ickelsamer, *Ein Teütsche Grammatica* (Erfurt, 1527) ('Alles in der Welt erfahren, wissen und ewig merken und behalten').

292   *Notes to pages 165–169*

Chapter 7 Printing Conquers the World

1. 'That is to say, that the always glorious and heavenworthy spirit of Nicolas of Cusa, Cardinal of St Peter in Chains, wished above all else that this holy art that was then seen emerging in Germany should be transported to Rome.'
2. Preface to the *Letters* of Gasparin of Bergamo (Basel, 1472): 'Even if Mainz established the art of printing,/It was Basel which drew it out of the original alluvium'.
3. Robert Teichl, 'Der Wiegendruck im Kartenbild', in *Bibliothek und Wissenschaft*, 1 (1964), pp. 201–65; Jean-François Gilmont, 'Les centres de la production imprimée aux XVe et XVIe siècles', in *Produzione e commercio della carta del libro secc. XIII–XVIII*, ed. Simonetta Cavaciocchi (Prato, 1992), pp. 343–64; Philippe Nieto, 'Géographie des impressions européennes du XVe siècle', in *Mélanges Aquilon*, pp. 125–74. See also the lists and studies on specific geographies: the catalogues of the British Museum and the works of Ferdinand Geldner (*Die Deutschen Inkunabeldrucker: ein Handbuch der Buchdrucker des XV. Jhts.* (Stuttgart, 1968), 2 vols); Haebler 1924, *passim*; Rouzet, *passim*; *Johannes Gutenberg: regionale Aspekte des frühen Buchdrucks* (Berlin, 1993). The maps reproduced here are taken from Nieto, 'Géographie des impressions européennes'.
4. J. C. Russell, 'Population in Europe, 500–1500', in *The Fontana Economic History of Europe*, ed. C. M. Cipolla, 2 vols (London, 1974), pp. 15–82; Paul Bairoch, Jean Batou and Pierre Chèvre, *La Population des villes européenes de 800 à 1850* (Geneva, 1988); Jean Delumeau, *La Civilisation de la Renaissance*, new edn (Paris, 1984).
5. Pierre Chaunu, *Histoire économique et sociale du monde*, vol. 1 (Paris, 1977); Pierre Chaunu, *Le Temps des Réformes, 1: La crise de la Chrétienté. L'éclatement, 1250–1550* (Paris, 1975).
6. *Mainz 2000*, p. 219.
7. Ruppel came from Hanau and appears in the 'Gutenberg dossier' under the name of Bechtolff von Hanauwe.
8. Johannes de Spira may have spent time in Mainz, according to Marino Zorzi: *Aldo Manuzio e l'ambiente veneziano, 1494–1515* (Venice, 1994), p. 13.
9. Karl Schorbach, *Der Strasburger Frühdrucker Johann Mentelin* (Mainz, 1932) ('Veröffentlichungen der Gutenberg Gesellschaft', 22); Ritter, *passim*; Haebler 1924, *passim*; Johann Daniel Schoepflin, *Vindiciae typographicae, passim*.
10. Judit Ecsedy, *A Könyvnyomtatás Magyarországon a kézisajto korában 1473–1800* (Budapest, 1999); *Chronica Hungarorum*, re-ed. with preface by Erzsébet Soltész (Budapest, 1973).
11. Haebler 1924, pp. 46, 75.
12. Ibid., pp. 264ff.

13. Prosopographie, 69. Bartfeld = Bardejov (Slovakia), in the north of Presov/Preschau. For the correspondences of toponymy in the geography of Central and Eastern Europe, see Péter Bencsik, *Helységnévváltosások köztes-Európában 1763–1995* (Budapest, 1997). For the old Ottoman geography, see Nuri Akbayar, *Osmanli yer adlari sözlügü* (Istanbul, 2001).

14. A significant value, even though the correlation is based only on a small population. This method of calculation by ranks makes it possible, in particular, to avoid the uncertainties associated with estimating precise population figures for each town.

15. The hypothesis of Bonderno and the year 1463 is disputed: Piero Scapecchi, 'Subiaco 1465 oppure [Bonderno 1463?]. Analisi del frammento Parsons-Scheide', in *La Bibliofilia*, CIII (2001): 1–21.

16. From Schwanheim, near Frankfurt am Main.

17. *Roma 1997, passim*. The last title is dated 12 June 1467 and Haebler, on the basis of the initials 'GOD. AL.' in the explicit, attributes it to a supposed 'Godefridus (or Godehardus) Alemanus': Haebler 1924, pp. 8–10. The same initials are found in Rome, in the work of Philippus de Lignamine.

18. J. Bignami-Odier, *La Bibliothèque vaticane de Sixte IV à Pie IX* (Vatican City, 1973).

19. *Roma 1997*, p. 41.

20. Anna Modigliani, *Tipografi a Roma prima della stampa: due società per fare libri con le forme, 1466–1470* (Rome, 1989).

21. Febvre et Martin, 2nd edn, p. 249.

22. Note on the copy in the BnF, Rés. C 477 (*Roma 1997*, illustration 19, p. 43).

23. Königsbach-Stein, near Pforzheim.

24. Robert Marichal, *Le Livre des prieurs de Sorbonne (1431–1485)* (Paris, 1987); Jacques Monfrin, 'Les lectures de Guillaume Fichet et de Jean Heynlin d'après le registre de prêts de la Bibliothèque de la Sorbonne', in *BHR*, XVII (1955): 7–23.

25. 'Ut sol lumen sic doctrinam fundis in orbem/ Musarum nutrix, regia Parisius/ Nunc prope divinam tu quam Germania novit/ Artem scribendi suscipe pro merita': Guillaume Fichet, 1470.

26. *Amerbachkorrespondenz* (Basel, 1942–), 11t. appeared in 12 volumes.

27. A. Vingtrinier, *Histoire de l'imprimerie à Lyon de l'origine jusqu'à nos jours* (Lyon, 1894); Anatole Claudin, *Histoire de l'imprimerie en France aux XVe et XVIe siècles* (Paris, 1900–14), 4 vols; Charles Perrat, 'Barthélemy Buyer et les débuts de l'imprimerie à Lyon', in *Humanisme et Renaissance*, 1 (1935), pp. 103–21, 234–75, 349–87; René Fédou, *Les Hommes de loi lyonnais à la fin du Moyen Age* (Paris, 1964); Prosopographie, nos 29, 87 (and illustration p. 262).

28. Guillaume Fau et al., 'L'imprimerie à Lyon au XVe siècle: un état des lieux', in *Mélanges Aquilon*, pp. 191–208, illustration.

29. Rouzet, pp. 34–7.

30. R. Deacon, *William Caxton: The First English Editor, Printer, Merchant and Translator* (London, 1976).
31. The bibliography of the Venetian incunabula typography is huge, from H. F. Brown, *The Venetian Printing Press* (London, 1891) and T. Dibdin, *Early Printers in the City of Venice* (New York) up to the books devoted by Martin Lowry to Aldus Manutius (Lowry, Martin J. C., *The World of Aldus Manutius: Business and Scholarship in Renaissance Venice* (Oxford, 1979)) and Nicolas Jenson (*Nicholas Jenson and the Rise of Venetian Printing in Renaissance Europe* (Oxford, 1991).
32. Gedeon Borsa, *Clavis typographorum librariorumque Italiae 1465–1600* (Baden-Baden, 1980), 2 vols.
33. Giorgio Montecchi, 'Dalla pagina manoscritta alla pagina stampata nei breviari in caratteri glagolitici', in *Il Libro nel bacino adriatico* (Florence, 1992), pp. 3–30, illustration.
34. Ernst Voulliéme, *Der Buchdruck Kölns bis zum Ende des 15.Jahrhunderts* (Bonn, 1903).
35. Frédéric Barbier, 'Construction d'une capitale: Leipzig et la librairie allemande, 1750–1914', in *Capitales culturelles, capitales symboliques* (Paris, 2002), pp. 335–57.
36. Severin Corsten, 'Universities and early printing', in *Bibliography and the Study of 15th Century Civilisation* (London, 1987), pp. 83–123.
37. Anatole Claudin, *Les Origines de l'imprimerie à Albi en Languedoc (1480–1484): les pérégrinations de J. Neumeister, compagnon de Gutenberg en Allemagne, en Italie et en France* (Paris, 1880); *Mainz 2000*, pp. 226–9, 379–84: Haebler 1924, pp. 55–6, 208–210.
38. Angela Nuovo, *Il Commercio librario nell' Italia del Rinascimento*, third edn (Milan, 2003), pp. 99–100.
39. Haebler 1924, p. 56.
40. *Mainz 2000*, GM 198; *Thesaurus librorum*, 99.
41. *Mainz 2000*, GM 199.
42. Prosopographie, no. 106.
43. Mathieu Desachy, ed., *Incunables albigeois* (Rodez, 2005), p. 27.
44. I will not deal here with the major problems linked to the Orthodox Church, involving the specific relationships between the political and religious spheres.
45. Eva Frimmova, 'Les incunables en Slovaquie – au temps passé et aujourd'hui', in *Mélanges Aquilon*, pp. 361–77, illustration.
46. Werner Schmitz, *Südslawischer Buchdruck in Venedig (16.–18. Jt.): Untersuchungen und Bibliographie* (Giessen, 1977).
47. *CNAM*, p. 236.
48. *Centralblatt für Bibliothekswesen* (Leipzig, 1900), pp. 429–31.
49. Josip Badalić, *Jugoslavica usque ad annum 1600: Bibliographie der Südslawischen Frühdrucke* (Baden-Baden, 1959); Lazar Plavšić, *Srpske Štamparije od kraja 15 do sredine 19 veka* [*Serbian Printing from the Fifteenth to the Nineteenth Century*] (Beograd, 1959). Two copies of the *Breviarum Zagrabense* are preserved today, one in Budapest (National Library), the other in Rome (Vatican library).

50. Christian Rother, *Siebenbürgen und der Buchdruck im 16. Jahrhundert; mit einer Bibliographie 'Siebenbürgen und der Buchdruck'; mit einer Geleit wort von P[eter] Vodosek* (Wiesbaden, 2002) ('Buchwissenschaftliche Beiträge aus dem Deutschen Bucharchiv München', 71).

51. Josée Balagna, *L'imprimerie arabe en Occident (XVIe, XVIIe et XVIIIe siècles)* (Paris, 1984).

52. Dennis H. Rhodes, *Incunabula in Greece* …: *A First Census* (Munich, 1980); Loukia Droulia et al., [Greek title:] Τὸ Ελληνιχο βιξλίο – or *The Greek Book, 1476–1830* (Athens, 1986); Loukia Droulia, 'L'imprimerie grecque: naissance et retards', in *Le Livre et l'historien* (Geneva, 1997) (Mélanges H.-J. Martin), pp. 327–41; Frédéric Barbier (ed.), *Le Livre grec et l'Europe, du modèle antique à la diffusion des Lumières*, in *RFHL*, 98–9 (1998); *Le Edizioni di testi greci da Aldo Manuzio e le prime tipografie greche di Venezia* (Athens, 1993).

53. Frédéric Barbier, 'Vienne et la Grèce. Notes de lecture', in *RFHL*, 98–9 (1998): 111–40, illustration.

54. The geographical areas defined by the *ISTC* correspond to the current political geography.

55. *Poitiers*, p. 6.

56. Paul Lacombe, *Livres d'heures imprimés conservés dans les bibliothèques publiques de Paris* (Paris, 1907).

57. Dominique Coq and Ezio Ornato, 'La production et le marché des incunables. Le cas des livre juridiques', in *Tours 1988*, pp. 305–22.

58. Yves-Bernard Brissaud, 'Pistes pour une histoire de l'édition juridique française sous l'Ancien Régime', in *HCL*, 1 (2005): 33–136, illustration p. 38.

59. Note that in 1362 Edward III imposed English as the normal language of the courts.

60. Nicolai Rubinstein, *The Government of Florence under the Medici (1434 to 1494)* (Oxford, 1997).

61. Mirjam Bohacová (ed.), *Česká kniha v proměnách staletí* [*The Czech Book over the Centuries*] (Prague, 1990); Mirjam Bohacová, 'Le Livre et la Réforme en Bohême et en Moravie', in Jean-François Gilmont (ed.), *La Réforme et le livre* (Paris, 1990), pp. 393–416; Zdeněk Šimeček, *Geschichte des Buchhandels in Tschechien und in der Slowakei* (Wiesbaden, 2002) (Geschichte des Buchhandels, 7).

62. Equations of interrogation of the *ISTC*: Column 1: <1481; all fields = tr.; language = Latin; language = not Latin. Column 2: > 1480 and <1501. Column 3: sum of the preceding figures.

63. Nuper ego stultos vulgari carmine scripsi:/ Est satis hic noster notus ubique labor./ Narragonum quando nobis fabricata carina est/ Theutonico qualem struximus eloquio/ Scommate pro doctis…

64. Descendants of Auson, one of the sons of Ulysses, poetically = the Italians.

65. Alexandre Lorian, 'L'imprimerie hébraïque, 1470–1550: ateliers chrétiens et ateliers juifs', in *Tours 1988*, pp. 219–29; J. Bloch, 'Early Hebrew printing in Spain and Portugal', *Bulletin of the New York Public*

Library, 42 (1938): 371–420; Lyse Schwarzfuchs, *Le Livre hébreu à Paris au XVIe siècle. Inventaire chronologique* (Paris, 2004); Adri K. Offenberg, 'The chronology of Hebrew printing at Mantua in the fifteenth century', *The Library*, 16/4 (December 1994): 298–315.

66. H 9370.
67. Offenberg, p. 34.
68. Gunzenhausen, between Nuremberg and Nördlingen.
69. Moses ben Nahman [Nahmanide, 1194–1270], [*Hidushei ha-Torah*], Lisbon, Eliézer ben Jacob Toledano, 16 VII 1489.
70. Giacomo Manzoni, *Annali tipografici dei Soncini* (Bologna, 1883–6), 2 vols (only).
71. Haebler 1924, p. 127.
72. Offenberg, 12; Delaveau/Hillard, 1345.
73. Haebler 1924, pp. 124ff.
74. Frédéric Barbier, 'Entre Montesquieu et Adam Smith: Leipzig et la Société des libraires', in *RFHL*, 112–13 (2001): 149–70, illustration.
75. Jean-Dominique Mellot, *L'Edition rouennaise et ses marchés (vers 1600–vers 1730). Dynamisme provincial et centralisme parisien* (Paris, 1998) (Mémoires et doc. de l'École nationale des chartes, p. 48).
76. Frédéric Barbier, 'L'impérialisme communicationel: le commerce culturel des nations autour de la Méditerranée aux époques moderne et contemporaine', Afterword to *Des moulins à papier aux bibliothèques* (Montpellier, 2003), 2 vols, vol. 2, pp. 675–704.

Chapter 8 The Nature of Text

1. Bibliothèque de Chantilly (XII H 9). Exhibition in the chateau of Chantilly on 'Antoine Vérard and the birth of the deluxe printed book'.
2. *Venezia 1501. Petrucci e la stampa musicale* (Venice, 2001).
3. Lucien Febvre, *Rabelais et le problème de l'incroyance au XVIe siècle*, new edn (Paris, 1968), pp. 27, 70 ('L'Évolution de l'humanité'), trans. B. Gottlieb as *The Problem of Unbelief in the Sixteenth Century: The Religion of Rabelais* (Cambridge, Mass., 1982).
4. Henri-Jean Martin, 'Culture écrite et culture orale, culture savante et culture populaire dans la France d'Ancien Régime', in *JS*, 2 (July–December 1975): 225–82.
5. Jaroslava Kašparová, 'Rabelais, Cervantès et la Bohème. À propos de la réception de leur oeuvre par les lecteurs tchèques du XVIe au début du XXe siècle', in *Est-Ouest. Transferts et réceptions dans le monde du (XVIIe–XXe siècles)*, ed. Frédéric Barbier (Leipzig, 2005), pp. 221–33 ('Europe en réseaux/Vernetztes Europa', 2).
6. Proceedings of the conference *I Dintorni del testo*, Rome and Bologna, 2004, in the press.
7. For the construction of the typographic space of the ancient book: <http.//www.enssib.fr/bibliotheque/documents/travaux/sordet/nav.liv.ancien.html?>. In addition to the English language classics of material

bibliography, see: Giorgio Montecchi, *Il Libro nel Rinascimento. Saggi di bibliologia* (Rome, 1994); Lorenzo Baldacchini, *Il Libro antico*, new edn (Rome, 2001).

8. Konrad Haebler, *Handbuch der Inkunabelkunde* (Leipzig, 1925), p. 45.
9. Margaret McFadden Smith, *The Title-page: Its Early Development, 1460–1510* (Newcastle, 2000).
10. *André Desguines. Les incunables. Catalogue* (Nanterre, 1992), p. 145 and illustration on p. 16.
11. *Auctor et auctoritas: invention et conformisme dans l'écriture médiévale*, ed. Michel Zimmermann (Paris, 2001).
12. *L'Ecrivain face à son public en France et en Italie à la Renaissance* (Paris, 1989); Jean-Claude Margolin, 'Érasme et ses publics', in *L'Auteur et son public au temps de la Renaissance* (Paris, 1998), pp. 27–56.
13. *Sébastien Brant, son époque et 'la Nef des fols'* …, actes du colloque de Strasbourg (1994), ed. Gonthier Louis Finck (Strasbourg, 1995).
14. Erasmus did no other (cf. Crousaz).
15. John Macfarlane, *Antoine Vérard* (London, 1900), pp. 74, 149.
16. *Poitiers*, p. 29.
17. *Mainz 2000*, GM 216 (Latin), 217 (German); H. W. Davies, *Bernhard von Breydenbach and His Journey to the Holy Land, 1483–1484* (London, 1911).
18. BnF Rés., Vélins 769.
19. *Trésors de l'Arsenal*, 274.
20. *Clarorum virorum epistolae latinae, graecae et hebraicae variis temporibus missae ad J. Reuchlinum* (BSB). A new edition was published by Tiguri (Zürich) in 1558.
21. Frédéric Barbier, 'Discours rapporté, citation, référence', in *Texte. Revue de critique et de théorie littéraire*, 31–2 (2002): 57–87, illustration.
22. According to *Des Alexandries, II: les métamorphoses du lecteur* (Paris, 2003), pp. 229–31.
23. CNAM, 58, p. 247; *Thesaurus librorum*, 108; Henri-Jean Martin, 'Politique et typographie à la Renaissance', in *Trois révolutions*, pp. 71–91, illustration.
24. Victor Bérard, *La Turquie et l'héllenisme contemporain: la Macédoine* (Paris, 1893).
25. Petro Bembo, *De Aetna* (Venice, Aldus Manutius, 1496).
26. Veyrin, pp. 161–88.
27. A converted Jew, born in the diocese of Evreux (La Neuve-Lyre), died 1340. S. A. Hirsch, 'Early English Hebraists: Roger Bacon and his predecessors', in S. A. Hirsch, *A Book of Essays* (London, 1905), pp. 1–72: Beryl Smalley, *The Study of the Bible in the Middle Ages* (Oxford, 1983); B. Walde, *Christliche Hebraisten Deutschlands am Ausgang des Mittelalters* (Munster, 1916).
28. For example, the Latin Bible (based on the Vulgate) printed by Johann Herbort for Johannes de Colonia, Nicolas Jenson and associates in Venice in 1481 (HC 3164).
29. GW 4282; Zehnacker 445.

30. Guy Bédouelle, *Le Quintuplex Psalterium de Lefèvre d'Étaples: un guide de lecture* (Geneva, 1979) ('THR').

31. Delaveau/Hillard, 1.

32. Paul Saenger, 'La naissance de la coupure et de la séparation des mots', in *Mise en page*, pp. 446–9, illustration; Paul Saenger, 'Coupure et séparation des mots sur le Continent au Moyen Age', in *Mise en page*, pp. 450–5.

33. Henri-Jean Martin, *La Naissance du livre moderne. Mise en page et mise en texte du livre francais (XIVe–XVIIe)* (Paris, 2000).

34. Achim Krümmel, *Das Supplementum chronicarum* (Herzberg, 1992).

35. *Dictionnaire de théologie catholique*, VII, 230.

36. Papias, *Vocabularium* (Venice, Pinzi, 1496), 2°.

37. 'Que quidem tabula in omni vocabulo per duos numeros procedit, quorum primus denotat librum, secundus capitulum tam libri Augustini quam tractatus supradicti'.

38. Adrian Wilson, *The Making of the Nuremberg Chronicle* (Amsterdam, 1976; 2nd edn, 1978); E. Rucker, *Die Schedelsche Weltchronik* (Munich, 1993); Stefan Füssel, *Die Welt im Buch. Buchkünstlerischer und humanistischer Kontext der Schedelschen Weltchronik von 1493* (Mainz, 1996); CNAM, pp. 207–11.

39. One of them was reproduced 101 times, making a total of 203 illustrations.

40. See the reproduction at: <http://gallica.bnf.fr/anthologie/notices/00975.htm>.

41. Nuremberg Museum.

42. Friedrich Winkler, *Dürer und die Illustrationen zum Narrenschiff. Die Baseler und Strasburger Arbeiten des Künstlers und der altdeutsche Holzschnitt* (Berlin, 1951) ('Forschungen zur deutschen Kunstgeschichte', 36); Hans Joachim Raupp, 'Zum Verhältnis von Text und Illustration in Sebastian Brants *Narrenschiff*', in *Bibliothek und Wissenschaft*, 19 (1985): 146–84.

43. Reproduced at: <http://www.ulg.ac.be/wittert/fr/flori/opera/durer/durer_apocalypse.html>.

44. *Le Siècle d'or de l'imprimerie lyonnaise* (Paris, 1972), pp. 48ff.

45. For *Les Subtiles Fables D'Ésope*, see the *Notice* of J. Bastin, Lyon [1926].

46. Macfarlane, *Antoine Vérard, passim*.

47. Leonhardt Fuchs, *De Historia stirpium commentarii* (Basel, Officina Isingriniana, 1542).

48. A. Vesalius, *De humani corporis fabrica* (Basel, Johannes Oporinus, 1543).

49. G. Agricola, *De Re metallica* (Basel, Johann Froben and Nicolaus Episcopius, 1556).

50. Konrad Gesner, *Historia animalium* (Zürich, C. Froschover, 1551–87), 5 vols; Alfredo Serrai, *Conrad Gesner* (Rome, 1990) ('Il bibliothecario').

51. *La Face cachée du livre médiéval. L'histoire du livre vue par Ezio Ornato* (Rome, 1997), p. 88.

52. Jaques Fontaine, *Isidore de Séville. Genèse et originalité de la culture hispanique au temps des Wisigoths* (Turnout, 2000) ('Témoins de notre histoire').
53. Jaques Monfrin, 'Humanisme et traduction au Moyen Age', in *JS* (1963).
54. Work in progress at the Centre de recherche en histoire du livre (Enssib, Lyon: <http://www.enssib.fr/article.php?id=85&cat=La+recherche&id_cat=85>).
55. Anthony Grafton, *The Footnote: A Curious History* (London, 1997).
56. *Thesaurus librorum*, 109.
57. Konrad Gesner, *Bibliotheca universalis* (Zürich, C. Froschover, 1545); Table systématique: *Pandectarum, sive partitionum universalium...libri XXI* (Zürich, C. Froschover, 1548–9), 2 parts in 1 vol.

Chapter 9 The Media Explosion

1. Carla Bozzolo, Dominique Coq and Ezio Ornato, 'La production du livre en quelques pays d'Europe occidentale aux XIVe et XVe siècles', *Scrittura e civiltà*, 8 (1984), pp. 131–60, especially p. 143.
2. Ritter, p. 482.
3. Brigitte Moreau, 'La libraire parisienne du début du XVIe siècle', in *L'Europe et le livre* (Paris, 1996), pp. 13–16.
4. Letter to Johann Faber, 1526, quoted by Crousaz, pp. 101–2 (my italics).
5. Jurgen Habermas, *The Structural Transformation of the Public Sphere: An Enquiry into a Category of Bourgeois Society*, trans. Thomas Burger with the assistance of Frederick Lawrence (Cambridge, 1989).
6. Georges Lefèbvre, *The Great Fear of 1789: Rural Panic in Revolutionary France*, trans. Joan White (New York, 1973).
7. AdRhône, 10 G 1378, 2; Henri Hours and Claude Dalbanne, 'Deux placards imprimés à Lyon en 1489', in *Gut. Jb.* (1954), pp. 137–42.
8. CNAM, 68, p. 262.
9. Brigitte Moreau et al., *Inventaire chronologique des éditions parisiennes du XVIe siècle* (Paris, 1972–) (1540, nos 1726, 1722, 1725); Jean-Pierre Seguin, *L'Information en France, de Louis XII à Henri II* (Geneva, 1961) ('THR', 44).
10. Jean-Pierre Vittu, 'Qu'est-ce qu'un article au *Journal des savants* de 1665 à 1714, in *RFHL*, 112–13 (2001): 129–48.
11. André Chastel, *The Sack of Rome*, trans. Beth Archer (Princeton University Press, c.1983).
12. Frédéric Barbier, 'Fin produzione e riproduzione: cos'e' il patrimonio librario?', in *Prometeo. Rivista trimestrale di scienze e storia*, 23/91 (September 2005): 16–25, illustration.
13. Crousaz, pp. 115ff; Jean-François Gilmont, 'Les humanistes face à *L'Ars impressoria*', in idem, *Le Livre et ses secrets* (Geneva, Louvain, 2003).
14. Letter to Martinius, Basel, 1528, quoted by Crousaz, p. 118.

15. Juliette Guilbaud, 'À Paris chez Guillaume Desprez'. Le livre janséniste et ses réseaux aux XVIIe et XVIIIe siècles, doctoral thesis, Paris, EPHE, 2005, 2 vols in typescript.

16. For example, in Georgius Agricola, *De Re metallica libri XII* (Basel, Johann Froben for Nicolaus Episcopius, 1556), 2o.

17. Delaveau/Hillard.

18. HC 6683*.

19. *Mainz 2000*, p. 418.

20. Ibid., p. 419.

21. Delaveau/Hillard, 3974; Bettye T. Chambers, *Bibliography of French Bibles. 1: Fifteenth- and Sixteenth-Century, French Language Editions of the Scriptures* (Geneva, 1994).

22. Frédéric Barbier, 'Nature des mots, ordre des textes, classement des choses: entre savoir et proscription, le livre hébreu en Occident (XIIe–XVIe siècle)', in *Normes culturelles et construction de la déviance* (Paris, 2004), pp. 49–69.

23. Graecogermania. Griechischstudien deutscher Humanisten. Die Editionstätigkeit der Griechen in der italienischen Renaissance (1469–1523) (Weinheim, 1989), p. 165.

24. Delaveau/Hillard, 1; Graecogermania, 106.

25. Delaveau/Hillard, 1396.

26. Ibid., 3976.

27. Sophie Kessler-Mesguich, 'L'enseignement de l'hébreu et de l'araméen à Paris (1530–1560) d'apres les oeuvres grammaticales des lecteurs royaux', in *Les Origines du Collège de France* (Paris, 1998), pp. 357–74; Antoine Augustin Renouard, *Annales de l'imprimerie des Estienne*, 2nd edn (Paris, 1843).

28. Delaveau/Hillard, 1350.

29. Ibid., 1398.

30. Holger Flachmann, *Martin Luther und das Buch: eine historische Studie zur Bedetung des Buches im Handeln und Denken des Reformators* (Tübingen, 1996) ('Spätmittelalter und Reformation', 8); Jean-François Gilmont, *Jean Calvin et le livre imprimé* (Geneva, 1997).

31. W.A., I, p. 528.

32. Pierre Chaunu, *Eglise, culture et société: essai sur Réforme et Contre-Réforme (1517–1620)* (Paris, 1981).

33. *Aspects de la propagande religieuse* (Geneva, 1957) ('THR', 28).

34. E. J. Dévereux, *Renaissance English Translations of Erasmus* (Toronto [et al.], 1983).

35. Febvre et Martin, 2nd edn, p. 419.

36. Mark U. Edwards, *Printing, Propaganda and Martin Luther* (Berkeley, 1994).

37. Denis Crouzet, *La Genèse de la Réforme française, 1500–1562* (Paris, 1996).

38. Bm Valenciennes, ms 703, fol. 31v.

39. Bm Valenciennes, Serbat 47g.

40. Jean-Marie Apostolidès, *Le Roi-machine. Spectacle et politique au temps de Louis XIV* (Paris, 1981).

41. Geoffroy Tory, *Champ Fleury* (Paris, Geoffroy Tory, Gilles Gourmont, 1529).
42. Joachim du Bellay, *La Deffence et illustration de la langue françoyse* (Paris, Arnoul l'Angelier, 1549).
43. Anatole Claudin, *Histoire de l'imprimerie en France*, vol. IV, pp. 86ff.
44. Elisabeth Armstrong, *Before Copyright: The French Book-Privilege System, 1498–1526* (Cambridge, 1990); Hélène Michaud, *La Grande Chancellerie au XVIe siècle* (Paris, 1967).
45. Frédéric Barbier, 'Entre Montesquieu et Adam Smith: Leipzig et la Société des libraires', in *RFHL*, 112–13 (2001).
46. Erasmus, quoted by Crousaz, p. 137; Mario Infelise, *I Libri prohibiti, da Gutenberg all'Encyclopédie* (Rome–Bari, 1999) ('Storia moderna').
47. BnF Impr. E 2401 (and *Le Livre*, no. 483).
48. Albert Labarre, 'La repression du livre hérétique dans la France du XVIe siècle', in *Mélanges Aquilon*, pp. 335–60; Augustin Renaudet, *Préréforme et humanisme à Paris pendant les premieres guerres d'Italie (1484–1517)* (Paris, 1953).
49. Letter of 1527, quoted by Crousaz, p. 153.
50. Quoted by Crousaz, p. 144.
51. *Journal d'un bourgeois de Paris sous le règne de François Ier*, ed. L. Lalanne (Paris, 1854), p. 104.
52. Louis Haureau, 'Louis de Berquin', *Revue des deux mondes*, 79 (1869): 454–81; Margaret Mann, 'Louis de Berquin traducteur d'Érasme', *Revue du XVIe siècle*, 18 (1931): 309–23.
53. Étienne Dolet (1509–46) (Paris, 1986) ('Cahiers V. L. Saulnier').
54. Ibid., p. 186.
55. Quoted by Crousaz, p. 131.

Conclusion

1. For the chronology of the history of the book: Frédéric Barbier, 'D'une mutation l'autre: les temps longs de l'histoire du livre', in *Trois révolutions*, pp. 7–18; Frédéric Barbier, 'La Révolution et le problème de la périodisation en histoire du livre', postscript to *Imprimés limousins* (Limoges, 1994), pp. 215–37; Frédéric Barbier, 'Économie de la lecture: quelques notes d'historiographie et de problématique', preface to *Lecture et lecteurs en Bourgogne* (Dijon, 2005), pp. 3–24 (Annales de Bourgogne, 77).
2. Martin Luther, *Grand écrits réformateurs* (Paris, 1992), pp. 130–2.
3. It might even be possible to make comparisons over the very long term; Robert Marichal reckons that, in Roman Egypt, 'for one declaration of ownership' that survives today, some 150,000 have been lost: Robert Marichal, 'L'écriture latine et la civilisation occidentale du Ier au XVIe siècle', reprinted in *Histoire et art de l'écriture* (Paris, 2005), p. 657.
4. Frédéric Barbier, 'Habermas et l'éditeur, ou Qu'est-ce que la médiatisation?', in *Buch-Kulturen*, Mélanges Wittmann (Wiesbaden, 2005), pp. 37–57.

Index

Page numbers in *italics* refer to figures.